THE FETTERS OF RHYME

The Fetters of Rhyme

LIBERTY AND POETIC FORM IN EARLY MODERN ENGLAND

Rebecca M. Rush

PRINCETON UNIVERSITY PRESS

PRINCETON AND OXFORD

Published by Princeton University Press
41 William Street, Princeton, New Jersey 08540
6 Oxford Street, Woodstock, Oxfordshire OX20 1TR

press.princeton.edu

Library of Congress Cataloging-in-Publication Data

Names: Rush, Rebecca M., 1987- author.
Title: The fetters of rhyme : liberty and poetic form in early modern
    England / Rebecca M. Rush.
Description: Princeton : Princeton University Press, 2021. | Includes
    bibliographical references and index.
Identifiers: LCCN 2020034537 (print) | LCCN 2020034538 (ebook) | ISBN
    9780691212555 (hardcover) | ISBN 9780691215686 (ebook)
Subjects: LCSH: English poetry—Early modern, 1500-1700—History and
    criticism. | English language—Rhyme. | Poetics. | Couplets,
    English—History and criticism.
Classification: LCC PR535.R48 R87 2021 (print) | LCC PR535.R48 (ebook) |
    DDC 821/.409—dc23
LC record available at https://lccn.loc.gov/2020034537
LC ebook record available at https://lccn.loc.gov/2020034538

British Library Cataloging-in-Publication Data is available

Editorial: Anne Savarese and Jenny Tan
Production Editorial: Ellen Foos
Jacket Design: Pamela Schnitter
Production: Erin Suydam
Publicity: Alyssa Sanford and Amy Stewart
Copyeditor: Kathleen Kageff

Jacket art: Facsimile of 16th century wood engraving, 1862 / The Print Collector / Alamy Stock Photo

This book has been composed in Miller

Printed on acid-free paper. ∞

Printed in the United States of America

10 9 8 7 6 5 4 3 2 1

CONTENTS

ACKNOWLEDGMENTS

THIS BOOK HAS BENEFITED IMMEASURABLY from the generosity and rigor of many readers and interlocutors. David Kastan, David Quint, and John Rogers shaped the project from its earliest stages and ensured that each chapter remained in touch with the subtleties of history and the richness of poetic language. The knowledge, guidance, and conversation of David Bromwich, Ardis Butterfield, Jill Campbell, Ben Glaser, Cathy Nicholson, and Ayesha Ramachandran also enriched many pages of this book. From the first days of my arrival at Virginia, conversations with Steve Cushman, Elizabeth Fowler, Bruce Holsinger, Clare Kinney, Katharine Maus, John Parker, Jahan Ramazani, and Chip Tucker sharpened my thinking about form and poetic reading. I am particularly grateful to Steve, Elizabeth, and John for reading drafts with such thoughtfulness and to Chip and Steve for discussing metrical matters. The comments of the two anonymous readers at Princeton University Press deepened the book by clarifying its stakes and rooting its poetic argument more firmly in history. I would also like to thank Aaron Pratt—the Carl and Lily Pforzheimer Curator of Early Books and Manuscripts at the Harry Ransom Center at the University of Texas at Austin—for going out of his way to help me obtain images of rhyme charts from Puttenham and Drayton. I am very grateful to Anne Savarese, Jenny Tan, Ellen Foos, Kathleen Kageff, and the staff at Princeton University Press for turning a bundle of pages into a real book.

My thinking about poetic form and my readings of particular poems have been formed in conversation with my students at University of Virginia, particularly those in my courses Renaissance Lyric; Renaissance Poetry and Poetics; and Milton.

I owe thanks to many of my compeers at Yale for their conversation and counsel, including Carla Baricz, Sam Fallon, Brad Holden, Matt Hunter, Seo Hee Im, Angus Ledingham, Tessie Prakas, Aaron Pratt, Palmer Rampell, Justin Sider, and Antonio Templanza, but I am particularly indebted to Maggie Deli for being a tireless listener, editor, and friend.

The foundations for this project were laid when I was an undergraduate at UNC, where Jessica Wolfe and Reid Barbour first inspired my interest in early modern literature. Reid taught me everything I know about Milton and seventeenth-century literature. And Jessica's knowledge, prudence, and bigheartedness guided me through the wandering wood and error's den many a time and oft.

Parts of the introduction and chapter two appeared as "Licentious Rhymers: John Donne and the Late-Elizabethan Couplet Revival," *English Literary*

History 84, no. 2 (Fall 2017): 529–58, © 2017 The Johns Hopkins University Press. It is reprinted with permission in expanded and revised form.

ABBREVIATIONS

ARTE   George Puttenham, *The Arte of English Poesie*, London, 1589.

CPMP   John Milton, *The Complete Poems and Major Prose*, edited by Merritt Y. Hughes, Indianapolis: Hackett, 2003.

ELEGIES   John Donne, *The Variorum Edition of the Poetry of John Donne*, edited by Gary A. Stringer et al., vol. 2, *The Elegies*, edited by John R. Roberts et al., Bloomington: Indiana University Press, 2000.

ESSAYS   Abraham Cowley, *The Essays and Other Prose Writings*, edited by Alfred B. Gough, Oxford: Oxford University Press, 1915.

FQ   Edmund Spenser, *The Faerie Queene*, edited by A. C. Hamilton, New York: Longman, 2007.

JONSON   Ben Jonson, *The Cambridge Edition of the Works of Ben Jonson*, edited by David Bevington, Martin Butler, and Ian Donaldson, Cambridge: Cambridge University Press, 2012.

MASQUE   John Milton, *A Masque Presented at Ludlow Castle*, in *The Complete Poems and Major Prose*, edited by Merritt Y. Hughes, Indianapolis: Hackett, 2003.

PL   John Milton, *Paradise Lost*, in *The Complete Poems and Major Prose*, edited by Merritt Y. Hughes, Indianapolis: Hackett, 2003.

SA   John Milton, *Samson Agonistes*, in *The Complete Poems and Major Prose*, edited by Merritt Y. Hughes, Indianapolis: Hackett, 2003.

SATYRE   "Satyre 3," in John Donne, *The Satyres*, edited by Jeffrey S. Johnson, vol. 3 of *The Variorum Edition of the Poetry of John Donne*, edited by Gary A. Stringer et al., Bloomington: Indiana University Press, 2016.

SATYRES   John Donne, *The Variorum Edition of the Poetry of John Donne*, edited by Gary A. Stringer et al., vol. 3, *The Satyres*, edited by Jeffrey S. Johnson, Bloomington: Indiana University Press, 2016.

SCOURGE John Marston, *The Scourge of Villanie. Three Bookes of Satyres*, London, 1598.

SP Edmund Spenser, *The Yale Edition of the Shorter Poems of Edmund Spenser*, edited by William A. Oram, Einar Bjorvand, Ronald Bond, Thomas H. Cain, Alexander Dunlop, and Richard Schell, New Haven, CT: Yale University Press, 1989.

VERSE LETTERS John Donne, *The Variorum Edition of the Poetry of John Donne*, edited by Jeffrey S. Johnson, vol. 5, *The Verse Letters*, edited by Jeanne Shami et al., Bloomington: Indiana University Press, 2019.

THE FETTERS OF RHYME

Introduction

IN HIS 1668 PREFACE to *Paradise Lost*, John Milton justifies his rejection of rhyme in the same language he had once used to defend beheading kings and founding republics.[1] Rhyme, he insists, is the "Invention of a barbarous Age," a product of "Custom" rather than reason. He therefore describes himself as the leader of a poetic revolution, offering the first example "in *English*, of ancient liberty recover'd to Heroic Poem from the troublesome and modern bondage of Riming."[2] The phrase has become familiar because it succinctly captures Milton's most fundamental poetic and political allegiances. As he had in his polemic writing of the 1640s, Milton declares himself to be a radical in the root sense of the term: he desires to return to the classical roots of poetry by stripping away gratuitous poetic ornaments tagged to verse by "modern" poets, that is, by centuries of vernacular writers (*CPMP*, 210). To be a "modern" rhymer is to be heedlessly "carried away" by contemporary custom, while to pursue a higher "measure" is to act deliberately and rationally to "recove[r]" a long-lost vision of "ancient liberty" (*CPMP*, 210). In pitting ancient liberty against modern bondage, Milton attributes the widest possible implications to what might seem like an innocuous stylistic decision. The rejection of rhyme is not simply a matter of personal taste or generic necessity, but an act of liberation that will echo across England. It is tempting to read Milton's effort to make prosody a battleground for liberty as the product of a bellicose temperament and a particularly heated historical moment. Eight years after the Restoration, the defeated Republican poet was making a final sally for liberty in one of the few forums still available to him. But *The Fetters of Rhyme* makes it clear that rhyme was a site of contention about liberty and binding long before Milton made his declaration. When Milton announced his opposition to the troublesome and modern bondage of rhyming, he knew very well that he was not initiating a new line of thought but entering into a battle that had been raging since at least the sixteenth century. *The Fetters of Rhyme* reveals how Milton's choice of liberty and measure over binding and rhyme draws on long-standing divisions within English poetics about the nature and purpose of formal limitation. By telling the dynamic story of rhyme from Elizabeth's reign—when the couplet, of all things, was a sign of ancient liberty—to the Restoration, this book investigates what it meant for poets to subject themselves to what they so often described as the bands or fetters of rhyme.

The Bands of Rhyme

In 1633, Thomas Carew's song "Incommunicabilitie of Love" was performed at Whitehall before Charles I and Henrietta Maria. The two-part song, which consists of a series of questions and answers, begins with an exchange about the origins of monogamy:

> **Quest.** By what power was Love confinde
> To one object? who can binde,
> Or fixe a limit to the free-borne minde?
>
> **An.** Nature.[3]

The question suggests that the "minde" is "free-borne," that in its original state the mind is not bound to any master or mistress; by nature, it is completely in its own power. In the following decade, revolutionary figures like Milton and John Lilburne would speak of "freeborn Englishmen" and "the free-born people of England" as they made radical cases that the English were free citizens rather than subjects and that they could therefore overthrow tyrannical rulers.[4] But for Carew, the fact that the mind is born free does not mean that it can or should remain free. In his song, the "answer" attributes the circumscription of the freeborn mind not to some external binding force like custom or religion or society, but to "Nature" itself. The exchange registers a paradox at the heart of discourse about liberty, in which a confidence that we have "minds that can wander beyond all limit" existed alongside a belief that limitation is nevertheless a natural, necessary, and perhaps even desirable aspect of political, religious, and romantic life.[5] Carew's position on the source of limitation is unambiguous, if also mysterious: he insists that limitation is as natural to the mind as the freedom with which it is born. Love (and also, by implication, politics) is therefore a choice among fetters; maintaining an independent will is either impossible or undesirable because the mind has a natural inclination to form passionate allegiances.[6] Carew builds the mystery of the naturally self-binding mind into the formal structure of his poem by playing with the rhyme between "mind" and "bind." There is no rational account for the likeness between "bind" and "mind." They are not linked by grammar—one is a verb and the other a noun. Nor is there an obvious connection between the meanings of the words; in fact, Carew insists that minds are precisely the sorts of things that abhor binding. And yet, just as a mysterious but natural power binds the freeborn mind, the power of a sonic coincidence binds the unrelated words together in a way that suggests an affinity between them deeper than grammar or logic.

This idea of rhyme as a binding force is fundamental to poetic theory in the sixteenth and seventeenth centuries. Early modern poets consistently imagined rhyme as a band, fetter, or link that tied the poem together. Indeed, many theorists believed that rhyme's connective function made it essential to the structural integrity of verse. In his 1603 *Defence of Rhyme*, Samuel Daniel argues that rhyme is "as the iointure without which [verse] hangs loose, and cannot subsist."[7] Poetic theorists of the period not only discussed the binding function of rhyme but made its connective power visible on the page by providing diagrams of rhyme schemes in which rhyming lines are connected by curved lines (see figures i.1 and i.2). These diagrams likely derive from the common medieval scribal practice of connecting rhyming lines with brackets. In an article on the elaborate bracketing in some manuscripts of Chaucer's "Tale of Sir Thopas," Judith Tschann suggests that scribes may have added brackets in order "to help the reader see the verse form" and, in the case of "Sir Thopas," to interpret that form and to show that the tale is "a masterful display of incompetence."[8] Though I have not encountered a theoretical description of rhyme as binding prior to the sixteenth century, this bracketing practice suggests that rhyme may have already been imagined as a connective force. Even if the original use of the brackets did not reflect a preexisting theory of rhyme and binding, the conspicuous linking of the brackets may in fact have produced or contributed to the idea that rhyme is a band or jointure. George Puttenham and Michael Drayton certainly draw on manuscript tradition, but they make the binding that is implicit in medieval brackets explicit and systematic in their visual representations of rhyme. In these figures, the words of poems are eliminated so that we can see the links formed by rhyme and the many "proportions" that can be made by "enterweaving" these links.[9] Form emerges as something separable from language itself. Rhyme becomes pure binding, abstracted from language.[10] This understanding of rhyme as a band, fetter, or jointure made it apt to be seen as an analogy for other types of bonds, particularly those that unite friends, lovers, or political communities.[11] Therefore the same questions that fascinated sonneteers and plagued political theorists—What powers can bind the freeborn mind? Are these powers natural or artificial? What is the scope of individual liberty? Can limitation be productive?—also animated debates about rhyme and its place in English verse.

For twentieth- and twenty-first-century poetic theorists, rhyme's binding effect continues to be one of its essential functions, but it is primarily an aural and cognitive phenomenon: as Donald Wesling puts it in *The Chances of Rhyme*, "Rhymed words leap easily from the page to the ear to the memory."[12] Premodern theorists were similarly intrigued by rhyme's ability to "give to the Eare an Echo of delightful report, and to the Memorie a deeper impression of

Poet muſt know to whoſe eare he maketh his rime, and accom-
modate himſelfe thereto, and not giue ſuch muſicke to the rude and
barbarous, as he would to the learned and delicate eare.

There is another ſort of proportion vſed by *Petrarche* called the
Seizino, not riming as other ſongs do, but by chuſing ſixe wordes
out of which all the whole dittie is made, euery of
thoſe ſixe commencing and ending his verſe by
courſe, which reſtraint to make the dittie ſenſible
will try the makers cunning, as thus.

Beſides all this there is in *Situation* of the concords two other
points, one that it go by plaine and cleere compaſſe not intangled:
another by enterweauing one with another by knots, or as it were
by band, which is more or leſſe buſie and curious, all as the maker
will double or redouble his rime or concords, and ſet his diſtances
farre or nigh, of all which I will giue you ocular examples, as thus.

Concord in

Plaine compaſſe   Entertangle.

And firſt in a *Quadreine* there are but two proportions,
for foure verſes in this laſt ſort coupled,
are but two *Diſticks*, and not a ſtaffe *qua-*
dreine or of foure.

The ſtaffe of fiue hath ſeuen proportions as,

whereof ſome of them be harſher and vnpleaſaunter to the eare
then other ſome be.

The *Sixaine* or ſtaffe of ſixe hath ten proportions, wherof ſome
be vſuall, ſome not vſuall, and not ſo ſweet one as another.

The ſtaffe of ſeuen verſes hath ſeuen proportions, whereof one
onely is the vſuall of our vulgar, and kept by our old Poets *Chau-*
cer and other in their hiſtoricall reports and other ditties: as in the
laſt part of them that follow next.

The

FIGURE I.I. Puttenham, George. *The Arte of English Poesie*. London:
Richard Field, 1589. Pforz 12 PFZ. Carl H. Pforzheimer Library,
Harry Ransom Center, University of Texas at Austin.

To the Reader.

all, but the same better aduise which hath caused me to alter the whole ; And where before the stanza was of seauen lines, wherin there are two couplets, as in this figure appeareth,

the often harmonie thereof softned the verse more then the maie-stie of the subiect would permit, vnlesse they had all been Gemi-nels, or couplets. Therefore (but not without new fashioning the whole frame) I chose Ariostos stanza of all other the most com-plete, and best proportioned, consisting of eight, sixe inter wouen, and a couplet in base.

    The Quadrin doth neuer double, or to vse a word of Heral-drie, neuer bringeth foorth Gemells . The Quinzain too soone. The Sestin hath Twinnes in the base , but they detaine not the Musicke, nor the Cloze (as Musitions terme it) long enough for an Epick Poem ; The stanza of seauen is touched before; This of eight both holds the tune cleane through to the base of the co-lumne (which is the couplet at the foote or bottom) & closeth not but with a full satisfaction to the eare for so long detention.

    Briefely, this sort of stanza hath in it maiestie, perfection, & soliditie , resembling the piller which in Architecture is called the Tuscan, whose shaft is of sixe diameters, & bases of two. The

A 3

other

FIGURE I.2. Drayton, Michael. *The Barrons Wars in the raigne of Edward the second. With Englands heroicall epistles.* London: Nicholas Ling, 1603. Carl H. Pforzheimer Library, Harry Ransom Center, University of Texas at Austin.

what is deliuered therein."[13] Yet they also had a sense that rhyme's mysterious binding force might amount to more than a physical or psychological effect of repeated sound. The bands of rhyme form patterns within verse, and these patterns had far-ranging significance because, as Lawrence Manley has argued, premodern writers tended not only to understand "human life to be governed by fundamental human laws or ends" but to "think of these same norms as isomorphic, applicable and operative in all spheres of human activity."[14] If poets could demonstrate that limitation and binding are essential in one sphere—whether in poetic composition or in love—then perhaps the same logic could be applied to theological or political questions.

This tendency to think about the world in isomorphic, or what I will call analogical, ways is a prominent feature of the formal readings offered in treatises of poetry in the sixteenth and seventeenth centuries. Drawing on Pythagorean and Augustinian understandings of music that remained deeply influential throughout the Middle Ages and early modern period, poets and theorists frequently argued that the purpose of poetry was to reflect the symmetry of the divine mind or of the product of that mind, the cosmos, which, according to an oft-quoted verse from the Wisdom of Solomon, God "ordered . . . in measure and number and weight."[15] Polydore Vergil, an Italian humanist and priest who was sent to England in 1502, captures this mode of thinking in a passage on the origin of meter in his book *De Inventoribus Rerum* (1499): "The beginner of meter [metrum] was God, whiche proporcioned the world, with all the contentes of the same, with a certain order, as it were a meter, for there is noone (as Pithagoras taught) that douteth, but that there is in thynges heauenly and yearthly a kynd of armonye, and oneles it were gouerned with a fourmal concorde and discribed nombre, howe could it long continue?"[16] George Puttenham likewise grounds his own account of "Proportion Poetical" on the idea that "God made the world by number, measure and weight" and that "all things stand by proportion, and that without it nothing could stand to be good or beautiful" (*Arte*, K1r). Both critics insist that proportion is the framework that allows the world and everything in it to "stand" and to endure. Poets should imitate the order God inscribed in nature not only because this is a devout task, but because "those numbers wherwith heau'n & earth are mou'd" represent a formal ideal that will make human fabrications as rational, beautiful, enduring, and structurally sound as the divine originals.[17] Rhyme did not simply forge sonic resonances between words but formed part of a deeper poetic structure that had larger cosmic and social resonances even when it went undetected by the reader.[18]

Rhyme's binding power was not the only feature that made it particularly charged for early modern poets. Rhyme is also insistent. As frequent comparisons of rhyme to "tinkling," "jingling," and "chiming" bells suggest, rhyme calls attention to itself and demands that poets and readers reckon with it.[19] Donald

Wesling argues that while "all poetic devices . . . are likenings," rhyme is more "clearly marked by the ear as an equivalence" than any other device; rhyme, therefore, "more boldly than meter is at once sign and symbol."[20] This symbolic boldness makes rhyme a stand-in for every manner of question about the purposes and functions of poetic form. Rhyme, as Wesling points out, is also "suspect" because its pleasure seems so irrational, because the idea that "two words with separate meanings should be similar in sound is a transgression of our deepest language habits."[21] Unease about rhyme's potential to detach itself from reason is visible in definitions of rhyme offered by both its detractors and its champions. Early modern rhyme skeptics tend to define rhyme in ways that depict likeness of sound as entirely accidental, as a mere "falling out of verses together in one like sounde."[22] Defenders of rhyme, in contrast, tend to use words that imply that rhyme is a kind of agreement or harmony rather than a mere sonic coincidence. William Scott calls it an "answerableness at the ends of our verses in likeness of sound."[23] George Puttenham consistently uses the word "concord" to refer to rhyme and describes rhymes as the "tunable consentes in the latter end of our verses" (*Arte*, L2r, L2v). And for Samuel Daniel, rhyme is "number and harmonie of words, consisting of an agreeing sound in the last sillables of seuerall verses."[24] Words like "answerableness," "concord," "consent," "harmony," and "agreeing" all have social as well as musical meanings, as if the words at the ends of lines are forming social bonds with one another or building little commonwealths within the poem. And theorists who described rhyme in this way tended to see it not only as an emblem, but as an instrument, of social connections. Rhyme's opponents, in contrast, tended to see its irrational binding as a form of "tyranny" or "bondage" or even as a Procrustean torture device.[25]

Rhyme also came under attack in the sixteenth century because classically trained English poets were wary of its conspicuous absence from Greek and Roman verse. Throughout the sixteenth century, writers like Ascham, Sidney, Spenser, Harvey, and Campion railed against the barbarism of rhyme and attempted to reform English verse to fit a classical model of quantitative poetry.[26] Yet they never succeeded in supplanting rhyme or even in producing a workable model of English quantitative meter.[27] They did succeed, however, in prompting their contemporaries to develop a theoretical language for talking about rhyme. As Samuel Daniel puts it in his 1603 *Defence of Ryme*, in the face of attacks from advocates of quantitative meter, "The Generall Custome and vse of Ryme in this kingdome" could no longer be "held vnquestionable."[28] The threat posed by the quantitative alternative, though it never proved viable, prompted writers of the period to approach rhyme with heightened attention and deliberation. As theorists like Puttenham and Daniel endeavored to defend rhyme against its detractors, they developed new ways of conceiving of its peculiar function in English verse.

A short excursion into the sixteenth-century debate about quantitative meter will reveal how contentions over rhyme were wrapped up with conversations about primitive life and the origins of society. In these debates, advocates of rhyme held it up as an exemplar of the possibility of reconciling natural energy with disciplined order. Humanist and one-time tutor to Queen Elizabeth Roger Ascham began the English attack on rhyme in *The Scholemaster* (published posthumously in 1570), where he beseeches English poets not to be "caryed by tyme and custome to content themselues with that barbarous and rude Ryming" but to follow the "*Greeks* in trew versifiying."[29] His account of rhyme as a barbarous custom "brought first into Italie by *Gothes* and *Hunnes*" contains all the seeds of later criticisms of like endings, including Milton's preface to *Paradise Lost*.[30] In his *Observations in the Art of English Poesy* (1602), Thomas Campion elaborates on Ascham's unflattering genealogy of rhyme, telling a tale of the decline "of the *Romaine* Empire and the pollution of their language through the conquest of the *Barbarians*," which left learning "most pitifully deformed till the time of *Erasmus*, *Rewcline*, Sir *Thomas More*, and other learned men of that age, who brought the Latine toong again to light, redeeming it with much labour out of the hands of the illiterate Monks and Friers."[31] The "vulgar and easie" rhymed verse "now in use throughout most parts of Cristendome" is the product of these "lack-learning times."[32] Both Ascham and Campion (and Milton after them) model their prosodic histories on the familiar humanist and Reformation arc of history: a pure age is followed by a descent into darkness that is at long last dispelled by the torchbearers of the early sixteenth century. Richard Helgerson has highlighted the ways in which this story of rhyme "presents an active model of self-fashioning" in which individuals and the English nation may choose to reject the passive acceptance of custom in favor of deliberately remaking themselves on an ancient model.[33] There is an irony in the fact that humanist poetics enjoined poets to shake off the familiar bonds of English poetic custom only to bind themselves as apprentices to ancient masters. Indeed, the prayer-book declaration that "service is perfect freedom" captures a central paradox of the humanist program as well as Reformation theology.[34] In humanist and Reformation arguments for a return *ad fontes*, there is a conviction that the most strenuous and serious liberty involves shaking off arbitrary, human bonds in order to submit oneself willingly to more divine, rational, or ancient restraints.

Because advocates of quantitative measure saw this act of uprooting native custom and replacing it with an extrinsic measure as central to the purpose of poetry, they use "artificial" as a term of praise in their writings.[35] During his own flirtation with quantitative meter, Spenser sent a sample of his experiments to Gabriel Harvey with this preface: "Loe, here I let you see my olde vse of toying in Rymes turned into your artificial straightnesse of Verse by this Tetrasticon."[36] While rhyming was a native and infantile habit, an "olde vse of toying" idly with language, versifying according to the rules of quantity requires the strenuous labor of hammering language into an artificial straightness. For its sixteenth-century opponents, to choose rhyme is not only to side with barbarous Goths and illiterate monks but to regress to poetic infancy, to surrender to the easy and irrational pleasures of what Campion calls a "childish titillation."[37]

Instead of contending against rhyme's detractors by insisting that rhyme is in fact artificial and sophisticated, advocates of rhyme often translated the charge of childishness and rudeness into a virtue. If you wanted to champion something in the Renaissance, it was always shrewd to claim that it was both old and universal. Defenders of rhyme therefore tried to outvie quantitative advocates in their claim to be returning to the most ancient models. Sidney takes precisely this tack in *Apology for Poetry*, contending that "Poetrie is of all humane learning the most auncient and of most fatherly antiquitie, as from whence other learnings haue taken theyr beginnings" and that "it is so vniuersall that no learned Nation dooth despise it, nor no barbarous Nation is without it."[38] In their poetic treatises, George Puttenham and Samuel Daniel convert Sidney's general argument about the antiquity of poetry into a defense of rhyme in particular. Building on the idea that there was rhyme in biblical Hebrew, Puttenham argues that the biblical precedent takes priority over the classical precedent described by Ascham:

> But the Hebrues & Chaldees who were more ancient then the Greekes, did not only use a metrical Poesie, but also with the same maner of rime, as hath been of late obserued by learned men. Wherby it appeareth that our vulgar running Poesie was common to all the nations of the world besides, whom the Latines and Greekes in speciall called barbarous. So as it was notwithstanding the first and most ancient Poesie, and the most vniuersall; which two points do otherwise giue to all humane inuentions and affaires no small credit. (*Arte*, C4r)[39]

Indeed, one of Puttenham's fundamental arguments is that poetry is primitive, that it is "most ancient from the beginning, and not as manie erroniously suppose, after, but before, any ciuil society was among men" (*Arte*, C2r). He can therefore make the case that "Poesie was th'originall cause and occasion" of political life; its sweetness enticed the "rude and savage" and "by that meanes made them tame" (*Arte*, C2r, C2v, C2v).[40] The fact that rhyme, too, is ancient and primitive is evidence that it plays this dual role of enticing and ordering.

Samuel Daniel likewise answers the charge that "all Ryming is grosse, vulgare, barbarous" by contending that "The vniuersalitie argues the generall power of it: for if the Barbarian vse it, then it shewes that it swais th' affection of the Barbarian: if ciuil nations practise it, it proues that it works vpon the harts of ciuil nations: if all, then that it hath a power in nature on all."[41] The "olde vse of toying" with rhymes should not be left behind because it is precisely rhyme's "childish titillation," its ability to sway the affections and work on the hearts of all human beings, that gives rhyme its power.[42] Daniel offers a more robust account of rhyme's "power in nature" than Puttenham, deriving its primitive influence from the fact that it is a force of energy and motion.[43] He argues that quantitative numbers will only take hold if the "world" finds that it can "feele" the "pulse, life, and enargie" in them that it now feels in rhyme.[44] Daniel's phrase expands on Philip Sidney's contention that rhyme is the "chiefe life" of "modern" versifying.[45] While we might see rhyme as an inert scheme or lifeless repetition, Daniel sees repetition as a sign of energy and argues that it is the pulsations of rhyme that enable it to perform "those offices of motion for which it is imployed; delighting the eare, stirring the heart, and satisfying the iudgement."[46] Daniel's account of rhyme's power is remarkably physical. The purpose of poetry is to "swa[y]," "work on," and "stir" an audience, and rhyme is the perpetual motion machine that makes these "offices of motion" possible by imparting its own energy to the ear, the heart, and the judgment.[47]

And yet in the same sentence in which Daniel attributes the "pulse, life, and enargie" of verse to "our Rymes," he adds a clause that makes rhyme the moderator as well as the fountain of motion: "whose knowne frame hath those due staies for the minde, those incounters of touch, as makes the motion certaine, though the varietie be infinite."[48] Daniel offers a fascinating series of metaphors to explain the role of rhyme: it is a "known frame," that is, a structure, framework, or lattice that acts as a "stay" or prop for a poetic mind that might otherwise run wild or collapse under its own weight.[49] Yet the idea that rhymes provide periodic "incounters of touch" for the mind is even more loaded and intriguing. The word "touch" could mean physical contact as it does today, but it could also mean an encounter with a touchstone that tests the purity of a precious metal (as in the phrase "put to the touch").[50] The sounds of rhyme might keep the poetic mind in touch with the physical senses of the body, or they might be a recurring test that keeps the poet honest. I would argue that the two senses of "touch" are both in play in this passage since the only true touchstone of verse for Daniel is whether we can "feel" life and energy within it. By returning to make contact with rhyme's energy at the end of every single verse, the poet also gives his poem regularity and certainty. Rhyme is like the regular push given to a child in a swing; the push imparts energy and motion, but it also makes the swing's motion regular.

In a rich and thought-provoking 2016 essay, Colleen Ruth Rosenfeld takes seriously Sidney's idea that rhyme could be the "chief life" of a poem, demonstrating in a reading of Spenser's Maleger episode that rhyme can be both artificial and generative. She also draws on this peculiar passage from Daniel, contending that here "rhyme's model of life might assert its mechanical existence onto the listeners of verse, remaking their rhythms . . . in the image of mechanical life. Under this model, the iterations of rhyme do not fold into the beating heart so much as act as defibrillator and pacemaker in one: rhyme 'makes the motion certain' rather than erratic."[51] Though I think that Spenser does in fact use rhyme as an artificial restraint that remakes erratic nature (I will return to this idea in the first chapter), it is not clear to me that this captures the tensions at the heart of Daniel's account of rhyme. Instead, I would argue that Daniel sees the assertion of certain motion as a return to rather than a departure from nature.[52]

Daniel makes the case that certainty is natural later in his treatise by taking on an extreme example of poetic limitation: the sonnet. He argues that the "certaine limit obserued in Sonnets" is not a "tyrannical bounding of the conceit, but rather a reducing it in *girum*, and a iust forme."[53] He goes on to compare the form of the sonnet with the form of the world after the divine act of creation:

> For the body of our imagination, being as an vnformed *Chaos* without fashion, without day, if by the diuine power of the spirit it be wrought into an Orbe of order and forme, is it not more pleasing to Nature, that desires a certaintie, and comports not with that which is infinite, to haue these clozes, rather than, not to know where to end, or how farre to goe, especially seeing our passions are often without measure.[54]

The "certaine limit" of the sonnet's rhyme scheme and the "clozes" of the end rhymes do not tyrannically impose an artificial order on nature. Just as Carew argues that nature is the origin of the freeborn mind's limitations, Daniel contends that the desire for "certaintie" is built into "Nature" itself. While the imagination and the passions are often "vnformed" and "without measure," there is something in "Nature" that is "pleas[ed]" with "order and forme." The poet's task is to "reduc[e]" the conceit "in *girum*," that is, to lead it back (*reducere*) into its own proper gyre or circuit. The metaphor of the gyre allows Daniel to reconcile the idea of rhyme as measure with the sense that rhyme is energy: an object moving in a gyre retains its motion even as it follows a set path. This dual capacity of rhyme is precisely what makes it a perpetual source of fascination and debate in early modern poetics. Each of the poets in this book has a different understanding of whether movement or measure predominates and whether each aspect is a boon or a hindrance to composition.

Daniel's idea that form is a natural and pleasing limitation of the imagination rather than a tyrannical bounding has much in common with Caroline Levine's recent efforts to overcome a lingering resistance in literary studies to "the containing power of form."[55] She argues that "containers do not afford only imprisonment, exclusion, and the quelling of difference"; rather, "bounded wholes" are necessary to political action and to scholarship itself since "*concepts* continue to do the work for us of imposing order on disparate materials: including and excluding, gathering specific examples while separating these from other categories of particulars."[56] Levine's invitation to reconsider the many "affordances" of poetic containment is fruitful, but the concept of "measure," a concept that runs through every chapter of this book because it was at the center of the poetics of this period, might offer a way of thinking about form that both includes and pushes beyond the idea of containment.[57] The word "measure" was used to translate the Latin words "metrum" and "modus." It had mathematical, musical, legal, and ethical meanings. It could mean limit, moderation, capacity (as in "full measure"), proportion, rhythm, and meter, among many other things. This complex of ideas brought together by the word "measure" was at the heart of what it meant to write in verse, for, as Samuel Daniel put it, "All verse is but a frame of wordes confined within certaine measure."[58] But in spite of consensus that measure was central to any understanding of verse, there was little agreement about which kind of measure ought to be pursued and how best to pursue it. While striving to tell a coherent story of rhyme's development from the 1590s to the 1670s, *The Fetters of Rhyme* aims to do full justice to the multiplicity and intricacy of concepts of measure in the period and to revel in the peculiar and colorful metaphors that poets used to represent their understandings of measure and form. Forms are compared not only to the familiar little rooms and well-wrought urns but also to orbs, gyres, frames, gowns, brick walls, soldiers, footsteps, and kisses. Each of these "fictions of form" carries with it a distinctive poetic theory.[59] By lingering with these metaphors and drawing out these theories over the course of this book, I hope not only to offer fresh insights into the complexities of early modern verse but to expand our notions of the ways form can be read.

Form and Analogical Reading

One of the aims of this book is to develop modes of formal reading that respond to the peculiarities of premodern verse making. *The Fetters of Rhyme* therefore builds on recent efforts by practitioners of "historical poetics" or "historical formalism" to historicize poetry, to peer around institutionalized twentieth-century understandings of "lyric" and "lyric reading" that often veil diverse and unfamiliar historical practices of reading and writing verse.[60] Critics like Virginia Jackson and Ardis Butterfield have made it clear just how much is lost by assuming that the deracinated lyrics printed in twentieth-century volumes tell the whole story. Butterfield begins a seminal article on medieval lyric with an invitation to "look at this page," to look closely at a legal roll and a sermon manuscript that contain texts we might want to call lyrics, deeply embedded in a multilingual, polygeneric context that is inevitably stripped away by the twenty-first-century editor.[61] Butterfield is building on Virginia Jackson's earlier invitation to look anew. In *Dickinson's Misery*, Jackson enlivens our understanding of the occasionality and materiality of Dickinson's poetry by recounting how the poet circulated and recirculated her poems and letters, sometimes even with a dead cricket or a pressed leaf attached.[62] But I am also wary of historical formalism's claim to offer a new understanding of poetry by clearing away modern prejudices and returning to the historical roots of poetry.[63] After all, that assertion sounds suspiciously similar to the dueling claims made by Renaissance prosodists from Ascham to Milton about the ancient roots of their theories. Practitioners of historical poetics are as subject to institutional predilections as new critics or new historicists were: Virginia Jackson's subtle examination of the cricket and the leaf in *Dickinson's Misery* and Yopie Prins's fine-tuned appreciation for the mediation of voice in "What Is Historical Poetics?" do not simply translate unadulterated the poetic realities of the past but reflect the unique and compelling passions of Jackson and Prins for materiality and mediation.[64] The presence of these unique interests, which are as much a product of the twentieth-century academy as the idea of lyric is, do not undermine their readings, only their claims to liberate us from troublesome and modern bondage. *The Fetters of Rhyme* endeavors to take up the historical formalists' call to think harder about bygone ways of engaging with form without making the claim that prior critics were uniquely estranged from Renaissance verse by their modern biases. "Historical" critics have been thinking deeply about form, and "formal" critics have been thinking deeply about history for much longer than historical formalists usually acknowledge.

Moreover, the work produced in the wake of calls for a reunification of history and form reveals what a wide range of methodologies can comfortably fit under the capacious umbrella of historical poetics. In the last two decades, a wave of edited volumes with variants of the words "form" and "Renaissance" in their titles has indicated that a lively and diverse group of scholars is dedicated to exploring the place of form in the early modern period.[65] Building on recent work in media theory and reception studies, Stephen Cohen invites readers to imagine form as a kind of "mediation" between "text and social context as well as author and audience."[66] Danielle Clarke and Marie-Louise Coolahan consider what it would mean to think about form as "a key element in reception, the interface between text and reader."[67] Joshua Scodel and Douglas Bruster consider how familiar concepts from historical scholarship such as source, intertextuality, and allusion can be used to illuminate the ways in which forms import ideologies from other texts.[68] And Raphael Lyne takes a "cognitive approach" to his analysis of Shakespeare's stanzaic poetry, describing "how form is shaped by the characteristics of human thinking."[69] Each of these methods expands our understanding of form by showing how it is in conversation with social, historical, and mental realms. But, as illuminating as these readings may be, they do not make it clear how far-reaching and, often, how strange premodern understandings of form and its correspondences with the wider world really were.

Premodern poetic theorists often interpret verse in ways that are familiar and immediately legible to modern critics. They dedicate considerable time to the intricacies of poetic craft, describing the architecture of stanza forms and meters and explaining how poets achieve particular sonic and verbal effects. Trained in humanist methods of classical philology, they also read form in historical or genealogical ways, tracing how particular meters, rhyme schemes, and genres derive from ancient or Middle English sources and how they import associations from their historical contexts.[70] But analogical reading, which was central to ancient, medieval, and early modern theories of music and poetry, has become less common since the Romantics and therefore often seems alien and backward. Premodern poets did not shrink from drawing analogies between forms and ideas and often maintained that the visual and verbal patterns inscribed in verse could be mapped onto social, moral, or cosmic structures.[71] Indeed, the numerological work of critics like A. Kent Hieatt and Alastair Fowler has revealed the mind-boggling lengths to which poets could take this idea that verse should reproduce the intricate structural patterns of the cosmos.[72] John Hollander has traced the gradual "untuning of the sky," that is, growing skepticism about the "physical and metaphysical reality" of the music of the spheres, from 1500 to 1700, but his study also testifies to the remarkable appeal of this account late into the seventeenth century, when poets went to great lengths to reshape ideas of heavenly harmony in the face of skepticism.[73] Though many complicated the correlation of cosmological and poetical proportion, every poet of the period had to reckon with this influential idea that the measure, number, and weight built into the form of verse made it a privileged mode for reflecting and perhaps even enforcing divine order.

I have chosen to describe this mode of reading as "analogical" because the term involves more than a simple arithmetical equality of two things.[74] "Analogy" comes from the Greek mathematical term for a ratio. As James Moxon defines it in his 1679 *Mathematical Dictionary*, it is "a double comparison, or proportion of Numbers or Magnitudes one to another: As when we say, as 4 is to 2, so 8 to 4."[75] Premodern interpreters rarely offer what I would call arithmetical readings, in which the sounds of the words in a line are equated with its local meaning.[76] Instead, they tend to make double comparisons: they carefully consider the patterns formed by rhyme, meter, line length, and so on and consider how these formal patterns correspond with other patterns inside and outside the poem. George Puttenham's account of "*Analogie*" shows just how difficult it was to detect and size up these correspondences (*Arte*, Ff4r). Though he defines analogy rather simply as the "louely conformitie, or proportion, or conueniencie, betweene the sence and the sensible," he reveals how many elements are involved in this proportion when he says that it "resteth in the good conformitie of many things and their sundry circumstances, with respect one to another, so as there be found a iust correspondencie betweene them by this or that relation" (*Arte*, Ff4r).[77] In fact, sorting out all the manifold relations between many things and their sundry circumstances seems like such a knotty task that Puttenham wonders who is even capable of performing it. He concludes that only the "discreetest man" who is "of much observation and greatest experience" can judge the correspondences of things, and even he only with the aid of "example" and "particular discussions" (*Arte*, Ff4v).[78] Although analogical thinkers posit a web of correspondences that should link poetic form to natural order, this idea does not make poetic composition a simple task of copying out conspicuous patterns. The patterns and correspondences are so difficult to discern and then to body forth in language that even the rule-loving Puttenham dictates few laws to govern analogy or decorum, instead leaving it to the discretion of particularly learned and experienced individuals.

The analogical manner of interpreting form not only is unfamiliar to contemporary critics practiced in the art of reading historically and for craft but also runs athwart two assumptions that underlie much post-Romantic poetic criticism: that mimetic theories of literature are rigid and reductive, and that the poet can do justice to melody or form only when he is liberated from the burden of representing anything beyond his own thoughts and feelings.[79] Both of these evaluative principles are on display, for example, in one of Simon Jarvis's seminal articles on "verse thinking."[80] In order to clear the way for much-needed attention to the manifold ways in which poets think in verse, Jarvis has attempted to banish "the doctrine of verbal mimesis" from poetic criticism, even as he acknowledges that two foundational figures in English poetics, Dryden and Pope, espoused this doctrine.[81] In "The Melodics of Long Poems," Jarvis maintains that Pope's most compelling verse indeed works against Pope's own mimetic theory. In a reading of "An Essay on Man," Jarvis argues that the poem's "continuous explosions of wit . . . think back against, detonate, those inert cosmological and moral schemas which they should, according to Pope's own poetics, meekly exemplify."[82] This reading presents a Manichaean vision of the struggle between the individual artist and communal norms.[83] The individual is complex, energetic, and free, while understandings of the cosmos and morality (which are always imposed by society) are dull, monolithic, and repressive. Since the melody of the poem is intricate and full of life, it must perforce be on the side of the individual and not the schemas. One need only read John Davies's 1596 poem *Orchestra, or A Poeme of Dauncing*, in which every aspect of the cosmos from the planets to the plants engages in its own lively dance, to see that the patterns detected within the cosmos were far from "inert."[84] And Spenser is somehow at his most melodious in *Epithalamion*, at the exact moment when he is most dedicated to versifying cosmological and moral patterns. Just as poets can think in and through rhyme, meter, and melody, Spenser is capable of thinking in and through the patterns of time and ceremony. Indeed, poetic theorists repeatedly argue that imposing strictures on the fancy enables rather than hampers composition. Poets, they insist, need not detonate "schemas" in order to be harmonious, witty, or free.

In fact, one of the pleasures of studying poetics is discovering the manifold ways poets of the period endeavor to build bridges between mind and world, verse and universe. Each of the poets considered in this book is building such bridges; that is, each is thinking about form in analogical ways. But, as much as I hope to draw out the resemblances and interconnections among these poets, I also hope to do full justice to the distinctiveness of each poet's account of form's correspondences. For Spenser, the bands of interwoven rhyme schemes are analogous to the coercive social bonds he believed were required to rein in the unruly passions of isolated individuals. Donne and the couplet poets of the 1590s in some ways anticipate the recent emphasis on "verse thinking" as they reshape poetry into an analogy for the struggle of discursive thought. In Ben Jonson's poetics of character, form is a "pattern" of ethical living: its order both reflects the inner character of the poet and provides readers with a model of the good life. And in the royalist theories I discuss in chapter 4, analogical thinking begins to border on magical thinking. Like Spenser, the Royalists were interested in the connection between rhyme and social bonds, but they go beyond Spenser in their belief that the orderly chime of rhyme might actually be a transrational force that can instill political order rather than simply reflecting it. Milton did not contest the royalist idea that rhyme can charm us into obedience, but he saw the royalist effort to use rhyme to manipulate the passions as a violation of poetry's rational purpose. His poetic theory therefore returns to the Donnean and Jonsonian correlations of form with individual thought and character. Though these poets do not share a politics or a world picture and in fact fundamentally disagree about the practices and the purposes of verse making, there is a remarkable consensus among them that verse patterns are in conversation with other patterns, whether the workings of the mind or the dance of the cosmos.

As I trace the history of rhyme in this project, I endeavor to read analogically as well as historically and for craft. My goal, like that of Susanne Woods in her essential study of early modern versification, is not to "reconstruc[t] and presen[t] what is archaic and irrelevant," but rather to "provide a context and a perspective for hearing . . . the art of Renaissance poetry."[85] I recognize that there are risks inherent in the enterprise of analogical reading. After all, if this brief survey of analogical approaches shows anything, it is that analogical thinking is flexible and that analogies are open to interpretation. Even when poets advertise their poetic theories explicitly, how can critics determine how these analogies play out within any given poem and when they are disrupted or displaced? But this risk is common to all poetic interpretation and to literary studies more generally. Interpretation always requires extrapolating from what we know (or think we know) about a poet or period. The precariousness of the critical enterprise and the slipperiness of poems are precisely what allow us to return to reinterpret "Satyre 3" and *Paradise Lost* again and again. I hope that other critics will correct the excesses and infelicities of my analogical extrapolations, just as they have done with previous readings that employ other interpretive methods. But I also hope to make it evident that analogical reading was a lively, demanding, and contested methodology that premodern thinkers believed had the utmost stakes for social and political life.

Though Jarvis's intimation that the poet's melody is directly opposed to moral and cosmological patterns betrays his reliance on a Romantic understanding of artistry that is inconsonant with the analogical thinking of earlier periods, his more fundamental objection to "verbal mimesis" still needs to be tackled.[86] His opposition to "word-painting" springs from a desire to revivify attention to the melody of a poem and from a very real fear—shared by most poetic scholars—of making form subservient to content.[87] Any teacher of poetry knows firsthand that the effort to make a poem's rhyme scheme or metrical patterns fit neatly with its message can produce remarkably far-fetched interpretations.[88] Students are liable to assert that they can actually hear the pigeons sinking into the abyss in the alliteration of Wallace Stevens's "Downward to darkness, on extended wings."[89] As teachers who know the delights of poetry's sounds, we should indeed encourage students to slow down and linger with the form of a poem, to attune their ears to the more subtle music of rhyme and meter rather than precipitately fixing their meaning. But I have found that analogical thinking can actually help students and teachers push beyond simple equations of local sound with local sense. By seeing Puttenham's figures of the bands formed by rhymes or hearing Jonson's ideas about the correspondence of language patterns and individual character, students develop a more expansive sense of the complex patterns that can be uncovered within verse. I am not contending that critics should themselves adhere to the view that form is in conversation with cosmic and social forces. But attending to and even temporarily immersing ourselves in analogical reading can not only open up new understandings of the historical resonances of particular poems but amplify our sense of what forms can do.

Moreover, a fine-grained reading of metaphors for form demonstrates just how premodern poetic dualism differs from the twentieth-century division between form and content questioned by Jarvis and, before him, by the New Critics. Cleanth Brooks in particular challenged the view that the poet has something to communicate and that form is just a "transparent pane of glass through which the stuff of poetry is reflected, directly and immediately" or "a kind of box, neat or capacious, chastely engraved or gaudily decorated, into which the valuable and essentially poetic 'content' of the poem is packed."[90] Premodern theorists do often speak of form in ways that make it secondary to the "stuff" of poetry. As David Scott Wilson-Okamura has emphasized, the preferred metaphor for form in this period is not a pane of glass or container, but clothing: they frequently describe verse as the "clothing," "rayment," "habit or livery," "Garb and dress" of poetry.[91] Even Samuel Daniel, dedicated as he is to the idea that rhyme is the life and pulse of verse, also calls rhyme "our kind and natural attire."[92] Though the metaphor of clothing undoubtedly makes the attire of rhyme secondary to the body of poetry, it is telling that Daniel

theoretical associations with measure—and because it was a feature of classical verse—it was rarely described as a suspiciously prerational threat to sense. Many poets insisted that rhyme was amenable to or even akin to restraint and reason, but it was clear that it was in many ways apart from reason. Much of the prosodic energy of the century was poured into negotiating rhyme's precise place between sound and sense because to decide how one felt about rhyme was to decide how one felt about the proper mixture of the sonic and the rational in poetry itself.

As my survey of the quantitative debate suggests, conversations about what to do with rhyme during this period almost always became conversations about which past or pasts should form the foundations of a new English verse. Because the same question of which past to follow was at the center of debates about the origins of the polity and the sources and limits of individuals' obligations to it, poets often draw more and less explicit correspondences between rhyme and politics. These parallels and explicit connections make it tempting to describe the history of rhyme outlined in this book as a *political* history of rhyme. But the addition of the adjective unnecessarily narrows the implications of freedom and binding. The poetical debates about liberty and bands I discuss in this book are always in touch with but never completely absorbed by the politics of the period. Rhyme was political, but it was never purely political. Indeed, the story of rhyme in the late sixteenth and early seventeenth centuries can often seem as much like a picaresque novel as like an epic: always getting into scrapes and regularly changing its disguises and companions, rhyme is present for the big political events of the period but also pursues many romantic and intellectual side adventures away from the centers of power. I have therefore resolved to follow rhyme's adventures where they lead and to reveal how the bands of rhyme gathered and cast off political, ethical, and social implications over the course of a century. As much as rhyme's interpreters in the period tried to claim that it had a fixed nature and meaning, rhyme's *malleability* is one of the constants of this story; rhyme's status as something between sound and sense, sensuality and reason, made it amenable to repeated reinterpretation over the course of the century. The understanding of the couplet, to take an extreme example, was overturned several times in the course of a century: it was in turn seen as a sign of radical licentiousness, of Stoic evenness, and of charming magic. But taking a long view of rhyme's many repurposings from the end of Elizabeth's reign to the Restoration reveals that there were many patterns within the mutability and that poets were engaged in a common debate about the purposes of measured writing. By telling a new story about the life of rhyme in the period, I hope not only to enrich knowledge of particular poets and poems but to reshape understanding of the aims and stakes of early modern verse making.

Before outlining the argument of *The Fetters of Rhyme* at the level of the chapter, I would like to take a moment to consider an Elizabethan prosodic innovation that represented a departure from the fundamental premises of the sixteenth-century debate over quantitative verse and rhyme. While all the defenders and opponents of rhyme I have discussed in this introduction were keen to claim that their version of poetry was the most deeply rooted in the ancient past, Catherine Nicholson's work has made it clear that Marlowe's blank verse was seen as an upstart Tamburlaine, bursting violently onto the scene without apologizing for its disruptive novelty.[107] Robert Greene sums up the sense of prosodic outrage with characteristic color when he complains of those

> who (mounted on the stage of arrogance) think to outbraue better pens with the swelling bumbast of a bragging blanke verse. Indeed it may be the ingrafted ouerflow of some kilcow conceipt, that ouerclioeth their imagination with a more than drunken resolution, beeing not extemporall in the inuention of anie other meanes to vent their manhood, commits the disgestion of their cholerick incumbrances, to the spacious volubilitie of a drumming decasillabon.[108]

The novelty of English blank verse was something of a fiction since Surrey's *Aeneid*, Grimald's translations, Norton and Sackville's *Gorboduc*, and Gascoigne's *Jocasta* and *Steel Glass* all preceded *Tamburlaine*, but the overflow that characterized Marlowe's drama played right into the fiction that blank verse was a swaggering upstart. Kicking loose from classical precedent on the one hand and from what he called the "riming mother wits" of native tradition on the other, Marlowe produced a form well adapted to accommodate the passionate speech of his overreaching protagonists.[109] Marlowe's willingness to embrace the disruptive reputation of his blank verse may partly account for the fact that the innovation remained nearly exclusive to drama for eighty years. His innovation was seen as too arrogantly newfangled, too willing to cut ties with ancient poetry. Not just the sixteenth-century controversialists I have considered, but every poet and theorist I will discuss in this book touted some ancient past—classical, Christian, or English—in justifying decisions about how to shape and reshape rhyme and meter. Dramatists like Kyd, Shakespeare, and Jonson were willing to follow Marlowe in his innovation because they found in blank verse a new and fruitful middle ground between prose and rhymed verse that was too well accommodated to the needs of drama to resist. (Though these poets understood the implications of the form very differently; as early as *Much Ado about Nothing* [c. 1598], Shakespeare's Benedick speaks of the "even road of a blank verse." Hardly Marlovian bombast.)[110] But epics, lyrics, elegies, and odes—even those written by the blank-verse dramatists themselves—continued to be written in some kind of rhyme.[111]

Perhaps even more strikingly, Milton himself confessed to the influence of Marlowe's, Shakespeare's, and Jonson's blank verse with only a brief and vague statement in the middle of his preface to *Paradise Lost* that "our best *English* tragedies" have "long since" rejected rhyme (*CPMP*, 210). This is not, I think, solely because he wanted to focus on his claim to be the first English heroic poet to cast off rhyme, but because he saw that Marlowe's dramatic innovation sprung from a desire for a different kind of prosodic freedom than that of *Paradise Lost*, that is, from a desire to imitate more freely the rhythms of the passions and of speech.[112] Milton saw his own rejection of "riming mother wits" as an effort to imitate not speech but the lofty harmonies of ancient poetry (classical and biblical). Though dramatic and nondramatic verse practice influenced one another in innumerable ways during this period, I have restricted myself to nondramatic verse because, in prosody at least, Marlowe's innovation made the gap between dramatic and nondramatic verse wider in this period than it was before the 1580s or after rhyme returned to the stage in the Restoration. Doing justice to the history of blank verse and rhyme in drama would require another monograph entirely, one that I hope someone will soon write.[113]

In honor of one of the great analogical thinkers of the seventeenth century, Thomas Browne, the five chapters of my book form a sort of quincunx.[114] The first two chapters and the last two chapters analyze contemporaneous poets who contended over the implications of rhyme. Chapters 1 and 2 examine two rival poetic camps that emerged in the final decade of Elizabeth's reign. Their prosodic debate over the merits of stanzas and couplets was entangled with a larger controversy about the proper balance between personal liberty and social constraint. Chapter 1 focuses on Spenser's experiments with interwoven rhyme patterns in *Amoretti*. In his sonnet sequence celebrating his betrothal to Elizabeth Boyle, Spenser depicts the drama of courtship as a small-scale version of the struggle to unite freeborn individuals in communities. Pointing to his interwoven rhyme schemes and the sonnet form itself as emblems of pleasant and beneficial confinement, Spenser argues that social life requires a form of voluntary captivity that is made palatable by its beauty. The second chapter reveals that John Donne played a formative role in a new school of couplet poetry that arose in the 1590s. The youthful poets who belonged to this school rejected the interwoven rhymes favored by many Elizabethans, insisting that elaborate rhyme schemes betrayed a preference for form over reason. Reacting against Italianate stanzaic poetry, these poets took up the Chaucerian pentameter couplet in order to flout imported poetic rules and return English poetry to its original state of rational liberty. They contended that the antiquated form, with its loose rhythm and enjambed lines, allowed them to restore verse to its proper function as a forum for free, argumentative discourse.

In the middle of the quincunx stands Ben Jonson, whom contemporaries viewed as the presiding spirit of seventeenth-century verse. The third chapter endeavors to explain why Jonson's measured couplets were seen as a watershed in the history of English poetry. I argue that the battle between the couplet and the stanzaic poets in the 1590s ended in a sort of stalemate. The young couplet poets eroded the influence of stanzaic poets like Spenser by associating stanzas with a cowardly submission to mistresses, conventions, and continental rules of poetry. Nevertheless, their separation of verse from measure was not particularly congenial to most seventeenth-century poets, who continued to hold to the view that poetic form should reflect divine or social order. By instituting a reform of English verse that reconciled the argumentative freedom of the couplet school with the measure of the stanzaic poets, Ben Jonson made the couplet a fitting vehicle for his ethical poetry, which celebrates a circumscribed, private kind of liberty. In doing so, he developed concepts of lyric freedom and a separate poetic sphere that would be taken up and reinterpreted by the subsequent generation of poets.

The final section of the book again analyzes two competing schools of rhyme: royalist lyric poets, who celebrated the affective power of rhyme's chime, and Milton, who categorically rejected the "jingling sound of like endings" in his preface to *Paradise Lost* (*CPMP*, 210). Focusing on the verse of Robert Herrick, Katherine Philips, and Abraham Cowley, the fourth chapter argues that royalist poets responded to a Civil War crisis of the passions by embracing the prerational charms of rhyme's chime and its connections to the most basic and natural bonds of the heart. In the final chapter, I recontextualize Milton's disavowal of rhyme in *Paradise Lost* by showing how it grew out of a career-long effort to reckon with rhyme's allures and to disentangle his own dedication to poetic sublimity and private liberty from the royalist retreat into the affections.

CHAPTER ONE

Sweet Be the Bands

SPENSER AND THE SONNET OF ASSOCIATION

IN 1796, COLERIDGE FOUND that he had extra paper lying around at the printer's office that he "could employ no other way," so he resolved to "amuse [him]self" by compiling a little pamphlet of sonnets by Charlotte Smith, Robert Southey, Charles Lamb, and others.[1] He prefaced his miniature anthology with a brief essay on the nature of the sonnet, which he defines succinctly as "a small poem, in which some lonely feeling is developed."[2] His definition typifies the Romantic association of lyric with individual subjectivity: the sonnet should be lonely because the proper subject of lyric is the individual mind, sequestered from political and social life so that it can meditate on itself.[3] The definition also implies that there is some correlation between the smallness of the sonnet and its lonely subject. The sonnet is peculiarly suited for such lonely explorations of the self, Coleridge suggests, because its "limited form" allows the poem to "acquire, as it were, a totality" that mirrors the integrity of the mind.[4]

The tacit association of lyric's formal circumscription with the secluded mind continues to inflect our understanding of the sonnet tradition that preceded Coleridge and to inform our evaluations about the merit and canonical status of individual sonnets and sonnet sequences. Critics, anthologists, and casual readers still gravitate toward sonnets that develop lonely feelings and overlook sonnets that, in G. K. Hunter's language, "run counter to the 'natural genius' of the Elizabethan love sonnet" by subsuming the ego into a larger "pattern" rather than focusing on the "tensions of individualism."[5] Recent calls to historicize poetic form and reconsider the ways in which genres signified without the distorting lens of Romanticism should prompt us to look anew at the sonnet and to consider just how "natural" this reclusive "genius" of the genre actually is: did early modern sonneteers connect the sonnet's limited form with the boundaries of the human mind, or did they have other ways of interpreting and utilizing the form's circumscription?

To some extent, this association of the sonnet with loneliness is embedded within the early modern sonnet tradition itself. The outsized and enduring influence of a single Italian sonneteer and his reclusive temperament made seclusion a common characteristic of the sonnet centuries before Coleridge's pronouncement. As Thomas Greene notes, Petrarch "was born deracinated," and his relative lack of "attachments to a class, a place, and a community" helped foster a "rootless, self-questioning personality, half in love with and half perplexed by its reflexive inquisitions."[6] Petrarch displays his admiration for the life of seclusion in his Latin prose works *De otio religioso* and *De vita solitaria*, but his vision of a "Solo et pensoso" lover, who seemed to be perpetually wandering through deserted fields with only "Amor" to converse with him, proved far more influential.[7] Indeed, Petrarch's isolation is so extreme that we cannot be sure he ever propositions Laura in person or hears her speak directly to him within the world of the sequence.[8] Like Romantic verse, Petrarch's reflections on the inner life of a lonely lover have an implicit politics: they help forge an idea of "autarkic individualism" in which human beings are more dignified and free when they are abstracted from political and social allegiances.[9] Petrarch's English imitators often tempered the extremity of Petrarch's solitude: Stella's voice and the voices of well-meaning friends at times puncture Astrophil's internal dialogue, and Shakespeare's speaker generally addresses his two lovers directly. But, despite these significant alterations, Tudor sonneteers generally followed Petrarch in recording the vicissitudes of unsuccessful love affairs and representing minds driven inward by frustrated love.[10]

Writing at the height of the late Elizabethan sonnet craze, Spenser tests the conventional limits of the genre and interrogates the political implications of its dedication to the solitary individual. Indeed, his work in *Amoretti and Epithalamion* has something in common with the avant-garde antilyricism of the twentieth century. As a group of Language Poets did in 1988 in their manifesto "Aesthetic Tendency and the Politics of Poetry," Spenser questions the prevailing view that "the maintenance of a marginal, isolated individualism" is "an heroic and transcendent project."[11] Yet he does so not by destabilizing the traditional narrative voice or by defending collective writing practices but by crafting a sonnet sequence that depicts the social integration rather than the isolation of the individual. As the diminutive title of his 1595 sonnet sequence *Amoretti* indicates, Spenser, like Coleridge, saw smallness as a fundamental characteristic of the sonnet, but, in his sonnets tracing a courtship that culminates in matrimony, Spenser makes the case that the circumscribed form of the sonnet is as suitable for reflections on the ties that bind human beings as it is for meditations on the deracinated mind. In converting the sonnet into a sociable genre, Spenser modifies its formal conventions accordingly, inventing his own interlocking rhyme scheme and adopting modes of address that advance his vision of mutual captivity. These revisions aid him as he inverts the Petrarchan paradigm by depicting a lover who is gradually driven out of, rather than into, himself. As *Amoretti* opens, both the speaker and the lady are engaged in the enterprise of the Coleridgean sonneteer—they are developing, perhaps even nursing, their lonely feelings. But Spenser's opening sonnets reveal that inordinate self-examination fosters the base passions that he believes subdue the fallen human mind, including lust and "self-pleasing pride."[12] Spenser contends that fellowship in general and the marriage bond in particular provide a remedy for the pitfalls of solipsism. Through his account of courtship and marriage, Spenser makes the case that artificial and restrictive "bands"—a term Elizabethans used to describe marriage and political obligations as well as rhyme—are essential to the establishment of all order, beauty, and community since they rein in unruly passions while allowing humanity's higher nature to flourish. Spenser shares his belief that the formation of societies requires individuals to relinquish a certain amount of sovereignty with many of his Elizabethan contemporaries. But in *Amoretti and Epithalamion* Spenser presents a distinctive account of human association that heightens the role of restraint in the formation of human bonds. After considering the merits of a contractual account of marriage and society, Spenser reveals that contract is insufficient to "knit the knot that ever shall remain" (*SP*, 6.14). Instead, he indicates that an enduring union requires both parties to sacrifice life and liberty in order to obtain a mysterious state of happiness within captive bonds.

The Bond of Association

I have chosen to describe Spenser's love poems as sonnets of "association" because the noun implies both the action of uniting and the union that is the product of that action. In his poetry, Spenser meditates on both existing social institutions and their genesis, but he is predominantly interested in the latter. Indeed, the sonnet of association is the culmination of a poetic career in which Spenser repeatedly represents the human struggle to convert isolation into attachment. Throughout his career, Spenser chose genres that allowed him to consider the interactions of individuals in a natural or pseudonatural state: pastoral and romance. And he begins his two major works in these genres, *The Shepheardes Calender* and *The Faerie Queene*, with figures who are detached from their surroundings and from one another before proceeding to explore whether and how they can be brought together. Although both his pastoral and romantic worlds are characterized by a dense web of social interactions, he tends to focus on the relations between pairs of individuals—Cuddie and Thenot, Redcrosse and Una, Britomart and Artegall—because these small units of society allow the poet to lay bare the mechanics of social interaction in their most elemental form.[13]

In Spenser's romantic poetry *love* is in fact *love*, but it is also *politics*. Because Spenser advertises his complex relations with the queen and incorporates topical allusions into his poetry, his verse has always invited political interpretations, and he was particularly favored as an object of new historicist criticism.[14] But, to some extent, critical fascination with court intrigue, colonial power, and, above all, Elizabeth herself has distracted from the ways in which Spenser's poetry is political in the broader sense of the term: it attempts to uncover the origins and ends of social formations. Spenser does not neglect the dynamics of homosocial interaction, but the emotional center of both *The Faerie Queene* and his minor works seems to be the bonds between "Knights and Ladies," perhaps because Spenser thinks, like Edwardian counselor and political theorist Sir Thomas Smith, that "the naturalest and first coniunction of two toward the making of a further societie of continuance is of the husband & of the wife."[15] Smith is drawing on Aristotle's description of the union between "male and female" at the beginning of the *Politics*; Aristotle argues that this conjunction "is formed not of deliberate purpose, but because, in common with other animals and with plants, mankind have a natural desire to leave behind them an image of themselves."[16] Because Smith follows Aristotle in seeing the family and its hierarchy as natural, he does not discuss how this "naturalest and first coniunction" is formed: he takes it for granted that the "societie of man, and woman" already exists in nature, and he carries on to describe how the labor and power are divided among men and women.[17] French political theorist Jean Bodin, whose *Les Six livres de la Republique* was published in 1576, places a similar emphasis on marriage and the family as the "true seminarie and beginning of euery Commonweale" but also treats the family as something that already exists.[18] Indeed, Bodin takes Aristotle and Xenophon to task for separating "the Oeconomical government from the political" and argues that good government in the family is the building block and "true model" of good government in the city.[19] In depicting marriage and the family as the elementary units of political life without inspecting the origins of this conjunction itself, Smith and Bodin choose to depict the order and hierarchy of the family as natural and therefore as a solid and unchangeable foundation for political order. Though Spenser does seem to see the marriage bond as the root of social life, he is far from believing that the formation of this bond is natural or easy. In his sonnets of courtship, Spenser endeavors to explore the making of this first conjunction and begins his account of association with two completely isolated individuals rather than a preexisting family. Indeed, although his marriage to Elizabeth Boyle doubtless involved complex negotiations with her relatives and friends, Spenser eliminates all other social interactions in order to focus on the pair of lovers, whom he depicts as warriors facing each other in a state of nature.[20] Because Spenser focuses on the lovers alone and speaks about them in his characteristic figurative manner, the lovers become what Peter Cummings describes as an "allegory" of all lovers.[21] But by repeatedly comparing the lovers to hostile warriors endeavoring to form a league and by playing with tropes of liberty and captivity, Spenser indicates that the sequence is also an allegory of all human bonds: the way in which his lovers negotiate the relation between freedom and restraint has ramifications not only for all other lovers, but for all other social associations. And Spenser suggests through his warring lovers that the marital "association" does not have the fixed meaning or natural stability that Smith and Bodin attribute to it. The lovers do not have a settled or shared understanding of what it means to unite themselves but must work it out in the midst of their battle. The conjunction of two that forms the basis of the polity is not natural and established but artificial and hard won.

In addition to describing both the process and product of social combination, the word "association" is particularly appropriate to Spenser because it captures the dynamic interplay between consent and constraint that animates his accounts of love and social life. At the beginning of book 3 of *The Faerie Queene*, Britomart lays down a fundamental premise of the book, and of Spenser's work more generally, when she insists that "loue" may not "be compeld by maistery" (*FQ*, 3.1.25). Elizabeth Fowler has argued that Spenser's interest in the idea that the "marriage contract" and "sexual consent" are "constitutive of the polity" was long-standing since the "episode of the marriage of Thames and Medway," which may have been one of the earliest portions of *The Faerie Queene* Spenser conceived, "ceremoniously asserts the voluntary contractual and reciprocal basis" of the polity.[22] In *Amoretti*, Spenser also depicts the league formed between the lovers as consensual and contractual; indeed, he famously describes the lady as "tyed" "with her own goodwill" in the betrothal sonnet that culminates the first stage of courtship. But he also questions the contractual model throughout the sequence and considers whether other metaphors and models might better capture his sense that social bonds curtail and thwart the individual will as much as they fulfill that will's longing for union.

The subtleties of Spenser's understanding of the interplay of consent and constraint in the process of association are illuminated by considering Richard Hooker's complex use of the word "association" in the first book of *Laws of Ecclesiastical Polity*, which was published in 1593, a year before Spenser's marriage to Elizabeth Boyle. Hooker connects the words "associate" and "association" with voluntary combination when he describes the church as a "supernaturall societie" in which "wee associate our selues." Although the church differs from human societies in that it is a union of "holy men" rather than "men simply considered as men," Hooker maintains that "it hath the selfe same original grounds which other politique societies haue, namely the naturall inclination which all men haue vnto sociable life, and consent to some certaine bond of association, which bond is the law that appointeth what kind of order they shall be associated in."[23] Hooker's slow-building prose style allows for a potential equivocation in the key phrase "bond of association." Since the term follows Hooker's remarks on humanity's innate inclination to social life, it initially appears that the "bond of association" simply refers to the natural bonds that unite individuals. But the dependent clause reveals that the "bond of association" is actually an artificial instrument of constraint, a positive law that imposes order by binding citizens to a particular form of government.[24] The natural bond that brings them together is translated into an artificial bond that holds them to an order.

The double meaning of "bond of association" captures the twofold foundation of Hooker's political philosophy. His understanding of secular and ecclesiastical politics is thoroughly imbued with the Aristotelian view that "by nature . . . a man is a civill and sociable creature."[25] But, as Alexander Rosenthal argued in his study of the origins of constitutionalism, Hooker does not think that natural social inclinations are sufficient grounds for the formation of a functioning commonwealth. In a fallen world in which sin distorts and destabilizes sociability, the artifice of a consensual covenant is required to constitute and maintain civil society.[26] This "bond" both fulfills and thwarts the inclinations of "natural man": it satisfies human beings' fervent desires for union while restraining the disruptive passions that impede harmony.

In his tales of lovers struggling to "eternally bind" the "lovely band" of matrimony, Spenser reveals that he, like Hooker, adheres to an Aristotelian view of human sociability in which artifice must supplement instinct (*SP*, *Epithalamion* 396). His knights and ladies display an unmistakable proclivity for social life and seem to long with every fiber of their beings to unite themselves to one another.[27] As Yeats puts it in his preface to a 1902 volume of Spenser's poetry, even when Spenser describes the stately pageants and houses that are the trappings of his official morality, "all the while he is thinking of nothing but lovers whose bodies are quivering with the memory or the hope of long embraces."[28] Although Yeats may exaggerate Spenser's sensuality and underestimate the significance of Spenser's morality, his statement underscores the fact that overwhelming desire for union is the motive force of Spenser's characters and his poems. But, despite his keen awareness of humanity's social inclinations, Spenser has less confidence than Hooker that these natural instincts can lead to lasting unions. Although he carefully considers a contractual account of association of the kind advocated by Hooker, in the end Spenser concludes that human beings require more coercive and unnatural bonds.

The Bands of Rhyme

In order to understand fully the social theory that Spenser promulgates in his sonnet sequence, we must attend not only to the complex negotiations recorded in the poems, but to their formal features, which reproduce, further, and shape the social lessons of Spenser's verse.[29] As their frequent use of the myths of Orpheus and Amphion suggests, the Elizabethans saw a connection between founding cities or nations and ordering language through verse.[30] Indeed, Spenser famously uses the language of political conquest to describe his vision of versification in his earliest extant pronouncements on verse, his letters to Gabriel Harvey on quantitative meter, which Henry Bynneman printed in 1580 as *Three proper, and wittie, familiar letters: lately passed betweene tvvo vniuersitie men: touching the earthquake in Aprill Last, and our English refourmed versifying*. As the loaded past participle in the title indicates, Spenser and Harvey saw an urgent need to "reform" English verse to bring it in line with a newly reformed English church and commonwealth. In their letters, Spenser and Harvey reveal that they have become "more in loue wyth . . . Englishe Versifying, than with Ryming" precisely because they desire the "artificial straightnesse" of quantitative meter. As Harvey puts it, their "new famous enterprise" is the "Exchanging of Barbarous and Balductum Rymes with Artificial Uerses."[31]

Although both Spenser and his former tutor agree that English verse has been allowed to develop in a helter-skelter manner for far too long and that they must organize the muddled language by imposing an artificial order on it, the two writers disagree about the extent to which this artificial program of English versification should accommodate the natural state of the English tongue. After discussing English words that are difficult to assimilate into the system of quantitative measure, Spenser concludes that the war against a recalcitrant tongue "is to be wonne with Custome, and rough words must be subdued with Vse."[32] As Richard Helgerson has argued, Spenser expresses a desire to "remake" the English language in the image of the classical tongues, and he is perfectly comfortable using the "language of sovereign power eager to subdue rough words and have the kingdom of them" to describe his linguistic project.[33] In contrast to Spenser, Harvey appeals to common usage, insisting that in "bring[ing] our Language into Arte" grammarians must ensure that the artificial order is "in all pointes conformable and proportionate to our COMMON NATURAL PROSODYE."[34] Harvey imagines nature and art on a continuum and suggests that natural language can be gently taken by the hand and led into orderliness, which can be "conformable" to nature, but Spenser sees a gulf between the current barbarism of the tongue and the civilized poetic language he envisions.[35] Only the violent imposition of rule will bring order. Although Spenser's flirtation with quantitative meters proved short-lived, he did not abandon his aspiration to bend and shape the English language to his will. Instead, he embraced rhyme as an alternative instrument of restraint.[36]

Although Harvey preserved Spenser's youthful meditations on poetic form for posterity by printing *Three proper, and wittie, familiar letters*, Spenser's later views on rhyme and meter must be extrapolated from his works themselves since no treatise on his poetic theory survives. In the argument to "Oc-

tober" in *The Shepheardes Calender*, Spenser's (likely fictional) commentator
E.K. suggests that such a treatise once existed. He notes that the new poet
discourses on poetic inspiration "els where at large . . . in his booke called the
English Poete, which booke being lately come into my hands, I mynde also by
Gods grace upon further advisement to publish."[37] This is a tantalizing remark
for historians of poetics—did this lost work contain an account of Spenser's
fundamental poetic principles in the manner of Sidney's *Defence* and Putten-
ham's *Arte*? It is uncertain whether the work really existed and was "looselie
scattered abroad" in manuscript and subsequently lost like Spenser's poem *The
Dying Pellican*, or whether the teasing allusion is one of E.K.'s many waggish
misdirections.[38] But the provocative possibility of a lost prose treatise should
not distract from the fact that we can uncover considerable information about
the development of Spenser's prosodic views by charting the poetic forms that
he used over the course of his thirty-year poetic career. Chronological analysis
of Spenser's verse forms reveals an intriguing movement toward stanzaic
poems with intricately interwoven rhyme patterns. In his works of the 1560s
and 1570s, Spenser used blank verse and couplets alongside interwoven forms.
When Jan Van der Noot commissioned Spenser to translate French, Italian,
and Flemish verse into English in *A Theatre wherein be represented as wel the
miseries and calamities that follow the voluptuous Worldlings* (1569), Spenser
composed his translations in blank verse as well as in rhyme. He wrote his
Chaucerian beast fable *Mother Hubberds Tale* (composed c. 1579) in iambic
pentameter couplets, and he used couplets and a rough four-beat accentual
meter for three of the twelve eclogues in *The Shepheardes Calender* (1579).
Indeed, in his appreciation of rudeness and roughness in general and of the
Chaucerian couplet in particular, the young Spenser of the 1560s and 1570s in
many ways anticipates the couplet poets of the 1590s I discuss in chapter 2.[39]
But after 1580, when he went to Ireland as private secretary to Lord Grey, who
became Lord Deputy of Ireland in that year, Spenser turned his back on blank
verse and couplets altogether.[40] Indeed, his conversion was so complete that
he even retranslated his translations of Du Bellay from *A Theatre* into tradi-
tional English sonnets sometime before they were published in a 1591 compila-
tion of his minor verse, *Complaints. Containing sundrie small Poemes of the
Worlds Vanitie*.

Spenser continued to experiment with verse forms until the premature end
of his career, but all his poetic experiments printed in the 1590s share distinc-
tive characteristics: with the exception of *Colin Clouts Come Home Again*,
which has a complex but nonstanzaic rhyme pattern, all of Spenser's late works
are stanzaic, have interlocking or alternating rhyme schemes, and conclude
with the chime of a couplet. Even Spenser's most complex and distinctive po-
etic configurations—the seventeen- to nineteen-line stanzas of *Epithalamion*
and *Prothalamion*—adhere to this basic pattern. The fact that Spenser know-
ingly rejected continuous couplets and continued to produce variations on the

same poetic theme throughout the second half of this career suggests that he found this form congenial not only to his particular habit of mind but also to his cosmic and social thought.[41]

The most important resource for interpreting Spenserian poetics is of course his poetry itself, in which he not only offers explicit meditations on the poetic enterprise but provides more general reflections on the benefits of artificial restriction that illuminate his preference for interwoven rhyme. But contemporary defenses of poetry and prosodic manuals like those by Gascoigne, Sidney, Puttenham, and Webbe can also help guide interpretations of Spenser by providing a small sample of the ways that Elizabethan readers interpreted complex rhyme patterns. In his *Arte of English Poesie,* published in 1589, George Puttenham offers more extensive and detailed analysis of what he calls "proportion poetical" than any other writer of the period. His analysis of rhyme patterns is particularly useful in interpreting Spenser's corpus since he, like Spenser, displays a decided preference for interwoven stanzas (*Arte,* K1r). Puttenham defends his preference by arguing that rhymes actually contribute to the solidity of a stanza. In his discussion of the "*Situation* of the concords," or the placement of rhymes, Puttenham offers guidance about how to craft a stanza that is "fast and not loose" (*Arte,* M2v). The secret to the firmly fixed stanza is what Puttenham calls "band," a term that he draws from the craft of masonry (*Arte,* M3r).[42] We can see "in buildings of stone or bricke," he notes, that the mason "giueth a band, that is, a length to two breadths, & vpon necessitie diuers other sort of bands to hold in the worke faste and maintaine the perpendicularitie of the wall" (*Arte,* M3r). In other words, the bricklayer does not just stack one brick directly on top of the other but finds a way of laying them in an alternating pattern so that the wall is more stable and does not fall to the ground. Similarly, the poet's stanza will "fall asunder" if he does not take care to "close and make band" through the proper placement of like and unlike sounds (*Arte,* M3r). Puttenham's comparison to the trade of bricklaying not only renders the nebulous idea of poetic proportion concrete and tangible; it also raises the stakes of rhyme's linking function, making it the principle of a poem's structural integrity. If the poet fails to use rhyme properly, all his work will be for naught since his stanza will crumble to pieces.

Puttenham maintains that the poetic craftsman can preserve the structural integrity of the stanza only by using "intangled" rhyme, by "enterweaving one with another by knots, or as it were by band" (*Arte,* M2v). He provides one of his "ocular example[s]" in order to illustrate the distinction between this "entertangle" rhyme and what he calls "concord in plaine compasse" (*Arte,* M2v; see figure 1.1). The image makes it clear that "entertangle" is equivalent to alternating rhyme while "plaine compass" is equivalent to enclosed or envelope rhyme. The fact that Puttenham uses these "ocular example[s]" instead of the alphabetical notation we now use to represent rhyme patterns has a significant bearing on his understanding of rhyme's function. While alphabetical notation

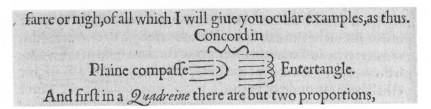

FIGURE 1.1. Detail from Puttenham, George. *The Arte of English Poesie*. London: Richard Field, 1589. Pforz 12 PFZ. Carl H. Pforzheimer Library, Harry Ransom Center, University of Texas at Austin.

draws attention to the scheme or pattern created by rhyme, Puttenham's method of drawing links between lines with like endings draws attention to the connective function of rhyme, its ability to recall the ear to an earlier moment in the stanza and hence to tie together disparate sections of the poem.[43]

Puttenham has confidence that his images straightforwardly represent the aural links produced by the sound of like endings since he maintains that "there is a natural *simpathie*, betweene the eare and the eye" and therefore "most times your occular proportion doeth declare the nature of the audible" (*Arte*, M1v). Thus, the lack of intersections or "knots" in the illustration of "plain compass" plainly demonstrates the shortcomings of this form, which does not sufficiently tie together the stanza. Because the sound of the second rhyme returns again "so nye and so suddenly," it is never "out of the eare" and immediately satisfies the listener's desire for closure (*Arte*, M2r). This instant gratification makes the couplet the "most vulgar proportion" since any "rude and popular eare" can detect and delight in it (*Arte*, M2r). Puttenham's disdain for the instantaneous chime of the couplet even extends to concluding couplets, for he maintains "*Chaucer* and others" do "a misse" by "shut[ting] up the staffe with a *disticke*, concording with none other verse that went before, and mak[ing] but a loose rhyme" (*Arte*, M3r). Though the sound of the couplet might satisfy the vulgar ear, the poet who indulges in concluding distichs risks undermining the structural integrity of his poem as the loose, unbanded couplet can simply fall off the end of the stanza. In contrast to the loose and vulgar couplet, complex entertangle rhyme requires both a skillful artificer and a "learned" audience: the poet "sheweth him selfe more cunning" and demonstrates that he has "his owne language at will" by finding multiple rhymes for a single word, and the auditors exercise their ears by holding multiple endings in suspension for a time—though the poet should never make them wait so long "that the eare by loosing his concord is not satisfied" (*Arte*, M2r, M3r). Thus, poems that interweave rhymes at a distance of two or three lines achieve the delicate balance between suspense and satisfaction required to maximize delight, harmony, and artfulness.

Puttenham's involved account of "plaine compasse" and entertangle rhyme reveals much about his understanding of the aims and methods of poetic composition. He maintains that the English language must be "fashioned and reduced into a method of rules & precepts" in the manner of the Greeks and Latins (*Arte*, C2r). This vision of the necessity of linguistic conquest derives from his larger understanding of the relationship between art and nature, which he expresses through the myths of Amphion and Orpheus. Puttenham presents a dark vision of humanity in a state of nature: they were "vagarant and dispersed like the wild beasts, lawlesse and naked, or verie ill clad" until the intervention of poetic lawgivers, who managed to "hold and containe the people in order and duety" (*Arte*, C2r-v). Puttenham's vision of the state of nature likely draws on Cicero's account in *De Inventione*. Indeed, his descriptions of prepolitical humanity as "vagarant" and "dispersed like the wild beasts" echo the language of Cicero's own account of the ancient world, when "homines passim bestiarum modo vagabuntur," men wandered here and there in the manner of beasts, and were "dispersos . . . in agros et in tectis silvestribus abditos," dispersed in the fields and hidden under sylvan roofs.[44] But, intriguingly, Puttenham's language is also a direct translation of Machiavelli's statement in the *Discourses* that at the beginning of the world men lived "dispersi, a similitudine delle bestie."[45] For Machiavelli, this dispersed, beastlike state came to an end when the world became more crowded and men chose robust and strong-hearted leaders to defend themselves. Puttenham, in contrast, takes a more Ciceronian approach and credits poets with taming beast-like humanity with "sweete and eloquent perswasion" (*Arte*, C2v). Yet Cicero, Machiavelli, and Puttenham are alike in questioning the Aristotelian premise that sociability is natural. Civil life is hard won and requires the few to manage the naturally unruly instincts of the rest through force or persuasion. Indeed, Machiavelli goes onto conclude that "men act right only upon compulsion; but from the moment they have the option and liberty to commit wrong with impunity, then they never fail to carry confusion and disorder everywhere."[46] In his writings of the 1590s, Spenser stands somewhere between Aristotle and Machiavelli. As I have suggested, the forces that stir his shepherds, knights, ladies, and sonneteers to set out on their quests are love and the desire for union. And he maintains throughout his poetry that gentleness, civility, and courtesy are "planted naturall" in at least some individuals (*FQ*, 6.1.2). But, inside these individuals as well as in the wider world, these courteous instincts are always jostling with a swarm of equally natural antisocial forces that threaten to thwart political life. Spenser's fears about these forces often lead him to defend root-level reformation in which natural beastliness is subdued by the bonds of art. This instinct for radically remaking nature was present in Spenser's work before he left for Ireland—it informed his longing to reform English prosody during his flirtation with quantitative meter—but it is most visible in the extreme cruelty of the approach to Ireland he advocated in his *Vewe of the Presente State of Ireland*. In the tract, which was likely written a few years after Spenser's marriage to Elizabeth Boyle but was not published until

1633, the interlocutors in Spenser's dialogue begin by asking what is necessary for "reducing that salvage nacion to better government and Cyvilitye" and conclude that the nation is in such an unruly state that it will be necessary to "new fram[e]" it "in the forge" and "alter the whole form of governement" by means of the sword.[47] The interlocutors in Spenser's dialogue convince themselves of the need for the alteration of form and frame with much reluctance and debate and depict this reformation as an extreme response to a peculiar legal, customary, and military situation in Ireland, but underneath all the debates about the best "plot" for "reformacion" there is the consistent suggestion that the natural state of human beings without "discipline" is "licentious barbarism" and "lewd libertie" in which the passions run wild.[48] Early in the dialogue, Irenius compares the Irish to "colt[s]" that were broken but then allowed to "rune loose at random"; once they "shoke of theire bridles," he charges, they "began to Colte anewe more licentiouslye then before."[49] Spenser's depiction of English intervention as an effort to rein in natural coltishness and impose civility through discipline was certainly a self-serving colonial fiction. His efforts to defend what he saw as his plot of ground in Ireland required considerable legal, and likely physical, wrangling. In 1589, his Old English neighbor Lord Roche wrote to Walsingham to accuse Spenser of "falsely pretending title to certain castles and ploughlands" and of "threatening and menacing the said Lord Roche's tenants," "seizing their cattle," and "beating Lord Roche's servants and bailiffs"; Spenser in turn accused Lord Roche of being a "traitor," imprisoning Spenser's "men," killing the "fat beef" of people who housed Spenser, and speaking contemptuously of the queen and her laws.[50] Whatever the reality that lies behind these mutual recriminations, it is clear that Spenser's residence in Ireland was far from peaceful and that he wanted to see all violence and repression on the part of the New English as efforts to defend civilization against barbarism.[51] But if Spenser's experience in Ireland deepened his suspicion of nature and his embrace of artificial bands, it did so across the board. He did not simply depict the Irish as the licentious, natural other but increasingly emphasized the naturally unruliness that threatens to undermine all civil life. Spenser's deepening suspicion of natural liberty is most visible in *Amoretti*, where the sonneteer and his lady are themselves portrayed as licentious colts that repeatedly revolt against the "bridle" of the marriage bond.

I see Spenser's turn to what we now view as his characteristic prosodic forms—the Spenserian stanza, the Spenserian sonnet, and the long interwoven rhyme patterns of his marriage odes—as directly tied to his growing belief that the containment of licentious natural instincts is the aim of both social and poetic artifice. It is telling that Puttenham's vision of vagrant and dispersed nature led him to a similar poetic remedy. Although he discusses other methods of organizing language, Puttenham makes the case that entertangle rhyme is the English poet's most effective instrument of discipline. In seeing rhyme as a way of bringing order and civility to English verse, Puttenham and Spenser were working against its reputation during the quantitative controversy as primitive, customary, and artless. With modifications, the "olde vse of toying in Rymes" could become a new way of reframing and civilizing the English tongue.[52] Stanzaic rhyme, especially the elaborately interwoven rhymes Puttenham and Spenser prefer, could provide the kind of artificiality and measure sought by advocates of quantitative verse.

While Puttenham's treatise provides a detailed theory of the aims of poetry and the effects of formal decisions that may illuminate Spenser's prosodic choices, William Webbe's 1586 *Discourse of English Poetrie* offers more direct evidence about contemporary understanding of Spenser's verse since it contains a meticulous prosodic analysis of *The Shepheardes Calender*. Webbe sees a wealth of poetical instruction in the *Calender*. In fact, he uses the poem as a rubric for his own directory of verse forms. Since there are "in that worke twelue or thirteene sundry sorts of verses which differ eyther in length or ryme o[r] destinction of the staues," he decides that a survey of the eclogues will "serue" to introduce readers to the principal "sortes of verses" available to the English poet.[53] Webbe's analysis of each eclogue includes an account of the number of syllables in each verse and of the rhyme pattern, followed by an explanation of how these poetic features are particularly "agreeable" to the "affections" expressed in that eclogue. His lengthy explanations of the poetic features of the eclogues often seem unnecessarily tortuous. The most extreme example is his account of the "March" stanza: "The third kynd is a pretty rounde verse, running currantly together, commonly seauen sillables or sometime eyght in one verse, as many in the next, both ryming together: euery two hauing one the like verse after them, but of rounder wordes, and two of them likewyse ryming mutually."[54] It would certainly have been simpler to state that the stanza rhymes AABCCB, but Webbe's befuddling description reveals much more about his understanding of verse than such a technical schema could capture. Like Puttenham's ocular examples, phrases like "running currantly together," "hauing one the like verse after them," and "likewyse ryming mutually" indicate Webbe's interest in the pattern of resemblances and interconnections among lines of verse, in the ways in which a poet can fashion a single "rounde" whole out of an assemblage of lines by carefully interweaving like and unlike. The socially inflected word "mutually" is particularly intriguing, and an investigation of Webbe's use of the word in the rest of the treatise indicates that he always applies the adverb to lines that rhyme across a distance, or "mutuallie crosse" as he puts it at one point, in this case the tail rhyme in the March stanza. This term—which, as far as I can tell, is unique to Webbe—perfectly suits a pastoral poem in which many of the songs are, as Webbe observes, "mutuallie sung betweene two."[55]

Indeed, whether wittingly or no, Webbe seems to have drawn out a connection between the rhyme scheme and the argument of the *Calender* that illuminates Spenser's movement toward interlocking rhyme. For the eclogues that contain these "mutual," interlocking rhymes are precisely those that depict the struggle for human association and the ways that it can be won out of sorrow and strife.[56] In contrast, Spenser reserves couplets and rough accentual meter for those dialogues that present a dark vision of the fallen world in which permanent and irresolvable difference thwarts the human desire for fellowship. E.K. classes all three couplet dialogues (February, May, and September) as "Moral" in the general argument, remarking that they "for the most part be mixed with some Satyrical bitternesse."[57] Spenser's couplet dialogues present a world that is so out of joint that no amount of human artifice can set it right. Thus, it is appropriate that the estranged interlocutors in these dialogues can speak only in couplets—they fail to "make band" with each other, and their speech falls asunder into detached units. In the distichic dialogues of the *Calender*, Spenser confronts the limits of poetry's ability to "hold and containe the people in order and duety" (*Arte*, C2r–v). Although he frequently returns to the antisocial themes of these dialogues, he never returns to continuous couplets. Instead, he opts for a poetic form that suggests that even the most recalcitrant and antisocial of elements can be incorporated into the artist's orderly pattern.

In their verbose accounts of English rhyme, Puttenham and Webbe suggest potential interpretations of Spenser's penchant for interlocking rhyme that must be tested against his verse practice. Both stress rhyme's role as a connective force that unifies the poem. While Webbe describes rhyme as a kind of sociability, Puttenham maintains that such unification can be achieved only with an element of coercion. For Puttenham, the artificial "bands" of rhyme, like the "bond of association," both satisfy and limit natural inclinations. Although Puttenham's general views about the binding function of rhyme can be fruitfully applied to Spenser's corpus, Spenser does not follow Puttenham in all the latter's poetic preferences. In particular, Spenser does not share Puttenham's categorical opposition to the use of couplet rhymes within an interwoven stanza or his objection to the Chaucerian concluding couplet. Spenser's *Faerie Queene* stanza, which rhymes ABABBCBCC, contains couplets in the middle and at the end, but each of the couplets in the stanza is linked to an earlier rhyme, allowing Spenser to combine the connective function of entertangle rhyme with the benefits of the couplet. Clare Kinney and Jeff Dolven have analyzed the effects of the couplets woven into the Spenserian stanza in detail. Kinney describes the B rhymes in the middle of the stanza as a "pivot about which the stanza doubles back on itself," and Dolven similarly argues that the central couplet of the stanza allows a "double-take in the middest," a moment of reflection that Spenser uses for both "disruption" and "closure."[58] For Dolven, the final couplet, with its concluding alexandrine line, serves a different function: it is "reflective, summary, or even epigrammatic," offering a "moment of provisional rest" in a "poem so wary of rest."[59] It would seem that these insights about the couplets within the Spenserian stanza could

Table 1.1

Spenserian Stanza	Spenserian Sonnet
A	A
B	B
A	A
B ⎤	B ⎤
B ⎦	B ⎦
C	C
B	B
C ⎤	C ⎤
C ⎦	C ⎦
	D
	C
	D
	E ⎤
	E ⎦

simply be applied to the Spenserian sonnet, which appears to be a mere exten-
sion of the Spenserian form from nine to fourteen lines. But there are two
differences between the stanza and the sonnet that complicate any easy cor-
relation of the two (see table 1.1). First, Spenser strictly follows sonnet conven-
tion in making each of his quatrains discrete syntactical units. The clear in-
dentation of the sonnets in Ponsonby's original edition accentuates the
separation of the quatrains, making the verse units perceptible even to an inat-
tentive reader. As a result of Spenser's strict adherence to the quatrain as a unit
of sense in his sonnets, the couplets formed between these quatrains do not
function in the same way as the middle couplet of the Spenserian stanza. In-
stead of providing a moment of meditation in the midst of the poem, they
serve the same function as the conjunctions—and, but, so, for—that Spenser
habitually uses to connect quatrains: they forcibly yoke together distinct ideas
and syntactical units.[60] Because these couplets are required to do more con-
nective work than those in the *Faerie Queene* stanza, they draw attention to
the labor and strain involved in the poet's task of wrestling his recalcitrant
words into a single, unified whole.

  The Spenserian sonnet also differs from the Spenserian stanza because the
final couplet of the sonnet is not linked to the body of the poem. As in the
traditional English sonnet, the couplet stands completely alone. Like those of
The Faerie Queene, these final couplets are often sententious and recapitula-
tive, but the fact that they do not rhyme with the body of the sonnet advances
the account of union Spenser provides in the *Amoretti*. Spenser often uses the
disconnected couplet to address the lady directly and signal the precariousness
of both courtship and the poetic enterprise, which depend on her reception of
the sonnets. The poet's artfulness can carry him only so far in courtship since

his attempts to bind the couple in the bands of matrimony require that the lady assent to his proposal and respond in kind. The loose couplet of the Spenserian sonnet also portends the fact that the association between the poet and the lady will not be realized within the confines of the sequence. In order to complete the union, Spenser introduces a new poetic feature—the refrain—in *Epithalamion*. Thus, Spenser crafted his peculiar sonnet form to draw attention to the connective function of rhyme and hence to the laborious effort required to gain kingdom over a barbarous and balductum language. Spenser's efforts to highlight the artificial straightness of verse through his rhyme pattern reflect his larger purpose in the sonnet sequence: examining the ways that naturally isolated individuals can become bound to one another.

Love's Soft Bands in Amoretti and Epithalamion

In contrast to Petrarch's sonnet sequence, which advertises its fragmentary nature and resists attempts to construct a seamless narrative, *Amoretti* has a more legible narrative structure, recounting the story of a successful courtship from the moment the lady begins to "entertaine" this "new loue" to the trying period of separation that follows betrothal (*SP*, 4.14).[61] Within *Amoretti's* complex account of the vicissitudes of courtship and betrothal, we can demarcate several distinct stages in the process of association. When the sequence and the courtship begin, the lovers are depicted as hostile warriors who exist in a sort of romantic state of nature: their desire for society is outweighed by their fear and alienation.[62] The speaker attempts to remedy this state of fear by proposing that the two enter into a limited contractual bond that will allow them to form an association without giving up their freedom (Sonnet 12). But this contractual logic proves insufficient to bind the lovers in a lasting band and, when he is involuntarily taken captive by the lady (Sonnet 12), the lover discovers that self-yielding and captivity are the proper path to enduring fellowship. After he makes this discovery and yields himself to the lady (Sonnets 29, 42), the lover must then convince her to take a similar risk, which she at length does in the well-known betrothal sonnet (Sonnet 67). Just as in matters of form, in his theory of marriage and society Spenser seems to be moving in the opposite direction from his contemporaries, who were embracing contractual accounts of marriage and, increasingly, of political institutions.[63] Spenser likely knew that the arguments of the foremost contractual theorist of his day, George Buchanan, led to the position that the social contract can be revoked when the monarch does not uphold his or her end of the bargain.[64] Decades later, Milton would not only apply this argument to the English monarchy, but extend it to the marriage contract.[65] Wary of the threat this contractual logic posed to the stability of marriage and society, in *Amoretti and Epithalamion* Spenser seeks to go beyond contractualism and form an indissoluble bond between the lover and the lady.

THE WEARY WAR: LOVERS IN A STATE OF NATURE

From the opening lines of *Amoretti*, Spenser indicates that his lovers have a natural inclination to sociable life but reveals that mutual wariness and fear predominate over mutual longing for the "soules long lacked foode" (*SP*, 1.12). This tension is visible in the opening quatrain of Sonnet 1, in which the poet alternates between desire and fear as he addresses the "leaves" that contain his verses:

> Happy ye leaves, when as those lilly hands,
>> which hold my life in their dead doing might
>> shall handle you and hold in loves soft bands,
>> lyke captives trembling at the victors sight. (*SP*, 1.1–4)

The sanguine first and third lines form a complete thought without the dependent clauses of the second and fourth lines: "Happy ye leaves, when as those lilly hands, / . . . shall handle you and hold in loves soft bands." In these lines, happiness consists not in amorous conquest, but in being held and restrained by the beloved. Though the "bands" of love may be soft and the lady's hands as delicate as a lily, they are agents of captivity and restriction nonetheless. These rhyming instruments of constraint will return throughout the sonnet sequence and again in a culminating moment of the marriage in *Epithalamion*, when the lady gives her "hand" as "The pledge of all our band" (*SP*, 238, 239). But at this point the outcome of the courtship is far from certain, so the language of captivity seems far more sinister. The interwoven second and fourth lines express the lover's anxiety about his captivity and set the tone for a sequence that depicts courtship as a terrifying and dangerous enterprise. For in order to win the lady's grace, the speaker must make himself vulnerable to her "dead doing might" by yielding his inner thoughts to her as captives in war. In disclosing the contents of his "harts close bleeding book," the lover puts himself at the mercy of the lady's judgment and risks her displeasure (*SP*, 1.8). Spenser's speaker acknowledges from the outset the very real possibility that the lady's "lamping eyes" will "reade the sorrowes" of his heart and nevertheless refuse to grant him grace (*SP*, 1.6, 7). The lover trembles at this prospect because he has already committed himself to her service: if the lady does not reciprocate, then the "soft bands" of mutual affection can easily become the hard fetters of unrequited love. Because we know that *Amoretti* culminates in betrothal, it is easy to overlook the uncertainties of its first sonnet, but the vulnerability and fearfulness of Spenser's speaker lays the foundation for the sequence's account of the painful process of association.

Spenser's desire to present alienation and trepidation as the natural state of human beings before the intervention of artifice accounts for a group of sonnets that have consistently puzzled critics. Expanding on the Petrarchan trope of the *dolce guerrera* (sweet warrior), Spenser composed a remarkable number of sonnets, fifteen to be precise, that depict the lady as a warrior or wild beast with which the speaker must battle.[66] These sonnets all occur in the first half of the sequence, before the betrothal sonnet, and, though there is a concentration of war imagery in Sonnets 10–14, the rest of the warrior sonnets are interspersed throughout the first half of the sequence. These images of the lady massacring enemies with her eyes and trampling on the neck of the lover are so extreme that they led J. W. Lever to posit "an attempted blending of two collections of sonnets, differing in subject-matter, characterization, and general conception." This hypothesis led him to excise eighteen sonnets from the sequence.[67] Later critics have responded to Lever's discomfort with the war poems in two ways: by arguing that the war between the lover and his "stubborne damzell" has a touch of playfulness and humor that Lever overlooked, or by maintaining that each "individual sonnet . . . represents not the completeness of vision of Spenser the author, but the emotional state of the lover at one stage of his development" (*SP*, 29.1).[68]

While both of these responses illuminate the tone and dramatic method of the sequence, they do not account for Spenser's singular preoccupation with the war trope. In the continental and English sequences that preceded and inspired Spenser's *Amoretti*, war was just one of many conceits to depict the trials of courtship and unrequited love, but Spenser makes it one of the governing tropes of his sequence. Though Spenser had long made connections between love and warfare, in *Amoretti* the idea that lovers view each other as combatants becomes fundamental to his account of courtship and marriage. I would argue that Spenser returns to the image of the battlefield so frequently in his sonnet sequence in order to underscore the idea that even the most fundamental unit of society, the "naturalest and first coniunction of two," does not spring up spontaneously.[69] Rather, the lady and the lover approach each other with all the wariness of inveterate enemies, unwilling to expose themselves to the "dead doing might" of the other (*SP*, 1.2). In depicting the natural relations between human beings as dominated by distance and fear, Spenser draws on two sixteenth-century discourses that emphasized the natural unruliness and estrangement of human beings: Reformation theology and poetic theory. Both of these discourses underscore the need for external intervention—whether of divine grace or of human artifice—by depicting the natural state of individuals as solitary, wild, and violent. In his sonnet sequence, Spenser fuses these two traditions together. For him, as for Sidney and Puttenham, human artifice can aid divine grace in counteracting the results of the fall by binding humanity's lower nature.

In the second poem of the sequence, Spenser reveals that the natural alienation between individuals can be credited to two innate vices: lust and pride. By disrupting his own rhyme pattern in this sonnet and failing to "make band,"

Spenser underscores the idea that these vices prevent the couple from being "fit for mate" (*Arte*, M3r; *SP*, 66.6). The sonnet is a dark parody of the opening sonnet of *Astrophil and Stella*, where Astrophil describes himself as "great with child to speak, and helpless in [his] throes," until his Muse at length acts as midwife, counseling him in the final line to turn back to his inner truthfulness: "'Fool,' said my muse to me; 'look in thy heart, and write.'"[70] Spenser's speaker is also great with child, but his "wombe" has been taken over by an "Unquiet thought," which the poet "bred / Of th'inward bale of [his] love pined heart" (*SP*, 2.4, 1, 1–2). Since he has daily "fed" his restive progeny with "sighes and sorrowes," it has become monstrous and "woxen" greater than his "wombe," writhing inside of him "like to [a] vipers brood" (*SP*, 2.3, 3, 4, 4, 6). The lover has no choice but to command the overgrown product of his passion to "Breake forth at length out of the inner part" in hopes that it can seek some "succour" for the lover in addition to sustaining its "selfe with food" (*SP*, 2.5, 7, 8). Spenser's images of self-impregnation and self-feeding hark back to his description of Error and her cannibalistic "brood" of children in book 1 of *The Faerie Queene* and anticipate Milton's perverse triad of Satan, Sin, and Death (*FQ*, 1.1.25).[71] This grotesque account of the lover's "inner part" challenges Sidney's sanguine call to look inward: when Spenser's lover looks in his heart to write, he finds only poison, darkness, and confusion within (*SP*, 2.5).

To some extent, this description of the roiling passions within the mind simply reflects Spenser's understanding of fallen human nature, in which the passions have usurped the seat of reason. Guyon summarizes this traditional view in book 2 of *The Faerie Queene* when he bewails the fact that our "mortalitie" and "feeble nature" allow "raging passion with fierce tyranny" to rob "reason of her dew regalitie" and make "it seruaunt to her basest part" (*SP*, 2.1.57). Yet, in addition to offering a general condemnation of human sinfulness, this sonnet specifically condemns the vices of the inward-looking Petrarchan lover who revels in his own passions.[72] The lover's narcissism and self-pity nourish these unruly passions until at length they break the boundaries of the self. By continually developing his lonely feelings, the Petrarchan speaker actually intensifies his natural alienation from the lady. His overgrown, viperous thoughts confirm the lady's trepidations about uniting herself to him.

In the middle of the poem, Spenser reinforces the idea that the lover's unruly desire makes him unfit to form an association with the lady by breaking his own rhyme scheme:

> Unquiet thought, whom at the first I bred
> > Of th'inward bale of my love pined hart:
> > and sithens have with sighes and sorrowes fed,
> > till greater then my wombe thou woxen art:

Breake forth at length out of the inner part,
    in which thou lurkest lyke to vipers brood:
    and seeke some succour both to ease my smart
    and also to sustayne thy selfe with food. ⎫
But if in presence of that fayrest proud   ⎬
    thou chance to come, fall lowly at her feet:
    and with meeke humblesse and afflicted mood,
    pardon for thee, and grace for me intreat.
Which if she graunt, then live and my love cherish,
    if not, die soone, and I with thee will perish. (*SP*, 1, bracket mine)

In the ninth line, in which the lover realizes that his unleashed thoughts may by chance stumble into the presence of the lady, the word "proud" should form a couplet with "food" that connects the central quatrains together, but the rhyme is noticeably partial.[73] Since Spenser is generally precise in his rhymes, the discord violates what John Hollander calls the poet's "metrical contract" with the reader and forcefully accentuates the disjunction between the lover's lustful pursuit of amorous "food" and the lady's chaste pride.[74] Spenser's couplet could be read as a juxtaposition of the base with the spiritual if we interpret the lady's pride as a praiseworthy "scorn of base things" as the speaker does in Sonnet 5 (*SP*, 5.6).

But the lady's pride is not unambiguously lofty and spiritual in Spenser's sequence.[75] The poet reveals over the course of the sequence that the lady's "self-pleasing pride," like the lover's unquiet thoughts, may spring from inordinate self-love and willfulness (*SP*, 5.14). He charges that her pride is a sign of undue confidence in her "weake flesh" and unsociable scorn for "others ayde" (*SP*, 58.1, 2). Indeed, with her pride and resistance to losing her freedom, Spenser's lady often seems to represent the "folly" that the Elizabethan "Homilie of the state of Matrimonie" depicts as one of the most deep-seated and universal obstacles to marriage: the "desire to rule, to thynke hyghly by our selfe, so that none thinketh it meete to geue place to another"; this "wicked vice of stubborne wyll and selfe loue," according to the homily, "is more meete to breake and to disseuer the loue of hart, then to preserue concorde."[76] Thus, two perverse wills clash in Spenser's couplet—the lover's erotic will and the lady's "stubborne will" (*SP*, 38.8). The poet's failure to form an aural connection between the will that desires "food" and the "proud" will causes the sonnet to fall apart in the middle, breaking into an octet on the lover's unquiet thought and a sestet on its imagined meeting with the lady (*SP*, 2.8, 9). Although the speaker concludes with a tentative hope that the lady will "pardon" his wild thoughts and "cherish" his love, Spenser suggests that reconciliation between the lover's looseness and the lady's hardness cannot occur until both of their recalcitrant wills have been reformed (*SP*, 2.12, 13).

ENTERTAINING TERMS: CONTRACTUAL
LOGIC IN *AMORETTI*

After establishing in the opening poems of the sequence that the lovers begin in a state of war with one another, Spenser recounts the speaker's attempts to find an artful remedy for this natural standoff. The speaker proposes that the lovers resolve their conflict by entering into a limited, contractual bond in which both lovers give up a small portion of their pride and self-love in order to form an association. The language of covenant runs through the sequence, but one of the most loaded scenes of negotiation comes in Sonnet 12, when the speaker reveals his desire "to make a truce and termes to entertaine" with the warrior lady (*SP*, 12.2). In the sixteenth century, the word "terms" in all its senses was still closely connected to the Latin *terminus* (boundary, limit, or end); thus, to establish the "terms" of a contract meant to delineate the limiting conditions.[77] In choosing this word, Spenser suggests that the "league twixt" the lovers requires them to give up only a limited portion of their liberty and personal sovereignty in exchange for security, peace, and fellowship (*SP*, 65.10). This limited covenant should be agreeable to both the lover and the lady since both sedulously guard their personal freedom throughout the courtship. The speaker notes in Sonnet 65 that the lady fears to "loose [her] liberty," and he reveals a similar defensiveness about his own sovereignty in the aphoristic couplet that concludes Sonnet 37: "Fondnesse it were for any being free, / to covet fetters, though they golden bee" (*SP*, 65.2, 37.13–14). If they can come to "terms," both parties will be able to retain most of the liberty they cherish.

The idea of a limited, consensual contract runs through the sequence and plays an important part in the culminating sonnets that surround the Easter sonnet to the Lord of Lyfe. In Sonnet 65, for example, the speaker calms his lady's fears about leaving the single state to enter into fellowship by describing wedlock as a "league" that "loyal love hath bound" and that is built on the foundation of "simple truth and mutuall good will" (*SP*, 65.10, 10, 11). Playing on the etymological connection between the word *league* and the Latin *ligare*, to bind, Spenser presents an account of association that is remarkably similar to Hooker's idea that political and religious institutions are formed when individuals "consent to some certain bond of association."[78] Though they restrict freedom and constrain viperous thoughts, the "bands, the which true love doth tye," seem to be "Sweet" because they are consonant with the natural inclinations of the lovers and freely chosen (*SP*, 65.5). As Spenser puts it in the betrothal sonnet, the lady is "with her owne goodwill . . . fyrmely tyde" (*SP*, 67.12). The ambiguous syntax of this culminating line of the sequence increases the sense that the lady consents to her bonds, for the phrase could mean either that the lady is firmly tied while giving her consent or, even more forcefully, that her "goodwill" is the very instrument or cord with which she is tied.[79]

This idea that freely chosen restriction can be satisfying as well as salutary plays an important role in Spenser's account of his turn to the sonnet itself. In the eightieth sonnet of the sequence, in which Spenser excuses himself for leaving *The Faerie Queene* "halfe fordonne," he compares the sonnet and its domestic subject to a "prison" to which a "steed" retires after long "toyle" in order to "rest" and become "refreshed" (*SP*, 80.3, 6, 5, 5, 3, 5). Although in the first two quatrains Spenser presents the love sonnet as a temporary escape from the more strenuous endeavors of epic, in the third quatrain he elevates his prison:

> Till then give leave to me in pleasant mew,
>> to sport my muse and sing my loves sweet praise:
>> the contemplation of whose heavenly hew,
>> my spirit to an higher pitch will rayse. (*SP*, 80.9–12)

Though in the first half of the sonnet the poet compares himself to a steed, in using the word "mew" in the ninth line he introduces a new animal metaphor. "Mew" could be used to refer to a cage or prison in general, but it was most frequently applied to the cages where hawks were kept while molting. Hence, "in mew" came to be used metaphorically for something in the process of transformation.[80] In combination with the Neoplatonic language of contemplation and spiritual transcendence in the subsequent lines, the "pleasant mew" suggests that limitation does not simply allow for temporary relaxation, but actually transforms and exalts the poet.[81] By restricting himself to the confines of the entertangled sonnet, Spenser provides a model of the freely chosen bands he recommends to the lady and suggests that a "mew" may actually be more "pleasant" and uplifting than boundless freedom.

This vision of marriage and poetry as restrictions to which we freely bind ourselves seems to place Spenser in the vanguard of romantic and prosodic thinking. Indeed, readers and critics of *Amoretti* have long celebrated Spenser's progressive understanding of marriage as a consensual and mutual contract between two equal parties who both have the power to set the terms of the contract. William Johnson even goes so far as to laud the poet as a "daring proponent of mutuality."[82] Although Spenser's earlier poetry certainly contributes to his reputation as the poet of married love, it is in *Amoretti and Epithalamion* that he presents his most idyllic vision of the woman's role in assenting to the contract. Unlike Amoret, the lady of the sonnets is not led away weeping "tender teares" and begging her lover to restore her "wished freedom" (*FQ*, 4.10.57). As Ilona Bell has argued, the powerful lady of the sonnets "seems less like a conventional sonnet lady than like Elizabeth I, declaring her right to remain single unless or until she finds a suitor who not only arouses her desire but who also acknowledges her liberty."[83] In the betrothal sonnet, Spenser seems to allow the lady to maintain her sovereignty even as she binds herself: because she has been tied with her own goodwill, she remains free.

Although the interpretations of Spenser's sonnet sequence offered by Bell and others highlight Spenser's surprisingly forward-looking understanding of marriage and gender relations, the idea that the lovers remain free when they choose the bands of matrimony does not capture all the nuances of Spenser's prosodic and social theories. Indeed, this interpretation requires considerable hermeneutic ingenuity to explain away the images of bands and cages that pervade even the postbetrothal portions of the sequence.[84] Critics have attempted to account for these images by describing them as relapses on the speaker's part, as signs that he does not quite comprehend the blissful notion of "mutuall good will" (*SP*, 65.11).[85] In order to do justice to the sequence, however, we should attempt to overcome—or embrace—our discomfort with these recurrent images of captivity, which occur even at the most idyllic moments of the sequence, and consider how they might contribute to Spenser's distinctive theory of matrimony and social combination. In presenting captivity as an essential component of human fellowship, Spenser moves beyond the contractual logic of Hooker and presents a much more surprising and original account of association as voluntary self-yielding and mutual captivity.

THE BIRD IN A CAGE: CAPTIVITY AND
THE BANDS OF MATRIMONY

Always a dedicated and alert reader of Spenser, John Keats can aid us in understanding Spenser's embrace of restriction.[86] In a letter to George and Georgiana Keats dated May 3, 1819, Keats records that he has been "endeavouring to discover a better sonnet stanza than we have," noting that he objects to the "pouncing rhymes" of the Italian sonnet and finds the "couplet at the end" of the English sonnet "has seldom a pleasing effect." Thus, he invents his own sonnet form with an interwoven rhyme scheme that would have warmed the cockles of Puttenham's heart (ABCABDCABCDEDE). In the sonnet itself, he explains his preference for this intricately entertangled pattern, explaining that "If by dull rhymes our english must be chaind," poets should at least strive to "find out . . . / Sandals more interwoven & complete / To fit the naked foot of Poesy." He aligns himself with Spenser, Harvey, and Puttenham in the lines that follow by suggesting that the artificiality of this stanza is precisely what makes it fitting—the complex pattern indicates that every word and sound has been weighed "By ear industrious & attention meet." Thus, in a paradox worthy of Petrarch, Keats suggests that a sonnet stanza actually seems to become more natural as it becomes more elaborate and artificial: only interwoven stanzas "fit" Poesy's foot. Keats does not offer a way out of the necessity of captivity—he seems to admit that English must in fact be chained by dull rhymes—but he does indicate in the final lines that, because of their artfulness, interwoven chains are less onerous to the muse than other kinds of fetters: "So if we may not let the Muse be free, / She will be bound with Garlands of her own."[87]

The concluding image of the Muse restrained by her own garlands recalls Spenser's lady tied with her own goodwill and prompts an interpretation of that betrothal scene and of Spenserian wedlock that better accounts for the persistence of images of captivity in the most blissful moments of Spenser's sequence. Spenser maintains that his lovers, like Keats's muse, must be bound by artificial bands, so their best hope is to be bound by garlands of their own. The speaker's confidence at the outset of the sequence that they can simply entertain terms, making limited sacrifices in order to form an association, proves misguided or, at least, incomplete. Instead, Spenser maintains that the lovers can bind the eternal band of matrimony only by sacrificing both life and liberty and yielding the self into the power of the other.

Indeed, if we return to Sonnet 12, the sonnet that begins with the speaker's proposal that the pair make a truce and entertain terms, we can see that the contract negotiations immediately fall apart as the lover becomes captive to the lady in the second half of the sonnet. As the "disarmed" speaker approaches the lady to begin negotiations, he suddenly falls prey to a "wicked ambush" that breaks forth from her eye (*SP*, 12.5, 6). Being "Too feeble . . . t'abide the brunt so strong," he is "forst to yield [his] selfe" into the hands of his fierce enemies who, after "captiving [him] streight with rigorous wrong," go on to hold him in "cruell bands" (*SP*, 12.9, 10, 11, 12). At this early stage in the courtship, the speaker is by no means reconciled to his bands and vociferously protests against his captivity as an injustice. But, in taking him captive, the lady may actually be teaching him a lesson in association. Only by yielding his whole "selfe" and submitting his unruly thoughts to the restrictive "bands" of the lady will he at length be able to form a bond with her (*SP*, 10, 12). In order to seal the bond of association, both lovers must eventually yield, but someone must be the first to throw down arms and risk death for the sake of fellowship. In Spenser's sequence, the male speaker must begin because he is both more powerful and more unruly: his "Unquiet thoughts" make him a threat to the lady's chastity as well as her sovereignty (*SP*, 2.1). Once he has yielded himself into her power, the lady can "frame [his] thoughts and fashion [him] within," making him a fit mate by reining in his "base affections" (*SP*, 8.9, 6). Thus, the sonnet sequence and the courtship it represents have the same goal as *The Faerie Queene*—"to fashion a gentleman or noble person in vertuous and gentle discipline"—but in *Amoretti* fashioning and discipline derive from a beloved human source.[88] The lover can become worthy of the lady only if he gives himself over to her to be reframed and refashioned in a more virtuous and gentle mold.

Although the speaker accidentally succumbs to captivity in the twelfth sonnet when he is surprised and "forst" into bands by the lady's dangerous eyes, as the sequence progresses he gradually and fitfully begins to embrace captivity as a means to unity with the lady (*SP*, 12.10). As early as Sonnet 29 he asks the lady to "accept [him] as her faithfull thrall" (*SP*, 29.10), but it is not until Sonnet 42 that he definitively welcomes thralldom and outlines the benefits of the lady's restraint:

> The loue which me so cruelly tormenteth,
>> So pleasing is in my extreamest <u>paine</u>:
>> that all the more my sorrow it augmenteth,
>> the more I love and doe embrace my <u>bane</u>.
> Ne doe I wish (for wishing were but <u>vaine</u>)
>> to be acquit from my continuall smart:
>> but joy her thrall for ever to <u>remayne</u>,
>> and yield for pledge my poore captyued hart;
> The which that it from her may never start,
>> let her, yf please her, bynd with adamant <u>chayne</u>:
>> and from all wandring loues which mote pervart,
>> his safe assurance strongly it <u>restrayne</u>.
> Onely let her <u>abstaine</u> from cruelty,
>> and doe me not before my time to dy.[89]

The sonnet opens with a quatrain that plays with Petrarchan contraries, relating that the "loue which . . . so cruelly tormenteth" the lover actually is "pleasing" even when the lover is in "extreamest paine" (*SP*, 42.1, 2, 2). This leads him to cultivate this painful love and "embrace" his "bane" (*SP*, 42.4). In the second quatrain, he focuses in particular on the pleasure of his captivity, revealing that he "joy[s] her thrall for ever to remayne, / and yield[s] for pledge [his] poore captyved hart" (*SP*, 42.7–8). The speaker's captivity is both voluntary and involuntary—his heart has already been "captyved" by the lady's ambushing eye-beams, but now he joyfully "yields" it himself as a pledge of his complete dedication to the lady.[90] The rhyme between "paine," "bane," "vaine," and "remayne" binds the first and second quatrains together and underscores the idea that pain and permanence are inextricably linked with one another. In fact, "paine" is one of Spenser's preferred rhyme words in the sequence, and the word is paired with "remayne" three of the seven times it occurs in *Amoretti*. The pair is consistently used to demonstrate that love that is "the harder wonne, the firmer will abide" (*SP*, 6.4).[91]

Here, Spenser takes the paine/remayne rhyme one step further, altering his usual rhyme scheme by continuing the B rhyme into the third quatrain. Spenser therefore interweaves this sonnet more tightly than his other sonnets in the sequence, making band between lines as far apart as the second and twelfth lines. This heightened use of rhyme's binding power is no coincidence since the subject of the final quatrain is the benefits of allowing the lady to "bynd" him with "adamant chayne" (*SP*, 42.10). Only by submitting to these chains can the lover finally be rescued from the internal turmoil that plagued him in the second sonnet, for the lady will restrain him "from all wandring loues which mote pervart" (*SP*, 42.11). Spenser leaves the object of "pervart" ambiguous—wandering loves would pervert the lover himself, but they would also pervert the love between the couple. By restraining the viperous thoughts and wandering passions within the lover, the lady both improves his moral state and lays the groundwork for a healthy union. As in Spenser's youthful theory of English prosody, in his mature theory of marriage coercion and restraint are essential to counteracting the shortcomings of nature—human beings cannot simply pursue their wild, natural inclinations but need the aid of an artificial bond.

Although the speaker yields his heart to the lady in Sonnet 42, she does not immediately respond in kind. She continues to guard her sovereignty for twenty-five sonnets. The enthralled speaker attempts to convince the lady to yield herself throughout this portion of the sequence, but his most powerful argument, and, I think, the one that ultimately convinces the lady, comes in Sonnet 65, two sonnets prior to the betrothal. As Kenneth Larsen points out in his notes, this sonnet corresponds with Maundy Thursday, the day on which churchgoers commemorated the Last Supper and the new covenant laid down in John 15:12: "This is my commaundement, that ye loue together as I haue loued you."[92] The traditional rite of foot washing performed during the Maundy Thursday service reinforced the idea of a covenant of mutual service. In his sonnet, Spenser draws on the themes of mutual covenanting by imagining a "league" of "mutuall good will" between the lovers in which, instead of washing each other's feet, they "salve each others wound" (*SP*, 65.10, 11, 12). Yet, even though the third quatrain of this sonnet presents a vision of a consensual covenant, the poem begins with a concession that the lovers must sacrifice their liberty in order to obtain this league.

As the poem opens, the speaker is chiding his "fayre love" for a "vaine" "doubt" that has hindered the progress of the courtship (*SP*, 65.1). But when the lover reveals the nature of the lady's doubt in the second line, it seems perfectly understandable: she fears to "loose [her] liberty" (*SP*, 65.2). In fact, Bishop John Jewel, in his homily on matrimony, acknowledges the reasonableness of female trepidations about marriage, noting that "they must specially feele the greefe and paynes of their matrimonie, in that they relinquish the libertie of their owne rule, in the payne of their traueling, in the bryngyng vp of their chyldren."[93] The speaker, moreover, has spent a large portion of the sonnet sequence regaling us with his own fears about captivity and maintaining that it would be "Fondnesse" for "any being free, / to covet fetters, though they golden bee" (*SP*, 37.13–14). Since he submitted himself to the lady's adamantine chain in Sonnet 42, he now reverses his position, insisting instead that it is the fear of lost liberty that is "vaine" and "fond" (*SP*, 65.1, 2).

The lover defends his newfound position by turning to the language of paradox: he does not argue that the lady will be able to keep her liberty by entering a contract limited by specific "terms," nor does he maintain that freely chosen bonds are not bonds at all. Rather, he attempts to reassure the lady with two enigmatic, aphoristic lines: "when loosing one, two liberties ye gayne / and make him bond that bondage earst did fly" (*SP*, 65.3–4). The lady must perform the "fond" and risky task of yielding her own liberty in hopes that she will receive two liberties in return. Although Spenser does not spell out the details of this arrangement, he must mean that the lady not only gains possession of the "liberty" of the lover whom she has bound, but, through some mysterious means, recovers the liberty she forfeited. Spenser's lines play with the paradoxical sacrificial logic of the New Testament, perhaps best exemplified in the declaration in Luke 9:24 that "whosoeuer wyl saue his lyfe shal lose it: But whosoeuer wil lose his lyfe for my sake, the same shall saue it."[94] Once again, Spenser adapts sonnet convention to his own purposes: he merges Petrarchan paradox with Christian paradox in order to demonstrate that a limited, conditional contract will never truly bind individuals—instead they must imitate the "Lord of Lyfe" in losing their life and liberty (*SP*, 68.1).

Spenser reinforces the idea that his vision of bound liberty is counterintuitive and mysterious by offering a comparison that seems to refute his claim to amorous freedom. In order to illustrate the fact that the "bands" of true love tie "without constraynt or dread of any ill," the speaker argues that "the gentle birde feeles no captivity / within her cage, but singes and feeds her fill" (*SP*, 65.5, 6, 7–8). In comparing the lady to a song bird, Spenser links her to the poet himself, who chooses to sing within the cage of rhyme and meter. Nevertheless, the cage is a troubling emblem of matrimony, and critics have repeatedly balked at the comparison, seeing it as a sign of the speaker's enduring desire to have impious "maistery" over his mistress or of Spenser's enduring misogyny.[95] Ilona Bell's compelling reading of the metaphor merges these two lines of argumentation: "To the bird's owner, it may look as if the bird 'feeles no captiuity'; however, to the caged bird, even if she is well nourished and free to sing her heart out, a cage still 'feeles' like a cage. . . . From the magisterial imposition of male authority to the acceptance of gender equality is not an instantaneous Ovidean metamorphosis, but a slow, painstaking process of social change."[96] The visceral discomfort readers like Bell feel when faced with the image of the caged bird does not, I think, spring from misreading the poem or imposing our own understanding of liberty and gender equality on a sixteenth-century text. In fact, I would argue that Spenser deliberately cultivates this unease. Like the Gospel paradox of gaining one's life by losing it, the concept of sweet bands and free captivity is not meant to be easily swallowed. If yielding the self were a naturally agreeable task, Spenser could have skipped the sonnets of courtship and proceeded straight to the celebration of marriage in *Epithalamion*. Instead, he composes an eighty-nine sonnet sequence that explores our deep-seated resistance to the image of the caged bird. And, from the opening poem, Spenser acknowledges that even the most fervent of lovers approach the bands of love with fear and trembling. In the end, it seems, both the lover and the lady must act in spite of this fear and faithfully accept the mysterious and paradoxical truth that a bird in its cage feels no captivity, that the bonds of association actually free the individual. His paradoxical language suggests that the lovers will not fully comprehend the liberty of the marriage bonds until they have been irrevocably bound together. And this lack of complete comprehension is precisely what makes the action of association so terrifying and so commendable: the lovers' willingness to encounter danger, to oblige the self to another without any guarantee, testifies to their faithfulness and enduring love.

Though the betrothal sonnet is presented as a culmination of the logic of sacrifice and captivity, Spenser by no means suggests that engagement concludes the struggle between the love of freedom and the bonds of association. In Sonnet 71, Spenser's speaker continues to address the lady's fears of captivity and, in doing so, brings together his meditations on marriage and art. When the sonnet opens, the speaker is commenting on the lady's "drawen work" (her embroidery), which depicts a spider catching a bee in his net (SP, 71.1). The lover immediately recognizes that she is "compar[ing]" herself to the bee and her lover to the spider and acknowledges the aptness of her comparison:

> Right so your selfe were caught in cunning snare
>> of a deare foe, and thralled to his love:
>> in whose streight bands ye now captived are
>> so firmely, that ye never may remove. (SP, 71.5–8)

The tone of the poem is decidedly more playful than the prebetrothal sonnets that contain images of captivity. But this playfulness does not undermine the sonnet's serious argument that the bands of love and marriage are restrictive and permanent.[97] In the subsequent quatrain the speaker introduces a second analogy between the lady's art and the lovers' situation:

> But as your worke is woven all about,
>> with woodbynd flowers and fragrant Eglantine:
>> so sweet your prison you in time shall prove,
>> with many deare delights bedecked fyne. (SP, 71.9–12)

While the first analogy of the poem, signaled by "Right so," points out how the lady's art imitates life, in this quatrain the "as . . . so" analogy inverts the customary logic of mimesis, encouraging the lady to imitate her own "worke" of art. Although artifice is an instrument of constraint in the poem, it is also a consolation for constraint, since the lady can make her bonds delightful through art, decking her prison with woodbine flowers and fragrant eglantine roses.

The speaker acknowledges that this transformation will not occur instantaneously—the lady's mew will only "prove" sweet "in time"—but the resulting harmony will prove perpetual as "all thensforth eternall peace shall see / betweene the Spyder and the gentle Bee" (*SP*, 71.11, 11, 13–14). Spenser describes the lady as "gentle" throughout the sequence, but he does so in particular when he is using animal imagery to describe and sweeten the lady's captive state—she is a "gentle deare" in the betrothal sonnet; a "gentle birde" in Sonnet 65, and a "gentle Bee" here (*SP*, 67.7, 65.7, 71.14). In selecting this adjective, Spenser suggests a fusion of art and nature in the lady. As he makes abundantly clear in book 6 of *The Faerie Queene*, Spenser believes that "gentlenesse of spright" was "planted naturall" in those of "gentle bloud," but he also maintains that gentleness requires cultivation and discipline (*FQ*, 6.1.2, 6.5.1). Indeed, the fact that premodern writers often used the word to describe plants or animals domesticated by human efforts testifies to the association between artifice and gentility.[98] By using an adjective that activates these implications, Spenser suggests that the lady will receive ample compensation for the fetters of domestic captivity when she enjoys the tranquility and refinement that accompany gentility.

This Spenserian belief that civilization requires a form of captivity that is rendered palatable by its beauty would be anathema to more radical proponents of liberty. Indeed, Rousseau uses this image of chains decked with flowers in his *Discourse on the Arts and Sciences*, railing against the fact that the arts "spread garlands of flowers over the iron chains with which they are laden, throttle in them the sentiment of that original freedom for which they seemed born, make them love their slavery, and fashion them into what is called civilized Peoples."[99] But, for Spenser, "original freedom" was not such a sweet prospect because it was marred by the vices and terrors of the natural state. The lovers of the early sequence are free from external restraint, but they are subject to the tyranny of pride and lust and, as a result, suffer from fear and alienation. Spenser suggests that such "salvage wylde" creatures can be bound together into an association that will salve the wounds of sin and lust only if they bind themselves, not in a limited social contract, but in complete mutual servitude (*SP*, 20.9). Although they resist confinement for the majority of the sequence, the speaker and the lady of *Amoretti* at length choose to escape the chaos of natural freedom by embracing the orderliness and fellowship of the captive state. Spenser's peculiar sonnet form, with its emphasis on linking disparate quatrains, is the emblem of and the testing ground for this bond of association. Spenser's career-long movement toward this interwoven form reflects his increasing sense that our barbarous and balductum English must be chained by dull rhymes. His best hope is to beautify the fetters by writing in elaborate interwoven rhyme schemes.

Though Spenser uses the sonnet sequence to depict the process of converting loneliness into association, *Amoretti* does not complete the project of association. After his lovers bind themselves in betrothal in Sonnet 67, Spenser makes it readily apparent in the sonnets that follow that their association is far from realized, that we must wait until *Epithalamion* for the lovers to "Eternally bind . . . this lovely band" (*SP*, 396). The twenty-one sonnets that follow the betrothal and Easter sonnets depict the trials of engagement, including absence, rumor, and resurging lust. Indeed, the sequence ends on a note reminiscent of the loneliness of more traditional sequences:

> Lyke as the Culver on the bared bough
> > Sits mourning for the absence of her mate:
> > and in her songs sends many a wishful vow,
> > for his returne that seems to linger late,
> So I alone now left disconsolate,
> > mourne to my selfe the absence of my love:
> > and wandring here and there all desolate,
> > seek with my playnts to match that mournful dove.
> Ne joy of ought that under heaven doth hove
> > can comfort me, but her own joyous sight:
> > whose sweet aspect both God and man doth move,
> > in her unspotted pleasauns to delight.
> Dark is my day, whyles her fayre light I mis,
> > and dead my life that wants such lively blis. (*SP*, 89)

Spenser's final sonnet certainly leaves more room for hope than the conclusions of sequences like Samuel Daniel's *Delia* and Philip Sidney's *Astrophil and Stella*. While Daniel's speaker is left "pensiue alone, none but despayre about" him and Astrophil's hopes of realizing his love for Stella have been utterly dashed by the end of the sequence, in *Amoretti* 89 temporal words like "now" and "whyles" hint that the speaker's solitary condition is temporary (*SP*, 89.5, 13).[100] As painful as this absence may be, in the end it will only heighten the lover's elation at his mate's "returne" in *Epithalamion* (*SP*, 89.4).

Nonetheless, it is significant that the marriage remains unrealized and the poet isolated at the conclusion of *Amoretti*. Although Spenser converts the sonnet sequence into a forum for meditation on the process of association, he is unable to complete that association within the confines of the sequence. The Spenserian sonnet is an imperfect emblem of the bands of union. Despite his efforts to unify each sonnet with entertangle rhyme and the sequence by superimposing the pattern of the liturgical calendar, formally each of the *Amoretti* sonnets remains cut off from the rest.[101] Spenser resolves this formal problem in *Epithalamion* and in his second marriage ode, *Prothalamion*, by introducing a new poetic feature to complement his lengthy entertangle stanzas—a couplet refrain.[102] As Heather Dubrow has pointed out, refrain was a common feature of the epithalamic convention Spenser inherited from classical poets like Catullus.[103] But many classical and continental marriage songs did not include refrains, so the implications of Spenser's poetic choice deserve careful consideration. Once more Puttenham's account of "band" sheds light on Spenser's poetic practice. After defending entertangle rhyme as the best way to "make band" in a stanza, Puttenham widens his scope: "And as there is in euery staffe, band, giuen to the verses by concord more or lesse busie: so is there in some cases a band giuen to euery staffe, and that is by one whole verse running alone throughout the ditty or ballade, either in the middle or end of euery staff" (*Arte*, M3r). Refrain serves the same connective function as entertangle rhyme, recalling the ear to an earlier part of the poem and thereby tying the entire "ditty" into one coherent whole. In *Epithalamion*, Spenser signals the achievement of the social bond of association by heightening the binding of his verse. Whereas each sonnet of *Amoretti* remained sonically separated from the rest, in *Epithalamion* his complexly interwoven stanzas are linked together by the band of refrain. This heightened binding also indicates that Spenser has widened the scope of his social reflections in *Epithalamion*. While *Amoretti* focused exclusively on the conjunction of two individuals, *Epithalamion* considers how the couple can be woven into a larger social and religious community. The couplets that conclude each stanza reflect on the connections and disjunctions between the couple and the wider world of gods, merchants' daughters, choristers, and angels. The repeated rhyme between "sing" and "Echo ring" indicates that what ties this community together is their willingness to echo back the song of another, to make themselves resemble one another or rhyme "mutually," in William Webbe's terms.[104]

But *Epithalamion*, like *Amoretti*, makes it clear that union is not just a product of human contract or agreement. The refrain is not an emblem just of communal mutuality, but of the ceremonial forces required to make and sustain it. Both in his account of refrain and in his later discussion of figures of speech, Puttenham notes that the Greeks "called such linking verse Epimone, the Latines *versus intercalaris*" (*Arte*, Bb4v). Puttenham does not discuss the Latin term *versus intercalaris* in any detail, but the etymology and history of the term, which was frequently used in early modern commentaries and often specifically associated with marriage poetry, indicates that it is particularly appropriate to the temporally conscious *Epithalamion*.[105] As E.K. notes in the "Generall Argument" to *The Shepheardes Calender*, the Romans used "intercalaris" to describe days inserted into the calendar to compensate for discrepancies between the calendrical and astronomical year (*SP*, 24). In his commentary on Virgil's eighth eclogue, fourth-century grammarian Maurus Servius Honoratus explains how the term came to be applied to refrains: "this verse is called intercalary that is frequently interposed after a few verses, just as days and months are called intercalary that are interposed so that the reckoning/ course [*ratio*] of the sun and of the moon may correspond [*conveniat*]."[106] Servius's account of the Latin term seems to be in tension with Puttenham's vision of the refrain as a "linking verse" that runs through the whole poem. Servius describes these verses as disruptive rather than connective: the "interposed" lines periodically punctuate the flow of the poem. But Servius also underscores the fact that these intrusive intercalary days, and by implication intercalary verses, bring order by compensating for the deficiencies in human attempts to systematize and organize. When the ordinary methods of human art prove insufficient, an additional layer of extraordinary artifice is necessary to make the reckoning correspond.

Servius's analogy between calendrical and poetic structures is particularly relevant to Spenser's marriage song, which, as A. Kent Hieatt convincingly demonstrated in his 1960 study of the poem, incorporates intricate temporal patterns into its form as well as its content.[107] Although he notes that Spenser shared his penchant for numerical symbolism with many poets of his own and prior generations, Hieatt argues that the amount of calendrical detail embedded in *Epithalamion* was unparalleled.[108] The complexity of the temporal structures Hieatt detects in Spenser's marriage poem requires an almost inconceivable level of artfulness—one wonders how Spenser managed to write any poem, much less such a mellifluous one, while simultaneously observing all the prosodic regulations he imposed on himself. Although Spenser had certainly held himself to a high standard of poetic complexity throughout his whole career, this heightening of artifice in *Epithalamion* stands out.

Taking a cue from Hieatt's numerological analysis, I would suggest that the couplet that lies at the exact center of *Epithalamion* provides the most succinct answer to the question of the poem's extraordinary artificiality. After commanding the merchants' daughters to "Open the temple gates" so that his lady may come "before th'almighties vew," in these central lines the bridegroom directs the merchants' daughters to complete their hierophantic duties:

> Bring her up to th'high altar that she may
> The sacred ceremonies there partake,
> The which do endlesse matrimony make. (*SP*, 204, 211, 215–17)

Although pomp and pageantry fill *The Faerie Queene*, Spenser uses the word "ceremony" or "ceremonies" only one other time in his entire corpus.[109] The fact that Spenser reserves this word for the crowning moment of *Epithalamion*, which is also one of the few moments in Spenser's poetic corpus when a marriage is actually realized, indicates that there is something extraordinary and rare about ceremony.[110] Indeed, Spenser attributes considerable power to the sacred ceremonies: they are not mere signs or symbols, but agents that actually "make" an everlasting union between the bride and bridegroom.[111] The verb connects ceremony to human artifice in general and to poetry in particular—as Puttenham was keen to point out in the opening line of his treatise, "A poet is as much as to say a maker"—but it also associates the marriage rite with the divine "Maker" (*Arte*, C1r). Indeed, in *Amoretti* Spenser repeatedly underscores God's role as artificer by using "Maker" more frequently than any other divine title (*SP*, 8.2, 9.13, 24.4, 53.14, 61.1). Ceremony, then, is the bridge between human and divine making, the extraordinary artifice that makes things correspond.

The *versus intercalaris* and the elaborate temporal patterning of *Epithalamion* are the formal corollaries of the poem's central argument that associations—even the "naturalest and first coniunction of two"—require layer upon layer of artful restriction.[112] In *Amoretti*, the lovers undergo a painful process of association, learning to abandon their all too human desires to maintain their own sovereignty so that they can yield to the "sweet . . . bands, the which true love doth tye" (*SP*, 65.5). But they cannot "eternally bind . . . the lovely band" without the addition of mysterious and divine ceremony (*SP*, 396). This making of endless matrimony represents not only the culmination of this particular marriage and poetic sequence, but the crowning achievement of Spenser's decades-long struggle to discover a poetic form that, in E.K.'s terms, was "well grounded, finely framed, and strongly trussed up together."[113] Spenser's dedication to elaborate poetic artifice and particularly to the fetters of interlocking rhyme reflects his general conviction that nature is more apt to drive human beings apart than draw them together.

Spenser's poetry in general and *Epithalamion* in particular represent a high-water mark for the appreciation of artificial restraint. During the same decade in which Spenser was making his case for the necessity and pleasure of restriction in society and poetry, a group of younger poets were conducting poetic experiments that combined libertine personae and celebrations of natural desire with elegiac couplets. Spenser and his poetic mode remained dominant until at least 1600, when the miscellany *Englands Parnassus* gathered together pastoral poetry in complex interwoven forms by Spenser and Sidney as well as living poets like Lodge and Drayton. But over the course of the seventeenth century the influence of Marlowe and Donne and, later, of Jonson and his descendants made the couplet so dominant that by 1687 Edward Howard felt the need to translate Spenser's romance into "Heroick Numbers," which he found much more "sutable" both "in respect of their Freedom & Pleasure."[114] And by 1762 Thomas Warton wondered how Spenser managed to compose his spirited poetry "laden as he was with so many shackles, and embarrassed with so complicated a BONDAGE OF RIMING."[115]

CHAPTER TWO

Licentious Rhymers

DONNE AND THE LATE
ELIZABETHAN COUPLET REVIVAL

TO MODERN READERS accustomed to encountering couplets in the poems
of Dryden, Pope, and their imitators, the form seems to represent the Enlight-
enment in miniature. The relentless chime of the end rhymes and the perfect
balance of the clauses seem tailor-made to transmit eighteenth-century views
of rational judgment, discipline, and order.[1] But the prominence of the bal-
anced eighteenth-century couplet has obscured an earlier, more risqué reputa-
tion of the form. Prior to 1600, iambic pentameter couplets were disdained by
sophisticated English poets, who associated the rhyme scheme with loose
verse and libertine thought. Though in the early seventeenth century Ben Jon-
son and his literary progeny converted the pentameter couplet into a form
congenial to neoclassical restraint and balance, sixteenth-century poets and
critics connected couplets with *The Canterbury Tales* and with an outmoded
kind of verse they deemed merry, light, and vulgar. In the mid-1590s, a group
of boisterous young poets revived and reimagined the couplet precisely be-
cause of its reputation as an ancient and licentious form. Reacting against the
elaborateness of Elizabethan stanzaic poetry, these poets took up the couplet
in order to flout newly established poetic laws and return English poetry to its
original state of liberty.

The couplet poets—Christopher Marlowe (1564–93), John Donne (1572–
1631), Everard Guilpin (1572–?), Joseph Hall (1574–1656), John Marston
(1576–1634), and Thomas Middleton (1580–1627)—belonged to what can be
loosely described as a new school of poetry that arose in the 1590s. Most of the
poets who belonged to this school were in their twenties, and many were stu-
dents or residents at the Inns of Court. They defined themselves in opposition
to contemporaries who saw Spenser and Sidney as their contemporary mas-
ters, who held up Virgil and Petrarch as their poetic forefathers, and who

favored genres like pastoral and the sonnet. The couplet poets of the 1590s instead chose to imitate witty and urbane Roman poets like Horace, Ovid, Martial, and Juvenal. They tested the boundaries of erotic propriety in love elegies and epyllia and deflated the pretensions of polite society in satires and epigrams.[2] And while their contemporaries preferred to write in stanzaic forms and interwoven rhyme schemes, the new poets chose to revive a form that had been used intermittently over the course of the previous century: iambic pentameter couplets.

Donne played a formative role in this late Elizabethan trend for writing in what Marlowe calls "looser lines."[3] In fact, Donne produced the largest and most varied body of couplet poetry in the 1590s. Donne's status as a couplet poet has long been overlooked since the portion of his early corpus favored by twentieth-century readers, his "Songs and Sonnets," consists largely of stanzaic poems.[4] But nearly everything else Donne wrote in the 1590s—his elegies, satires, epigrams, and most of his verse letters—is in iambic pentameter couplets.[5] Even in the "Songs and Sonnets," where Donne rarely repeats a rhyme scheme, continuous couplets are by far the most frequently used verse form, occurring in eleven of fifty-five poems, including such well-known poems as "The Flea." Moreover, the few records that remain of Elizabethan and Jacobean engagement with Donne's verse indicate that early readers did not privilege the "Songs and Sonnets" as we do and that they may have actually preferred his couplet verse.

By considering Donne's early experiments with the couplet, I aim to provide a new perspective on a period of Donne's career that has often proved elusive for several reasons: the lack of surviving Elizabethan manuscripts of Donne's verse, Donne's reserve about his verse practice and poetic influences, and the diversity of personae and moral positions that he adopts in his early poetry. Attending to verse forms can shed new light on Donne's youthful thought as well as the controversies that embroiled the Inns of Court in the 1590s because premodern poets and theorists did not isolate formal questions from social, political, and ethical concerns and, in fact, often endeavored to defend and recommend the art of poesy by attributing larger implications to formal features like rhyme and meter. They recognized that verse forms, like genres, carry considerable freight along with them and allow poets to associate themselves implicitly with particular figures and epochs in literary history. This chapter endeavors to reveal the larger stakes of Donne's prosodic choices by responding to two questions: what prompted Donne and his youthful contemporaries to take up the iambic pentameter couplet in the 1590s, and how did they adapt it to their purposes?

Throughout this chapter, I have avoided using the term "heroic couplets," which has forced me to use precise but at times tiresome formulations like "iambic pentameter couplets" and "decasyllabic couplets." I have gone out of my way to avoid the familiar adjective not only because it is not an Elizabethan

term but because prior to 1600 the decasyllabic couplet was anything but he-
roic. In the 1590s the phrase "heroical verse" was used to refer to *ottava rima*
rather than couplets.[6] Indeed, Elizabethans consistently associated decasyl-
labic couplets with *The Canterbury Tales* and other light and comic works
produced by England's "auncient rymers" (*Arte*, Lɪv).[7] In their poetic manuals,
theorists like George Gascoigne and George Puttenham accepted a late medi-
eval distinction between couplets and stanzaic verse that depicted couplets as
native, light, and unrefined and stanzaic forms as foreign, grave, and sophisti-
cated.[8] Disdain for the couplet stemmed from analogical readings of its formal
features as well as from its association with outdated verse: because the Chau-
cerian couplet was often characterized by enjambment, loose placement of the
caesura, and slant rhyme, strict poetic lawgivers like Puttenham rejected it as
a licentious form beneath the dignity of a courtly artificer (*Arte*, Lɪv). The
distinction between loose couplets and grave stanzas was not simply theoreti-
cal but reflected the practice of sixteenth-century poets. Before the rage for
pentameter couplets in the 1590s, the form was used infrequently over the
course of the century, but, when it was used, it was primarily for lighter fare
like beast fables, romances, ballads, epigrams, and satires. Many of these
works, like the couplet epigrams of Donne's maternal grandfather, John Hey-
wood, look back nostalgically to Chaucer's age as a time when the English were
bawdier but also more virtuous since they used wit and homespun wisdom to
check the newfangled vices of civilized society.[9]

Donne and his contemporaries took up the form because of these associa-
tions with the light but upright verse of the ancient rhymers of England. Scorn-
ing the high level of artifice cultivated by their poetic elders and contempo-
raries as well as inveighing against the increasing sophistication of London life,
the new poets frequently expressed their desire to return to a time before "free
borne" men "disclaime[d] Natures manumission" and made "themselues bond
to opinion."[10] This longing for an ancient state of liberty is a central preoccupa-
tion of the new poets and links the Stoic satires of Hall with the libertine erotic
verse of Marlowe and Donne. All these poets look back to a more natural Sa-
turnian age: in his first moral satire Hall mocks continental apparel and ap-
peals to a time when "that homely Emperour" Saturn dressed with less pomp
than a contemporary "vnder-groome of the Ostlerie," and in a mythical digres-
sion within *Hero and Leander* Marlowe depicts Mercury and Cupid—figures
of scholarship and love—conspiring to end Jove's violent rule and return Sat-
urn to his rightful seat.[11] The turn toward the pentameter couplet was inter-
twined with this radical naturalism and disdain for fashionable artifice. Just
as Elizabethan satirists mocked the imported apparel, the "far-fetched liuery,"
of the fashionable London set, they often ridiculed interwoven stanzas as su-
perfluous foreign finery.[12] As Chapman put it in a colorful 1598 preface to
Achilles Shield, "octaues, canzons, canzonets" and other such "fustian" forms
were "affect[ed]" only by the "strooting lips" of "quidditicall Italianistes."[13]

Thus, to reject the stanza was to liberate oneself from French and Italian poetical tyranny and return to "free-bred poesie."[14]

It was also to overturn what they saw as an Elizabethan preference for form over reason. Because the open couplet does not require the poet to wrap up a thought or sentence within a prescribed number of lines, it is particularly conducive to lengthy arguments, extended comparisons, and dramatic speech. These are all, of course, characteristic features of Donne's verse. I will make the case that Donne developed aspects of this characteristic and influential style by experimenting with the loose couplet in his early years as a student at the Inns of Court. Donne chose the couplet in the 1590s because it was associated with unpretentious poetry and liberty of thought. But his early apprenticeship to the couplet in turn shaped his style and his conception of poetic liberty in ways that would profoundly influence seventeenth-century poets like Jonson and Milton.

Auncient Rymers: Couplets in Elizabethan Poetic Theory

The term "couplet" did not become widespread until the seventeenth century, though it was first used to describe one of the shepherds' poetical "sports" in Sidney's *Arcadia*.[15] Since no single term was settled on before 1600, poetic theorists used a delightful jumble of terms, including "distich," "couple of verses," "cooples," "geminels," "riding rhyme," and, less concisely, "The verse . . . that consists of five feet, and the rhyme each verse immediately returned."[16] This inconsistency of vocabulary makes comments on the couplet difficult to locate in prefaces and poetic treatises. However, bringing together these scattered remarks reveals remarkable consistency in Elizabethan views of the verse form: whatever term theorists choose, they almost invariably connect the couplet to "our Mayster and Father *Chaucer*" and his imitators and associate it with light and bawdy narrative verse.[17]

George Gascoigne provides one of the earliest Elizabethan commentaries on couplets in his brief poetic handbook *Certayne notes of Instruction*, which was included in his 1575 collection of poetry *The Posies of George Gascoigne, Esquire*. At the conclusion of his treatise, Gascoigne offers guidance about how to choose among the "sundrie sortes of verses which we vse now adayes" by tracing their historical genealogies and noting the generic associations of each "kinde of ryme." On the final page of the book, Gascoigne suddenly remembers that he left something out: "I had forgotten a notable kinde of ryme, called ryding rime, and that is suche as our Mayster and Father *Chaucer* vsed in his Canterburie tales, and in diuers other delectable and light enterprises." After further apology for bringing in this "remembrance somewhat out of order," Gascoigne goes on to say that "this riding rime serueth most aptly to wryte a merie tale" while another Chaucerian verse form, "Rythme royall," is "fittest for

a graue discourse." Gascoigne desires to provide clear-cut "Notes of Instruc-
tion" for prospective English poets, so he attempts to use historical precedent
to establish a fundamental rule that correlates certain "sorts of verse" with
certain "enterprises." Since Chaucer is the "Mayster and Father" of English
poetry, the prosodic divisions within his corpus become prescriptive for all
subsequent versifiers.[18]

This association of the short couplet with light verse was not simply a ret-
rospective invention of Gascoigne. Traces of the distinction between light cou-
plets and grave stanzas can be found in the works of Middle English poets.
Chaucer apologizes for his octosyllabic couplets in his early poem *House of
Fame*, remarking in the invocation to the third book that his "rym ys lyght and
lewed" since he did no "diligence" to show "craft" but only "sentence."[19] The
social implications of Chaucer's description of his verse as "lewed"—that is,
unlearned, unskillful, and low—become more apparent when it is read along-
side a more extended discussion of rhyme in the verse prologue to Robert
Mannyng's fourteenth-century chronicle *The Story of England* (c. 1338). Man-
nyng relates that he was advised "many a tyme" to "turn" his story "in light[e]
ryme," that is, in four-beat couplets, because this form is "lightest in mannes
mouthe" and most manageable for "lewed men" and the "comonalte."[20] If he
had instead chosen to "turne" the poem "in strange ryme" and "in baston," that
is, in a French stanzaic form like "ryme couwee" (tail rhyme) or "enterlace," the
common performer and listener would have been utterly "fordon."[21] On the
one hand, Mannyng associates the stanza with the educated and refined classes
and with a "strange" or foreign poetic craft advanced enough to have complex
terms of art, while on the other he connects the couplet with simple and intel-
ligible native verse that provides "solace" for his common "felawes."[22] Man-
nyng's belief that interwoven rhyme is too demanding for untrained ears is
curious and makes one wonder how exactly he thought rhyme at a distance
would confound a lewd listener, but it is clear that Mannyng prefers wide-
spread comprehension of his "story of Inglande" to recognition for his prosodic
dexterity and that he, like Chaucer, considers the short couplet to be the most
appropriate form for those who prefer sentence to craft.[23]

Two hundred and fifty years later, Elizabethan theorist George Puttenham
would draw on this distinction and its social implications in order to uphold
the artful stanza over the common couplet. In the brief history of English verse
he provides in book 1, Puttenham, like Gascoigne, distinguishes between the
"graue and stately" rhyme royal "staffe" of *Troilus and Criseyde* and the "verse
of the Canterbury tales," which he calls, with patent disapproval, "but riding
ryme" (*Arte*, I1v). He reveals the source of his disdain in his analysis of rhyme
schemes, where he argues, in the vein of Mannyng, that rhyme at a distance is
better accommodated to the "learned and delicate eare" while short couplet
verse is more fitting for the "rude and popular eare" (*Arte*, M2r).[24] Puttenham
attempts to establish a quantitative rule for determining the lightness of a

form: the more "speedily" the rhyme "return[s]," the lighter and more vulgar the poem (*Arte*, M1v–M2r).

Because the purpose of Puttenham's book is to show that English verse can be just as refined and artful as Greek and Latin verse, he becomes exercised about the vulgarity and licentiousness of the "too speedy returne" of rhyme (*Arte*, M1r). In a colorful and revealing rant, he suggests that such verse is only fitting for

> small & popular Musickes song by these *Cantabanqui* vpon benches and barrels heads where they haue none other audience then boys or countrey fellowes that passe by them in the streete, or else by blind harpers or such like tauerne minstrels that giue a fit of mirth for a groat, & their matters being for the most part stories of old time, as the tale of Sir *Topas*, the reportes of *Beuis* of *Southampton*, *Guy* of *Warwicke*, *Adam Bell*, and *Clymme* of the *Clough* & such other old Romances or historicall rimes, made purposely for recreation of the common people at Christmasse diners & brideales, and in tauernes & alehouses and such other places of base resort, also they be vsed in Carols and rounds and such light or lasciuious Poemes, which are commonly more commodiously vttered by these buffons or vices in playes then by any other person. Such were the rimes of *Skelton* (vsurping the name of a Poet Laureat) being in deede but a rude rayling rimer & all his doings ridiculous, he vsed both short distaunces and short measures pleasing onely the popular eare: in our courtly maker we banish them vtterly. (*Arte*, M1r)

In his harangue against short distances between rhymes, Puttenham manages to paint a vivid picture of what a more sympathetic or sentimental observer might have called "merry old England": a world of taverns, minstrels, tales of old times, Christmas dinners, weddings, and bawdy songs.[25] Puttenham's rant sounds excessively vehement and has the ring of an aspiring gentleman trying to dissociate himself from his rude country relatives. If the English are to prove that they are "nothing inferiour to the French or Italian for copie of language, subtiltie of deuice, good method and proportion in any forme of poeme," they must rid themselves of all the trappings of their unsophisticated past (*Arte*, H8v). In banishing the too speedy return of rhyme, Puttenham attempts to banish a whole vision of England that he thinks has prevented his country from producing a refined courtly maker.

Puttenham has disdain not only for the "vulgar proportion" used in *The Canterbury Tales* but also for the continuous and enjambed character of its riding rhyme (*Arte*, M2r). When he complains that "our auncient rymers, as *Chaucer*, *Lydgate* & others" do not keep the caesura "precisely" or mind the end of the line, his condemnation takes on a moral tinge (*Arte*, L1v). In letting "their rymes runne out at length," these ancient poets ignore a "law" and "rule

of restraint" intended to "correct the licentiousnesse of rymers" (*Arte*, L1v).
Puttenham disparages rhymers so reckless that they "will be tyed to no rules at
all, but range as [they] list" (*Arte*, L1v). They may manage to express them-
selves, to "vtter what [they] will," but their work is undeserving of the lofty
name of poetry and should be labelled "ryme dogrell" (*Arte*, L1v, L2r). Al-
though Gascoigne and Mannyng establish a hierarchy of "light" and "grave"
verse, for them the distinction is largely a question of fitness and knowing one's
audience. For Puttenham, the choice between enjambed couplets and end-
stopped entertangle rhyme becomes a serious aesthetic and even moral ques-
tion—to write in riding rhyme is not simply light and merry but vulgar, loose,
and licentious. By failing to uphold the rules of measure and number, the licen-
tious rhymer forsakes his primary responsibility as an Orphic poet, which,
according to Puttenham, is to act as a "lawgiver" and "hold and containe the
people in order and duety by force of good and wholesome lawes" (*Arte*, M2r).
Since "proportion poetical" not only reflects cosmic order but produces social
order, Puttenham fears that the result of stylistic licentiousness would be noth-
ing less than moral decay and social chaos (*Arte*, K1r).

"Let my lines in freedome goe": Discursive Couplets in Elizabethan Satire

George Puttenham was buried at St. Bride's, Fleet Street, in London on Janu-
ary 6, 1591, less than two years after the anonymous publication of *The Arte of
English Poesie*, so he did not live to see the rise of the new school of poetry in
the final decade of the sixteenth century.[26] But it is not difficult to imagine
what Puttenham would have thought of the new poets since every complaint
that he lodges against Chaucer and the ancient rhymers also applies to Donne
and his fellows. In addition to breaking Puttenham's law against speedily re-
turning rhymes, they heavily enjamb their lines, place the internal caesura
loosely, and use an inordinate number of feminine and slant rhymes. For the
most part, the young couplet poets silently break the rules of refined poetry
without announcing the reasons for their mutiny, but the satires of Donne's
peers Hall and Marston contain a wealth of information on style and prosody
that illuminates the poetic program of this new school. In their poems on Eliz-
abethan poetic trends, Hall and Marston indicate that their loose couplet style
is intimately connected with the central goal of their satires: liberating Eliza-
bethan society from the tyranny of fashion and opinion. They depict their re-
jection of the stanza and turn to the couplet as a deliberate effort to overturn
the artificial rules of courtly makers and return English poetry to a natural
state of liberty.

Though his satires were written later than those of Hall and Donne, John
Marston is the most explicit about his poetic intentions and offers a manifesto
of sorts for the couplet poets in his poem "Ad Rithmum." While Puttenham

despises the rhymer who "will be tyed to no rules at all, but range as he list," Marston declares that he would prefer to "freely range" rather than "wrest some forced rime" (*Arte*, L1v; *Scourge*, E2r). He exemplifies his licentiousness even as he proclaims it, breaking nearly every Puttenhamic law in the space of three lines:

> Then hence base ballad stuffe, my poetrie
> Disclaimes you quite, for know my libertie
> Scornes riming lawes. (*Scourge*, E1r)

To name just a few transgressions, the clauses recklessly overflow the line endings, and both final nouns are polysyllabic and would be classified by Puttenham as dactyls.[27] Indeed, Puttenham argues that although "libertie" may not be a "precise *Dactil* by the Latine rule," it will "passe wel inough" for a dactyl in "our vulgar meeters" because it is "usually vulgarly pronounced" as one (*Arte*, P2v). He warns against such polysyllabic and dactylic line endings, which, like the couplet, he associates with vulgar rhymes: they "make your musicke too light and of no solemn grauitie" and "smatch more of the school of common players than of any delicate Poet *Lyricke* or *Elegiacke*" (*Arte*, M2r). Marston has little regard for such courtly delicacy. Instead, he proudly describes himself as a poetic bull in a china shop in a passage that Ben Jonson would repeatedly mock:[28]

> I cannot hold, I cannot I indure
> To view a big womb'd foggie clowde immure
> The radiant tresses of the quickening sunne.
> Let Custards quake, my rage must freely runne. (*Scourge*, B8v)

The custard is a fitting emblem not only of courtly refinement—Dekker describes it as a pastry "stiffe with curious art"—but of the instability of such artifices: the truth-disclosing rage of the poet makes the egg-based delicacy quiver and quake.[29] Marston's verse is certainly wilder than that of Hall or Donne, but in his custard-quaking declaration of liberty, he simply amplifies the central concern of all late Elizabethan satires. The satirists of the 1590s aimed to expose the ways that their contemporaries had made themselves slaves to a host of unnatural masters: to Petrarchan mistresses and abject sensuality, to moneylenders and patrons, and, above all, to fashion and the conventions of polite society. It is striking how infrequently the satirists use metaphors of looseness or laxness to describe the vices and follies of the times. Instead, all the sins of London society are depicted as forms of restriction and "servile service" (*Scourge*, C2r). In fact, Marston uses a recurring rhyme to set up an antithesis between all kinds of "controule" and the free and rational "soule." He repeats the pair so frequently that it becomes a kind of refrain or motto for the satire book as a whole:

But yee diuiner wits, celestiall soules,
Whose free-borne mindes no kennel thought cont[r]oules . . .
  (*Scourge*, B3r)

But as for me, my vexed thoughtfull soule,
Takes pleasure, in displeasing sharp controule. (*Scourge*, B5r)

O that the boundlesse power of the soule
Should be subiected to such base controule! (*Scourge*, G2r)[30]

The adjectives Marston uses to describe the human soul in these refrains—
"celestiall," "free-borne," "thoughtful," and "boundlesse"—hint at the philosoph-
ical underpinning of his belief that all vices are forms of slavery.

He explains his position in more detail in a passage that seems to have been
accidentally left out of the 1598 edition of *Scourge of Villanie* but that was re-
stored in the 1599 edition. The restored lines, addressed to "Gallants," argue
that we all have a "part not subiect to mortality" that is given "wings" by
"Boundlesse discursive apprehension."[31] This immortal part "should grudge &
inly scorne to be made slave" to humors within and masters without and
"should murmur, when you stop his course."[32] Belief in a rational, immortal
part of the soul was common in the period, but Marston's depiction of reason
as a wandering, boundless faculty and his suggestion that virtue is a result of
releasing the soul from all stops and limits is less conventional. The passage is
one of the most philosophical and argumentative in Marston's work, and, not
coincidentally, it is also one of the most enjambed: in the fourteen-line pas-
sage, the end of the sentence corresponds with the end of the line only twice.
With his swift, overflowing lines, Marston reproduces the activity of his bound-
less discursive apprehension.

In fact, Marston's multivalent adjective "discursive" captures many facets
of the couplet poets' characteristic style. Derived from the Latin verb *discur-
rere*, to run off in different directions, it means (1) expansive or digressive, (2)
related to speech or discourse, and (3) characterized by reasoned argument or
thought.[33] The stylistic tendencies of Marston and Donne, particularly their
tendency to imitate familiar speech and to let arguments and conceits run their
full course, originates in the belief that reason should be set free from the im-
position of burdensome "riming lawes" (*Scourge*, E1r). But why did these poets
consider the couplet particularly conducive to such boundless discourse? After
all, sixteenth- and seventeenth-century theorists described all forms of
rhyme—not just stanzas—as restrictive "bands" or "fetters."[34] Moreover, we
tend to associate couplets not with boundless speech but with tiresome repeti-
tion and uniformity.[35] But many early modern writers thought that couplets
actually fostered variety and mobility. Sir John Beaumont praised couplets
because

Their forme surpassing farre the fetter'd staues,
Vaine care, and needlesse repetition saues.[36]

Ben Jonson agreed with Beaumont's assessment of the couplet as a liberating form: he told Drummond that he preferred couplets and considered "cross-rhymes and stanzas" to be "forced" because "the purpose would lead him beyond eight lines to conclude."[37] Even Puttenham confirms that the distich, though "not to be accompted a staff, serues for a continuance" (*Arte*, K2r).[38]

Looking back on the Elizabethan period through the lens of Milton's reaction against the couplets of Civil War and Restoration poetry, it is difficult to connect couplets with free verse and thought. But for Marston and the young poets of the 1590s, stanzas were the "troublesome and modern" verse form while couplets restored "ancient liberty" (*CPMP*, 210). This rapid inversion of the reputation of the couplet between the end of Elizabeth's reign and the Restoration reveals the importance of keeping a close eye on the shifting implications of poetic forms. If we assume that verse forms had the same implications in 1590 as they did in 1690 or 1790, we are liable to misread the prosodic signals issued by early modern poets and misunderstand controversies like the late Elizabethan war over fashionable artifice and English liberty.

Far-Fetched Livery, Homespun Thread, and Full Nakedness: Rhyme, Clothing, and the Pursuit of Nature

In his work on Spenser's style and early modern ornamentalism, David Scott Wilson-Okamura draws attention to the fact that premodern poetic theorists (he cites authors from Dante to Samuel Johnson) saw language as the garment of thought, an idea that he notes often seems alien and distasteful to post-Cartesian critics. Wilson-Okamura argues that this disconnect is part of why "ornamentalism still makes us uncomfortable"; there is a "suspicion that ornament is something external, detachable, or superficial—like a façade on a building or frosting on a cake."[39] Wilson-Okamura's analysis of the deeper philosophical division that informs critical discomfort with the clothing metaphor illuminates not only Spenser's stylistic choices but the broader understanding of form and its aims in the period. I would like to build on Wilson-Okamura's insight about the garment of style by thinking through how much room there was for play and disagreement within the metaphor. For, as the satirists of the 1590s make very clear, there are many different kinds of garments available to the gallant and the poet—and some garments are in fact gaudy and superficial. Indeed, attitudes toward dress are frequently a litmus test for poets' opinions on the proper balance between nature and artifice. The poets whom I have described as licentious rhymers all make it clear that their prosodic and philosophical aim is to discard unnecessary frippery in order to return to homespun clothing or, more radically, to the nakedness of Adam and Eve.

All the satirists look back nostalgically on an idealized English past that was free from the fetters of fashion and opinion, but Joseph Hall spends the most time fleshing out the idea of ancient liberty. The fifth book of his satires is dedicated entirely to abuses of land and property that have crept in since the days of "our Grandsires . . . in ages past."[40] And in his first "moral" satire of the third book, Hall offers a vivid, if somewhat conventional, account of the golden age when men lived on acorns and berries and "naked went: or clad in ruder hide: / Or home-spun *Russet*, void of forraine pride."[41] This recollection of the simplicity of homespun ancient dress causes Hall to rail against the imported fopperies of courtiers:

> But thou canst maske in garish gauderie,
> To suit a fooles far-fetched liuery.
> A *French* head ioyn'd to necke *Italian*:
> Thy thighs from *Germanie*, and brest fro *Spaine*:
> An *Englishman* in none, a foole in all:
> Many in one, and one in seuerall.[42]

Like Jonson's character Amorphus the traveler in *Cynthia's Revels* (which was acted in 1600), Hall's courtier is "so made out of the mixture and shreds of forms that himself is truly deformed"; his pursuit of the newest and most "far-fetched" fashions from France, Italy, Germany, and Spain make him a monster who is alienated from his native Englishness.[43] Hall's admiration for the simple sartorial choices of the golden world contrasts starkly with Puttenham's distaste for the time before the arrival of civilizing poets, when "the people" were "vagarant and dipersed like the wild beasts, lawlesse and naked, or verie ill clad" (*Arte*, C2r–v).

Elizabethan poets on both sides of the stanza-couplet debate saw courtly dress as an emblem for elaborate continental poetic forms like the stanza. Puttenham uses comparison to the "courtly habiliments" of "Madames of honour" in order to bolster his argument for elaborate poetry in the opening portion of his section on "ornament poeticall" (*Arte*, Q3v–Q4r). But Joseph Hall draws on the same sartorial analogy to depreciate both stanzaic and quantitative poetry. In the opening lines of the book of "Poeticall" satires, he uses the image of dressed-up stanzas to distinguish his own work from Spenser's romance:

> Nor Ladies wanton loue nor wandring knight,
> Legend I out in rymes all richly dight.[44]

Hall chooses his language carefully here. Spenser frequently uses the word "dight," which could mean ordered, arranged, clothed, or adorned, but he uses the phrase "richly dight" in particular to describe Duessa: "Most false *Duessa*, royall richly dight, / That easie was t'inueigle weaker sight" (*FQ*, 1.12.32). In

adopting the phrase, Hall accuses Spenser of crafting stanzas in which adorn-
ment covers nether parts as "wanton" as those of his most appealingly false
character. In the sixth satire of his first book, Hall condemns English efforts to
write quantitative verse as equally contrived: those who "scorn the home-spun
threed of rimes" and pursue the "loftie feet" and "numbred verse that *Virgil*
sung" are working against the natural rhythms and native attire of English
verse.[45] Hall presents couplets as a middle way between two forms of preten-
sion. He agrees with Samuel Daniel that rhyme is the "kinde and naturall at-
tire" of English poetry and that the "single numbers" of quantitative meter will
never "doe in our Climate."[46] Though Spenser uses the homespun thread of
rhyme, he weaves it into overdressed stanzaic patterns that Hall considers
equally contrived.

Marston echoes Hall's language and makes the denunciation of ornately
dressed stanzas more explicit in his first book of satires. His first attempts at
satiric poetry were printed in a 1598 volume that also included his Ovidian
poem "The Metamorphosis of Pygmalion's Image," which was composed in a
common stanzaic form rhyming ABABCC. In a transitional poem between the
two works, Marston claims that his Ovidian poem was a parody and mocks his
own "stanzaes," comparing them to "odd bands / Of voluntaries, and mercenar-
ians"; like "Soldados" of the current "age" the stanzas

> March rich bedight in warlike equipage:
> Glittering in dawbed lac'd accoustrements,
> And pleasing sutes of loues habiliments.
> Yet puffie as Dutch hose they are within,
> Faint, and white liuer'd, as our gallants bin.[47]

Marston describes the ornament of his stanzas in nearly the same words Hall
uses for Spenser's stanzaic rhymes: they are "rich bedight." Marston, charac-
teristically, cannot leave it at that but expands the image of sartorial richness.
Like many of the characters of Marston's satires, his soldier-stanzas are covered
in layer upon layer of deceptive artifice. The stanzas initially appear to be im-
ages of martial discipline and order—they may be richly dressed, but they are
warlike and marching in order. But in the next two lines, it becomes clear that
their suits not only are glittering and lacy but are the "habiliments" of love
rather than war. Not only are the soldier-stanzas dressed as lovers rather than
warriors, but even this costume is only a cover for the empty puffery of their
insides. As he gradually demotes stanzas from soldiers to lily-livered gallants,
Marston exposes the pretensions of courtly versifiers who claim that their
finely wrought stanzaic forms are emblems of the restrained order and beauty
of civilized life. Instead, Marston charges, stanzas are nothing but form—stan-
zaic poets spend so much time interweaving their rhymes and decking out
their lines that they forget to attend to the matter of their poetry. By turning

against his own stanzas, Marston attempts to position himself as a defender of inner truth against the encroachments of excessively elaborate rhyme.

Hall and Marston are explicit about the connections between their prosodic choices and their dedication to natural liberty, while the two better-known members of the couplet school, Marlowe and Donne, less frequently speak of stanzas and couplets. But these poets do think about clothing, fashion, and nakedness in their couplet verse in ways that connect them with the other members of the school. In fact, attending to the question of ornament and natural dress in Donne and Marlowe brings out new continuities within and between their work. In his first satire, which Marotti argues "especially reflect[s] the Inns-of-Court setting" in which it was composed, Donne's satirist contends with a "motley humorist" who sizes up the wealth of all he meets on the street by searching their clothing for "silke" and "gould" and "to that rate / So high or low do[es] vaile [his] formall hatt."[48] Donne accuses his companion of enjoying the "nakedness and bareness" of his "plump muddy whore, or prostitute boy" but then castigates the humorist for despising another kind of nakedness:

> Why shouldst thou . . .
> Hate vertu though she be naked and bare?
> At birthe, and death our bodyes naked are:
> And till our Soules be vnapparelled
> Of bodyes, they from blis are banished.
> Mans first blest State was naked, when by Sin
> He lost that, yet he was clothd but in beasts skin.
> And in this coarse attire which I now weare
> With God and with the Muses I confer.[49]

This is the serious version of the more sophistic argument in "To his mistress going to bed":

> Full nakednes, all ioyes are due to thee;
> As Soules vnbodied, bodyes vncloth'd must bee,
> To tast whole ioyes.[50]

This argument that stripping away gets us closer to the "naked" essence of bodies and souls runs through Donne's early work. To some extent naked truth and naked virtue are unattainable—the fall has alienated humanity from that blessed state in the time between birth and death—but Donne contends that in the meantime, while conferring with God and the muses, one should at least stick with the "course attire" given by God to cover Adam and Eve after the fall. Like Hall, Donne's satirist depicts plain, ancient attire as an antidote to the ever-changing "fashiond hats," "ruffs," and "Suites" worn by "supple-witted antick Youths."[51] By discarding the newfangled trappings of those who follow fashion and custom, Donne's satirist hopes to draw nearer to the naked, natural truth.

In *Hero and Leander*, Marlowe displays a similar concern with stripping away clothing to get to the nakedness beneath, though he approaches the equation of nakedness and truth with more irony than Donne. We can hardly take Leander at his word, for example, when he claims in his sophistic speech to Hero, "My words shall be as spotlesse as my youth, / Full of simplicitie and naked truth."[52] But, for all of Marlowe's irony, Leander's association of youth and naked truth does capture something about the poem's push to uncover the rudiments of desire.[53] In *Hero and Leander*, Marlowe strips down Eros to its bare, youthful, reckless, love-at-first-sight essence. When she makes her entry into the poem, Hero—with her ridiculously ornate sacerdotal robes featuring "*Venus* in her naked glory" and the blood of slain lovers, her veil of artificial flowers, and a pair of boots with chirruping birds that her handmaid must periodically refill as she walks—is too artificial by half, while "Amorous *Leander*, beautifull and yoong" is adored by the narrator for the natural beauty of his body.[54] As the story of wooing and winning unfolds, Hero is literally and figuratively defrocked. After Leander points out the incongruity of being a celibate "Nun" to Venus and woos her to exchange her vow of chastity for "*Venus* sweet rites," Hero trades her ceremonial vestments for a "lawne" through which her "limmes" "sparkl[e]."[55] And the penultimate image of the (perhaps) unfinished poem, bookending the opening description of her contrived costume, is the revelation of Hero's body after she tries to sneak away from the bed but is caught by Leander:

> Thus neere the bed she blushing stood upright,
> And from her countenance behold ye might
> A kind of twilight breake, which through the heare,
> As from an orient cloud, glymse here and there.
> And round about the chamber this false morne,
> Brought foourth the day before the day was borne.
> So *Heroes* ruddie cheeke, *Hero* betrayd,
> And her all naked to his sight diplayd.
> Whence his admiring eyes more pleasure tooke,
> Than *Dis*, on heapes of gold fixing his looke.[56]

The unveiling—or "betray[al]"—of Hero in all her unadorned splendor does seem to be a moment of aesthetic transcendence in the poem. Marlowe quickly undercuts that transcendence with Leander's miserly gaze and with the concluding image of night "o'recome with anguish, shame, and rage, / Dang[ing] downe to hell her loathsome carriage."[57] I am persuaded by Gordon Braden's argument that the false morning produced by Hero's blush invites us to think for a moment that "we are almost on the verge of a giddy affirmation such as John Donne makes in his own contrarian *aubade* in scorning everything the daytime represents. . . . But we aren't; this poem is not that one. The real dawn comes on cue, and it is imperious and loud and sweeps everything before it."[58] The fact that Marlowe shatters the vision while Donne bears it out is significant. Yet it is also significant that these two poets are united in imagining the elemental force of Eros warring against and outbraving—even just for a moment—the orderly force of the sun. The vision is more brittle in Marlowe, but it is powerful nonetheless. Indeed, it is telling that Marlowe's Saturnian digression—in which he aligns lovers and scholars with Saturn and Ops and against Jove and the Fates—has no counterpart in Musaeus's Greek.[59] The poem as a whole seems designed to uncover and revel in the pre-Olympian natural passions that spring up spontaneously in Hero and Leander and to cut through their customary pretensions and posturing. The erotic desire that Marlowe reveals within his youthful characters is not sweet—in fact, it is "deaffe and cruell"—and is fated to end in destruction, but it is undeniably a mighty and elemental force akin to the forces Marlowe unleashes in his plays.[60]

Gordon Braden has noted that the passage in which Hero's blush produces a false morn echoes a passage from Marlowe's youthful translation of Ovid in which Corinna's "Starke naked" "selfe" is also "Betray'd" to the eye of the speaker.[61] Indeed, *Hero and Leander*, which was likely one of the last things Marlowe wrote before his untimely death in May 1593, is in many ways a revisiting of his Ovid translation, which he likely composed during his time at Cambridge between 1580 and 1587.[62] As Heather James has suggested, Marlowe was attracted to Ovidianism (as were many of his contemporaries) because "the audacity and licentiousness of Ovidian elegy represent a deliberately risky and playful kind of speech, developed for Roman imperial subjects to express their residual dissent from the heroic and patriotic line of thinking that had, in Ovid's day, become an inescapable institution rather than a novel proposition."[63] James contends that Ovid's political disruptiveness is built into the Latin elegiac distich, which yokes together a dactylic hexameter and a pentameter line.[64] But, in Englishing Ovid, Marlowe leaves behind the disruptive unevenness of his lines and pursues other kinds of prosodic looseness. In both *All Ovids Elegies* and *Hero and Leander*, Marlowe (who was born and raised in Canterbury) rendered the naturalism of Ovid in the pentameter couplets of Chaucer. In *All Ovids Elegies*, Marlowe describes his Ovidian verse as "looser lines," significantly transforming Ovid's "*teneris . . . modis*," tender or soft measures.[65] Marlowe's "looser" implies all the prosodic and moral licentiousness Puttenham attributed to reckless rhymers, and his substitution of "lines" for Ovid's "modis" also suggests that Marlowe's verse may be less measured even than his model. The looseness of Marlowe's couplets in both translations is different from the enjambed looseness of Donne and Marston. He tends to close his couplets and to emphasize his rhymes (in *Hero and Leander* this is often to humorous effect; indeed, the rhymes in Marlowe's epyllion often seem to undercut the sententious wisdom offered by the narrator).[66] But Marlowe's couplet poems also contain the seeds of the licentious rhyming of the 1590s: in spite of their end-stops, Marlowe's couplets allow for a looser and more continuous narrative than sonnets or stanzas. (Comparing *Hero and Leander* to Shakespeare's stanzaic *Venus and Adonis* makes the significance of the couplet very apparent; Shakespeare's poem does not hurtle onward like *Hero and Leander* but lingers over and elaborates metaphorically on the lovers and their exchanges in a manner that recalls Spenser more than Marlowe.)[67] And, particularly in his Ovidian elegies, Marlowe plays with loose rhythm and varied placement of the caesura to cultivate a witty, conversational voice that resounds in Donne's later Ovidian experiments.[68] But, above all, Marlowe's couplet verse anticipates the work of the couplet school in its association of the couplet with a licentiousness that strips away custom and artifice in order to gain access to the naked nature beneath.

John Donne, Couplet Poet

The discovery and restoration of natural liberty is the central preoccupation of Donne's early corpus, unifying an otherwise discordant body of poetry.[69] In his verse letters, Donne defines poetry as free discourse among friends and makes the case that rational speech cannot always be pressed into measured verse. In his elegies, he adopts the persona of the libertine as a skeptical position from which he can interrogate the boundaries of desire and distinguish its natural limitations from the arbitrary restraints of poetic and social custom.[70] And in his satires, he applies the same test to social and religious practices, discovering few that meet his standards of natural liberty. Indeed, Donne is more extreme than the other couplet poets in his resistance to all forms of restraint. Hall and Marston use the loose couplet to counteract what they see as the social and stylistic excesses of an earlier generation, but they are unwilling to extend their critique of control to marital, political, or religious customs. The young Donne is willing to take on these forbidden subjects and to inspect the grounds of every manner of obligation. He maintains that a certain amount of natural limitation is built into every realm of human life but that the restrictions of nature are less onerous than the dictates of custom. As he argues in *Pseudo-Martyr*, there are "obligations" that are "*natural*, and borne in us" and consequently consistent with "rectified reason."[71] These natural obligations are the only ones that truly bind since "any resolution which is but new borne in us, must bee abandon'd and forsaken, when that obedience which is borne with us, is requir'd at our hands."[72]

But Donne also believes that it is extremely difficult to distinguish natural from artificial obligations, and, in contrast to most of his contemporaries, he argues that while deliberating we should refrain from binding ourselves at all. On the rare occasions when Donne gives an account of his own life, he describes himself as a man who, with the notable exception of his clandestine marriage, spent the first forty years of his life avoiding obligations. In the oft-quoted preface to *Pseudo-Martyr*, he confesses his "Indulgence" to "freedome and libertie" in both academic and religious realms: he "did not betroth or enthral" himself "to any one science, which should possesse or denominate" him, and he "used no inordinate hast, no precipitation in binding [his] conscience to any locall Religion."[73] These confessional passages suggest that Donne was interested in cultivating a particular kind of liberty that I will call discursive liberty. Discursive liberty is the liberty to explore a variety of possibilities and argumentative positions rather than binding oneself to a particular institution or system of thought. Discursive liberty can be distinguished from ethical liberty, which is the focus of Ben Jonson's work. In his poetry, Jonson suggests that he already knows what constitutes the ethical life and that he simply seeks to carve out a circumscribed realm in which he is free to live this life. Where Jonson uses images of standing and dwelling to describe his ideal liberty, Donne uses images of seeking and wandering. And while both Donne and Jonson considered the couplet an apt form for cultivating rational discourse, each poet crafted a peculiar couplet style to accommodate his particular understanding of liberty.

This chapter focuses on Donne's Elizabethan couplet verse not only because Donne was at the vanguard of this new poetic movement but because the surviving records of Elizabethan and Jacobean engagement with Donne's poetry indicate that early readers knew Donne primarily, and perhaps exclusively, as a poet who wrote in couplets. Not a single allusion to the "Songs and Sonnets" has been found prior to 1609, when an anonymous version of "The Expiration" was set to music in *Ayres: by Alfonso Ferrabosco*.[74] There is much more evidence that Donne's satires, elegies, and epigrams were being circulated, read, and imitated around the turn of the century: it is clear that Hall and Guilpin had access to Donne's verse in manuscript, and A. J. Smith's *John Donne: The Critical Heritage* records seven references to the verse letters, elegies, epigrams, and satires between 1600 and 1612.[75]

Though these scattered allusions suggest that Donne's couplet poems were better known than the "Songs and Sonnets," the brief comments of two poets connected to Inns of Court literary circles—Francis Davison and Ben Jonson—reveal more about the portions of Donne's early corpus that were favored by early readers. In a manuscript dated circa 1606, Francis Davison, a poet and anthologist who was admitted to Gray's Inn in 1593, explicitly mentions only couplet verse in his list of "manuscripts to get."[76] He notes that he would like to acquire "Satyres, Elegies, Epigrams, etc. by John Don."[77] Next to this note, Davison jots down two potential sources for Donne's verse: "some from Eleaz. Hodgson, and Ben Johnson."[78] Davison was right to see Jonson as a likely source for Donne manuscripts. Jonson's epigram "To Lucy, Countess of Bedford, with Master Donne's Satires" indicates that he sent a copy of Donne's satires to their shared patroness.[79] He also testified to William Drummond that he was particularly impressed with Donne's youthful verse, affirming "Donne to have written all his best pieces ere he was twenty-five years old," that is, before 1597.[80] Since Jonson opens the conversations with Drummond with the revelation that he had written a treatise proving "couplets to be the bravest sort of verses," it is likely that Jonson's appreciation of Donne's youthful verse is due, at least in part, to Donne's role as a couplet pioneer.[81]

In fact, these allusions may suggest that Donne wrote exclusively in couplets during his early career at the Inns of Court. Since no sixteenth-century manuscripts of Donne's poetry survive, we can only speculate about why the couplet poems circulated more widely than the "Songs and Sonnets." However, Helen Gardner and Arthur Marotti argue that the lack of early references to the "Songs and Sonnets" is due to a deliberate effort on the part of the poet to restrict their circulation.[82] Gardner posits that Donne guarded the "Songs and Sonnets" more jealously than the couplet poems because he composed them after 1597, when his appointment as Sir Thomas Egerton's secretary might have made him reluctant to circulate libertine lyrics.[83] If Gardner's hypothesis is correct, then Donne dedicated himself entirely to couplet verse during his years at the Inns of Court. This apprenticeship to the couplet would explain much about Donne's innovative approach to stanzaic poetry. Donne learned the poetic trade by working in the medium of the loose Chaucerian couplet. When he began to write the "Songs and Sonnets," he loosened up the "fetter'd staves" by applying tools he had developed for the elegies and satires: he continued to bend poetic form to accommodate dramatic speech and discursive thought by inventing his own stanzaic patterns for each poem and by using enjambment and rough rhythm.[84]

Donne's verse letters from his earliest years at the Inns of Court provide a window into his early conception of his poetic project and suggest that his harsh and conversational style grew out of his attempts to cast off the strictures of measure and redefine poetry as free discourse among friends. In one of his earliest verse letters, "To Mr. T.W.," Donne provides a clear, if unsystematic, account of his poetic priorities. He presents the poem as an apology for his poetic shortcomings, but it is also an apologia for a new poetic mode:

> Haste thee harsh Verse, as fast as thy lame measure
>   Will give thee leaue, to him my payne and pleasure.
> I have given thee, and yet thou art too weake,
>   Feete, and a reasoning Soule and tong to speake.
> Plead for me, and so by thyne and my labor,
>   I am thy Creator, thou my Sauior.[85]

The fourteen-line poem could almost be described as an antisonnet: instead of displaying his mastery of poetic artifice with an intricate rhyme scheme, Donne offers a loose gathering of seven enjambed couplets.[86] And instead of cultivating the "sweet" and "sugared" style generally associated with the sonnet, Donne declares in the third word of the poem that his verse is "harsh."[87] The claim to harsh and lame verse is not simply self-deprecating rhetoric since Donne then proceeds to break the most basic rules of Elizabethan prosody as laid out by Puttenham and Gascoigne. Over half of the rhymes in the poem are feminine, and Donne immediately departs from the regular iambic line. In the first line, unexpected stresses on "harsh" and "lame" emphasize the phrases "harsh Verse" and "lame measure":

> /   x   /   /   x   / x   x   /   / x
> Haste thee harsh Verse as fast as thy lame measure.

It is no accident, of course, that the misplaced stresses fall on the key adjectives Donne uses to characterize his halting measure.

Decades later, Ben Jonson would object to such intentional roughness in a passage on style in his commonplace book. After complaining about those who labor only for ostentation, Jonson piles equal opprobrium on those who "in composition are nothing, but what is rough and broken. . . . And if it would come gently, they trouble it of purpose. They would not have it run without rubs, as if that style were more strong and manly, that struck the ear with a kind of unevenness. These men err not by chance, but knowingly, and willingly."[88] Jonson views such deliberate unevenness as a mere eccentricity, equivalent to trying to distinguish oneself sartorially with "some singularity in a ruff, cloak, or hatband."[89] Donne, however, offers a more philosophical justification for his knowing and willing disregard of poetic rules in the sixth line of the verse letter quoted above, where he describes himself as a poetic "Creator" who has given his verse "Feete, and a reasoning Soule and tong to speake" (*Verse Letters*, 6, 4). Playing with scholastic definitions of man, Donne defines his verse as a rational creature that is capable of speech. This definition of poetry echoes throughout Donne's verse letters, where he repeatedly suggests that the purpose of poetic exchange is to allow "friends absent" to "speake" and thereby "mingle" their "reasoning Soule[s]."[90] But what is striking about this particular verse letter is not simply that Donne emphasizes rational speech, but that he decouples reason from measure. Donne's poetic elders insisted on the preeminence of number and measure in poetic creation, touting it as a sign of rationality and even divinity since, as Puttenham notes, "God made the world by number, measure and weight" (*Arte*, K1r). But Donne turns the creator-creature analogy against advocates of measure: since the essence of the creature lies in its "reasoning Soule," it would be foolish to obsess over the condition of its "Feete" (*Verse Letters*, 4). Just as a rational soul can be joined to lame feet, rational verse can be joined to halting measure.

In the verse letters, Donne attempts to make poetry a forum for intimate and rational speech by loosening the restrictions of measure, but his love elegies offer a more sustained attack on artificial limitations. At times, the erotic radicalism of the elegies seems to spring from sheer youthful delight in impertinent wit. But, when the elegies are read alongside Donne's early satires and verse letters, it becomes apparent that they engage thoughtfully with questions of romantic freedom and thralldom. Like the satires of Hall and Marston, Donne's elegies suggest that the fashions of courtly love poetry have actually spoiled love affairs for both sexes by making men into servile but swaggering gallants.[91] Although the elegies do not constitute a unified book because Donne uses a variety of male personae, some whining and some truculent, they are unified by their attempts to free English poetry from "servile imitation" of Petrarchan tropes and English youths from debasing slavery to their mistresses.[92]

One of Donne's primary methods for liberating young men from the spell of Petrarchism is to use shock and disgust to shatter ideals about the youth and beauty of the mistress, as he does in "The Anagram," "The Comparison," and "Autumnal," or about her virtue and chastity, as he does in "Nature's Lay Idiot," "Change," and "Oh Let me not serve so." In one of his most obscene and misogynistic elegies, "Love's Progress," which waggishly proposes that a woman's "Centrique part" is "the right true end of loue," Donne defends his erotic iconoclasm by arguing that art deforms love:

> And Loue is a Bear-whelp borne; if we ouer-lick
> Our Loue, and force it newe strange shapes to take
> Wee erre, and of a lumpe a Monster make. (*Elegies*, 36, 2, 3–5)

The lines refer to an ancient myth that bear whelps were born as lumps of matter without form and subsequently licked into an ursine shape by their mothers.[93] The most well-known use of the bear-whelp story is in the final book of Ovid's *Metamorphoses*, where Pythagoras uses it as an instance of the mutability of the natural world:

> The Bearwhelp also which
> The Beare hath newly littred, is no whelp immediatly.
> But like an euill fauored lump of flesh alyue dooth lye.
> The dam by licking shapeth out his members orderly
> Of such a syse, as such a peece is able too conceyue.[94]

Donne's allusion imports some of the larger cosmological implications of the Ovidian original: he uses the bear-whelp image to suggest that variable and wild forces are a permanent feature of the natural world.[95] Ovid uses the image to indicate that art can restrain these forces and produce order out of the "euill fauored lump" of nature. But Donne adds a new twist to the metaphor by arguing that there is a danger of applying too much art and forcing Eros into "strange shapes" (*Elegies*, 4). This is what Petrarchan poets have done for centuries, producing forced and "strange" conceptions of love in poems that take the "strange shapes" of Italianate sonnets.

In the elegy titled "Change," Donne once more explores humanity's natural wildness and wonders whether even the expectation of constancy and monogamy is a "strange shape" that custom has forced on love. The poem exemplifies Donne's understanding of verse as rational speech since it opens with a decidedly argumentative word—"Although"—and immediately launches into what sounds, for a moment, like a theological disputation among friends:

> Although thy hand, and fayth and good works too
> Haue seald thy love which nothing should vndoo,
> Yea though thou fall back, that Apostasee
> Confirme thy love; yet much much I feare thee. (*Elegies*, 1–4)

Donne uses the same licentious play with the language of theology that we saw in "Hast[e] thee harsh verse," but here Donne's sexual puns raise serious questions about the guarantees of romantic fidelity. Since the twelfth century, Christian marriage had required two "seals": a present tense vow—the giving of "hand and fayth"—and consummation—the "good works" Donne attributes to his lady.[96] In the first three lines, Donne seems to hold up the primitive seal of erotic deeds as a more reliable confirmation of love than the bands of marriage. But in the fourth line, the witty play and its celebration of desire come to an abrupt halt at the caesura as the speaker admits his crippling fear. The passion and pathos of the confession make it difficult to discern which of the six monosyllables after the caesura should be accented:

> x / x / ||
> Confirme thy love; yet much much I feare thee.

After commending the lady for her physical good works in the first three lines, the speaker suddenly reveals that he mistrusts even this corporeal seal of love. Neither the more primitive seal of consummation nor the communal seal of marriage is sufficient to secure the love of his mistress or guard him from fears and doubts.

In a series of conditionals and comparisons that show his wavering mind at work, the speaker then goes on to explain that the source of his fear is nature itself, which he maintains is governed by change. In order to demonstrate that natural love has no permanent or particular object—that "Women are made for men, not him nor mee"—he turns to the animal world:

> Foxes and Gotes, All beasts change when they please,
> Shall women, more hott, wyly, wild then these
> Be bound to one man, and did Nature then
> Id'ly make them apter to'endure then men? (*Elegies*, 10, 11–14)

The lines play on the ancient belief that women are changeable and men constant, but here feminine mutability is naturalized through the comparison with beasts. The speaker presents himself with a choice between two equally unappealing forms of degradation: female erotic liberty may be "natural," but it is associated with base and lecherous beasts like foxes and goats, while masculine constancy is associated with artificial instruments of slavery—clogs and chains.

Though the speaker expresses his distaste for the "hott, wyly, wild" liberty of women, he argues that men must follow suit or endure the one-sided enslavement characteristic of the asymmetrical courtly love tradition.

After expanding on the charge that women are licentious by comparing them to "plough-land" and the "sea," the speaker reaches an impasse in a passionate outburst:

By Nature which gaue it, this libertee
Thou lov'st, but Oh, canst thou love it and mee? (*Elegies*, 17, 17,
  20–22)

The lines sit near the center of the elegy and encapsulate the conflict between two irreconcilable desires that Donne attempts to negotiate in this poem: the desire for liberty and the desire to love and be loved by a particular individual. The desires are gendered here, but in other poems Donne reverses the roles, associating men with liberty and women with fidelity.[97] This suggests that Donne sees the tension as a fundamental feature of human love rather than a result of female vice. The tension is familiar from more idealistic love poetry like Spenser's *Amoretti*, where the speaker must address his own resistance to the golden "fetters" of matrimony and his lady's reluctance to "loose [her] liberty" (*SP*, 37.14, 65.2). But Donne rejects the Spenserian solution in which both lovers embrace the "Sweet . . . bands" of mutual servitude (*SP*, 65.5). He maintains that the natural love of freedom must be accommodated since no manner of artifice can overcome it.

In the remainder of the poem, the speaker attempts to find a middle ground between the desire for freedom and the desire for constancy. After reiterating the point that loving one woman would be "Captiuity" and loving all would be "a wild roguery," the speaker uses a final natural metaphor to present his middle way:

Waters stinck soon yf in one place they bide
And in the vast Sea are worse putrifide:
But when they kisse one banke and leauing this
Neuer look backe but the next banke do kis
Then are they purest. Change is the Nurcery
Of Musick, Ioye, Life, and Eternity. (*Elegies*, 29, 30, 31–36)

This conclusion, particularly the claim that change is the nursery of eternity, has sometimes been dismissed as "characteristic sophistry" since it is directly opposed to the more orthodox Spenserian view that "Eternity . . . is contrayr to *Mutabilitie*" (*FQ*, 7.8.2.).[98] But William Rockett has made the case that the poem is a genuine "argument for liberty and pleasure" that rests on the "pseudo-Epicurean idea" that flux and change are generative.[99] The poem is certainly not a serious philosophical case for change; at most it is an exploration of what it would mean to reconcile liberty and constancy in love. But the conclusion, with its emphasis on purification through movement, is consistent with a dedication to accommodating roughness and energy that runs throughout Donne's early verse. Since a restless desire for change and a love of freedom seem to be natural to us, he argues, we should embrace these qualities and use them to purify ourselves from putrid obligations and ideas. In a world where love is a bear whelp and women are foxes, it is best to preserve a free mind and heart rather than hastily binding oneself to imperfect creatures.

Donne offers a more sustained and plausible argument for the productivity of mobility and struggle in "Satyre 3," which is titled "Of Religion" in some manuscripts. In the poem, which critics have dated to 1593–98 primarily on the basis of Donne's religious biography, Donne inverts the theological double entendres of the elegies. Instead of connecting his love affairs to religious debates, he explores the "Soules deuotion" to "our Mistres fayre Religion."[100] It is no coincidence that Donne uses the metaphor of a mistress in the opening lines of the poem and in the famous section in which he compares religious inclinations to "Lecherous humors" (Satyre, 53). "Satyre 3" addresses the same question about fidelity and freedom that concerned Donne in the love elegies: given the natural desire for freedom and the unreliability of earthly objects of devotion, how can we permanently bind ourselves to a particular mistress—whether that mistress is a woman or a church? With his well-known image of the "high hill" of truth, he argues that the pursuit of knowledge requires freedom from arbitrary human laws and tolerance for imperfections and roughness (Satyre, 79). In the satire, Donne uses his rough style more precisely and effectively than in any of the couplet poems. By presenting his argument for religious liberty in the loosest verse of his career, Donne makes the case that it is the task of poetry to reproduce rather than restrain the disorderly effort involved in the "minds endeauors" (Satyre, 87).

Despite its religious subject, "Satyre 3" is in line with the courtly satires of the 1590s in its condemnation of custom and fashion. The poem endeavors to expose what Donne would later call "*fashionall*, and *Circumstantiall christians*, that doe sometimes some offices of religion, out of custome, or company, or neighborhood, or necessity."[101] In the satire, Donne argues that such Christians are bound to particular churches because they are too literal minded in their response to the passionate question posed by the satirist: "Seeke true Religion; Oh where?" (Satyre, 43). The first three satiric characters attempt to locate religion in particular, earthly places: Mirreus thinks religion has been "vnhous'd" from England and therefore looks for her "at Rome" (Satyre, 44, 45). The reformed Crants also attempts to circumscribe religion to a particular place, tying himself to her "only" who is called religion "at Geneua" (Satyre, 50). Donne declares his resistance to such circumscription of religion to a particular location in a letter to his close friend Sir Henry Goodyer: "You know I never fettered nor imprisoned the word Religion; not straightning it Frierly, *ad Religiones factitias*, (as the *Romans* call well their orders of Religion) nor

immuring it in a *Rome*, or a *Wittemberg*, or a *Geneva*."[102] Playing on the ety-
mological connection between the word "religion" and the Latin for fettering,
ligare, Donne depicts religious orders and churches as factitious, man-made
prisons. The adherents of these religions have immured themselves within
comfortable, safe, and definite theological systems and opted out of the search
for "true Religion" (Satyre, 43).

Mirreus and Crants may restrict religion to Rome and Geneva, but they are
at least described as leaving home and "Seek[ing]" religion (Satyre, 45). Graius,
the representative of the Church of England, is the most captive to place since
he "stayes still at home here" and thinks that "Shee / Which dwells with vs is
only perfect" (Satyre, 55, 57–58). Donne may be particularly hard on the
Church of England because it was the most comfortable and obvious choice
for the young English lawyers he addresses in the satires, but he objects in
particular to the fact that the English derive their religious obligations from
"lawes / Still new, like fashions" (Satyre, 56–57). Graius's godfathers are hypo-
critical as well as misguided since they try to pass off rules that are as new as
the latest sartorial fashion as if they were eternal and permanently binding
laws. In the remainder of the satire, Donne attempts to check the errors of
"*fashionall . . . christians*" by depicting the pursuit of true and natural religious
obligations as a rugged and laborious enterprise.[103]

The end of "Satyre 3" is unique among the Elizabethan satires since it does
not simply censure contemporary society, but offers a positive statement of
Donne's own religious ideals. For the circumscribed places admired by the
devotees of false religion, Donne substitutes a metaphorical place, the "high
hill" where "Truthe dwells" (Satyre 79, 80). A hilltop is a naturally rather than
an artificially circumscribed place, protected by the steepness of the ascent
rather than factitious walls. In order to ascend the huge hill, Donne argues,
the religious seeker must be willing to accommodate the irregularities of the
path. The lines that describe this painful inquisition are among the roughest
in Donne's licentious early corpus. Indeed, the rough rhythm of this passage
can be interpreted in any number of ways. Here is one effort to capture its
idiosyncrasies:

```
    x   /  x   /   x   / x    /  x  /
To'adore or scorne an Image, or protest,
    x  /  x  /    /    / x  x   /     /
May all be bad; doubt wisely; In strange way
    x   /  x  / x   /   x   / x   /
To stand inquyring right is not to stray.
    x   /   x  /    /   / x  x  /    /
To sleepe, or run wrong, is. On a high hill,
    /  x  x   /      /     /  x   / x  (?)
Ragged and steepe Truthe dwells; and he that will
```

```
 /   x  x  /   /   x  x  /   /
Reach it, about must, and about go¹⁰⁴
 x     /   x   /  x x  x /    /    /
And what th'hills sodainnes resists, winne so. (Satyre, 76–82)
```

Every detail of these couplets is calculated to reinforce the argument that the steep hill of knowledge can be surmounted only by ponderous and disorderly effort.¹⁰⁵ Long, inverted sentences wind about the verse paragraph, overflowing line endings and couplet units. Frequent caesuras and an extremely irregular rhythm produce a halting pace. And Donne punctuates this paragraph of couplets with heavily accented, monosyllabic verbs—aske, seeke, doubt, stand, goe, winne, strive—that issue a call to intellectual action culminating in a final, emphatic command: "To will, implyes delay, therfore now do" (Satyre, 85).

Donne plays with this relationship between will and deed in a remarkable enjambment between lines 80 and 81 ("will / Reach"). Here, he not only separates the auxiliary verb from the main verb but, in doing so, violates one of our most fixed expectations about the pentameter line: that it will conclude with a heavily accented word. Donne carefully chooses an auxiliary verb—"will"—that can be accented or unaccented and then follows it with a trochaic foot on the next line. While the metrical contract makes it seem natural to stress "will" at the end of the line, stumbling over "Reach" at the beginning of the next line prompts a debate: should "will" be left unaccented because it is the auxiliary verb next to an accented main verb, or should it be accented because it is in a strong position at the end of the line?¹⁰⁶ Donne's careful manipulation of accentual expectations across the line ending reinforces the idea that the rules of the pursuit are far from settled and that the "will" to knowledge is insufficient without the messy struggle to "Reach" the top of the rugged hill. Donne's loose use of measure and number is an essential component of the attack on human measures that was also at the heart of the verse letters and elegies. At their best, the "minds endeauours" are far from ordered and neat, and to circumscribe their discursive movements would be to cut off the search for truth (Satyre, 87).

Donne's efforts to represent the discursive struggle in poetic form are even more striking if we read this passage alongside a comparable one from a poet who dedicated himself to interwoven, stanzaic verse. The passage from book 1 of Spenser's *Faerie Queene* describes a portion of Redcrosse Knight's journey to redemption within the House of Holiness. Spenser, like Donne, expands on the adage from the Sermon on the Mount that the way that leads to life is narrow (Matthew 7:14):

> The godly Matrone by the hand him beares
>> Forth from her presence, by a narrow way,
>> Scattred with bushy thornes, and ragged breares,
>> Which still before him she remou'd away,

> That nothing might his ready passage stay:
> And euer when his feet encombred were,
> Or gan to shrinke, or from the right to stray,
> She held him fast, and firmely did vpbeare,
> As carefull Nourse her child from falling oft does reare. (*FQ*, 1.10.35)

While the religious struggle described in Donne's poem is a solitary one, Spenser's hero is accompanied and all but carried up the path by the "godly Matrone" Mercy. Though the "narrow way" to heavenly contemplation may be strewn with rocks and surrounded with thorns, Spenser's prosody controls rather than imitates the roughness of the ascent. Like Redcrosse Knight's divine guide, Spenser's regular iambs, end-stopped lines, and interwoven rhymes firmly bear up the stanza. Spenser does not shrink from difficulty or disorder in his romance, but his dedication to measure produces a constant undercurrent of order in the most chaotic scenes of the poem. The prosodic differences between these two passages about religious struggle reveal much more than a difference of style or temperament. They reveal that Spenser and Donne fundamentally disagree about the purpose of poetic form and the way that it should interact with the matter of the poem. For Spenser, at least in his later years, form should contain an unruly language and make poetic art a reflection of divine creation. For Donne, form should reflect not the ideal of heavenly order but the reality of earthly struggle.[107] This belief that poetry can serve its proper function only when it is freed from the strict limitations of "riming lawes" was at the heart of Donne's early verse and of the poetic rebellion he initiated (*Scourge*, E1r). For the new poets of the 1590s and their Inns of Court audience, the discursive couplet was not simply a badge of a philosophical and social revolution, but a way of embodying critique at the level of form.

CHAPTER THREE

An Even and Unaltered Gait

JONSON AND THE POETICS OF CHARACTER

IN 1599, THE ELIZABETHAN AUTHORITIES tried to rein in licentious rhyming. The enigmatic Elizabethan document known as the Bishops' Ban of 1599 has long inspired critical discussion and speculation. Recorded in the Stationers' Register without any context or commentary, the document simply begins with a list of works and genres (satires and epigrams) that should not be "printed hereafter" and that, if found, should "bee presentlye broughte to the Bishop of London to be burnte."[1] John Whitgift and Richard Bancroft do not advertise their motives in the terse document, leaving scholars to debate whether the bishops proscribed these works because they were sexually licentious or because they were satirical and potentially libelous.[2] While Donne's satires and elegies escaped specific interdiction because they were circulated in manuscript rather than print, the satire books of Hall, Marston, and Guilpin were listed by name, as was Marlowe's translation of Ovid's elegies. While I would hardly suggest that Archbishop Whitgift and Bishop Bancroft were motivated by animus toward the couplet itself, it is intriguing to note that, of the nine poetic volumes relegated to the fire, eight consist largely or entirely of iambic pentameter couplets.[3] The overrepresentation of the couplet in the list of banned books underscores the idea that writing in couplets meant something very different in 1599 than it would even a decade or two later. The poet who contributed most to snatching the couplet from the fires and bringing it into polite society was Ben Jonson.

Though Ben Jonson was born in the same year as Donne, he was in many ways a poetic descendant of his more precocious contemporary. Drummond reports that Jonson "esteemeth Donne the first poet in the world for some things."[4] The "some things" Jonson appreciated and imitated include Donne's use of the couplet, his direct and argumentative style, and his definition of poetry as rational discourse among friends. Indeed, in addition to believing "couplets to be the bravest sort of verses," Jonson often chafed against the constraints of form in ways that recall the protests of the couplet poets.[5] He insisted that "cross-rhymes and stanzas" were "all forced" compared to couplets, and he conveyed his disdain for the sonnet and its founder to William Drummond with characteristic vehemence: "He cursed Petrarch for redacting verses to sonnets, which he said were like that tyrant's bed, where some who were too short were racked, others too long cut short."[6] His comparison of the Petrarchan sonnet to Procrustes's bed is borrowed from Thomas Campion, who also uses it to condemn "Quatorzens" or sonnets.[7] But the borrowing is apt since the image of an instrument of torture is a graphic representation of Jonson's conviction that complex, fixed rhyme schemes like the sonnet force poets to mangle reason to fit arbitrary rules. Jonson's concern about the tyranny of form, and of stanzaic form in particular, aligns him with the couplet poets' defense of discursive verse.

Jonson extends his attack on coercive form to rhyme itself in his satirical tail-rhymed poem "A Fit of Rhyme against Rhyme," where he condemns rhyme in terms that echo his criticism of the sonnet as a Procrustean bed.[8] Rhyme is a "Tyrant" and "the rack of finest wits, / That expresseth but by fits / True Conceit" (*Jonson*, 46, 1–3). Jonson follows Sidney in seeing "Conceit" as the "True" core of poetry and as something that exists independently in the mind of the poet prior to its "express[ion]" in form.[9] But even in his tongue-in-cheek rebuke of rhyme, Jonson reveals his distance from Donne's and Marston's attempts to separate reason from poetic measure. For Jonson sees rhyme as a "Tyrant" not just because it distorts reason, but because it commits atrocities against language itself: "Wresting words from their true calling, / Propping verse, for fear of falling / To the ground; / Jointing syllabes, drowning letters, / Fastening vowels, as with fetters / They were bound!" (*Jonson*, 7–12). The pursuit of rhyme leads poets to disregard all other rules of language and prosody, binding things that should be free and loosing things that should be bound. In other words, Jonson does not maintain that rules of measure always work against reason but objects when "True Conceit" is out of line with "true measure" (*Jonson*, 45).

Indeed, Jonson's insistence on the correspondence between conceit and form, between the mind and the language that issues from it, is one of his best-known adages from his commonplace book: "Language most shows a man: speak, that I may see thee. It springs out of the most retired and inmost parts of us, and is the image of the parent of it, the mind. No glass renders a man's form or likeness so true as his speech."[10] In spite of the decisiveness and plainness of his language, Jonson's effort to articulate the connection between "language" and "man" is layered and rewards close inspection. One particularly striking aspect of the passage is his repeated use of metaphors of sight and image. He does not command his imagined interlocutor, "speak that I may *know* thee," but rather, "speak that I may *see* thee." The implication, of course, is that we can learn something as soon as the "man" opens his mouth that we cannot see when we simply pass him on the street. But, in the sentences that follow, Jonson expands on the idea of seeing through language: it is an "image" of its parent, a "glass" (i.e., a mirror) that offers a "true" rendering of a man's "form, or likeness." Jonson is repeatedly drawn to the idea of language as an image or form for the same reason that Puttenham is drawn to "ocular example[s]": thinking of language as an image or form allows him to emphasize that it is more than just a series of words (*Arte*, M2v). It is a pattern composed of many elements, including "greatness, aptness, sound, structure, and harmony." Rhyme is to blame in "A Fit of Rhyme against Rhyme" because poets so often pursue it at the cost of this larger pattern of poetic language. Poets chop, prop, joint, and fetter other elements of verse in order to satisfy the dictates of rhyme, and readers are in turn hoodwinked by the semblance of order: rhyme "cozen[s] judgment with a measure, / But false weight."

And yet this acknowledgement that rhyme could distort did not prevent Jonson from seeing it as an important piece of the larger pattern of verse. For the wit of "A Fit" (which was apparently entertaining enough to be printed in the 1654 miscellany *Recreation for ingenious head-pieces*) is that the form of the poem undermines its charge that rhyme is always at war with reason.[11] Jonson remains in firm control of rhyme throughout the poem, using tail rhyme and feminine rhyme to humorous effect. The poem concedes Campion's point that rhyme can lead to poetic abuses but nevertheless shows that in the hands of a deft rhymer like Jonson (or Campion, for that matter) it can be consonant with true conceit and true measure. But, as Jonson received it from Donne and the licentious rhymers, the couplet was not the vehicle of measure that Jonson needed it to be. He therefore set out to reform it. Jonson's attempt to reconcile "true measure" with Donne's discursive style resulted in a new kind of couplet verse that would become the favored form of seventeenth-century poets.[12] Jonson regularized the couplet's meter, largely restricted himself to precise and masculine rhymes, and used enjambment more sparingly. His measured couplet began to overtake the loose couplet in the early years of James's reign, and by the time Donne died in 1631, the Jonsonian couplet all but dominated the Caroline poetic scene. Indeed, the 1633 first edition of Donne's poems testifies to the enormous influence of Donne's couplet verse but also to the ways in which his poetic legacy had already been modified and chastened by seventeenth-century poets. All but one of the commemorative "Elegies upon the Author" appended to the end of the volume are written in iambic pentameter couplets.[13] But they are the couplets of the sons of Ben—even gaited, restrained, and anything but licentious.[14]

Wither, Jonson, and the Gait of Verse

A decade after the bishops' ban of satire and epigram, the satiric spirit of the licentious rhymers found a new home in the bosom of a young George Wither.

The work of David Norbrook and Michelle O'Callaghan has illuminated
Wither's connections with a group of Spenserian poets who, despite their
many disagreements, were all in some way in opposition to James and who
kept "alive the traditions of Protestant prophetic poetry which were beginning
to lose favour at court."[15] But especially in his Jacobean satirical works, *Abuses
Stript, and Whipt* (1613), *Satyre: Dedicated to His Most Excellent Majestie*
(1614), and *Wither's Motto* (1621), Wither's loose couplet style and bold-
speaking persona also have much in common with the Elizabethan writings of
Donne and Marston. Wither warns his readers in the preface to *Abuses Stript*
not to look for "Spencers, or Daniels wel composed numbers; or the deep con-
ceits of now flourishing Iohnson," but only "honest plain matter."[16] Although
Wither associates himself throughout his long and prolific career with the
Spenserians and prophetic poetry, here he distances his loose verse from the
carefully composed measure and number of Spenser's poetry as well as from
the carefully plotted conceits of Jonson's writing. Wither depicts his own verse
as unpremeditated, loose, and plain. In the *Motto*, readers are cautioned that
"The Language is but indifferent" since the poet affects "*Matter* more than
Words. The *Method* is none at all."[17] In a Marstonian vein, he goes on in the
Motto to describe his "lines" as "free-borne," and in the following year pro-
claims in *Faire-virtue* that his "free discourse" is not bound "to chuse / Such
strict rules as Arts-men use."[18] This rejection of rules and external authorities
extends to every aspect of his prosody: he will "for no mans pleasure / Change
a syllable or measure" and further declares,

> I disdaine to make my Song,
> For their pleasures short or long.
> If I please Ile end it here:
> If I list Ile sing this yeere.[19]

In his unwillingness to bind his song to others' pleasures or strict measures,
Wither embraces the unruliness that Jonson found so distasteful in Marston
and Donne. Norbrook has emphasized how inimical Wither's freewheeling
style and prophetic claims were to Ben Jonson's court poetry and has drawn
attention to Jonson's parody of Wither's "ambling and diffused iambic cou-
plets" in his masque *Time Vindicated*, which was performed at Whitehall in
January 1623.[20] And yet, as much as Jonson went after Wither in the masque
because the popular and prolific poet was a foil for Jonson's own labored court-
liness, Jonson may also have felt the need to distinguish Wither's inward-
looking poetics from Jonson's own.[21] Wither's claim to affect matter over words
echoes Jonson's own claim in the prologue to *Cynthia's Revels* (1600) that his
"poesy . . . affords / Words above action, matter above words."[22] Michelle
O'Callaghan describes *Wither's Motto* as a "portrait of the inner man, his mo-
tivations, and character. Yet this interior self simultaneously has a public as-
pect whereby his friends if they 'liked the forme of it they might (wherein they

were defectiue) fashion thier owne mindes thereunto.' "23 Nearly every aspect of this description could apply as much to Jonson as to Wither. Jonson's focus throughout his career, in his drama and his verse, was on expressing inner character, and he hoped that his poetry of character could serve as a pattern or mirror of virtue for his readers. And like Wither, he thought that the couplet was one of the best vehicles for poetry of character.

Yet, for Jonson, the loose Witherian couplet was fundamentally at odds with the upright character required of the poet. In *Time Vindicated*, Jonson has his parodic version of Wither, Chronomastix, or time-whipper, declare that his "muse hath rid in rapture / On a soft ambling verse to euery capture."24 The image of Wither's verse as an ambling horse recalls the (usually derisory) description of Chaucerian couplets as "riding rhyme," but the comparison of prosodic style to a horse's pace is particularly significant here since throughout Jonson's corpus the gait is a key metaphor for character.25 In a *Discoveries* passage that is a rough translation of Seneca's "Epistle CXIV," he argues that

> There cannot be one colour of the mind, another of the wit. If the mind be staid, grave, and composed, the wit is so; that vitiated, the other is blown and deflowered. Do we not see, if the mind languish, the members are dull? Look upon an effeminate person: his very gait confesseth him. If a man be fiery, his motion is so: if angry, 'tis troubled, and violent. So that we may conclude: wheresoever manners, and fashions are corrupted, language is.26

The gait, for Seneca and Jonson, is the perfect emblem of the continuity between inner and outer, mind and body, character and style.27 The idea that the gait or manner of moving involuntarily "confesseth" the temperament or identity of the individual was already an established trope when Seneca wrote his epistles, and it was often linked with notions of gender, as it is in the Seneca passage, or with ideas about nobility. Aristotle notes that his great-souled man will have a "slow gait" since to "walk fast denotes an excitable and nervous temperament, which does not belong to one who cares for few things and thinks nothing great."28 And in book 1 of the *Aeneid*, it is Venus's *incessus*, her step or gait, that reveals her divine nature to Aeneas and allows him to detect her even in disguise.29 And in the masque of Cupid in book 3 of *The Faerie Queene*, the narrator remarks that Fancy's "vain and light" nature "by his gate might easily appeare" (*FQ*, 3.12.8). These examples suggest that the gait is directly tied to temperament and difficult to adjust or disguise at will.30 It is seen as a reliable external sign of an internal state. Although he believes that all aspects of language similarly mime the internal state of individuals and whole societies, Jonson is particularly concerned with the connection between the rhythms of verse and the manners of the poet since meter is the most evident and constant source of measure in the poem. For Jonson, Wither's soft ambling reveals that he is not what he claims to be. Jonson mocks Wither for insisting that he is riding in the grips of a "rapture" of poetic and religious inspiration even as his verse moves at a "soft ambl[e]."[31] Through his parody, Jonson charges that Wither's self-characterization as a prophet who disregards the rules of art is merely a cover for a mind that is disorderly, lazy, and mercantile. Jonson does not deny that Wither's verse expresses the poet's inner nature; rather, he contends that the nature it reveals is incompatible with (Jonson's understanding of) the poetic calling.[32]

For, as one early Jacobean response to Jonson's verse suggests, Jonson's vision of the poet was intimately tied up with the idea of measure. The assessment of Jonson is buried in an unlikely place: an account of Sir Thomas Smythe's diplomatic mission to Russia, published in 1605. In one passage that longs for "some excellent pen-man" to describe the unexpected political turbulence the mission met with in Russia, the writer (Gavin Alexander has suggested that the writer might be William Scott, author of *The Model of Poesy*, who went on the expedition) praises "our Lawreat worthy *Benjamen*" as "the elaborate English *Horace* that giues number, waight, and measure to euery word, to teach the reader by his industries."[33] The passage has many of the hallmarks of later assessments of Jonson and, indeed, of Jonson's own understanding of his poetic strengths: Jonson is associated with Horace, with laborious art ("elaborate" includes the now obsolete sense of "produced by labor"), and with carefully measured language.[34] This early assessment of Jonson supports both aspects of J. G. Nichols's account of "Renaissance taste," which, he argues, "enjoyed poems which were unashamedly didactic, which buttonholed the reader and positively insisted on giving him sound advice, and also poems which, far from offering advice, said very little about anything but said it with style, poems where the artifice was everything. Neither kind of poem has much to do with the common modern demand for poems which reveal the poet's state of mind."[35] But what is striking about this formulation is that it collapses Nichols's distinction between didactic and formal poems. It is precisely Jonson's formalism—his efforts to weigh and measure language—that enables him "to teach the reader."[36] As Jonson himself put it in *Discoveries*, poetry is the art of "expressing the life of man in fit measure, numbers, and harmony," and "the study of it . . . offers to mankind a certain rule and pattern of living well and happily."[37] In this precis of his poetic principles, Jonson draws on the familiar language of cosmic harmony from the Book of Wisdom, but he does not say that form's primary function is to reflect heavenly order. While Spenser reads poetic form as an analogy for cosmic, temporal, and social patterns, Jonson confines his attention more narrowly to the relationship between poetry and the "life of man."[38] And that relationship runs in two directions: poetry draws on, or rather "express[es]," human life, but it also aims to shape human life by offering a "pattern," or, more forcefully, a "rule," of "living well and happily."[39] And, as the passage from *Sir Thomas Smithes Voiage* suggests, Jonson believes that it is form that allows poetry to be both expressive and edifying.

For Jonson, poetry does not reflect life exactly as it exists, but transmutes it into something more orderly and formal by expressing it "in fit measure, numbers, and harmony."[40] Only this transformed image of life can serve as a "pattern" for ethical living.[41] The idea of poetic form as a pattern of living is a middle ground between the Spenserian and Donnean conceptions.[42] The youthful Donne argues that form should accommodate the rough and uneven progress of a rational mind at work, while Spenser depicts form as an external imposition that, like the bands of the polity, of marriage, and of religion, is necessary to restrain the natural unruliness of the heart. Like Donne, Jonson is suspicious of external fetters and sees poetry as a reflection of the inner workings of the rational mind, but he insists that the marker of the rational mind is its adherence to fixed rules of living. Yet he also maintains that these fixed rules must be freely chosen rather than imposed from without. Poetry is therefore a pattern or exemplar of the free but measured life rather than an emblem of unruly nature subdued by the order of art.

Contemporaries recognized and frequently celebrated the correlation between form and ethical reform in Jonson's verse. While Donne's elegists in the 1633 edition of his poems associate his verse with wit, raptures, fancy, and fire, Jonson's elegists in the memorial volume *Jonsonus Virbius* use words like *reform*, *refine*, *order*, *proportion*, *measure*, and *harmony*, and they hold him up as the *"Prince of Numbers"* and the "great refiner of our Poesie."[43] In order to understand why so many of Jonson's contemporaries celebrated and imitated his "proportioned Witt," it is useful to take stock of the state of English poetry at the beginning of James's reign.[44] The dominance of Petrarchan poetry was much more short-lived in England than on the continent, in part because Sidney's example had inspired such a craze for sonnet sequences in the 1590s that the trend exhausted itself within a few years, and in part because the young couplet poets of the 1590s succeeded in puncturing the Petrarchan bubble by associating the continental tradition with servile lovers and fettered verse. Though their criticism helped topple the prevailing poetic mode of the previous generation, the young poets of the 1590s did not succeed in developing a new poetic mode that could sustain itself into the Jacobean age. The erotic, religious, and political radicalism of the couplet school made them liable to run afoul of authorities—as they did in 1599—and made ambitious young men who sought places at court or in the church unlikely to follow their example. And, as Jonson himself discovered in the war of the theaters, the extreme satirical pose of these poets began to look reactionary, peevish, and uncharitable if carried on for long. Moreover, the rough styles of the couplet poets were difficult to imitate. Marston's verse was so wild and clotted that it often became incomprehensible, and Donne's calculated roughness required a rhythmic prowess that very few possessed. More significantly, though the young poets convinced many of their contemporaries that the stanza and the sonnet were too constraining, their attempt to separate rational verse from numerical measure was not particularly congenial to most poets of the period, who continued to insist that measured language was poetry's distinctive strength.

Faced with this poetic vacuum at the turn of the century, Ben Jonson was highly conscious of the unique opportunity it afforded him to craft a new kind of English verse. His admiration for Donne and his desire for continuity in his verse informed his lifelong preference for the couplet, but his dedication to measure led him to initiate a prosodic reform of the Chaucerian form. While Hall, Marston, and Donne had embraced the couplet's Elizabethan reputation as a radical verse form associated with the erotic and political freedom of England's ancient past, Jonson worked to convert the form into a middle way between license and slavery by regularizing its meter and pauses. Criticizing the servility of Elizabethan sonneteers, Jonson developed a new poetry that focused on sociability, manners, and individual character rather than love.[45] This concern with manners and character is at the heart of all of Jonson's writing, beginning with his early humor plays. Katharine Maus has noted that, even before Jonson gained his reputation as a "classical" dramatist, seventeenth-century readers celebrated his dramatic characterization as one of the most salient and successful aspects of his plays.[46] Jonson's concern with character may have grown out of his early experience as an actor and dramatist, but his approach to character is remarkably different in his lyric poetry than it is in his plays. As Thomas Greene's influential account of images of the center and the circle in Jonson's works revealed, in the plays even the upright characters are involved in a messy world that makes constant inroads on their peace and inner stability.[47] But in lyric poetry Jonson sees a unique opportunity to offer a pattern of a self that can—at least for a moment—separate from a disorderly and servile world.[48] This distinction between the visions of the plays and the poems is reflected in their prosody and style. Jonas Barish and Russ McDonald have drawn attention to the deliberate asymmetries of Jonson's prose and blank verse, which become especially apparent when he is read alongside Shakespeare.[49] While I think they overstate Jonson's "spiky irregularity" in the plays by selecting his most irregular passages, it is undeniable that his dramatic writing is far more "unbalanced, anti-symmetrical, and accumulative" than his lyric poetry.[50] These characteristics are visible even in more regular passages from Jonson's early drama, like this one from *Sejanus*:

> Well, all is worthy of us, were it more,
> Who with our riots, pride, and civil hate
> Have so provoked the justice of the gods;
> We that within these fourscore years were born
> Free, equal lords of the triumphed world,
> And knew no masters but affections,
> To which, betraying first our liberties,
> We since became the slaves to one man's lusts,

And now to many. Every minist'ring spy
That will accuse and swear is lord of you,
Of me, of all, our fortunes, and our lives.[51]

The piling up of phrases and clauses, the inversions, and the enjambment not only make it seem as if Silius is thinking through the origins of political subjection as he speaks but also reveal the ethical complexities of the corrupt world in which he is enmeshed in the play. As McDonald puts it, "the verse is unbalanced because the world is tilted."[52] In his lyrics, Jonson speaks in his own person and more often traces out his ideal ethical patterns, so he cultivates a style that reflects his understanding of the measured self. As we will see, the asymmetrical characteristics of Jonson's drama at times enter into his nondramatic verse, usually when he momentarily looks out on the unruly forces of the world, but in his lyrics Jonson consistently strives to counter these forces of disorder by enclosing himself and his objects of praise within a circumscribed world where only individual character matters. Jonson's vision of lyric poetry as a place of retreat would prove remarkably appealing as his poetic descendants faced the Civil War and its aftermath. By championing measured forms of poetic and political liberty that could weather any kind of political storm, Jonson secured his position as the presiding spirit of seventeenth-century verse.

Jonson's Liminal Poems: Redefining the Poetic Collection

Although Jonson's short verse circulated in manuscript during his early career, only a few scattered verses, mostly dedicatory, reached print before the publication of his folio in 1616. Jonson's 1616 *The Workes of Beniamin Ionson* included two separate collections of short verse, *Epigrammes* and *The Forrest*, which he placed in between his plays and his masques. Unlike *The Underwood*, which was published posthumously in 1640, these two collections were carefully selected and arranged by Jonson. The collections, like the folio as a whole, were constructed to display both Jonson's range as a poet and his carefully defined poetic program.[53] He experiments with a variety of genres, including epigrams, elegies, epistles, odes, songs, hymns, and even a mock-epic, and he endeavors to represent and size up a variety of human types, from "Gut" the glutton to King James himself.[54] The heterogeneity of the two collections testifies to Jonson's ambition to imitate all aspects of human life not through the continuous narrative of epic but through the accumulation of a multitude of discrete lyric moments. But Jonson is dedicated to measuring and judging life, not simply representing it, so he sets strict formal and thematic limits on his verse. The two collections could be described as a series of experiments with the couplet: 118 of the 133 epigrams and ten of the fifteen poems in *The Forrest* are written in couplets.[55] And Jonson carefully defines the subject and tone of his verse by rejecting the two rival schools of poetry that had dominated the Elizabethan poetic scene. He uses the liminal poems in each sequence to carve out a new realm for poetry distinct from Petrarchan and Ovidian love poetry on the one hand and libertine satire on the other. Jonson makes the case that his new poetry of manners and his measured couplets chart a middle way between the licentiousness of the Elizabethan couplet poets and the slavishness of the sonneteers.

After seeking the "protection of truth, and liberty" in his dedicatory epistle to William Herbert, third Earl of Pembroke (and son of Mary Sidney),[56] Jonson lays the groundwork for his collection by distinguishing between his own vision of poetic liberty and the satirical license of the couplet poets of the 1590s in his second epigram, "To My Book." Jonson focuses in particular on the scurrilous reputation of the English epigram, but the genre also stands in for the satirical couplet school in general. While many critics and poets took care to distinguish epigram from satire, the genres were often conflated or associated, whether by poets like Everard Guilpin or by the bishops who banned them in 1599.[57] Addressing his book directly, Jonson worries that when some see the "title, 'Epigrams,'" they will expect his book to "be bold, licentious, full of gall, / Wormwood, and sulphur; sharp and toothed withal."[58] As Jack D. Winner has argued, Jonson's harsh adjectives echo the language that many of the couplet satirists used to describe themselves.[59] They proudly laid claim to the bitter satirical mode, arguing that boldness and licentiousness are signs of the righteous indignation and free thinking required to correct the vices of the times. Joseph Hall titled the second volume of *Virgidemiarum* "byting satires," Marston repeatedly described himself as a "sharp-fang'd Satyrist," and the epigrammatist Thomas Bastard "confesse[d]" that that there was a "biting" and "sharpenesse" in his epigrams, likening it to the "salt which bites the wound, but doth it good."[60] Jonson complains elsewhere in his collection that such claims to morally efficacious, witty "salt" are covers for mere bawdry.[61] In an epigram "To Playwright" (who may be Marston), he responds to a critic who "damns" Jonson's epigrams for their lack of "salt" (*Jonson*, 3).[62] Jonson claims to see depravity lurking behind this criticism: "I have no salt. No bawdry he doth mean. / For witty, in his language, is obscene" (*Jonson*, 3–4). The plainness and syntactical balance of the two lines of the couplet emphasize the ease with which Jonson decodes the obfuscating language of the satirists: their supposedly medicinal "salt" is nothing more than bawdry, and their "wit" is merely obscenity.

The satirists and epigrammatists of the 1590s not only embraced the bitterness and sharpness of the satirical mode but anticipated criticisms like Jonson's. Joseph Hall, the least wild and most Jonsonian of the couplet satirists, warns in a postscript to his first volume of satires that "true and natural Satyre" is "not for euery one," "being of it selfe besides the natiue and in bred bitterness and tartnes of the perticulers, both hard of concept, and harsh of stile"; it "therefore cannot but be vnpleasing both to the vnskillful, and ouer Musicall eare, the one being affected with onely a shallow and easie matter, the other with a smooth and currant disposition."[63] Everard Guilpin likewise predicts in an epigram, "To the Reader," that some tender ears will be offended by his rollicking satires of social vices:

> *To the Reader. 69.*
> Some dainte eare, like a wax-rubd Citty roome,
> Wil haply blame my *Muse* for this salt rhume,[64]
> Thinking her lewd and too vnmaidenly,
> For dauncing this Iigge so lasciuiously:
> But better thoughts, more discreet, will excuse
> This quick *Couranto* of my merry *Muse*;
> And say she keeps *Decorum* to the times,
> To womens loose gownes suting her loose rimes.[65]

Both Hall and Guilpin depict their potential critics as dainty ears in order to dismiss their objections as the products of offended taste rather than indignant morality. Because their tender ears are chafed by the "harsh stile," "loose rimes," and rapid, "Iigge"-like pace of the satirical couplets, such critics wrongly conclude that the verse and the poet himself must be "lewd" and "vnmaidenly." In addition to depicting such criticism as mere fussiness, Hall and Guilpin defend their rough and loose styles as reflections of the corrupt nature of the world and the "times." In order to castigate vice, they contend, the satirist must be willing to expose its filthiness.

Jonson sounds much like the overmusical and dainty ear these Elizabethan satirists foresaw when he rejects the bitter and loose satirical style and protests that his epigrams will not stoop to gain fame from "another's shame / Much less with lewd, profane, and beastly phrase" (*Jonson*, 10–11). Jonson's triad of adjectives raises the stakes of licentious verse: the rough "phrase," or style, of satirists not only injures the objects of satire but offends against sexual propriety, divine laws, and even human nature itself. Indeed, the Jonsonian counterargument to Hall and Marston's defense of rough style is that the liberties the satirists takes with language, conventions of courtesy, and sexual mores reflect on their own characters.[66] And Jonson uses adjectives like "licentious" and "lewd" that combine sexual, social, and stylistic implications to suggest that these different varieties of license cannot be separated from one another (*Jonson*, 3, 11). For Jonson, the poet cannot remain unscathed while using his discursive liberty to test transgressive ideas. As he insists in the final line of the epigram, scurrility and bawdiness, even in the service of exposing vice, taint the "honesty" of the biting satirist (*Jonson*, 14).

Any stylistic excesses that blemish the honesty of the poet must be avoided because honesty is the quintessential Jonsonian virtue. He boasted to Drummond that "of all styles he loved most to be named honest, and hath of that an hundred letters so naming him."[67] As Joshua Scodel explains, building on William Empson's analysis of "honesty" in *The Structure of Complex Words*, Jonson uses the word in both the older sense of "honorable" or "dignified" and in the newer anti-aristocratic sense of plain and humble but virtuous.[68] Though the word points to the Jonsonian ideal of an independent individual who is "round within himself and straight," the way he presents himself to the world is not an indifferent matter.[69] As Jonson's boast about that heap of letters naming him honest reveals, public opinion, or at least the opinion of the noble and virtuous, has significant weight in his self-evaluations and his ethics. The style of the satirist matters because it matters how one is styled by others.

The belief that speech is a direct reflection of character is one of Jonson's most deeply held positions and one of the central concerns of his *Timber: Or, Discoveries; Made vpon Men and Matter*, but one passage in particular illustrates his belief in the moral stakes of ordered speech: "Neither can his mind be thought to be in tune, whose words do jar; nor his reason in frame, whose sentence is preposterous; nor his elocution clear and perfect, whose utterance breaks itself into fragments and uncertainties."[70] Ben Jonson's simple and carefully proportioned phrases make the pairs of nouns in each section stand out and reinforce his equation of mind and words, reason and sentence, elocution and utterance. But Jonson does not simply argue that jarring speech reflects the mind of the speaker. Worse still, he goes on to argue, "disordered speech" does "injury" to "things in themselves," which fall into "disproportion and incoherence" when they are so "negligently expressed."[71] While Jonson often presents himself as an advocate of *res* above *verba*, "matter above words," here he suggests that the two are inseparable and adds a third term to the classical pair: *mens*.[72] It is incumbent on the poet to attend to the order of his speech because it is a mirror not only of his own mental state, but of the world of things themselves.

The opening of *Epigrammes* defines one limit of Jonson's poetic program by rejecting the "too-much license of Poetasters," but he is equally concerned about the dangers of poetic slavishness.[73] He uses the first poem of *The Forrest*, "Why I Write Not of Love," to announce his freedom from the god who had long reigned over lyric verse. This poem has frequently been connected with the opening poem of Ovid's *Amores*, in which Cupid thwarts Ovid's epic ambitions, his intention to sing of arms and violent wars (*arma ... violentaque bella*) in the fittingly grave meter (*gravi numero*) of dactylic hexameter, by stealing the final foot of his verse.[74] As Ovid vehemently objects to this power grab by the boy god, Cupid strikes him with an arrow of love, and the poet resigns himself to a subject that befits the lighter meter (*numeris levioribus apta*) of the elegiac couplet.[75] Jonson's liminal poem, which also features Cupid and plays with the relationship between verse form and subject, is certainly indebted to *Amores* 1.1, but it also engages with the entire love poetry tradition from Anacreon and Ovid to Petrarch and Sidney. In particular, it inverts the conventions of the most popular and formalized kind of poetic collection of the period: the sonnet sequence. Jonson's curses against Petrarch and the formal tyranny of the sonnet reflect his concern about another kind of distorting tyranny he believed Petrarchism had imposed on English verse. Like the couplet poets of the 1590s, Jonson endeavors to free young men from the Petrarchan posture of servility to a mistress and the god of love.[76] But he does not, like Donne and the licentious poets, use shock and bawdry to challenge the norms of love poetry and overturn the idealization of women; instead, he claims that he will abandon the subject of love altogether.

In the opening lines of "Why I Write Not of Love," Jonson introduces the question of the poet's ties to the conventions of love poetry and to love itself by playing with ideas of binding and loosing:

Some act of Love's bound to rehearse,
I thought to bind him in my verse:
Which when he felt, Away (quoth hee)
Can Poets hope to fetter mee? (*Jonson*, 1–4)

At first glance, the past participle in the opening line seems to express the poet's own will: he is "bound," as in "bound and determined," to rehearse an act of love. But Jonson's use of the word "bind" in the second line makes one reconsider the meaning of "bound" in the first. Perhaps the poet is not determined to write of love, but is actually "bound" by poetic convention, which obliges him to rehearse (re-hearse, etymologically, to rake or harrow again) the old, familiar theme of Cupid's exploits. Forty years later, in his preface to his own collection of poems, Jonson's poetic descendant Abraham Cowley would explain the binding power of amorous poetic conventions by comparing them to the obligations imposed by a trade guild or religious order: "Poets are scarce thought *Free-men* of their *Company*, without paying some duties, and obliging themselves to be true to *Love*. Sooner or later they must all pass through that *Tryal*, like some *Mahumetan Monks*, that are bound by their Order, once at least, in their life, to make a *Pilgrimage* to *Meca*."[77] Highlighting the paradoxical language of traditional institutions like the guild, Cowley announces that he is willing to become a slave to love if doing so will allow him to become a freeman in the company of poets. And in the opening poems of his sequence *The Mistress*, Cowley carries out his promise: in "The Request" he begs Cupid to strike him, and in the "Thraldom" he is duly taken prisoner. In the first two lines of his opening poem, Jonson seems to be toeing the line of amorous convention as well. Bound by the traditions of his poetic order, Jonson attempts to begin his poetic collection by setting out on a pilgrimage to love.

But, instead of binding himself as a follower of love as Cowley does, Jonson immediately tries to turn the tables on Cupid, binding up the wild god in the chains of measured verse. Cupid does not take kindly to this attempted enslavement: "Away (quoth he) / Can poets hope to fetter me?" (*Jonson*, 3–4). The universality of Cupid's objection is worth noting. Critics have often read this poem as a personal confession in which Jonson admits that he can no longer write love poetry because he has "grow[n] old" (*Jonson*, 12). But Cupid dashes the hopes of all "poets"—not just Jonson's. The myth suggests that slippery Eros can never "be got" "Into . . . rhymes . . . by any art" and supports Donne's depiction of love as a bear whelp that cannot be forced into strange shapes (*Jonson*, 9–10). Love is simply too wild to be bound by the rules of verse. Donne responds to this conflict by adapting his verse to Cupid's bear-whelp nature, writing his elegies in loose measures and licentious couplets. But Jonson decides to give up on Love rather than on the fetters of verse. As he puts it in the tenth poem of *The Forrest*, "light Venus" and her "looseness" do not "sort" with his measured kind of "making" (*Jonson*, 16, 18, 18, 18).

In attempting to tie up Cupid at the beginning of his collection, Jonson also takes on the sonnet tradition by intentionally inverting the order of the sonnet sequence. In their work on Shakespeare's sonnets, Katherine Duncan-Jones and John Kerrigan note that English sonnet sequences frequently follow a tripartite structure in which the sonnets are followed by a small group of Anacreontic poems, usually concerning the antics of Cupid, and then by a longer complaint poem.[78] The Anacreontic poems, which are frequently written in tetrameter couplets, often attempt to provide a conclusion for the unsuccessful love affair of the sequence by portraying Cupid being wounded or disarmed.[79] But another common structural feature that explains why the wounding of Cupid was such a popular conclusion to the sequence seems to have gone unnoticed: many Elizabethan sonnet sequences open with a depiction of Cupid wounding and binding the lover in the second or third sonnet of the sequence. The convention derives from Ovid and Petrarch, who are both captured by Cupid in the second poems of their amorous sequences. In *Amores* 1.2, Ovid submits to the chains (*vincula*) of love and is led bound in a triumph by savage Cupid (*ferus . . . Amor*) and his companions Error and Furor.[80] Petrarch records in the second and third sonnets of *Canzoniere* how he was struck, captured, and bound by Cupid's arrows and blows, which dart from his lady's eyes.[81] When Elizabethans began to compose complete sonnet sequences in the 1580s and 1590s, they closely followed the example of Ovid and Petrarch. In the opening poem of the first known English sonnet sequence, *Hekatompathia*, Thomas Watson complains, "Cupid hath clapt a yoake upon my necke / Under whose waight I liue in seruile kinde," and many of the sequences printed during the sonnet vogue of the subsequent decade followed suit by beginning with a sonnet in which the lover submits to love's captivity.[82]

Though the concern with loss of liberty runs through the entire amorous tradition, it is particularly pronounced in the sonnet sequences of the members of the Sidney circle, who were also the primary dedicatees of Jonson's *The Forrest*. Astrophil famously laments in the second sonnet of *Astrophil and Stella* that he has been so conquered by love that he no longer even retains the "footstep of lost liberty" but, "like a slave-born Muscovite," he calls "it praise to suffer tyranny."[83] In his unfinished sonnet sequences, which survive in an autograph notebook that was rediscovered and attributed in the early 1970s, Philip's younger brother Robert expands on the theme of tyranny by playing with the language of predestination: "Long ere I was, I was by destiny / vnto yowr loue ordained, a free bownd slaue."[84] And Lady Mary Wroth, Robert Sidney's daughter, makes the loss of freedom one of the central tensions of her sequence. In her fourteenth sonnet, Wroth's speaker bridles at her captivity, wondering why she should "bee servile" and "still" while Love "captive leads [her] prisoner bound, unfree," but she ultimately resigns herself in the final line to a life of amorous servitude: "I love, and must: So farwell liberty."[85] Wroth's "must," which echoes the final line of Philip Sidney's fifth sonnet, draws attention to one of the central concerns of all the Sidney sonnets and, indeed, of most Elizabethan sequences: the limitations of the human will. Their verses repeatedly underscore the fact that no amount of Neoplatonic philosophy or English independence can save the lover from the snares of desire. And unlike Petrarch and Spenser, the Sidneys do not suggest in their sonnet sequences that the captive will can be redeemed by captivity to a higher power.

The sonnet-writing Sidneys are at the center of Jonson's *The Forrest* and are the dedicatees of four of its most celebrated poems: "To Penshurst" celebrates the estate of Robert Sidney, "To Sir Robert Wroth" praises Mary Wroth's husband, "Epistle to Elizabeth Countess of Rutland" addresses Philip Sidney's daughter, and "Ode to Sir William Sidney, on his Birth-day" commemorates the twenty-first birthday of Robert's eldest son and Jonson's one-time pupil.[86] Though Jonson goes out of his way to heap praise on even the most undeserving members of the Sidney family, he also uses his collection to revise, and at times to contradict, the poetic and aristocratic ideals expressed in their sonnet sequences. As the Sidneys were well aware, the Petrarchan trope of the lover's captivity was intertwined with courtly and chivalric traditions of service to a mistress and a monarch. Not only in "Why I Write Not of Love," but throughout *The Forrest*, Jonson works to undermine female rule and restore masculine freedom. In one of the central poems of the collection—"Song. That Women Are But Men's Shadows," which Drummond reports was written in response to a dispute between Mary Sidney's son William Herbert, third Earl of Pembroke, and his wife, Mary Talbot—Jonson encourages men to abandon the endless amorous pursuit that is the central drama of sonnet sequences:[87]

Follow a shadow, it still flies you;
Seem to fly it, it will pursue;
So court a mistress, she denies you;
Let her alone, she will court you. (*Jonson*, 1–4)

This poem, like Donne's elegies, is an attempt to restore male sovereignty by suggesting that men will be more successful in love if they abandon the fruitless courtship ritual that characterized Petrarchan verse. But Jonson believes that he is also rescuing women from the merry-go-round of courtship and the vices of courtly life. Instead of recording the trials of unsuccessful and unequal courtships, Jonson fills his collection with images of the domestic lives of married men and women who have removed themselves from the court. Indeed, independence and integrity are two of the primary virtues celebrated in *The Forrest*. As he puts it in "To the World: A Farewell for a Gentlewoman, Virtuous and noble," written in the voice of the gentlewoman herself, freedom consists in shaking oneself "loose" from "all the nets," "baits," "snares," "engines," and "golden gyves" (that is, golden fetters) that the fashionable world sets "To take the weak" (*Jonson*, 28, 8, 12, 18, 34, 24, 19). Jonson refuses to grant the Sidneian thesis that the human will is destined to be enslaved by the passions.[88] He argues that poets and their pupils should free themselves from the distorted vision of human life presented by the sonneteers and recover their freedom and equilibrium by embracing a life of mental stability and domestic leisure.

The allusions embedded in the formal features of Jonson's renunciation of love also suggest that Jonson is defining his poetic sequence in opposition to the conventions of the sonnet sequence. The liminal poem's octosyllabic couplets and its concern with the exploits of Cupid marked it as an Anacreontic poem.[89] Anacreon's lines were seven syllables in the original Greek and in the Latin translation printed alongside the Greek in the popular Estienne edition of the nine lyric poets, *Carminum Poetarum novem, lyricae poesieos principum fragmentum*. Jonson owned and marked the 1598 Heidelberg edition of this volume, which was bound with Aemilius Portus's edition of Pindar.[90] English Anacreontics were generally written in iambic tetrameter couplets or seven-syllable couplets that are sometimes described as "headless iambic tetrameter couplets."[91] The Anacreontic poems were not translated into English in large quantities until the 1650s, when two young sons of Ben, Thomas Stanley and Abraham Cowley, included translations of Anacreon in iambic tetrameter couplets in their collections, but early imitations are scattered in nearly every genre of Elizabethan writing.[92] Nicholas Breton used octosyllabic couplets to bid "farewell to loue" in his 1600 volume *Melancholike humours, in verses of diuerse natures* (for which Jonson wrote the dedicatory poem), and Lyly used the form for his song "O Cruell Love!" in *Sapho and Phao* (1584).[93] The prose narrative *Greenes Vision* (1592), which was supposedly written by

Robert Greene "at the instant of his death," opens with an octosyllabic ode "on the vanitie of wanton writings" in which Greene laments following the wanton example of Ovid, Martial, and Anacreon.[94] It is no coincidence that all these poems contain lamentations or renunciations of Cupid's tyrannical power. English Renaissance authors frequently cited Anacreon as a poet who knew through hard experience that love was a tyrant, a form of madness, and an enemy of reason.[95]

But most Elizabethan Anacreontics are contained in the volumes of sonnets printed between 1593 and 1595. Most often, Anacreontics signal the conclusion of the sequence. While Shakespeare writes his two Anacreontics in sonnet form and Spenser experiments with a variety of stanzaic forms, many sonneteers conclude their sequences with odes in octosyllabic or heptasyllabic couplets. Giles Fletcher's *Licia* (1593), Thomas Lodge's *Phillis* (1593), and Richard Barnfield's *Cynthia* (1595) all conclude with a single poem titled "An Ode" in these short couplets.[96] By beginning his sequence with an octosyllabic couplet poem that bids farewell to Cupid, Jonson therefore signals that his verse picks up where the sonnet sequence leaves off: with life after love. Framing the volume in this way is somewhat disingenuous since Jonson does write of love in *The Forrest*: the volume includes not only celebrations of chaste love like "Epode" but seduction songs like "5. Song to Celia" (from *Volpone*); "6. To the Same"; and "9. To Celia" (the stunning "Drink to me only with thine eyes"). Jonson may wish to make it clear that he was once capable of writing of love in the most dulcet verse. But it is nonetheless telling that these poems are in the middle of the volume, hedged in by the framing poem and by his more austere explorations of aristocratic virtue. In opening his volume with a renunciation of the subject that had been at the center of Elizabethan lyric poetry, Jonson reveals his intention to redefine the poetic collection for a Jacobean age and clears space for a new poetry of manners and ethics.

An Even and Unaltered Gait: Jonsonian Couplets and Ethical Liberty

Though Jonson's liminal poems define his new poetry of manners negatively by rejecting the two dominant poetic schools of the previous generation, the majority of the poems that make up his two collections present a positive account of his ethical and poetic principles. Two poems that sit near the beginning and end of *The Forrest*—"To Sir Robert Wroth" and "An Epistle to Katherine, Lady Aubigny"—present Jonson's concept of circumscribed liberty in particularly clear terms and demonstrate how his moral argument is intertwined with his couplet style. In these poems, Jonson champions a kind of liberty that is distinct from the discursive liberty of the couplet school. Instead of freedom of thought and argument, his idealized aristocrats enjoy ethical freedom or freedom of character. By retreating from the turmoil of political and commercial life, Jonson's virtuous individuals are able to live in accordance with their own standards of upright living.

The Forrest draws on the couplet's association with ancient liberty and the golden age. But instead of using the ancient past as a foil to highlight the vice and profligacy of the current age as the Elizabethan satirists had, Jonson aligns the modern country estates of aristocratic families like the Sidneys with the golden world. This is most apparent in the poem "To Sir Robert Wroth," which is closely modeled on Roman poems in praise of the country life, including Virgil's second Georgic and Horace's second epode; Jonson translated the latter sometime between 1616 and 1618.[97] The form of the poem also advertises its Horatian heritage: Jonson alternates between iambic pentameter and iambic tetrameter in imitation of the alternating distiches Horace uses in most of the epodes. At least one early modern reader seems to have picked up on this formal allusion since the poem is titled "To Sr Robt Wroth in praise of a Cuntry lief, Epode" in an early seventeenth-century manuscript miscellany.[98] And Jonson goes out of his way to ensure that his readers do not overlook his efforts to associate Wroth's country life with the golden age. Describing the "mirth, and cheer" of Wroth's banquet hall, Jonson notes that it was "as if in Saturn's reign it were" and then, only thirteen lines later, reminds us that "Such, and no other, was that age of old, / Which boasts t'have had the head of gold" (*Jonson*, 49, 50, 63–64). Like the couplet satirists, Jonson emphasizes the liberty that comes from rejecting elaborate artifices and returning to nature: Wroth is "securer" far from the city and court since he lives "Free from proud porches, or their gilded roofs, / 'Mongst lowing herds, and solid hoofs" (*Jonson*, 13, 15–16).

But the primary freedom Wroth enjoys in his golden world is leisure or *otium*, freedom from action and business. Jonson reserves the most active verbs of the poem for the city and court dwellers whom he disdains.[99] The gawkers who go to view court masques "*throng* . . . to have a sight / Of the short bravery of the night"; bragging soldiers "*enter* breaches, *meet* the cannon's rage"; ambitious lawyers "*sweat*, and *wrangle* at the bar" and, more disturbingly, "*blow up* orphans, widows, and their states"; and greedy merchants "*heap* a mass of wretched wealth" (*Jonson*, 9–10, 69, 73, 79–81, emphases mine). The good life, in contrast, consists primarily of such low-energy activities as lying in bed listening to the "loud stag speak" and sending the "jolly wassail" round the table (*Jonson*, 22, 59). Even when Jonson mentions country activities that involve exertion and violence—hunting, hawking, and shooting—he manages to describe them as if they were as placid and innocuous as a croquet match. His description of deer hunting in particular is masterfully oblique: "Or with thy friends, the heart of all the year, / Divid'st, upon the lesser deer" (*Jonson*, 25–26). And when he does explicitly admit that Wroth and his guests engage in hunting and shooting, he rushes to assure the reader that these activities are nonetheless leisurely since they are done "More for . . . exercise, than fare" and in order to "with some delight the day outwear" (*Jonson*, 30, 35). Jonson depicts the sports that take place on Wroth's estate as pastimes rather than laborious enterprises in part because he wants to underscore his patron's freedom from necessity and want. But Jonson goes beyond his classical sources in deemphasizing the activity of the country life because his ethical thought privileges manners over action.

Jonson's concern with ways of living rather than ways of acting is particularly apparent in two key couplets of the epode. After describing the wassailing at Wroth's table and comparing his estate to the golden age, Jonson issues an imperative: "And such since thou canst make thine own content, / Strive, Wroth, to live long innocent" (*Jonson*, 65–66). Unlike Donne, who punctuates his verse with imperatives and exclamations, Jonson rarely issues commands to his addressees, who are often aristocratic patrons. But what is most striking about Jonson's imperative is that, despite using the strenuous verb "Strive," Jonson is not spurring Wroth to action. Instead, he is encouraging him to cultivate a serenity of mind that he already possesses, to "live long innocent" (*Jonson*, 66). After recounting all the vices of the busy world that sweats and wrangles for advancement, Jonson expands on this ideal of living well, telling Wroth, "Thy peace is made; and when man's state is well, / 'Tis better, if he there can dwell" (*Jonson*, 93–94). Jonson plays on the many meanings of "man's state," including his mental condition or state of being, his social status or standing, and his property or estate. All these meanings are closely related to the etymology of the noun, which derives from the Latin verb *stare*, to stand. For Jonson, as for Milton after him, standing is the posture of the virtuous.[100] Wroth's "state is well" because he enjoys mental, social, and physical fixity. As Jonson puts it later in the poem, roughly translating Juvenal, Wroth should celebrate the blessings of "A body sound, with sounder mind" (*Jonson*, 102).[101] Jonson gives little sense in this poem or elsewhere in his verse of how a sound mind is acquired. Though he draws on classical distinctions between the active and contemplative life, he does not generally depict his heroes and heroines engaged in study or contemplation. Their task, instead, is simply to maintain a virtuous state, to live long innocent.

While Donne and the Elizabethan couplet poets attempted to make poetry a forum for wandering and seeking, that is, for the unfettered exploration of ideas—even transgressive and licentious ones—Jonson is more interested in what I have called ethical freedom, the freedom to "live," "dwell," and "stand" in a state of virtue. This concept of liberty is much more circumscribed than that of Donne and the satirists and much less likely to incur the ire of the censor. It can easily be reconciled with obedience to traditional religious, political, and sexual laws. This is part of what made Jonson's poetry so attractive to Royalists both before and after the Civil War. While the Stuarts remained on the throne, Jonson's vision of ethical virtue allowed Royalists to claim liberty and independence while still proclaiming their dedication to the king.

Indeed, the anecdote of King James and Prince Henry dropping by for a sudden visit near the end of "To Penshurst" seems perfectly to represent Jonson's concept of loyal independence. Penshurst and its lady are not disturbed by the surprise visit because the king is just another guest, and the house is always "dressed" for visitors, whether they be the "farmer and the clown" or the king himself (*Jonson*, 87, 48). Jonson's focus on manners and the country life makes service to the king seem like a simple matter of occasional hospitality. For the remainder of the year, the Sidneys live as the free and undisturbed lords of their own estates. Though he credits the lord and lady of Penshurst for teaching their children the "mysteries of manners, arms, and arts," the middle term—the Sidneys' aristocratic obligation to provide armed service to their monarch—is contained and all but eliminated by Jonson's focus on manners and arts (*Jonson*, 98).[102] Indeed, it is intriguing that Jonson never mentions Philip Sidney's reputation as a Protestant military hero or his death in the Netherlands in his many paeans to the Sidney family. For Jonson, aristocracy and poetry are no longer defined by the battlefield or the court, but by the country estate. If this Jonsonian vision of freedom in a leisurely, secluded life appealed to many Royalists during the reigns of James and Charles, it was perhaps even more attractive after the defeat of Charles I. During the Civil War and Protectorate, the Jonsonian account of ethical liberty as retreat from the world was perfectly congenial to defeated Royalists who continued to live quietly in England.

While Jonson's two estate poems "To Penshurst" and "To Sir Robert Wroth," positioned at the beginning of the sequence, promulgate Jonson's vision of the good life and liberty in retirement, Jonson focuses more intensely on the internal state of the virtuous individual in two epistles to aristocratic women, "Epistle to Elizabeth, Countess of Rutland," written in 1600, and "Epistle to Katherine, Lady Aubigny," written in 1612.[103] Elizabeth Manners, Countess of Rutland, was the daughter of Sir Philip Sidney; Jonson reported to Drummond that he enjoyed the hospitality of the Countess of Rutland in spite of her husband's unhappiness that "she kept table to poets."[104] Jonson also told Drummond that he considered her "nothing inferior to her father in poetry."[105] Though the epistle to the Countess of Rutland meditates on patronage and the independence of the poet by contrasting gold and verse, Jonson's later epistle to Lady Aubigny is a more mature and sustained reflection on poetic liberty. Jonson associated Lady Aubigny with the support and security frequently offered to him by one of his most faithful patrons, Esmé Stuart, Seigneur d'Aubigny. Esmé Stuart was a Catholic cousin of King James who accompanied the king in his progress to England in 1603 and lived in a house in Blackfriars. Jonson lived at Aubigny's Blackfriars house for years at time when he was separated from his wife; Ian Donaldson notes that this allowed the recusant Jonson to hear a private mass and avoid the interrogations of the Consistory court.[106] Aubigny also played a role in saving Jonson from prison and possibly from having his nose and ears cut after writing against the Scots in *Eastward Ho!* in 1605.[107] Esmé Stuart married Katherine Clifton, daughter of Baron Gervase Clifton, in 1609. Sara van den Berg suggests that Lady Aubigny is depicted as a figure of fixity in the midst of strife in Jonson's epistle in part because her irascible father had been at feud with the Aubigny family from her marriage to the birth of her first child in 1612; van den Berg points out that he praises Lady Aubigny for siding with her husband in lines 110–14.[108] Jonson seemed to see some similarities between himself and Lady Aubigny when he composed the poem in 1612; she, like Jonson, was dependent on Esmé Stuart and the protection afforded from the strife of the outer world by the walls of his Blackfriars house. In his epistle, which focuses on the way poet and patroness mirror one another, Jonson endeavors to make the case that Lady Aubigny, and the poet who praises her, are made safe and free more by their inner character than by any outward support. It is no accident that Lady Aubigny was likely pregnant at the time Jonson wrote the poem. As Katharine Maus has shown, the womb became for many male writers of the period, including Jonson, a "topos of resistance to scrutiny, of an inner truth not susceptible to discovery or manipulation from outside."[109] The association is abundantly clear in the poem, as Jonson proceeds directly from praise of Lady Aubigny for shunning the world, comparing her to a boat that has "early put into harbor and all passages shut against storms or pirates," to the claim that she is therefore "worthy" of the "glad increase / Of [her] blest womb" (*Jonson*, 94–95). Jonson sees in a pregnant Lady Aubigny a figure of the kind of fruitful self-enclosure he pursues in his verse.

In addressing his couplet epistles to aristocratic patronesses, Jonson indicates that he is redefining Donne's youthful epistolary mode. While Donne's early verse letters depicted verse as a forum for intimate and free discourse among young men, in Jonson's epistles to patronesses, verse becomes the vehicle for a more formal and constrained conversation.[110] Indeed, the epistle to Lady Aubigny focuses on the preconditions and features of ethical praise poetry. Jonson spends the first fifty lines of the poem responding to such questions as: What is the relationship between the praise of the few and the common voice? Does the character of the praiser inflect the praise? Can verse accurately reflect the virtue of the lady? And which qualities of the lady should the praiser extol? As he meditates on these questions about the nature of praise, Jonson demonstrates the connection between his ethical thought and his couplet style.

In this verse epistle, Jonson capitalizes on the flexibility of the couplet form by balancing pithy sententiae against lengthy arguments. The poem opens with three enclosed, sententious couplets as Jonson describes the current state of affairs:

> { 'Tis grown almost a danger to speak true
> {   Of any good mind, now: || there are so few.
> { The bad, by number, are so fortified,
> {   As what they've lost t'expect, || they dare deride.
> { So, || both the praised and praiser suffer: || yet
> {   For others' ill || ought none their good forget. (*Jonson*, 1–6,
>   brackets mine)

Though Jonson does not divide each couplet into four even parcels as Pope often does, he does attend to the internal proportions of each pair of lines. The first two couplets have the same proportions: the first line of each is continuous and enjambed, and the second line is divided into two sections of six and four syllables. The structure emphasizes the last section of the couplet and was sometimes used by epigrammatists to underscore a final turn or punch line, as Donne does in his epigram "Antiquary":

> If in his Studie Hammon hath such care
> To hang all old strange things,|| let his wife beware.[111]

Jonson uses the structure to emphasize not a witty quip but his melancholy summaries about the weakness of the good—"there are so few"—and the boldness of the wicked—"they dare deride." He uses his carefully structured, closed couplets to reinforce the idea that he is conveying unalterable truths about the ways of the world that lay the foundation for his poetry of praise. This use of the closed couplet for sententiae is familiar from Marlowe's practice in *Hero and Leander*, where memorable closed couplets such as

> It lies not in our power to love or hate,
> For will in us is over-rul'd by fate.

or

> Where both deliberat, the love is slight:
> Whoever lov'd, that lov'd not at first sight?

communicate the fundamental laws of desire that govern Hero and Leander's affair.[112]

But Jonson's epistle does not consist entirely of closed, sententious couplets. After using three closed couplets to establish the preconditions of praise, Jonson demonstrates the stylistic range of the couplet form by immediately launching into a breathless, enjambed, fifteen-line sentence in which he gives an account of himself as a poet and a person. The syntactical and prosodic asymmetries of the passage resemble those that McDonald detects in Jonson's dramatic blank verse.[113] This resemblance is no accident: in this passage, Jonson draws closer to the worlds of his comedies and tragedies as he attempts to articulate the relation between the upright individual and the corrupt world.

The subject of this lengthy sentence is the first word of the seventh line—"*I, therefore, who profess myself in love*"—but we must wait until the twenty-first line to finally discover the main verb, as Jonson repeats the subject and finally concludes, "I, Madame, *am become* your praiser" (*Jonson*, 1, 21, emphasis mine). The intervening fourteen lines contain two relative clauses that lay out Jonson's ethical qualifications for praising. After detailing the ways in which his love of virtue has caused him to be besieged and slandered by the vicious, Jonson describes his steadfastness in the face of this onslaught:

/ x x / x / x / x /
I, that have suffered this, and though forsook
x / x / x / x / x /
Of Fortune, have not altered yet my look,
x / x / x / x / x /
Or so my selfe abandoned, as because
/ x x / x / x / x /
Men are not just, or keep no holy laws,
x / x / x / x / x /
Of nature, and society, I should faint;
x / x / x / x / x /
Or fear to draw true lines, 'cause others paint. (*Jonson*, 15–20)

Jonson's intellectual and stylistic debts to the satirical couplet school are particularly evident in this portion of his epistle. Like Donne, Hall, and Marston, Jonson adopts the persona of the Roman satirists: an exasperated and upright critic of contemporary social mores.[114] He appeals to natural law and depicts himself as a plainspoken man who utters the naked truth in order to expose the elaborate vices and lies that burden civilized society. Framing his poetic style accordingly, he writes in monosyllables and commonplace language.[115] And he does not subject his verse to the fetters of the stanza, but capitalizes on the couplet's association with discursive continuity, overflowing the line endings and placing his caesuras throughout the line rather than after the fourth syllable as Puttenham and Scott prescribe.[116]

For all the similarities between Jonson's couplet style and Donne's, a few key differences signal Jonson's departure from the poetic program of the licentious couplet poets. A brief passage from Donne's "Satire III" helps illustrate the distinction (reading the two passages aloud in succession makes the contrast more apparent):

Foole and wretch wilt thou let thy Soule be ty'de
To Mens Lawes, by which She shall not be tryed
At the last day? (Satyre, 93–95)

Reading these passages side by side illustrates why Jonson was so perturbed by Donne's "not keeping of accent."[117] Like Puttenham, Jonson reads metrical license as a moral deficiency. Beneath the breathlessness and syntactical ambiguities of his lines, the steady beat of the iambs is crafted to reinforce the idea that his character is resolute and unalterable in the face of injustice and deception. But the contrast between Jonson's use of "accent" and Donne's is not a simple matter of adherence to the iambic pattern. Though there is always a hierarchy of accents in the English line, the difference between Jonson's heaviest and lightest accents is comparatively small, giving his lines a steady and even rhythm across the line. Donne, in contrast, frequently uses extremes of heavy and light accents and manipulates the hierarchy of accents so that lines that scan as iambic pentameter can nonetheless disrupt readers' expectations. This careful manipulation of accents is a significant component of Donne's famously passionate and conversational verse.

Jonson's lines also have a conversational tone, but it is the conversation of an ethicist rather than a libertine. Indeed, as Wesley Trimpi has outlined in remarkable detail, Jonson's poetic style is indebted to the Latin prose *sermo* style, which Cicero described as "loose but not rambling; so that it may seem to move freely but not wander without restraint."[118] Jonson endeavors to craft precisely such a free—but not licentious—poetic style. He adopts the Donnean practice of overflowing line endings and couplet units because this flexibility allows him sufficient room to expound on the independent character of the virtuous individual without being fettered by stanzas or complex rhyme schemes. The form allows him to switch back and forth between two-line sententiae and fourteen-line excurses on his own uprightness. But he also takes care to distinguish his ethical poetry from the passionate and irregular verse of Donne and Marston by speaking in a steady pace and minimizing interjections and outbursts.

This metrical distinction between Jonson and Donne springs from a disagreement about the value of earthly rules and measures that is visible in the two poets' contrasting uses of the word "laws" in the passages quoted above. In his fervent rebuke of the "Foole and wretch" who obeys the dictates of religious and political authorities, Donne heaps scorn on "Mens Lawes" (Satyre, 93, 94). In this passage at least, he sees very little continuity between divine and human law and suggests that obeying divine laws often requires breaking human laws, including those that demand evenness and measure. Donne's primary goal in his youthful verse is to free us from the burden of man-made laws so that we can engage in the messy and disorderly search for truth. Jonson, in contrast, laments not adherence to false laws but the fact that most people "keep no holy laws / Of nature or society" (*Jonson*, 18–19). In describing not only the laws of nature, but the laws of society as "holy," Jonson reveals himself to be much closer to Spenser than to Donne on the question of the binding power of human laws. And his condemnation of the unjust is strikingly similar to his poetic condemnation of Donne: they "keep no holy laws," and Donne deserves hanging for "not keeping of accent."[119] For Jonson, the human laws that govern social life and poetic practice must be observed because they are reflections— or at least approximations—of divine order. The laws are ready at hand; they need only be "kept."

Indeed, in a central passage of his epistle to Lady Aubigny, Jonson directly addresses Donne's vision of the rough and disorderly ascent to truth. Like Donne, Jonson imagines the upright individual pursuing a solitary path: Lady Aubigny "tread[s]" the "way / Of virtue," a way that is "Far from the maze of custom, error, strife" (*Jonson*, 54, 54–55, 60). Jonson's use of the word "virtue" rather than Donne's "truth" is significant because it indicates a focus on character, on the internal state of the individual rather than the external goal that he or she pursues. This focus continues in the following lines, where he does not, as Donne would, describe the difficulties and irregularities of this virtuous "way." Instead, he praises the lady for "keep[ing] an even, and unaltered gait; / Not looking by, or back" (*Jonson*, 61–62).[120] Jonson's lady does not accommodate herself to her path but concentrates on regulating her own step so that it reflects her unwavering dedication to virtuous living. Jonson does not bother to specify where the lady's steady gait will carry her. Her "comfort" is not in making progress about the hill of truth, but in her own pure "conscience" and the knowledge that she is measuring her step according to her own internal metronome (*Jonson*, 68, 69). And throughout the epistle, Jonson makes the case that his verse is the "truest glass" to reflect the lady's "form" because he too is known for keeping an even and unaltered gait, both ethically and prosodically (*Jonson*, 122, 123). His use of measured and even iambic couplets is thus central to his depiction of himself as a lover and defender of virtue. By teaching the formerly rough and wild couplet to walk with an even and unaltered gait, Jonson reinforces his focus on the continuity between the manners and the integrity of the individual.

Containing Pindar: Jonson's Couplet
Ode on Cary and Morison

Though I have focused thus far on Jonson's nonstanzaic poetry, Jonson experimented with the stanza and strophe, and with the classical ode in particular, throughout his career. Jonson employs a variety of rhyme schemes in his odes, but couplets often make up a significant portion of even his most complex strophic patterns. This is particularly true in his most renowned ode, "To the Immortal Memory and Friendship of That Noble Pair, Sir Lucius Cary and Sir Henry Morison," which was written in 1629 and published in *The Underwood* after Jonson's death. The poem imitates the strophic structure of the Pindaric ode, but, with the exception of a pair of alternating rhymes in each "Stand," each strophe is composed of couplets. The status of Jonson's ode as the "first

true Pindaric ode in English" has long obscured the fact that Jonson and Pin-
dar make strange poetic bedfellows.[121] While Jonson's contemporaries praised
him as the "*Prince of Numbers*," early modern critics, following the Romans,
viewed Pindar as a poet who had liberated himself from the laws of num-
bers.[122] In an ode addressed to Augustus, Horace compares the immeasurable
(*immensus*) Pindar to a rushing river overflowing its established banks
(*notas . . . ripas*), borne along by numbers set free from law (*numerisque fer-
tur / lege solutis*).[123] In the tenth book of the *Institutio Oratoria*, Quintilian
affirms Horace's assessment of Pindar and his liquid metaphor, declaring Pin-
dar the foremost of the nine lyric poets because of his river of eloquence (*elo-
quentiae flumine*).[124] In his collection of "Pindarique Odes," first published in
his 1656 *Poems*, Abraham Cowley translates Horace's ode in "Praise of Pindar"
and cites Quintilian's assessment in his footnotes to the poem, but in an origi-
nal Pindaric poem, "The Resurrection," he chooses a new metaphor that un-
derscores the unruliness and lawlessness of the Greek lyricist's prosody.[125] He
describes the "*Pindarique Pegasus*" as

> an unruly, and a *hard-mouth'd Horse*,
>> Fierce, and unbroken yet,
>> Impatient of the *Spur* or *Bit*.
> Now *praunces* stately, and anon *flies* ore the place,
> Disdains the *servile Law* of any settled *pace*,
> *Conscious* and *proud* of his own *natural force*.[126]

With their images of a rushing river and an unbroken winged horse, Horace
and Cowley associate Pindar with the force and fury of nature, which they
explicitly contrast with artificial poetic law. Cowley even goes so far as to de-
scribe the rule that demands a "settled *pace*"—that is, a regular, Jonson-like
meter—as a "*servile Law*." In the sixteenth and seventeenth centuries, this
phrase was generally used to contrast the Old Testament law, especially the law
of circumcision, with the liberty Christians enjoyed under the new covenant of
grace.[127] In linking metrical law with ceremonial law, Cowley aligns himself
with Donne and the couplet poets of the 1590s, who depicted unwavering dedi-
cation to the rules of rhyming as a symptom of a servile preference for man's
laws over God's. For many admirers of Pindar, the poet represented a kind of
poetic furor that transcended earthly laws.

Pindar's reputation as a poet of action and furor was a product not simply
of his metrical practice, but of his heroic subjects. At least in the Pindaric
poems that survive in complete form, the victory odes, he is a poet of action
and athletic prowess. In the fifth Nemean ode, he gives an account of his poetic
program and its relation to his characteristic style, declaring in the opening
lines that he is not a "sculptor" who "fashion[s] stationary / statues that stand
on the same base," instead bidding his song to "go forth" on "every ship" and
"spread the news" of victory far and wide.[128] He expands on this idea of mobile

and active song in the second strophe, where he declares that if he is to sing of "happiness, strength of hands, or steel-clad war," "someone" must "dig . . . a jumping pit far from this point" since he "has a light spring in [his] knees, and eagles leap even beyond the sea."[129] Paul Fry notes that "Pindar's sublimity has always been imputed to his long leaps, concealing transition, from one figure to another."[130] Leaping is not an action one readily associates with the ponderous Jonson. Indeed, his preferred image of the even and unaltered gait is directly opposed to Pindar's image of lightly springing, as Jonson makes clear in a *Discoveries* passage where he argues that in writing, we should endeavor to "keep our gait, not leap."[131] Having rejected the dynamic subjects of love and war, Jonson dedicates himself to carving well-formed likenesses of virtuous individuals in measured verse.

Moreover, the occasion of Jonson's ode—the death of the twenty-one-year-old Henry Morison of smallpox in 1629—encouraged Jonson to deepen his dedication to celebrating character over action. Morison had hardly lived long enough to perform great actions, and his death by disease did not lend itself to a heroic account; Jonson therefore praised his character and his potential rather than his deeds.[132] The measured consolation Jonson offers in his ode also seems to have been prompted by Lucius Cary's own elegy on the death of his friend, in which the young Cary doubts the efficacy of philosophy, reason, and character:[133]

> Th'use of philosophy hath allwayes beene
> To pump out passions leakes haue taken in;
> This use compar'd to follye's use is small,
> A thick skin'd sence can neuer leake at all.
> Besid's theise heauie tart afflicksions
> Unteach all Seneca's instruktions,
> And greife breakes by its chaine shot batterye
> The reason-rampart of philosophye.[134]

Jonson's ode, which draws heavily on Seneca's epistles, is a powerful effort to rebut Cary's despondent misgivings about the use of Senecan instructions.[135] In particular, Jonson strives to answer Cary's images of a leaky ship and a fallen rampart. Against Cary's claim that the philosophical are vulnerable to invasion from without while the foolish are thick-skinned, Jonson makes the case that the virtuous individual is completely self-protecting and cannot be altered by time, fate, or the passions. Once again, Jonson's aim, to defend Stoic fixity, seems ill suited to his measureless Pindaric model. Since both the occasion of the poem and Jonson's own poetical and ethical disposition are in tension with the Pindaric mode, his choice of models seems counterintuitive and even counterproductive to his poetic goals.

But I would argue that this tension between Pindar's leaping poetry and Jonson's measured verse is precisely why Jonson chose Pindar as a model.

Jonson's adaptation of the Pindaric ode is an attempt to reckon with the Greek lyricist rather than a straightforward imitation. He reproduces formal characteristics of the Pindaric ode that critics associated with its ceremonial nature—the strophic structure and variable line lengths—but he also endeavors to produce a more restrained version of Pindar by using regular meter, midline caesuras, and couplet rhymes as sluice gates to regulate the rolling floods of Pindaric eloquence.[136] As he does in the epistle to Katherine, Lady Aubigny, Jonson adjusts his couplets to meet the changing demands of his subject: he often uses enjambed couplets to convey the hurry and strife of the world and closed couplets to offer sententious wisdom or describe the solid virtue of the exemplary pair of friends. By imposing measure on *immensus Pindarus*, Jonson reveals his intent to reform Pindar's poetic and heroic ideals for a new age. Indeed, the ode makes the case that poetic and heroic ideals are indistinguishable from one another and that the best life is the one that resembles a well-proportioned poem.

In reproducing the strophic structure and variable line lengths of the Pindaric ode, Jonson engages with the mobility associated with ancient choral poetry. Early modern critics derived both features from the original performance context of the odes. As Annabel Patterson has shown, sixteenth-century continental critics frequently noted that strophe, antistrophe, and epode (which Jonson translates "The Turn," "The Counter-Turn," and "The Stand") were stage directions of a sort for the Greek chorus. Scaliger argues that their movements to the left and right represented the motion of the spheres and the planets, respectively, and that their final stand represented the stability of the earth.[137] Thus, the strophic structure represented both the mobility of nature and the containment of that mobility by the forces of art and cosmic order. This vision of choreographed, proportional movement can be reconciled with Jonson's dedication to poetry that expresses the life of humanity in number, weight, and measure and offers a pattern of the good life.[138] Indeed, his masques repeatedly stage such measured dances as emblems of political and cosmic order.[139] In one Jacobean masque, *Mercury Vindicated from the Alchemists at Court*, Jonson prefaces "*the main dance*" with a defense of well-proportioned motion as an essential component of the order of nature:

CHORUS	Move, move again, in forms as heretofore.
NATURE	Tis form allures.
	Then move; the ladies here are store.
PROMETHEUS	Nature is motion's mother, as she's yours—
CHORUS	The spring whence order flows, that all directs,
	And knits the causes with th'effects.[140]

Though Jonson incorporates motion because, as Prometheus insists, motion is a child of nature, the focus of the passage, as ever in Jonson's poetry, is on the "forms" rather than the motion itself. While the young Donne argues that movement and change are the "nursery / Of Musick, joy, life, and eternity" in "Elegy III," for Jonson it is always "form" that "allures" (*Elegies*, 35–36). Jonson is attracted to the strophes of the Pindaric ode because Pindar, for all his leaping, moves in forms. The irregularity and wildness of his numbers is contained within the ceremonial turning, counterturning, and standing of the strophic pattern.[141]

Jonson's adoption of Pindar's variable line lengths is more difficult to reconcile with his poetic program since this variability seems to be a key component of Pindar's measureless style. But early modern critics also derived this feature of Pindar's odes from their original performance context. Though he generally scorns "shorter measures," George Puttenham allows the intermingling of short and long lines in one particular case:

> vnlesse it were in matters of such qualitie, as became best to be song with the voyce, and to some musicall instrument, as were with the Greeks, all your Hymnes & *Encomia* of *Pindarus* & *Callimachus*, not very histories but a manner of historicall reportes, in which cases they made those poemes in variable measures, & coupled a short verse with a long to serue that purpose the better, and we ourselues who compiled this treatise haue written for our pleasure a litle brief *Romance* or historicall ditty in the English tong of the Isle of great *Britaine* in short and long meetres, and by breaches or diuisions to be more commodiously song to the harpe in places of assembly, where the company shalbe desirous to hear of old aduentures & valiaunces of noble knights in times past, as those are of king *Arthur* and his knights. (*Arte*, G1r)

It is shocking to learn that Puttenham, who so vehemently expresses his horror at short lines and "tales of old times" in his rant against "small & popular Musickes," would write a "brief Romance or historicall ditty" in "short and long meetres" (*Arte*, M1r, G1r). Ben Jonson must have been struck by this confession as well because he marked this portion of the passage with one of his characteristic marginal symbols in his own copy of Puttenham's *Arte*.[142] Puttenham justifies his uncharacteristic foray into variable line lengths by pointing to the examples of Pindar and Callimachus and by arguing that the form is accommodated to the voice and musical instruments. Michael Drayton makes a similar connection between line lengths and musical accompaniment in his 1606 collection of odes, one of the first printed in English. In his preface, he defines an ode as a "song moduled to the ancient harp, and neither too short breathed as hasting to the end, nor composed of longest verses as vnfitte for the suddaine turnes and lofty tricks with which Apollo vsed to manage it" and then goes on to mention Pindar, Anacreon, and Horace as the prime exemplars.[143] Drayton's rare participle, "moduled," suggests that the lines of the ode are indeed measured and regulated, but according to the needs of the harp and the voice rather than the conventional laws of number. The sudden turns and tricks of the lines are the signs of a higher Apollonian order that joins verse to music.

Jonson retains the variable line lengths of the Pindaric ode with their faint hint of a musical order in the background, but he is not willing to leave his readers to imagine a ceremonial context and a musical accompaniment to lend stateliness and form to the variability. Instead, he carefully regulates the variation himself by establishing fixed patterns for his turns, counterturns, and stands. All his "Turn" sections are ten lines and adhere to a set pattern of line lengths: 8 syllables, 8, 10, 10, 6, 6, 8, 8, 10, 10. His ten-line "Counter-Turn" sections follow an identical pattern, except for the seventh line, which has ten syllables instead of eight. And his twelve-line "Stand" sections follow a slightly more complex pattern: 10, 4, 10, 4, 6, 6, 10, 6, 6, 8, 10, 10. Though he accepts the formal aspects of Pindar's verse associated with the ceremony of the chorus and the lyre, Jonson's revisions of Pindar reveal a discomfort with the freedom from measure that was also an essential component of Pindar's reputation for sublimity.

The tension between Jonsonian and Pindaric poetics is immediately visible not only in Jonson's revisions of Pindaric form but in the oft-discussed opening image of the infant of Saguntum. Indeed, the first two words of the ode—"Brave infant"—dramatically signal Jonson's intent to overturn conventional views of heroism and bravery (*Jonson*, 1). The infant, whom Pliny mentions among other "prodigious and monstrous births" in the seventh book of his *Natural History*, was born in the midst of Hannibal's destruction of the Spanish city of Saguntum, which set off the Second Punic War.[144] On seeing the turmoil of his city, he reportedly returned to his mother's womb to die. While Pliny depicts the infant's "reversus" as a prodigy, Jonson inverts his source, describing the Carthaginian conqueror as "prodigious Hannibal" (*Jonson*, 3).[145] Jonson emphasizes the monstrousness of Hannibal, who stands in for all the vices that the Romans associated with Carthage and that Jonson most detests: fierceness, cruelty, fury, and impiety. In the first "Counter-Turn," Jonson describes Hannibal's "sack" as a "trampl[ing]" of a host of characteristically Roman virtues: "shame, faith, honour, and regard of right" (*Jonson*, 12, 14, 14). But instead of contrasting Hannibal with the Roman military leaders who eventually thwarted his imperial ambitions, Fabius Maximus or Scipio Africanus, Jonson holds up a newborn infant from the little-known Spanish city of Saguntum as a foil to the Carthaginian commander.[146] The choice of Saguntum is significant not only because its sack initiated the Second Punic War, but because, according to Livy, the city sat near the border between the Roman and Carthaginian empires in Spain and, under a treaty with Hannibal's brother-in-law Hasdrubel, had been allowed to preserve its "libertas" from both powers.[147] By destroying the walls of the city in an eight-month siege, Livy claims, Hannibal violated not only the treaty with Rome, but the independence of a free city.

Thus, the "razing" of the "immortal town" of Saguntum, the first sight Jonson's infant sees when he "look[s] . . . about" as he leaves his mother's womb, represents the destruction of the kind of liberty Jonson celebrates in the estate poems of *The Forrest* and throughout his corpus—the liberty enjoyed in a home protected from strife (*Jonson*, 4, 4, 5). The infant judges that life is not worth living when this liberty has been eliminated and returns to the only secure place left to him, the circumscribed "urn" of his "mother's womb" (*Jonson*, 8). The infant of Saguntum could be read as a dark parody or exaggeration of the ode's ethical argument that "in short measures life may perfect be" (*Jonson*, 74). Indeed, in his peerless reading of the ode, Richard Peterson has argued that the image of the infant is a "small antimasque" and must be "immediately and wholly—though sympathetically—ironic."[148] But Peterson's addition of "sympathetically" is revealing. None of the lessons of the poem contradicts Jonson's praise of the infant, and, more importantly, the story is an extension, if an extreme and grotesque one, of Jonson's career-long dedication to character over action.

Indeed, in the first "Counter-Turn" of the poem, which continues the argument of the "Turn" by describing the horrible sack of Saguntum, Jonson continues his tendency to associate vice with frenetic action. Just as they do in the poems to Sir Robert Wroth and Lady Aubigny, the villains of the poem monopolize the active verbs.

> Did wiser Nature draw thee back
> From out the horror of that sack?
> Where shame, faith, honour, and regard of right
> Lay trampled on; the deeds of death and night,
> Urged, hurried forth, and hurled
> Upon th'affrighted world:
> Sword, fire, and famine with fell fury met,
> And all on utmost ruine set;
> As, could they but life's miseries foresee
> No doubt all infants would return like thee. (*Jonson*, 11–20)

Jonson manipulates the formal characteristics of the line to underscore the hurry and confusion of the moment. Unlike many of the stanzas in the ode, this "Counter-Turn" consists of one long sentence that is more enjambed than the rest of the poem. Jonson also uses the variable line lengths of the strophe both to emphasize and to restrain Hannibal's chaotic action. The three key verbs, "Urged, hurried forth, and hurled" sit in the middle of the "Counter-Turn," where the rhyme between *hurled* and *world* returns quickly (to use Puttenham's language) because of the short trimeter lines (*Jonson*, 16).[149] The hourglass shape of Jonson's strophes seems designed to enclose these short lines within graver octosyllabic and decasyllabic lines.[150] In this "Counter-Turn," Jonson surrounds his account of violence and strife with two longer couplets that offer the infant's melancholy wisdom as an antidote to the confusion of the sack.

Though he opens the poem with a direct assault on the active heroism characteristic of the Pindaric odes, in the first "Stand," Jonson seems to reconcile himself to a life judged according to action as he asks in lines that echo Seneca's *Epistles*, "What is life if measur'd by the space, / Not by the act?" (*Jonson*, 21–22).[151] And in the second "Counter-Turn," he comes closest to the Pindaric mode as he praises Henry Morison as a soldier:

> Alas, but Morison fell young:
> He never fell; thou fall'st my tongue.
> He stood, a soldier to the last right end,
> A perfect patriot, and a noble friend.
> But most a virtuous son.
> All offices were done
> By him so ample, full, and round,
> In weight, in measure, number, sound,
> As, though his age imperfect might appear,
> His life was of humanity the sphere. (*Jonson*, 43–52)

Jonson begins the "Counter-Turn" as if he were about to launch into a tale of action: "Alas, but" is an uncharacteristically passionate interjection, and the simple "Morison fell young" seems to promise a tale of battlefield derring-do (*Jonson*, 43). But Jonson thwarts these expectations after chastising his tongue for using the morally questionable word "fell" to describe the upright Morison (*Jonson*, 43). What follows the correction is characteristic Jonsonian praise of states rather than actions. Morison's only action is standing firm to the "last right end" (*Jonson*, 45). Jonson then focuses on the "offices" that the young man occupied: "A perfect patriot, and a noble friend. / But most a virtuous son" (*Jonson*, 49, 46–48). As he does in his discussion of the moral implications of disorderly speech in *Discoveries*, Jonson divides his lines into carefully balanced phrases, in this case, into three adjective-noun pairs that describe Morison's fixed relationship to his country, his friends, and his family. Though Jonson frequently uses enjambment elsewhere in the poem, in this antistrophe all but one of the lines end with a pause, emphasizing the chime of the couplet rhymes and dividing his account of the virtuous individual into discrete, carefully measured units. And, as he does throughout his corpus, Jonson uses a steady iambic meter here, with light accents that do not disrupt his account of moral solidity. As Jonson redefines heroism, soldiering, and victory as states rather than actions, standing rather than leaping, he uses caesuras, couplets, and even meter to rein in the hard-mouthed horse of Pindaric verse.

Indeed, in this "Counter-Turn" and throughout the ode, Jonson argues that the best life should approximate the form of a lyric poem, or at least the form of a measured Jonsonian lyric poem. Jonson's focus on Morison's offices recalls his argument in *Discoveries* that the "study" of poetry "offers to mankind a certain rule, and pattern of living well, and happily; disposing us to all civil offices of society."[152] In the ode, Jonson flips the analogy between life and poetry. Instead of looking to poetry for a pattern of living well, Jonson suggests that Morison's well-lived life has become a model of poetic perfection; he describes the young man as "sound" "in weight, in measure, number," the triad Jonson and his contemporaries associated with the structures of verse (*Jonson*, 50). In lines that sit near the center of the ode, Jonson expands on the poetic analogy as he defends Morison's short but well-proportioned life:

> for life doth her great actions spell
> By what was done and wrought
> In season, and so brought
> To light: her measures are, how well
> Each syllabe answered, and was formed, how fair:
> These make the lines of life, and that's her air. (*Jonson*, 59–64)

For a moment, Jonson seems to return to a more conventional idea of action-centered heroism, defined by what is "done and wrought" (*Jonson*, 60). But he uses the enjambment between line 60 and line 61 to add a twist: great actions are primarily defined not by the deeds themselves, but by their seasonableness or fitness. And as Jonson continues to describe his version of heroism, he leaves action behind altogether as he elaborates on the idea of fitness. The "measures" of life are "how well / Each syllabe answered, and was formed, how faire" (*Jonson*, 62, 62–63). The first half of the line is difficult to decipher since Jonson does not provide an object for the verb "answer," but he seems to use it in the sense of to correspond or act in conformity with something (*Jonson*, 63).[153] The implied object, then, is some law or standard—each syllable must answer to the rules of meter or to the higher law of cosmic harmony that the laws of linguistic measure are intended to reflect. The second half of the line suggests that each syllable must not only conform to a larger pattern but have a "fair" form in its own right (*Jonson*, 63). Once more, Jonson depicts virtue as an abstract form or pattern rather than a way of engaging with or reacting to the imperfect world. If every syllable and line of life is in its proper place, it doesn't matter what the Hannibals of the world do. In adopting this view of the best life, Jonson rejects the Donnean argument that the pursuit of truth requires the liberty to struggle, wander, and strive. For Jonson, liberty consists in dwelling in a state that is well, and he develops a couplet style that corresponds with his dedication to this staid kind of freedom.

And yet Jonson does not simply withdraw from energetic strife. In the third "Counter-Turn" of the ode, he faces up to all the lively impulses built into the classical tradition of the ode. He begins by restoring Anacreontic mirth, bidding Lucius Cary to "Call . . . for wine," "let [his] looks with gladness shine," and "plant" a "garland" on his "head" (*Jonson*, 75, 76, 77). Since Jonson tells us

that there were no "Orgies of drink" at Cary and Morison's "feasts," we can as-
sume that Jonson offers a measured form of Anacreontic mirth, that (like Jon-
son's companions in "Inviting a Friend to Supper") Cary will "sup free, but
moderately" of the wine (*Jonson*, "Immortal Memory," 104; "Inviting," 35). But
there is nothing moderate about the central consolation Jonson offers Cary in
this "Counter-Turn." "Morison's not dead," he insists; rather,

> He leaped the present age,
> Possessed with holy rage,
> To see that bright eternal day. (*Jonson*, 78, 79–81)

Jonson does not renounce Pindaric leaping but concentrates it into one giant
leap that carries Morison right out of this age and into eternity.[154] Jonson's
answer to the "fell fury" Hannibal hurls on the world is "holy rage" or *furor*,
which can lift his hero out of this world altogether (*Jonson*, 17, 80). Concentrat-
ing Pindaric energy into a single transcendent leap allows Jonson to reconcile
his dedication to fixity and measure with the movement of the ode. Morison
remains sound in weight, measure, and number on either side of the leap; his
fixed character is simply translated to the skies. Moreover, it is no accident that
Morison's holy rage, like Hannibal's fury in the first "Counter-Turn," is packed
into the central trimeter couplet of Jonson's hourglass strophe. Even as Jonson
embraces Pindaric leaping, he contains it, assuring us with his well-measured
lines and perfect rhyme between age and rage that Morison's leaping is done
in season, that it contributes to rather than deviates from the perfect round-
ness of his life.

And yet immediately after containing the energy of Morison's leap into
heaven, Jonson once more complicates his account of measured motion. Jon-
son's well-known enjambment of his name across the "Counter-Turn" and
"Stand" breaks the strophic container and registers some unease about whether
the poet, too, can be translated intact to the heavens:

> He leaped the present age,
> Possessed with holy rage,
> To see that bright eternal day,
> Of which we priests and poets say
> Such truths as we expect for happy men,
> And there he lives with memory, and Ben.
>
> *The Stand*
> Jonson, who sung this of him, ere he went
> Himself to rest,
> Or taste a part of that full joy he meant
> To have expressed,
> In this bright asterism. (*Jonson*, 79–89)

Peterson sees the enjambment as a "dancelike leap that straddles heaven and earth," a way of "mediating between the two friends" and showing that the "distance is after all not so great if it can be thus agilely crossed by a poet of this weight."[155] But it is not entirely clear to me that Jonson succeeds in making the leap here. He looks forward to dwelling in the bright eternal day with Morison, but he is acutely aware that he is not yet there, that his song must actually be sung "ere" he himself crosses over to heaven (*Jonson*, 85). Moreover, the poet, for all his priestliness, does not seem to have privileged access to the heavens. He is not, in other words, possessed with the holy rage that transports Morison. If he transcends, he must do so not through an inspired vision but through the more humble means of imagining the future: he can only speak of the truths he "expect[s]" for the happy (*Jonson*, 83).

In addition to emphasizing the gap between the heaven-dwelling Morison and the earth-bound singer, Jonson betrays some doubt about the transcendence of his expression with a striking use of the perfect infinitive: in the future, he tells us, he will taste the "joy he *meant / To have expressed / In this bright asterism*" (*Jonson*, 87–89, emphasis mine). He is far from confident that his poetic speech will in any way reach the reality of divine experience.[156] Compared to the resolute, and resolutely metrical, couplets in which Jonson assures Cary of his friend's survival in the afterlife ("Accept this garland, plant it on thy head / And think, nay know, thy Morison's not dead"), these lines are circuitous and irresolute (*Jonson*, 77–78). They do not have the jarring roughness of Donne's call for wise doubt, but they do depart from the even-gaited poetry Jonson has taught us to expect from him. The phrases "who sung this of him, ere he went" and "he meant / To have expressed" resist the poem's temporality and its iambic pattern (*Jonson*, 85, 87–88). Jonson's moment of hesitation about the relationship between the poet's words and the things they are meant to have represented shows that, in spite of his emphasis on the character of the poet, Jonson's poetic program is not built on the unshakeable belief that "God infused all perfection / Into [his] soule alone," as Marston charged in *Jack Drum's Entertainment*.[157] In comparison to earlier poems like the epistle to Katherine, Lady Aubigny, the ode rarely mentions the poet or his ethical qualifications for praise.

Jonson recovers his equilibrium after hesitating over his own transcendence by turning instead to his noble pair of subjects. The conclusion of the ode is a paean to the power of example. The friends, who had grown to be "cop[ies]" of one another, then

> lived to be the great surnames
> And titles, by which all made claims
> Unto virtue. Nothing perfect done
> But as a Cary or a Morison. (*Jonson*, 112, 113–16)

The perfection of an action is judged by comparing it not to other actions or to principles, but to paradigmatic characters. The key is not what is done but how it is done: it must be performed "as," that is, in the characteristic manner of, "a Cary, or a Morison" (*Jonson*, 116). In becoming the paradigms by which human deeds can be measured, the pair of friends have taken on the role Jonson assigned to poetry in *Discoveries*. Just as poetry "offers to mankind a certain rule and pattern of living well and happily," Cary and Morison are themselves the "fair example" and the "law . . . left yet to mankind" (*Jonson*, 117, 120).[158] In spite of the "force" of the friends' example, it is clear that many, or perhaps even most, "durst not practice it" (*Jonson*, 117, 119). Yet even these nonpractitioners are "glad" that they may "read and find" friendship in Cary and Morison (*Jonson*, 119, 122). The ode is the culmination of Jonson's poetics of character, as Cary and Morison become indistinguishable from the ideal poem that teaches the reader through number, weight, and measure. Jonson's celebration of Morison's short life as the pattern of good living is also the culmination of his defense of circumscribed liberty. When he argues that "In small proportions we just beauties see: / And in short measures life may perfect be," he makes the case that the small proportions of a private country life focused on curating one's own character may be superior to an active but messy life in the larger political sphere (*Jonson*, 73–74). Jonson's focus on maintaining one's internal proportions and living far from the strife of the court and the city was eminently appealing in a century of radical political change because it allowed individuals to guard their inner selves from the vicissitudes of politics and war.

In the Cary and Morison ode, Jonson also offers his most forceful case that the "short measures" of lyric may actually offer a better pattern of moral life than epic (*Jonson*, 74). Jonson reportedly told Drummond that "he had an intention to perfect an epic poem, entitled *Heroologia*, or the worthies of the country roused by fame, and was to dedicate it to his country. It is all in couplets, for he detesteth all other rhymes."[159] Though Drummond's report provides little information about the prospective Jonsonian epic, the title and description make it sound more like a catalogue of exemplary individuals than a continuous narrative of heroic action. Indeed, one wonders whether a couplet catalogue of Jonsonian heroes—who would surely be Stoic, rather than martial, heroes—would look much different from *Epigrammes* and *The Forrest*.[160] Epic heroes (and dramatic characters) must enter into the messy, striving world of action and therefore blur the outlines of their characters. But within the "short measures" of Jonson's epigrams, epistles, and odes, individuals like Cary and Morison may approximate Jonson's ideal of the perfectly proportioned life.

CHAPTER FOUR

Rhyme Oft Times
Overreaches Reason

MEASURE AND PASSION AFTER THE CIVIL WAR

IN 1629, JONSON STILL HAD HOPE that his measured couplets could re-
strain the flow of Pindar's unruly eloquence, instruct Lucius Cary's immense
grief, and carve out a place for a composed life in the midst of a chaotic, striv-
ing world. Jonson's poetic theory suggested that desperate times call for po-
etic measures, so it no surprise that, in the chaotic and striving years that
followed Jonson's death in 1637, Jonson's literary progeny followed his lead
and turned to the couplet to bring order to the rage.[1] Abraham Cowley, who,
like Jonson, enjoyed the patronage of Lucius Cary, tried his hand at using the
pentameter couplet to rein in the fury in his epic poem *The Civil War*.[2] Cow-
ley's formal decision to write about civil war in couplets had some precedent:
while Marlowe's translation of Lucan's *Pharsalia* was in blank verse, Arthur
Gorges's 1614 translation was in tetrameter couplets and Tom May's 1626
translation in pentameter couplets. In his commendatory poem to the 1627
edition of Tom May's translation, Jonson had described the poem as a tri-
umph of poetic control in which the extreme forces of the Roman civil war—
"*Pompey's* popularitie, / *Caesar's* ambition, *Cato's* libertie, / Calme *Brutus*
tenor"—were not allowed to "start," that is, to leap or bound, but were kept in
"due proportion" by "number" and "measure."[3] Cowley seems to be striving
for precisely such containment, but his epic runs up against the limits of Jon-
sonian measure at precisely the place where it draws nearest to Jonson's Cary
and Morison ode. While Jonson's Pindaric hero Morison had been felled by
the smallpox, his friend Lucius Cary did in fact fall in battle, in the First Bat-
tle of Newbury in September 1643. At this decisive point in the Civil War,
Cowley's epic poem turns into an elegy for Falkland and then breaks off al-
together. The unfinished epic registers Cowley's uncertainty about whether

poetry could impart measure to the exorbitant passions he saw in his enemies and in himself.

In 1642, Cowley was, as he puts it in his autobiographical essay "Of My self," "torn" from Cambridge "by that violent publick Storm which would suffer nothing to stand where it did, but rooted up every Plant, even from the Princely Cedars to me the Hyssop" (*Essays*, 218–19). He joined the Royalists in Oxford sometime that year and began work on his epic poem in the summer or autumn of 1643.[4] He would abandon the poem after the First Battle of Newbury in September 1643, claiming in his preface to the 1656 edition of his poems that "the succeeding *misfortune*" of the Royalists "stopt the work; for it is so uncustomary, as to become almost *ridiculous*, to make *Laurels* for the *Conquered*."[5] Cowley suggested in the preface that he had burned copies of the poem, but part of book 1 was published in 1679 as *A Poem on the Late Civil War*, and two manuscript copies of the three-book poem were discovered in the 1970s.[6]

Cowley's account of the Civil War begins, as the Cary and Morison ode had, with fury, neatly expressed in couplets:

> What rage does *England* from it selfe divide
> More than Seas doe from all the world beside?
> From every part the roaring Canon play;
> From every part *blood* roares as loud as they.
> What English Ground but still some moisture beares
> Of young mens blood, and more of Mothers teares?
> What aires unthickned with some sighs of Wives!
> And more of Mayds for their deare Lovers lives![7]

The epic opening offers some hope that Cowley can truly answer the question "What rage?" and that in answering that question, in understanding the nature and origins of this national rage, he might be able to tame its fury.[8] But there is also something strange about his efforts in the opening couplets to size things up; he repeatedly tells us that one thing is "more" than the other. Rage divides England "More" than the seas divide it from the world, blood roars "as loud" as Canons, the ground is wet "more" with mother's tears than with their sons' blood, and the air is thickened "more" with the sighs of maids than of wives. All this measuring and comparing—and the incessant internal rhyme between "roar" and "more"—only serves to heighten the sense of the ultimate immeasurability of the rage, blood, tears, and sighs that pervade every particle of English water, air, and soil. There is an ominous suggestion that Cowley will not, like Jonson, be able to transmute the fury of the world into a transcendent, holy rage that can lift his heroes above the fray. Instead of containing or transforming the rage, the poet is simply standing in the midst of a deluge of human passions and fluids, vainly comparing one to the other.

Cowley shows further signs that poetry will be unable to give order to the fury of the Civil War a mere 141 lines into the epic in his account of the Earl of

Strafford's trial for treason and execution in May 1641. Cowley does not let on that many who would later choose the royalist side—including Falkland—had spoken against Strafford as an evil counselor responsible for the Personal Rule.[9] Ignoring parliamentary debate, Cowley focuses on the crowds that gathered in the streets: the "many-mouthed Rout" called for justice and blood so loudly that

> In the sencelesse Clamours and confused Noyse,
> We lost that rare and yet unconquered voice.
> So when the sacred *Thracian Lyre* was drown'd
> In the *Bistonian Woemens* mixed Sound,
> The wondering stones, that came before to heare,
> Forgot themselves and turn'd his *Murderers* there.[10]

The comparison of Strafford to Orpheus suggests that Cowley's horror at the clamor is as much poetical as political.[11] In a sanguine ode, "On the Prayse of Poetry," included in the second edition of his *Poeticall Blossomes*, published in 1636 when he was eighteen, Cowley had wondered

> What cannot verse? when *Thracian Orpheus* tooke
>   His Lyre, and gently on it stroke;
> The learned stones came dancing all along,
>   And kept time to the charming song.[12]

In 1636, verse could do anything, but Orpheus's charming sounds are not so omnipotent by the 1640s. Indeed, Cowley's couplet rhymes in the *Civil War* passage focus on the struggle between different kinds of sound. The first couplet contrasts the "Noyse" of the crowd with the single, "rare" "voice" of the defeated statesman. The second couplet plays with the meaning of "drown'd": Orpheus was dismembered and drowned in the Hebrus, but only as a result of a prior sonic drowning. The music of his "sacred Thracian Lyre" was first "drown'd" out by the "mixed Sound" of the women who attacked him. In the Ovidian account of Orpheus's death, the poet "vanquisht" the first lance and stone thrown at him by the women, and "the sweetenesse of his song" would have "Appeasd all weapons" were it not for the fact

>   that the noyse now growing strong
> With blowing shalmes, and beating drummes, & bedlem howling out,
> And clapping hands on euery syde by *Bacchus* drunken rout,
> Did drowne the sownd of *Orphyes* harp Then first of all stones were
> Made ruddy with the prophets blood, and could not giue him eare.[13]

The poet "who neuer till that howre / Did vtter woordes in vaine, nor sing without effectuall powre" is defeated by the mere volume of his opponents' noise.[14] Cowley, like Milton and many of their contemporaries, is clearly haunted by this idea that the clamorous, confused noise of the Bistonian

women is able to convert, to "turn," the "wondering stones" that were once
Orpheus's willing audience into his *"Murderers."* Though before they could
"heare" the lyre, now they are bloody murderers simply because they happened
to be "there"—carried away from "themselves," their reasonable selves, by the
senseless, confused noise. Cowley's allusion to Orpheus is certainly not inher-
ently royalist. Indeed, it recalls Milton's lament in "Lycidas" that the muse was
not able to protect Orpheus from the "rout that made the hideous roar" that
sent "His gory visage down the stream."[15] The two poets agree that Orphic
music is threatened by disorderly noise, but they disagree about the origin of
the noise. For Cowley, the danger of the Civil War is that the solitary voices
defending what he later calls "well establisht things" will be powerless against
the deafening noise produced by the "sick Fancies" of the multitude.[16] Though
he carries on in his account of the origins of the Civil War, this early specter of
Orphic drowning hints that he, like Milton six years before, was wondering
what it booted to write poetry.

But Cowley's horror at Strafford's downfall hardly prepares us for the lam-
entations that follow the death of Falkland in book 3:

> Ah Godlike Falkland! Thee each Hill and Vale,
> Thee all the Trees, and Fields, and Floods bewayle,
> Thee all the Graces wept, and Muses all;
> Amoung the rest thus mine bemoan'd thy Fall.[17]

The restraint of Jonson's ode for Morison is utterly swept away in Cowley's la-
ment for Falkland.[18] With the extravagance of his pathetic fallacies, Cowley
endeavors to mend the rift between the hero and the natural world he railed
against in his Orphic vision of Strafford's death. Now, the natural elements are
properly aligned with the poet: the hills, vales, trees, fields, and floods likewise
"bemoa[n]" the "Fall" of Falkland. But as Cowley continues, he makes it more
and more apparent that this harmony is a product of his own grief-stricken
fancy. After the initial lament for Falkland, Cowley relates an angelic vision:

> I saw meethoughts, the Conquering Angell fly
> From Newb'ury Fields towards Oxford through the Sky.[19]

"Methought" is often used in literature of the period to indicate a dream or
vision, as when Bottom awakes in *A Midsummer Night's Dream*:

> I have had a dream past the wit of man to say what dream it was. Man
> is but an ass if he go about t'expound this dream. Methought I was—
> there is no man can tell what. Methought I was, and methought I
> had,—but man is but a patched fool if he will offer to say what
> methought I had. The eye of man hath not heard, the ear of man hath
> not seen, man's hand is not able to taste, his tongue to conceive, nor his
> heart to report, what my dream was. I will get Peter Quince to write a

ballad of this dream. It shall be called "Bottom's Dream," because it hath no bottom.[20]

Cowley similarly piles on "meethoughts" as he attempts to expound the bottomless woe that follows his visionary discovery of Falkland's death:

> Some mighty man is slaine there, and (ah mee!)
> Something within will needes say Falkland's Hee.
> An aesterne wind from Newb'ury rushing came,
> It sigh'd, meethoughts, it sigh'd out Falklands Name.
> Falkland, meethoughts, the Hills all Eccho'ed round,
> Falkland, meethoughts, each Bird did sadly sound.
> A Muse stood by mee, and just then I writ
> My Kings great acts in Verses not unfit.
> The trowbled Muse fell shapelesse into aire,
> Instead of Inck dropt from my Pen a Teare.
> O 'tis a deadly Truth! Falkland is slaine;
> His noble blood all dyes th'accursed plaine.[21]

While in his initial elegy for Falkland the pathetic fallacy is unmediated, here the repetition of "meethoughts" marks the sighing winds and singing hills as visions spun out of the imagination of the mourning poet. In a note in book 3 of his other effort at epic writing, *Davideis*, Cowley describes the word "methought" as a way of designating and softening hyperbole:

> This perhaps will be accus'd by some severe Men for two swelling an *Hyperbole*; and I should not have endur'd it my self, if it had not been mitigated with the word *Methought*; for in a great Apprehension of Fear, there is no extraordinary or extravagant Species that the Imagination is not capable of forming.[22]

Cowley's multiple uses of "meethoughts" in *The Civil War* likewise mark the swelling, extravagant hyperboles formed by the fancy.

Both the hyperboles and the repetition of "meethoughts" also indicate a turn away from Virgilian epic. In his account of the differences between epic and lyric, Tasso had pointed to such hyperbolic visions of nature reflecting the passions and fancies of the lover as the distinctive stuff of lyric. Where Virgil praised the beauty of Dido with the utmost simplicity—*"forma pulcherrima Dido,"*—"if Petrarch as a lyric poet had to describe this same beauty," he would have been much more extravagant in his conceits:

> He would have said that the earth laughs round about her; that it glories in being touched by her feet; that the grass and the flowers desire her to tread upon them; that, struck by her rays, the sky is inflamed with chastity; that it delights in becoming clear because of her glance; that

the sun is mirrored in her face since it can find its peer nowhere else. The poet would invite love to join him so that together they could contemplate her glory.[23]

In Petrarchan poetry, nature is made to bow to the beauty of the beloved and the imagination of the lover. Hyperbole is needed to convey the realities of extreme passion. Though Sidney and the sonneteers of the sixteenth century had captured many aspects of the Petrarchan mode, the English poet who seized on Petrarchan hyperbole and ran with it was Donne. While the libertine poetry I described in chapter 2 deflated many of the conventions of the love poetry tradition by exposing the tyranny of custom and of mistresses, his metaphysical poetry tests the conventions of lyric poetry in a different way, by pushing the hyperbolic imagination of the lover to its extremes. In "The Good Morrow" he considers what it means for love to "contro[l]" "all love of other sights," making "a little room an everywhere"; in "A Nocturnal Upon Saint Lucy's Day," the bereaved is the "quintessence" of "nothingness" and the "elixir" of the "first nothing"; and the governing conceit of "The First Anniversary: An Anatomy of the World" is that the death of Elizabeth Drury threw the whole world out of joint.[24] Ben Jonson famously objected to Donne's immoderate praise of Elizabeth Drury as blasphemous.[25] Hyperbole (which Puttenham glosses as the "loud lyer" or the "Ouer reacher") was beyond the ken of Jonsonian poetics.[26] For Jonson, poets should insist on measure in metaphor as well as form, avoiding the "far fet" and "affected."[27] Jonson's formal influence on Cowley in *The Civil War* is undeniable, but Cowley's elegy for Falkland crosses over into the far-fetched and affected lyric realm of Petrarch and Donne. In Falkland, he proclaims,

> They killd a Man, whose Knowledge did containe,
> All that the Apple promis'd us in vaine.
> The farthest lands of Art did hee invade,
> And widestretcht Nature was his Triumph made,
> What unjust weights into the Scale were hurl'd?
> We gain'd a Field, and lost in him a World.[28]

Jonson's Cary was perfect and a world in himself, but not because he absorbed the entire world. Rather, he stoically separated himself from it. In declaring that Falkland is the whole world and that that world is utterly lost in him, Cowley chooses to focus on the immoderate grief of the bereaved rather than the moderate life of the fallen. For a moment, though, it seems as if he will answer this Donnean lament with Jonsonian consolation:[29]

> Whether are all those thowsand Notions fled,
> Whether, alas? for sure they are not dead.
> I see, I see each Virtue and each Art.

If Jonson were writing this elegy, he would "see" virtue and art living on in memory or in the bright asterism of his own poem. But Cowley continues,

> Crowd through the gapeing Wound from out his Heart.
> In a long row through the glad aire they runne,
> Like Swarmes of guilded Atomes from the Sunne.
> There flew the happy Soule, and with it they;
> A track of heav'enly Light still signes the Way.[30]

Where Jonson had seen a single leap of holy rage, Cowley sees a dribble of arts and virtues that "Crowd" through a "gapeing Wound." The simile comparing the "long row" to "swarmes of . . . Atomes" hardly dignifies or organizes the horde of virtues, even if the atoms are "guilded." It is as if the poet's imagination only makes the death of Falkland more disorderly, turning virtues into swarms of atoms.[31] His use of the Orpheus story early in the epic suggests that poetic fury is powerless against the furious noise of the crowd, and his elegy for Falkland resists the Jonsonian idea that the poet can restore order even in the face of death and horror by celebrating the measure of a life. All the poet's imagination can do is amplify the wailing by extending it, in a lyrical manner, to winds and trees and birds.

As Gerald MacLean and Nigel Smith have argued, this intrusion of the elegiac need not amount to the failure of Cowley's epic (as Trotter charged) since epics were supposed to contain all the lesser genres (as *Paradise Lost* does).[32] And, in a thoughtful reading of Cowley's use of the Virgilian hemistich, Henry Power has argued that the broken ending of the poem is intentional, that "Virgilian incompleteness is co-opted by Cowley and presented as a feature of his finished product."[33] I am persuaded by the idea that the incompleteness and generic multiplicity of the epic were by design, particularly since I see them as consistent with the hints of doubt expressed in the opening lines and lament for Strafford in book 1.[34] Cowley knew from the beginning that it would be a struggle to account for the rage of the Civil War. In the famous descent into Hell in book 3, he turns to allegory and satire in order to explain what he sees as the fanatical unreason of the other side: the passionate forces that move the rebels exceed the explanatory powers of epic realism and must be attributed to "subtile Feinds . . . steal[ing]" like dreams into the heads of Londoners to "wound" reason and "unchaine" the "rebell passions below . . . / And license that wild Multitude to raigne."[35] But by the end of book 3, it is Cowley who is subject to the hyperbolic excesses of passion and fancy as he bemoans the loss of Falkland. In the moment of mourning, passionate excess seems like the only appropriate response to a death that Cowley believes represents the death of all learning. But, deliberate and appropriate as the ending may be, it nonetheless reveals a Cowley who is uncertain about the efficacy of verse. If poetry can only release more disorderly and excessive passions into the air like the gilded atoms that fly from Falkland's gaping wound, is it restraining or rather contributing to the "confused noyse"?

Cowley's doubts about poetry were not short-lived and were not altered by his experience of exile and return to England. He attempted to complete another epic, this time with King David as his hero rather than King Charles.[36] In the Virgilian opening of the poem ("I Sing the *Man* who *Judahs Scepter* bore"), Cowley depicts David as an Aeneas-like hero of "unwearied *Virtue*" whose many trials "exercise[d]" his "*Patience*" and his "*Sword*."[37] But the biblical story of David is not particularly Virgilian; David is consistently connected with the "heart" and seems to follow his passions (for music, for his friend Jonathan, for God, and, later, for Bathsheba) rather than acting like a patient and duty-bound Roman (1 Samuel 13:14). Cowley is attracted to the passionate nature of David's story—the second book contains "a digression concerning the nature of Love"—but throughout the poem the language of the heart jars against what he calls in the preface the "*Patern* of our Master *Virgil*."[38] This friction perhaps contributed to his declaration in the preface that he had neither "Appetite" nor "Leisure" to finish the work and to his disgust at the fact that so much contemporary verse was nothing "but the *Cold-meats* of the *Ancients*, new-heated, and new set forth."[39] Someone, Cowley suggests, should write the biblical epic of the heart, but his "weak and imperfect attempt" could do little more than inspire "some other person."[40] Christopher D'Addario has detected a "retreat from faith in the importance of poetry" in Cowley's 1656 volume of poetry and has argued that throughout the volume Cowley explores and equivocates on whether poetry can make anything happen.[41] This ebb in faith, I suggest, was due to his recognition that a new kind of poetry was needed to address the passions properly and his uncertainty about how to reconcile that recognition with his classical leanings and training.

In the wake of the Civil War, a question that had always occupied poetic theorists—should verse bind or release the passions?—gained new urgency as it became clear that the "voice" of rational persuasion was often powerless against the "confused noyse" of a passionate crowd, and of the passions within the poets themselves.[42] By the end of Cowley's poem, and even more so by the end of the Civil War itself, it was evident that the passions needed to be reckoned with, but it was far from evident how that could be done. The Stoicism built into Jonson's understanding of measure did not seem, for Cowley at least, to be able to accommodate the very real and very extreme grief of a mourning nation.[43] But, as the repeated reinterpretation of rhyme between 1590 and 1640 has shown, poetic theory was flexible, and many poets of the period (especially Royalists who remained in England) had ample leisure to meditate on the best way to retain the Jonsonian couplet but make it responsive to the passions. In order to alter the implications of the couplet, they had only to draw on aspects of rhyme's sixteenth-century reputation. After all, rhyme had a double legacy. Jonson had emphasized its role as a force of order in the poem, but it was also associated with the primitive passions and with the irrational pleasure of jingling sound. As Samuel Daniel had in his *Defence of Rhyme*, the royalist poets of the midcentury saw this dual nature of rhyme as its peculiar strength: rhyme could simultaneously appeal to the deep-rooted passions within the heart and marshal the wild energy of those passions into an orderly form. In other words, rhyme, to use a word that appears again and again in royalist verse written in the wake of the Civil War, could "charm" its listeners. "Charm" comes from the Latin *carmen*, meaning both song and magical incantation, and the English word still retains some of the mystical implications of the Latin. To charm a person can simply mean to please or delight him, but it can also mean to control him with supernatural powers. In the decades that followed the outbreak of the Civil War, royalist poets played up the charming, mystical aspects of the rhyming couplet.[44] Rhyme therefore became an emblem of the grounded sublimity that poets like Robert Herrick, Katherine Philips, and Abraham Cowley, who will serve as my primary case studies in this chapter, pursued in their verse. They endeavored to make the case that the form and matter of their verse were linked, on the one hand, to the most deep-rooted, primitive desires of the heart and, on the other, to the higher harmony of the cosmos. If the Civil War was, as Cowley suggested, a crisis of unleashed passion, embracing the charming, prerational nature of rhyme seemed like one way to reconnect those passions to forces of political, social, and cosmic order.[45]

The Countercharm: Royalist Poetic Theory and the Politics of Rhyme's Chime

One of the most pithy and forthright statements of royalist poetic theory I have encountered is a commendatory poem to Alexander Brome's 1661 *Songs and Other Poems*. Brome, a lawyer and poet, was part of a Civil War literary circle that Nicholas McDowell has drawn attention to in *Poetry and Allegiance*. The circle, which was mostly (though not exclusively) royalist, formed in the mid-1640s at the Middle Temple under the patronage of Thomas Stanley and included Stanley's kinsmen Edward Sherburne and Richard Lovelace as well as James Shirley and Robert Herrick.[46] McDowell details how, with the end of the war, Stanley and publisher Humphrey Moseley worked to encourage "new work that demonstrated the potential for literary studies in England to revive and even develop, primarily through the incorporation of classical and continental models."[47] Alexander Brome seems to have participated in this project, but his contributions are more cheerful and Anacreontic, less scholarly and Stoic than those of Lovelace and Stanley.[48] In spite (or perhaps because) of the merriness of his verses, a young barrister named Robert Napeir credits Brome with the utmost political power:[49]

Thou (*Brome*) to cure the Kingdoms wrong
Didst hatch new *loyalty* with a *song*.
Musick (as once *Saul's* eldest Devil)
Fetter'd *Rebellious* rampant evil;
Rhime oft times over-reaches *reason*;
A verse will counter-charm a *Treason*.[50]

Though Napeir's lines lack the metrical polish characteristic of the sons of Ben, the young lawyer does manage to encapsulate the royalist understanding of verse in three closed tetrameter couplets. He conflates poetry and music, referring to "song," "Musick," "Rhime," and "verse" as if they were interchangeable.[51] In royalist poets' efforts to emphasize verse's passionate and transcendent qualities, they frequently played up poetry's connections to music and song. When Napeir argues that verse can "counter-charm" treason, he also plays on the double meaning of "charm" as song and magical incantation. Napeir points to the episode from 1 Samuel 16 in which the young David drove an evil spirit out of Saul by playing his harp as evidence that poets had long had the power to "counter-charm" unruly forces of evil because of the transcendent affective power of verse, because "*Rhime* oft times over-reaches *reason*."[52] In *Davideis*, Cowley had used the same episode as an opportunity to reflect on the "mystick powers that in blest numbers dwell."[53] Cowley argues that "*Davids Lyre* did *Sauls* wild rage controul" because there is a natural "*sympathy*" between the "*Proportions*" and "*Harmonie*" of human beings and the measures of music.[54] Napeir likewise attributes the stabilizing power of verse to the restraints built into the form of the poem. Drawing on Puttenham's idea that rhyme acts as a band or fetter, he claims that rhyme "Fetter'd" the "*Rebellious* . . . evil" that ran amuck during the English Civil War. Using the analogical thinking so common in premodern accounts of form, Napeir suggests that the formal restraints built into verse allow it to have a restraining effect on the English nation, spellbinding an evil political spirit with its charming sounds.

Napeir certainly did not invent the idea of verse's transcendent powers to move the human mind. As his allusion to David indicates, the idea of poetry's affective charms was deeply embedded in the inherited biblical and classical traditions that informed Renaissance poetic theory and practice. Indeed, a passage on Orpheus from George Sandys's 1632 translation and mythologization of Ovid testifies to the endurance of this view:

> Yet musick in it selfe most strangely works vpon our humane affections. Not in that the Soule (according to the opinion of the *Platonists*) consisting of harmony, & rapt with the sphearicall musick before it descended from Heauen to inhabit the body, affects it with the like desire (there being no nation so barbarous, or man so austere and stupid, which is not by the melody of instruments and numerous composures, either incited to pleasure or animated to Virtue) but because the Spirits

which agitate in the heart, receaue a warbling and dancing aire into the bosome, and are made one with the same where with they haue an affinity; whose motions lead the rest of the Spirits dispersed through the body, raising or suppressing the instrumentall parts according to the measures of the Musick; sometimes inflaming: and againe composing the affections: the sence of hearing stricking the Spirits more immediatly, then the rest of the sences.[55]

John Hollander quotes this passage to mark a shift in the seventeenth century from an "older tradition of world harmony" to a "quasi-mechanistic model" in which music works more directly and physically on the affections.[56] The royalist poets discussed in this chapter draw on both the older and the newer models of music and the affections; in fact, Katherine Philips is particularly adept at weaving the two visions together in her verse. But for all their uncertainties and disagreements about how exactly music works on the affections, the poets are united in their emphasis on making written verse more closely resemble strangely affective Orphic song. Arguments about rhyme's ability to overreach reason were used more frequently and with an increasing sense of urgency as Royalists began to insist that verse represented their last best hope for turning back the revolution. Moreover, Royalists' emphasis on the affective and super-rational aspects of poetry was not simply theoretical but informed every aspect of their poetic practice, from their choices of subject to their decisions about genre and poetic form.

Though Caroline and royalist poets wrote in a wide variety of genres, meters, and rhyme schemes, nearly all the prosodic forms they favored were associated with ancient or contemporary song. Ben Jonson and his imitators have often been credited with ushering in the neoclassical mode that would reign until the late eighteenth century, but it is important to specify which particular classical models held sway between the publication of Jonson's folio in 1616 and the Restoration in 1660.[57] The most frequently celebrated, translated, and imitated poets during this period were the Greek and Roman lyric poets: Pindar, Anacreon, Horace, and Martial. Seventeenth-century volumes of poetry were dominated by genres that had been considered minor modes in sixteenth-century poetic hierarchies: elegies, songs, hymns, epigrams, and odes. Indeed, when Michael Drayton published a collection of odes in *Poemes Lyrick and pastorall* in 1606—the first English book known to use the word "lyric" on its title page—he was clearly conscious of the fact that the ode in particular and the lyric mode in general were comparatively foreign to his English audience. After a detailed preface that outlines the history of the grave and light ode by discussing the contributions of Pindar, Horace, and Anacreon, Drayton claims in the opening poem, addressed "To himselfe and the harpe," that his volume is doing poetry a great service by "reuiu[ing]" the "Lyrick kinde."[58] Though the actual influence of Drayton's volume is unclear, the "Lyrick kinde" did in fact enjoy an astonishingly rapid revival in the early seventeenth century, and by the 1640s the ode had become an essential component of any distinguished collection of verse.

It is tempting to describe this surge of lyric solely in a negative way, as the failure of leading poets like Jonson and Cowley to carry out their epic ambitions. But, as Arthur Marotti's work has suggested, the idea of a poetic career dedicated mostly or entirely to writing lyric became more legitimate in the wake of the posthumous publication of Herbert's *Temple* and Donne's *Poems* in 1633.[59] Moseley, Marotti argues, was building on this model when he published the single-author volumes of Milton, Waller, Crashaw, Shirley, Suckling, Cowley, Carew, Cartwright, Stanley, and Vaughan in the 1640s and 1650s.[60] Lyric was also congenial to poetic theories that increasingly emphasized the affective power of verse. Nigel Smith has argued that the Civil War "internalized" epic as "epic and heroic language was made to refer to inward states of human constitution and consciousness."[61] At the same time that poets were experimenting with a new heroic poetry of the mind and psyche, they were also turning to a genre already associated with the internal realm. In lyric, poets of the Civil War period found a genre that was simultaneously internal and ceremonial, that had long combined prolonged meditation on individual passions with larger patterns of ritual, sound, and thought.[62]

Though historians of lyric like Roland Greene and Virginia Jackson have rightly noted that in the early modern period the term was not consistently linked with ideas of subjectivity and was often simply used to describe genres associated with the ancient lyre, it is important to distinguish between the post-Romantic association of lyric with subjectivity and a much earlier association of lyric with interiority.[63] The connection between lyric and interiority was certainly available as early as 1599, when William Scott, pointing to Scaliger's expansive use of the term, noted that the word *lyric* could be construed to include all "those poesies wherein we imitate and discover our affections and moral or natural conceits, more sudden and short yet pithy and profitable."[64] Scott's definition is remarkably similar to the twentieth-century *OED* definition of the term: "Now used as the name for short poems (whether or not intended to be sung), usually divided into stanzas or strophes, and directly expressing the poet's own thoughts and sentiments."[65] Both definitions associate lyric with the representation of internal states, and both are careful to specify that lyrics can contain the operations of the mind ("conceits" or "thoughts") and of the heart ("affections" or "sentiments"). And both avoid explaining how the two parts of their definitions—the shortness of lyric and its representation of thoughts and affections—relate to one another. Despite the resemblances between these two definitions, two apparently minor differences reveal the gulf that separates premodern and post-Romantic poetics. The first is a distinction in the verbs: Scott's lyrics "imitate" and "discover," while the *OED*'s "express." The verbal distinction neatly encapsulates the nineteenth-century shift from a mimetic theory of poetics in which verse imitates the nature of the world to an expressive theory in which verse gives voice to the idiosyncratic workings of an individual mind.[66] The second distinction between the definitions appears even more inconsequential at first glance. Scott speaks of "our affections and . . . conceits" and the *OED* of "the poet's own thoughts and sentiments." The difference between Scott's "our" and the *OED*'s "the poet's own" could simply be attributed to the demands of genre and audience—Scott's inclusive possessive adjective is appropriate for a poetic treatise addressed to his fellow poets, while the third person of the *OED* befits the detachment of a reference work. But the shift from first to third person parallels a historical revolution in understanding of poetry in general and lyric in particular. Under the post-Romantic critical regime, the thoughts and sentiments presented in lyrics are depicted as "the poet's own" and not as the shared possession of a community or, indeed, of humanity in general. Lyric, in this account, is a way of externalizing, "expressing," the peculiar thoughts and passions of distinct individuals. Though early modern writers likewise associate lyric with the internal workings of the mind, they often suggest, as Scott's "our" does, that thoughts and passions are largely shared, that there is a "common sense" that unites poet and audience.[67] Cowley's horror at what he sees as the devilish passions of his opponents in *The Civil War* springs in part from a fear that the idea of shared affections was being shattered. He does his best in the descent into Hell to depict the roiling passions of the parliamentary side as an aberration, but, as I have suggested, by the end of the poem he is unsure whether either side can escape the tyranny of excessive personal passion. The royalist poets who turned to lyric in the middle of the seventeenth century hoped to tap into a universal web of affections to restore old ties, but they were often uncertain whether this web existed any longer. The poets that I consider in this chapter respond to their uncertainty about the affections in a variety of ways: by insisting that the natural affections remained constant and universal in spite of the Civil War, by lowering their sights and trying to root poetry in the most basic and therefore most common human affections, or by retreating into the self and trying to make sense of the idea that affections are private and personal.

This dedication to meditating on the affections informed not only the mid-century interest in lyric but the particular genres and verse forms that filled the verse miscellanies and single-author collections that circulated from the Civil War through the Restoration. In many ways Robert Herrick's nearly four-hundred-page verse collection *Hesperides* epitomizes the formal preferences of his age. Herrick did not publish the volume until 1648, two years after the arrival of the New Model Army drove him from of his vicarage in Devon, but the volume contains Herrick's life's work, including poems he wrote as early as the 1610s.[68] *Hesperides* therefore encapsulates not only the royalist poetry of the Civil War era but also the gradual development of the royalist lyric style over the course of several decades.[69] Detailed analysis of the pattern of verse forms in *Hesperides* reveals that the apparent miscellaneity and "sweet neglect" of the volume is a piece of characteristic Herrickian *sprezzatura*.[70] Of the 1,130 poems in *Hesperides*, over 90 percent are written in couplets or triplets.[71] Iambic tetrameter and pentameter couplets dominate the volume, but Herrick takes care to intersperse other verse forms throughout the lengthy octavo. Stanzaic poems with noncouplet rhyme schemes occur one in every ten poems, breaking up the couplet poems that dominate the volume. Herrick's preferred stanzaic form is the pattern used in the Sternhold and Hopkins psalter, rhyming ABAB and alternating between tetrameter and trimeter lines, which Isaac Watts would later dub "common meter."[72] He also favors an AABCCB rhyme pattern that may derive from tail rhyme. Both pseudo–tail rhyme and common meter were used by ballad and song writers of the Caroline and Civil War periods. In his effort to use forms associated with ancient and contemporary song in his printed lyrics, Herrick aligns his work with the Stanley circle's project of lyric revival. Even more intriguingly, Herrick uses the seven-syllable headless iambic tetrameter couplets associated with Anacreon more frequently than any previous poet—to be precise, 130, or about 12 percent, of the poems in *Hesperides* are written in this unusual form, and, more strikingly, the poems are distributed throughout the volume with a consistency that suggests deliberate effort.[73]

Herrick's metrical allusion to Anacreon connects his collection to the nine lyric poets, who represented not only the excellence but also the range of ancient Greek melic verse.[74] Renaissance theorists frequently depicted Anacreon and Pindar as representatives of the light and the grave, the amorous and the heroic aspects of lyric poetry.[75] Herrick explicitly names Anacreon many times in *Hesperides*, associating him with wine-fueled poetic "raptures" and with the "frantick," "wilde and wanton" verse Herrick desires to cultivate, but he also uses form to reveal his view of the ancient lyricist in more subtle ways.[76] Late in *Hesperides*, for example, Herrick connects the seven-syllable Anacreontic couplet with homespun English lyric by using the form for a series of short poems that he describes as "mystick charms" to protect the home from supernatural "harms."[77] Herrick's decision to write his magical charms in seven-syllable couplets draws on the English dramatic tradition. In late Elizabethan and early Jacobean plays and masques, seven- and eight-syllable couplets were frequently used for the charms, spells, and blessings of supernatural creatures: from the nefarious incantations of the weird sisters in *Macbeth*,

> The weird sisters hand in hand,
> Posters of the sea and land,
> Thus do go about, about,
> Thrice to thine, and thrice to mine,
> And thrice again to make up nine.
> Peace! The charm's wound up;[78]

and of the witches in Ben Jonson's *Masque of Queens*,

> *First Charm*
> Dame, Dame, the watch is set:
> Quickly come, we all are met.
> From the lakes and from the fens,
> From the rocks and from the dens,
> From the woods and from the caves,
> From the church-yards, from the graves,
> From the dungeon, from the tree
> That they die on, here are we;[79]

to the more benevolent, if misdirected, spells of Puck in *A Midsummer Night's Dream*,

> Churl, upon thy eyes I throw
> All the power this charm doth owe.
> When thou wak'st, let love forbid
> Sleep his seat on thy eyelid.
> So, awake when I am gone.
> For I must now to Oberon;[80]

and the restorative charms of the River God in John Fletcher's *The Faithfull Shepherdesse*, a model for Milton's masque at Ludlow,

> *God.* what powerfull Charmes my streames doe bring
> Backe againe vnto their spring?
> With such force that I their god,
> Three times stricking with my rod,
> Could not keepe them in their Rancks
> My fishes shute into the bankes.
> . . .
> If thou bee'st a Virgin pure,
> I can giue a present cure,
> Take a droope into thy wound
> From my watry locks more round
> Then Orient Pearle, and farr more pure,
> Then vnchast flesh may endure.[81]

The short couplets Herrick uses are markers not only of supernatural creatures but also of language at its most effective and affecting: the charms in these dramas have the power to cure bodies and break hearts, to kindle desire and inspire loathing. Since charms represent verse at its most efficacious and mysterious as well as its most primitive and earthy, it is easy to see why Herrick would want to associate his poetry with the supernatural versifiers of English drama. But, coming as they do at the tail end of a volume filled with explicit allusions to Anacreon and Anacreontic verse, Herrick's heptasyllabic charms point in two directions. Through his metrical allusion, Herrick links together the ancient Greek lyric tradition and the native tradition of spell writing.[82] As Thomas N. Corns has argued, Herrick's particular kind of English neoclassicism is intended to counter the millenarianism of his time: "the Anacreontic and Horatian may be rehearsed by poets throughout time as they contemplate the givens of human mortality."[83] Herrick's effort to draw out affinities between the raptures of ancient lyric and the customary rites of the English countryside is at the heart of the project of *Hesperides*.

While the Anacreontic and magical associations of the seven-syllable couplet make it easy to see how this form harmonizes with royalist theories about the superrational appeals of verse, Herrick and other Royalists' preference for pentameter and tetrameter couplets seems more difficult to square with their theoretical commitments since Donne and the poets of the 1590s associated couplets with natural reason and discursive argument. And, in spite of his efforts to rein in the license of the couplet poets, Jonson had reinforced their idea that poetry should be a forum for rational discourse and that the couplet was the ideal vehicle for poetry of reason and conversation. Moreover, the enjambed Donnean couplet, with all its associations with freewheeling, plainspoken reason, had survived in the verse of George Wither and in the satire, invective, and drollery written on both sides.[84] David Norbrook credits Wither with "democratiz[ing] the sublime" in his Civil War verse, and, in readings of *Vox Pacifica* (1645), Norbrook details how Wither "describes his inspiration as an inward voice, which emerges from the sublime inner depth of his heart."[85] In his earlier Civil War book *Campo-Musae* (1643), Wither also describes his poetic style as the product of a moment of political crisis:

> He that hath matter that concerns the King,
> Comes not and ringles at the doore with feare;
> But knockes, untill he mekes the Palace ring,
> And spurnes it open, if they will not heare:
> > Ev'n so do I; and thinke I have done well
> > To make my language like the tale I tell.[86]

The striking image of Wither forcefully banging at the door of the palace rather than timidly "ringl[ing]" (the bell or iron knocker?) sums up his theory of political verse: what he has to say is too vital and too urgent to be subjected to formalities. His verse is a vociferous cry like the one at the beginning of Campo-Musae: "Ho! *Englishmen*! / Awake and be your selfe, yet, once agen."[87] Wither was not the only Civil War writer to see the appeal of the satiric voice of Marston as a model for political speech. An epigraph that heads the October 31–November 8, 1648, edition of the Leveller newsbook *Mercurius Militaris* demonstrates both the influence of this voice and how it had been mixed up with Jonson's legacy. The epigraph, which reads,

Ramp up my Genius, be not retrograde,
  But boldly nominate a spade, a spade;
Let baser Varlets serve to paint the times,
  And fairly varnish Kings, and great mens crimes:
This (like Joves thunder) shall pride and vice controul,
  The honest Satyre hath the happiest soul,[88]

sounds like one of Marston's boldest satires claiming liberty from the decep-
tions and strictures of polite society. But the reason it sounds like the satires of
the 1590s is because the author, John Harris, has fused together couplets from
Jonson's *Poetaster* (1601), which (among other things) endeavors to correct
what Jonson saw as Marston's satiric and poetic excesses while defending a
more restrained Horatian vision of satire.[89] The first couplet of the *Mercurius
Militaris* passage is from Jonson's parody of Marston's verse, while the third
couplet is from Jonson's defense of the true satirist. The middle couplet seems
to be the invention of Harris. Harris had been an actor before becoming a
printer during the Civil War, and quotations from other Jonson plays and from
Shakespeare appear elsewhere in his newsbook.[90] It's not clear whether Har-
ris's citation of Jonson's parody of Marstonian satire to defend his ramped-up
satirical genius is intentionally or unwittingly ironic, but the vision of poetry
as the unguarded and unceremonious thoughts of an honest observer in
Wither and Harris does illustrate one Civil War model of the political couplet
against which royalist poets were working as they crafted the form into a ve-
hicle for disengaged and passionate lyric. There are some connections between
the two uses of the couplet: Wither and Civil War satirists, like the royalist lyri-
cists, emphasize poetry's links to the heart. But Wither and the couplet satirists
of the period are more likely to depict their rhyming couplets as a disorderly
outpouring of the heart while royalist writers emphasized the ways in which
the order of rhyme could work its way into the deepest parts of the heart.

  Though the English produced a large body of technical and theoretical
writing on poetry in the final decades of the sixteenth century, extended discus-
sions of the craft of verse making are comparatively rare in the seventeenth
century, perhaps in part because the poetic works produced by Sidney and
Spenser had reassured anxious contemporaries that the English tongue was in
fact capable of fostering versifiers on a par with the most illustrious continental
poets. In the absence of lengthy volumes of formal analysis, paratextual materi-
als like prose prefaces and commendatory poems are the best resources for
uncovering seventeenth-century poetic theories and attitudes about particular
verse forms like the couplet. When seventeenth-century writers explicitly men-
tion the couplet in these contexts, they almost invariably connect the form with
musical, social, and amorous concord. They frequently play on the verbal con-
nection between couplet and couple by describing couplets as lovers kissing or
embracing one another.

A commendatory poem to Thomas Beedome's *Poems, Divine, and Humane*
(1641) celebrates the deceased poet's verses for

> The sweet,
> And gentle cadence of their ordered feet,
> Whose couplets kisse, with so divine an Art,
> As if the Sibills had about thy heart,
> Layd their propheticke Spells.[91]

Little is known about Thomas Beedome other than what can be gathered from
his posthumous volume, and his poetic allegiances within the book are decid-
edly mixed: one epigram to "the excellent poet Wither" praises him for his
"heaven-bred boldnesse," but another poem thanks "great Johnson" for "such
lines as equall profit with delight" and that are "so neate, so sweet."[92] Beedome's
own couplets within the volume vacillate between the Witherian and the Jon-
sonian, but this commendatory poem focuses on his orderly Jonsonian aspect.
The praise of the sweet and gentle cadence of Beedome's "ordered feet" recalls
Jonson's dedication to even-gaited verse, but the metaphors that follow con-
nect orderly couplets not with reason but with love and prophecy. The image
of couplets kissing like a pair of well-matched lovers puts a more human and
affective spin on the commonplace idea that rhyme acts as a band or connec-
tive force tying the poem together. But this kissing is also beyond human; it
reveals a "divine art" in the "heart" of Beedome, as if he has been charmed by
the magical spells of the sybils. These ways of imagining Beedome's couplets
suggest that they are not simply verbal coincidences but strong mutual attrac-
tions, or even magical affinities, between words.

The conceit of couplets as embracing lovers also appears in a commenda-
tory poem that Alexander Brome wrote for Thomas Stanley in 1656. Stanley's
poems and verse translations of ancient and continental poets like Anacreon,
Moschus, Bion, Johannes Secundus, and Tasso were printed in several differ-
ent volumes between 1647 and 1652; later, in 1656, composer John Gamble set
eighty-five of Stanley's poems in *Ayres and Dialogues*.[93] The volume is pref-
aced by a group of commendatory poems written by the members of Stanley's
circle. The poems dwell so insistently on images of harmony and musical rap-
ture, including Apollo, his lyre, and the music of the spheres, that Richard
Lovelace's brother Dudley contributed a poem that begins, with playful exas-
peration, "Enough, enough of orbs and spheres."[94] In his own contribution,
which embraces the music of the spheres theme by praising "Stanley the Dar-
ling of Apollo," Alexander Brome points to the couplet in particular as one of
the sources of Stanley's alluring harmony:

> How thy words flow! How sweetly do they *Chyme*,
> When thy pure *Couplets* do imbrace in *Rhyme*![95]

Like the poem in Beedome's volume, Brome's verses associate couplets with sweetness and amity. The image of couplet rhyme as a pure embrace is particularly apt for Stanley's verse, since his project was to form a society of poets that could sustain English verse in the wake of the Civil War. The embrace (more than the kiss in May's poem) is an image of stability and closure as well as affection. The couplets do not simply kiss and part; rather, they clasp one another. The result of this loving embrace between lines is the much-maligned "chime" of rhyme. What opponents of rhyme saw as a hollow sonic coincidence, a jingling or tinkling of bells, Brome depicts as an enduring concord.

While Brome does not elaborate on the effects of this concord, Sir John Beaumont, a recusant poet who was a relative and follower of the Duke of Buckingham (and the brother of playwright Francis Beaumont), had offered a detailed psychological account of the way the couplet's chime works on the mind in a poem to King James on the "true forme of English Poetry":[96]

> The rellish of the Muse consists in rime,
> One verse must meete another like a chime.
> Our Saxon shortnesse hath peculiar grace
> In choise of words, fit for the ending place,
> Which leaue impression in the mind as well
> As closing sounds, of some delightfull bell.[97]

The concept of the mental "impression" is now a dead metaphor and no longer calls up images of a sensory object forcefully pressing its mark onto the mind, but it was still vivid and corporeal in the seventeenth century and was often used to clarify accounts of sense perception.[98] Beaumont's use of the word suggests that the chime of end rhymes forcefully alters the mind of the listener and lingers long after the ringing sound has passed.

In particular, Beaumont maintains that couplets—especially when they are made up of "Saxon" monosyllables—leave the listener with an impression of closure akin to the ringing of a "closing" bell, perhaps an allusion to the curfew bell that signaled the end of the day. Beaumont's theory of closure draws on centuries of English poetic practice, since individual couplets had long been used to signal the ends of scenes in drama and to conclude complex stanzaic forms like rhyme royal, the English sonnet, and the Spenserian stanza.[99] But Beaumont extends the idea of the satisfying chime of a single concluding couplet to poems that are made up entirely of couplets. Instead of using the couplet to resolve a stanza or scene, poets should offer this pleasing sense of closure again and again throughout the poem.

Beaumont's focus on closure overturns the couplet's Elizabethan reputation as a free-flowing argumentative form. Indeed, Donne and Marston had insistently disrupted the finality of the "ending place" of the line. In addition to enjambing their lines more frequently than other poets of the period, they often diminished the punch of the couplet rhyme by lightening the final accent or using near rhymes.[100] Thus, the chiming couplets that Beaumont praises are not the disruptive couplets of the radical Elizabethan poets of his youth but the measured couplets of Ben Jonson and other Jacobean versifiers. This shift in the couplet's style and reputation is indicative of a larger shift in views about the purpose of poetry. Beaumont, like the Elizabethan couplet poets, rejects the extreme restriction of the "fetter'd stave" favored by Spenser and Puttenham, but he also rejects the Marstonian argument that poetry should be a forum for the unrestricted movement of "boundless discursive apprehension."[101] For Beaumont, verse should appeal not only to reason but also to prerational instincts for pleasing repetitions and well-ordered, enclosed parcels of speech. By emphasizing how the couplet satisfies these instincts, Beaumont registered and perhaps contributed to an incremental shift in the meaning of the couplet over the course of the seventeenth century. Rhyme's chime came to seem the ideal vehicle for the new kind of poetry favored by the Royalists, centering around the private and emotional connections that they believed overreached reason. By the middle of the seventeenth century, then, the implications of the couplet had been modified to align with the rise of the new lyric kind and with theories of verse's sublime power over the heart. While many of Herrick's couplet poems, particularly his epigrams, nod to the older idea of couplets as vehicles for rational discourse, in the majority of his poems in iambic and tetrameter couplets, as in his poems in Anacreontic couplets or common meter, Herrick endeavors to "Stand by the *Magick* of [his] powerfull Rhymes / 'Gainst all the indignation of the times."[102] His rhymes' primitive, mystical power made them the ideal force to stand against what he hoped was the passing outrage of "the times." Like Jonson, Herrick contrasts his permanent things with the flux of fortune, but for Herrick the fixed things are magical and passionate.

Herrick's dedication to the magical, incantatory aspects of couplet verse is visible from the opening poems of *Hesperides*. As Jonson does in his two verse collections of 1616, *Epigrammes* and *The Forrest*, Herrick takes considerable care to define his poetic program in the liminal poems that frame *Hesperides*. After beginning the volume with a series of poems addressed to his muse and his book, Herrick turns to offer the reader guidance about the proper occasion and setting for his poetry in "When he would have his verses read":

> In sober mornings, doe not thou reherse
> The holy incantation of a verse;
> But when that men have both well drunke, and fed,
> Let my Enchantments then be sung, or read.
> When Laurell spirts i'th' fire, and when the Hearth
> Smiles to it selfe, and guilds the roofe with mirth;
> When up the *Thryse* is rais'd, and when the sound

Of sacred *Orgies* flyes, A round, A round.
When the *Rose* raignes, and locks with ointments shine,
Let rigid *Cato* read these Lines of mine.

    * A *JAVELIN* TWIND WITH *IVY*.   *SONGS TO *BACCHUS*.[103]

As the original seventeenth-century footnotes glossing the words "Thryse" and "Orgies" indicate, Herrick associates his poetry with Bacchus and the sensual trappings of the Dionysian cult: twining ivy and roses, ointments, song, and, of course, ample food and wine. Royalists did not celebrate wine and baccha-nalian revelry simply in order to thumb their noses at the teetotaling moralism of the parliamentary side—though that was certainly a powerful motivation. As Richard Lovelace suggests in "The Vintage to the Dungeon," when he speaks of "Drink[ing] oth' strong, the Rich, the Old," wine was a fitting emblem for preserving old customs and social bonds since dusty bottles from the cellar were superior to new bottles and provided a physical link to bygone merri-ment.[104] The atmosphere of mirth that Herrick conjures up in "When he would have his verses read" builds on the idea that a full life is one that em-braces all the senses and faculties of the human heart. And, as Herrick's rhyme between "fed" and "read" suggests, the poem makes the case that the desire for the "Enchantments" of song is as natural and as essential as the desire for food and drink.

Indeed, Herrick's use of the word "Enchantments," as well as the character-istically Herrickian phrase "holy incantation of a verse," sums up the poetic program of his volume and of the midcentury Royalists in general. Both "in-cantation" and "Enchantments" derive from the Latin verb, *cantare*, meaning to sing, chant, foretell, or enchant. *Cantare* is the frequentative form of the verb *canere*, to sing, and is used in particular to describe the kinds of repetitive but rapturous verse associated with oracles, religious rites, and magical spells.[105] The concept of incantation brings together the wild and the ceremo-nial aspects of Herrick's poetry and accounts for the particular characteristics of his couplet style. Every line of his poem is iambic and each couplet is end-stopped, but Herrick's couplets gambol rather than walk with the even and unaltered gait of Jonson's Stoic hero. The pulse of his iambs and the chime of his enclosed couplets are designed to charm the heart of the listener with their skipping but mesmerizing order.

Our Own Beloved Privacy: Property, Privacy, and Personal Affections in Royalist Verse

Though Herrick calls up a scene of Bacchanalian revelry in "When he would have his verses read" in order to associate his verse with the satisfaction of primal desires, he characteristically domesticates the orgies of the wild Roman god by situating them in front of a roaring English "Hearth" instead of the forest traditionally associated with the ecstatic rites. Indeed, the rhyme between mirth and hearth, which Herrick repeats elsewhere in *Hesperides*, announces one of the primary aims of Herrick's lyric collection: to fuse Bacchus with the "private *Larr*," as he calls it in a Horatian epode celebrating his brother Thomas's retirement to the country.[106] The Lares, the ancient Roman household gods that survived the Romans' adoption of the Greek pantheon, stand in for all the homely pleasures, personal ties, and ancient customs that Herrick celebrates in his collection. Herrick's focus on the joys of hearth and home in *Hesperides* is representative of a larger movement toward personal affections in royalist verse.

Earl Miner's influential study *The Cavalier Mode* described the poetry of Jonson and his descendants as "social," distinguishing it from the "private" verse of the metaphysicals and "public" verse of Milton and Dryden.[107] Miner's distinctions have proven useful and influential, but decades of scholarship on royalist writing have complicated these categories and revealed the manifold ways cavalier poets blurred the categories of publicity, privacy, and sociability. In the 1980s, Leah Marcus uncovered the politics of the holiday pastimes and mirthful gatherings that Caroline and midcentury Royalists often depicted as escapes from politics, Kevin Sharpe thought through the politics of Caroline Neoplatonism and cavalier love poetry, and Lois Potter offered an idea of "secret" writing that allowed her to advance a nuanced idea of political engagement from a position of retreat.[108] Building on these efforts to complicate notions of privacy and political engagement, Timothy Raylor and, more recently, Nicholas McDowell have brought to light the lively literary societies that survived royalist defeat; as Raylor suggests, knowledge of the club background reveals how verse that may appear "escapist, consolatory, or quietest" can often be "politically engaged" and "subversive."[109] These are only a few salient instances from a large body of scholarship that has worked to expand our understanding of the royalist literary community by revealing, as Christopher Burlinson suggests in a recent issue of *Seventeenth Century* that reassesses the cavaliers, that "the different modes of poetry—public and private" are far from "clearly separable and negotiable."[110]

As revealing as these debates about publicity and privacy, engagement and escapism, have been, I want to consider a distinctive characteristic of royalist verse that at first blush seems related to questions of privacy and political engagement but actually cuts across these categories. Royalist poets as different as Philips and Herrick seem to share a way of looking, an angle of approach to both political and amorous subjects. Whether they are writing of the king, Julia, or her crimson stomacher, many royalist poets tend to look at their subjects through the eyes of personal affections. Miner himself notes that cavalier verse is more dedicated to particular loves; he remarks that Jonson's children and Herrick's maid, Prew, are named in their poetry while Donne does not mention the names of his children or lovers.[111] He goes on to describe the experience of cavalier poetry as "intimate and yet inclusive."[112] Metaphysical poetry is absorbed by private, intimate loves, but these loves are abstracted so that they become reflections on the nature of love in general: beyond a few hints about riverbanks or beds, Donne's poems are not located in a particularized setting, and they offer no insights into the appearance or distinctive character of the beloved. In contrast, as Gerald Hammond compellingly argues in his 1990 study *Fleeting Things*, one of the unique charms of so-called cavalier verse is its dedication to the particular, the material, and even the trivial.[113] While Donne and the metaphysicals most often explore the nature of love and intimacy in the most abstract terms, poets like Herrick and Lovelace are interested in the affective bonds individuals form with this place, this person, this thing.[114] They try to think through what ties individuals to what they call their "own" and to consider whether and how these local loyalties interact with higher political and religious allegiances. This fascination with the whole spectrum of loyalties springs out of the royalist effort to wrestle with the problem of the passions. Ruth Connolly has argued that in spite of the fact that nearly all critics recognize the "significance of feeling" in cavalier writing it is rarely "an explicit focus of attention."[115] In her fine-tuned reading of the tiny creatures of Lovelace's *Posthume Poems* (1659), she sees the poems as a "self-reflexive poetic engagement with their own disordered political moment that are principally concerned with the political and aesthetic consequences of the dissipation of once powerful feeling, feeling previously embodied, literally, in the monarch."[116] Indeed, royalist poets seem to pursue these scattered feelings wherever they can find them, which most often leads to the fireside. They are interested in private life not only because they are excluded from political life or because retirement allows them to claim a degree of self-sufficiency and liberty (though these are also powerful motivations) but also because they find that the strongest and most deeply rooted passions are particular and homely. The bonds of intimacy, like the bands of rhyme, promise to unite primitive passions with rooted order.

This royalist pursuit of dispersed but powerful passions dovetails with these poets' preference for short verse and the rapid rise of the "Lyrick kinde" during this period.[117] Marjorie Swann has highlighted the ways in which this interest in the particular corresponds with the fragmentary aesthetic of Herrick's *Hesperides*, which "transforms all aspects of experience into a collection of discrete *things*," united only by their relationship to an authorial proprietor.[118] This formal and thematic discontinuity is visible not only in *Hesperides*, but in most of the single-author volumes of lyric poetry printed in the mid-seventeenth century, which are indebted to Jonson's *The Forrest* and to the Latin and continental *silvae* tradition that inspired Jonson's collection. As Poliziano puts it in his commentary on Statius's *Silvae*, such little books lacked the weight (*pondere*), heft (*mole*), and continuity of epic poems, but they displayed the poet's range and skill through their multiplicity of argument (*argumentorum multiplicitate*) and variety of stylistic artifices (*dicendi vario artificio*).[119] Turning away from historical poems and epics that chronicled the political fates of kings and nations and endeavored to provide a unified, all-encompassing account of the world, the poets of the mid-seventeenth century hold up the variety of the lyric collection as more representative of the multiplicity of human affections and experiences. Petrarch and the English sonneteers of the 1590s had used the discontinuity of the lyric collection to represent the changeability of the lover, but the repetition of the sonnet form and the loose narrative structure gave sonnet sequences a unified sense of purpose.[120] The stylistic and argumentative variety of the midcentury collection amplified the sense of lyric discontinuity and contributed to the idea that poetry's role was to represent the deep and passionate bonds that tie individuals not only to their mistresses and friends but also to the apparently trivial appurtenances of daily life.

There is no doubt that the royalist poets' turn to the personal and the particular was in part a response to the economic, academic, and political deprivations that accompanied defeat in the Civil War.[121] Since they were expelled from their positions in the church and universities, banished from London, or, at times, forbidden to "pass or remove above five miles" from their dwellings, it is no wonder that poets like Herrick, Cowley, and Mildmay Fane celebrated the life of retirement and focused on the "Liberty of a private man in being Master of his own Time and Actions," as Cowley puts it in his essay on liberty (*Essays*, 108).[122] Though the idea of private liberty certainly offered some compensation for the degradations of the Civil War, the events of the 1640s were not the sole cause of this literary movement toward the personal, already evident in the verse of poets who died before the eruption of the Civil War, including Ben Jonson, Thomas Carew, Richard Corbett, and Thomas Randolph, as well as in the poems Herrick composed between 1610 and 1640.[123] As Alastair Fowler argues in the introduction to his extensive anthology of estate poems, the "contemplative turn" was not merely a compensation for "enforced seclusion during the Interregnum" but "needs to be related to larger and longer changes" that had begun much earlier in the seventeenth century.[124] Building on Ben Jonson's idea of circumscribed liberty and drawing on classical exemplars like Horace and Martial, royalist poets extended a turn toward celebrations of the home and table that was already at work in the Caroline tradition. But they made a significant change as they interpreted Jonson's legacy. While for Jonson retirement was praiseworthy because turning away from the world allowed upright individuals to cultivate a measured life untroubled by the exorbitant passions of court and city, midcentury interpreters of Jonson (Herrick and Philips chief among them) often confined their desires to the hearth in order to concentrate and strengthen, rather than restrain, them.

Herrick proclaims in the programmatic opening poem of *Hesperides* that he sings, among other things, of *"Times trans-shifting,"* and his volume is indeed uniquely positioned to represent the gradual progression of the inward turn Fowler describes.[125] Herrick's 1648 collection includes early poems like his "Panegyrick to Sir Lewis Pemberton," which has been dated to the late 1610s or early 1620s, that participate in the early tradition of the country house poem by celebrating the "warm-love-hatching gates" and communal tables of his patrons that restore the ancient virtue of hospitality.[126] But in his later verse, including the framing poems written just before publication, he lowers his sights, bidding his muse to "stay at home" and pipe among the "poore and private *Cottages*."[127] In "His content in the Country," which was written sometime between 1630 and 1646, Herrick provides an account of domestic life that displays his heightened concern for property and for limiting himself to the fruits of his own possessions and bit of land:

> *His content in the Country*
> HERE, here I live with what my Board,
> Can with the smallest cost afford.
> Though ne'r so mean the Viands be,
> They well content my *Prew* and me.
> Or Pea, or Bean, or Wort, or Beet,
> What ever comes, content makes sweet:
> Here we rejoyce, because no Rent
> We pay for our poore Tenement:
> Wherein we rest, and never feare
> The Landlord, or the Usurer.
> The Quarter-day do's ne'r affright
> Our Peacefull slumbers in the night.
> We eate our own, and batten more,
> Because we feed on no man's score:
> But pitie those whose flanks grow great,
> Swel'd with the Lard of others meat.
> We bless our Fortunes, when we see
> Our own beloved privacie:
> And like our living, where w'are known
> To very few, or else to none.[128]

After beginning with a repetition that precisely locates his dwelling place "HERE, here," Herrick proceeds to draw impermeable boundaries around his plot of ground, assuring the reader that nothing comes into or out of his personal realm. No currency is exchanged since he pays nothing to the "Landlord" and borrows nothing from the "Usurer." And no goods are exchanged since he and his maid Prew "eate" only their "own" at their private board.[129] Though they eat only the "mean . . . Viands" of peas and beans grown in their own garden, they pity those whose luxurious lives and fat "flanks" require dependency on "others meat." The poem not only rejects the new order of commerce in favor of rural independence but also turns away from the old vision of social and economic community presented in earlier country house poems.[130] While Jonson, Carew, and the young Herrick himself depict country estates with "warm-love-hatching gates" that "stand wide open" so that the "farmer and the clown," the "lanke-Stranger and the sowre Swain," may "all come in" and enjoy the fruits of the "open table," Herrick concludes this poem with a celebration of the near-complete isolation of the poet and his maid.[131] They do not simply retreat into their "own beloved privacie" as a temporary respite from the trials of active life but seem to relish total anonymity, being "known / To very few, or else to none." While Herrick's vision of the country life allows for no form of engagement with the world beyond his property line, it is nonetheless consistent with intimate companionship, in this case that of his longtime maid Prudence Baldwin. Indeed, in the phrase "Our own beloved privacie," the modifiers are more important than the noun: privacy is prized not for its own sake but because it allows for perfect dedication to what is "our own" and "beloved." Herrick and Prew cut all feudal ties on the one hand and all commercial contacts on the other in order to nestle in "HERE, here" amid the simple, unattenuated bonds they form to their land, crops, and one another. Herrick responds to the problem of unleashed passion by envisioning a complete submersion in the most natural and primitive affections. The bounded life of Herrick and Prew in "content in the Country" is a kind of fantasy of affective purity, a prototype of the passionate life royalist poets depicted as the potential root of a stable and loyal commonwealth.

This poem, and Herrick's volume in general, is compelling evidence for Alastair Fowler's argument that the inward turn of country poetry was not solely a result of royalist seclusion. If this poem had been printed a few years later and by a different royalist poet, it would be easy to read "content in the Country" as a royalist effort to make destiny a choice, to transform the five-mile tether that restrained the movement of many Royalists and often made hospitality impossible into a freely chosen "beloved privacy." But the Civil War actually obliged Herrick to leave the country for the city: he was driven from country living in Devon into London in 1646, where he lived on the hospitality of family and friends, including Mildmay Fane.[132] Most of the poems in *Hesperides* were written in the decades before Herrick's return to London, and the book was probably submitted to the press in September 1647, after the first parliamentary measures to exclude Royalists from London in 1646, but before Royalists were confined to their estates in 1650.[133] As Thomas Corns and Alan Rudrum have argued, the publication of *Hesperides* was undoubtedly a political act, and his Caroline verse took on new implications in 1648.[134] But it is nonetheless telling that Herrick's early verse was so amenable to political reinterpretations. The Civil War did not initiate the turn to beloved privacy in country poetry: it was already at work in Jonson, Herrick, and others well before the 1640s. But the Civil War and Interregnum did accelerate the pace of the inward turn and led two poets of the subsequent generation, Katherine Philips and Abraham Cowley, to dedicate themselves more fully to the idea of personal and passionate liberty that is only one strand among many in *Hesperides*.[135]

Numbers Gentle and Passions High, or Katherine Philips Composes Her Thoughts

Philips and Cowley, who exchanged commendatory verses during their lives and who were both published in a 1663 Dublin collection of *Poems, by Several Persons*, were frequently linked in the decades immediately following their premature deaths in the 1660s.[136] A commendatory poem preceding Samuel Woodford's 1667 paraphrase of the Psalms, for example, notes that "this fruit-ful age" has produced "one" illustrious poet "of each sex," "*Cowley* and bright *Orinda*," and a 1674 commendatory poem to Thomas Flatman predicts that he will equal "Cowley or Orinda's fame."[137] As Elizabeth Scott-Baumann's work on the retirement odes of the two poets has made abundantly clear, during the 1660s Philips and Cowley were engaged in a poetic conversation about the relationship between retirement and liberty that would also shape Marvell's Restoration verse on retreat.[138]

Both of these poets turned to Donne during the Interregnum as they endeavored to form a new model of poetry that could accommodate excessive passion. Cowley wrote his most metaphysical verse during the 1650s, but Philips's engagement with Donne was much more sustained and serious as she worked to reshape his Neoplatonic verse to fit her own understanding of the bonds of romantic friendship. The passionate friendship poems that Katherine Philips wrote for her female friends have often been celebrated as ground-breaking explorations of the love between women.[139] But as critics like Carol Barash, Catharine Gray, Hero Chalmers, and Penelope Anderson have emphasized, Philips's Sapphic verse cannot be disentangled from her royalist understanding of social and political concord.[140] Building on the Neoplatonic idea that "Love chaines the differing Elements in one / Great harmony," Philips sees her theory of friendship as the foundation of the larger argument of her verse that "Submission and Conformity" are the fountains of human happiness.[141]

Philips's effort to root political allegiance in the bonds of love is evident in "Upon the double murther of K. Charles, in answer to a libellous rime made by V.P.," which was written during the 1650s in response to a poem by Welsh Fifth-Monarchist preacher Vavasor Powell.[142] "Upon the double murther" is the first poem in the unauthorized 1664 edition as well as the authorized 1667 edition of Philips's verse, but Gillian Wright has pointed out that in the auto-graph Tutin manuscript, which is divided into philosophical and personal sections, this poem was included among the personal poems while her only other overtly political poem of the Interregnum, "On the 3d of September," was included among the philosophical poems.[143] Despite the allusion to the regicide in the title, the poem opens with a disavowal of political engagement, followed by an apology for speaking out in response to what Philips describes as a political emergency:

> I thinke not on the state, nor am concern'd
> Which way soever that great Helme is turn'd,
> But as that sonne whose father's danger nigh
> Did force his native dumbnesse, and untye
> The fettred organs: so here is a cause
> That will excuse the breach of nature's lawes.
> Silence were now a Sin: Nay passion now
> Wise men themselves for merit would allow.[144]

Most readings of the poem have highlighted the ways that Philips's opening deftly manages to disown and defend female political speech simultaneously, and critics like Sarah Ross have depicted the poem as an emblem of the "emergence of political poetry by women in seventeenth-century Britain as a whole."[145] Though Philips's adroit lines certainly respond to contemporary gender norms governing propriety in speech, her claim to political disengagement might be more than a feint since it anticipates her celebration of the "unconcern'd" life throughout the volume.[146] Moreover, the particular analogy she uses to defend her entry into the political conversation links her speech not with political debate and the public sphere but with intense familial love. Philips draws on the oft-cited story from Herodotus of King Croesus's mute son, who "broke into speech" when his father was in "imminent peril," crying out, "slay not king Craesus."[147] Philips therefore domesticates her political verse by likening it to an outcry to rescue a father. She suggests that her poetry, though it addresses a political subject, springs from the same passions that bind father and son. This strategy builds on the long-standing royalist trope of the king as the father of his people. In *The Trew Law of Free Monarchies*, for example, James I illustrates the idea that there is "a mutuall and reciprock band" between the king and his subjects by comparing the king to a "natural father."[148] Under Charles I, love and marriage replaced fatherhood as the primary royal image, but the Caroline politics of love nonetheless built on the idea implicit in the Jacobean image of the king as father, that the natural and intimate passions should be tapped and depicted as corollaries of political allegiance.[149]

Though Philips's depiction of her affection for the king as filial had its roots in Stuart images of kingship, it was by no means an inevitable aspect of royalism by the 1650s. David Scott has described two factions in the royalist side from the 1640s: one (led by Henry Jermyn and John Culpepper) that adhered to a Lipsian and Hobbesian view that force and prudence were the foundations of a stable regime, and another (represented by Edward Hyde and Edward Nicholas) that stressed the affection between king and people and saw "monarchy not simply as a political phenomenon . . . but also as a moral force, rooted in a reciprocal relationship of trust and loyalty between king and people, and indivisible from the honour of the English nation."[150] Since Jermyn remained Henrietta Maria's close counselor, the prudential party retained significant influence over the exiled court in France (and over Cowley, who served as Jermyn's secretary). In imagining her connection to the dead king as a bond of affection, Philips is choosing a particular strand of royalism. This emphasis on private passions is particularly suited to a Royalist who remained in Wales (with visits to London) during the Interregnum. Depicting her bond with the king as a passionate, familial tie not only protects Philips from charges that her public speech violates gender norms but also allows her to maintain her allegiances under the Protectorate. Her opponents may be able to sequester royalist lands and suppress publication of royalist sermons and newsbooks, but surely, she suggests, they cannot regulate royalist affections.

This strategic personalization of the political continues throughout the poem, in which Philips's primary concern is not the Civil War or even the regicide itself but the ways that "every asse" has "kick'd" the "dying Lion," that is, the many personal indignities that Charles suffered before and after his execution: the betrayal of his "Unfaithfull friends" and the slanders of "ignoble enemies."[151] Philips argues that print attacks on the deceased Charles, like the poem by Vavasor Powell to which she responds, are akin to committing the sacrilege of "tear[ing] up a Tomb" on top of the treason of "pull[ing] downe a crowne."[152] In focusing on the "horrour" of denying Charles a "quiet grave," Philips appeals to the ancient sanctity of burial: "Tombes have been sanctuaryes," she claims, and even "Theeves lye here / Secure from all their penaltie and feare."[153] And, she insists, "any heathen" who had been the king's "foe" would have been more in touch with his natural affections and would have "wept to see him injur'd so."[154] By depicting Vavasor Powell's verse attack on Charles as a violation of the sanctity of the grave rather than an intellectual or political crime, Philips associates herself with Greek heroines like Antigone who defended the sanctity of the body, familial ties, and the religious rites of burial against Creon's claim that infidelity to the polis outweighed these concerns. Philips grounds her appeal on what she calls "our common sense," insisting that Powell and his allies not try to "sequester" basic reason and decency as they have the lands of the Royalists.[155] Philips "admire[s] not" that Powell has gone so far as to break open the tomb, since "No bounds will hold those who at scepters flye."[156] The charge suggests that there is at least some psychological connection between political "bounds" and the "bounds" of common-sense decency—he who breaks through one will not hesitate to transgress the other. Philips's verse works to restore broken "bounds" by building from the ground upward: she maintains that she "think[s] not on the state," but, in her friendship and devotional poetry as in this explicitly political poem, she endeavors to strengthen the bonds of passion and show how they are connected to higher forces of order.[157]

Like Spenser, the Sidneys, and other Elizabethan sonneteers, Philips points to the paradoxes of Petrarchism, Neoplatonism, and the love poetry tradition more generally as evidence that human beings not only require but actively seek out restraint and obligation.[158] Philips's interest in probing the contradictions built into the discourse of love is nowhere more apparent than in "Friendship's Mysterys, to my dearest Lucasia," the first of her friendship poems in the authorized 1667 edition of her verse. As the title suggests, she builds on contemporary associations of verse and mystical powers, proposing to "move" "men's faith" by offering a litany of paradoxical "wonder[s]" and "Prodig[ies]" of the love between friends.[159] In the second stanza, she uses the theological language of free will and divine design to argue that the fact that friends were "design'd t'agree" in no way diminishes their "liberty" since their "election" of each other is as free as that of the angels, who are "yet determin'd" to their "choice."[160] The word "determin'd" could imply either internal resolution or external compulsion. Philips implies in the paragraph that in the mysterious realms of religion and friendship both meanings apply: the particular natures of individuals lead them freely to choose their divinely ordained companion. Throughout her poetry, Philips holds up friendship as an emblem of liberty through acceptance of divinely ordained ties. The affinities between friends cannot be explained or altered, but yielding to the "eternall destiny of Love" makes one freer because it satisfies deep-seated natural desires for harmonious union.[161] Drawing on Donne's images of ecstatic mixing, she repeatedly depicts love as a "mixture" in which two souls become inseparable and indistinguishable from one another.[162] As Spenser does in *Amoretti*, Philips rejects a contractual account of human relationships in favor of a theory of mutual captivity. But she goes beyond Spenser's argument that the "prison" of the married life can be rendered sweet by the artful "bedeck[ing]" of the lady, that the chains can be covered by flowers.[163] She claims instead that the "intent" of the "fetters" that bind friends is not "bondage" at all but "Ornament."[164] The word "ornament" did not simply signify an embellishment or decoration but bore a more robust symbolic significance. Etymologically connected to the word *ordinare*, to set in order, the word could signify either "a well disposed order of things," as La Primaudaye put it, or the embellishments that acted as signs of one's place in that social or cosmic order.[165] Thus, Philips is not simply claiming that the fetters of friendship beautify rather than coerce but suggesting that this love bond is the sign and even the foundation of a larger order of things. The way in which she manipulates the poetic legacies of Donne and Jonson is calculated to reinforce this vision of deeply rooted order.

In her religious poem "Submission," for example, Philips reinterprets the Donnean argumentative couplet in order to defend a philosophy of resignation. Like many of Donne's verse letters and elegies, the poem is organized into a series of propositions linked by the language of argument and analogy: "For as," "So," "Yet," "Hence," "But though."[166] From the opening lines, Philips demonstrates that she has mastered the exclamatory, intimate style of Donne's early couplet verse:

> 'Tis so, and humbly I my will resign,
> Nor dare dispute with Providence divine.
> In vain, alas! we struggle with our chains,
> But more entangled by the fruitless pains.[167]

Though chatty phrases like " 'Tis so" and "alas!" reveal her debt to Donne, Philips inverts the libertine principles of the Elizabethan couplet writers. Her defense of resignation is much more in line with Donne's Jacobean religious poetry, including Holy Sonnet 2, which begins with the same sentiment and rhyme word: "As due by many titles I resigne / My selfe to thee (o god)."[168] Yet even in his holy sonnets, in which he adopts a traditional Italian sonnet form and an extreme position of surrender to the divine will, Donne's rhymes rarely chime, and his meter rarely observes strict rules of measure. He continues to use enjambment, caesura, and irregular meter to disrupt expectations of order and to produce a sense that his conversations with God, like his conversations with friends and lovers in his youthful verse, are characterized by spontaneous outbursts and discursive struggle. Though she too depicts her religious verse as a conversation with herself, Philips uses even-gaited, end-stopped lines, and perfectly chiming rhymes to reinforce the idea that all things "Are held so fast, and govern'd with such art, / That nothing can out of its order start."[169] Verse, for Philips, is designed to reinforce and even enforce divine order.

Philips's revision of the couplet builds on Jonson's metrical alteration of the form to make it align with his ethics of the even and unaltered gait. Philips, too, signals her dedication to "That serious evenness that calmes the Brest."[170] But, while Jonson generally focused on the mind as an internal source of order, Philips depicts measure as externally dictated. The world, she claims, is "God's watch" in which "the least pin" cannot be "misplac'd" without undermining the timekeeping function of the whole.[171] But no pin will be lost since the watch is overseen and maintained by the divine watchmaker:

> It beats no pulse in vain, but keeps its time,
> And undiscern'd to its own height does climb;
> Strung first, and daily wound up by his hand
> Who can its motions guide and understand.[172]

Like Jonson, Philips tends to maintain a strict equality of accent across her iambic pentameter lines and pause at the end of each line to accentuate the chime of the couplet rhyme. There are some exceptions of course; variations from the iambic pattern in the line about God stringing and winding the cosmic clock suggest that order requires divine exertion. But, with the rise and fall of her largely monosyllabic lines on either side of this line, Philips signals that the order of her verse corresponds with the cosmic pulse or ticking of God's watch. The unexplained transition from the biological metaphor of the pulse to the mechanical metaphor of the timepiece suggests that the throbs of life that animate the world are just as uniform as the click of an artificial instrument. The suggestion of a kinship between the liveliest and most mechanistic aspects of life reinforces the counterintuitive royalist theory that rhyme's chime appeals to the passionate part of the human psyche precisely because of the mesmerizing charms of regularity. And the conclusion of "Submission" indicates that Philips's regular couplets are in fact intended to lull the reader into a resigned orderliness. Philips concludes the poem by revealing that the informal discourse of the previous seventy-six lines was a conversation with herself in a moment of intellectual insubordination: "Thus," she says, "I compose my thoughts grown insolent."[173] Though she draws on the same association of pentameter couplets with argument and casual speech as Donne, Marston, and Hall, her aim is to restrain rather than unleash unruly thought. By working through arguments and counterarguments in her verse, Philips "composes" her thoughts, that is, she calms them by putting them in their customary place through the transrational force of rhyme and meter.

Although "Submission" offers a more explicit defense of order than many of her other poems, the religious poem captures something fundamental about Philips's poetics throughout her corpus. The ardent "pulse" of her friendship poetry always "keeps its time."[174] Indeed, Philips, like Herrick, is remarkably adept at pouring passion into iambic regularity, into what Saintsbury called her "metre of soar and throb."[175] This practice of making measure the conduit of passion differs markedly from Donne's career-long practice of venting passion by breaking meter. Philips admits extremity of passion into her verse in the form of soaring, hyperbolic Donnean conceits, but passion never disrupts her larger vision of cosmic and poetic order. In a commendatory poem that was published in the 1663 Dublin of *Poems, by Several Persons* and then appeared at the front of the unauthorized 1664 edition of Philips's verse, Abraham Cowley praises Philips for precisely this fusion of "numbers gentle" and "passions high."[176] Philips's effort to contain high passions within gentle numbers represented one possible answer to the problem raised by Cowley's *Civil War*. Philips allows ample room for the exaggerated Donnean "meethoughts" of friends and lovers and makes the case that high passions are in touch with a higher order. Cowley's post-Restoration writing has much in common with Philips's passionate unconcern, but in his *essays*, the final work that he produced before his own untimely death, he chose a different way of bringing together passions and numbers. Cowley finds in the irregular forms of the essay and the Pindaric ode a way to accommodate the natural affections that issue from the heart.

Never since Left Ringing: Cowley's Essays and the Rhyming Language of the Heart

Who now reads Cowley? ...
Forgot his epic, nay Pindaric art,
But still I love the language of his heart.

—ALEXANDER POPE, "IMITATIONS OF HORACE"

With the return of Henrietta Maria to England in 1660, Cowley hoped that he would be rewarded for his services to Jermyn and the former queen with the mastership of the Savoy, which had been promised to him by Charles I and Charles II.[177] Their promises were not kept. After grousing in "The Complaint" that "The *Rachel*, for which" he had worked "twice seven years and more" was "Giv'n to another," Cowley retired to the country.[178] But Philips, who may have visited him in retirement at Barn Elms, skillfully converted his disgruntled retreat into a Stoic triumph in "An ode upon retirement, made upon occasion of Mr. Cowley's on that subject," which was printed right after Cowley's ode on her high passions and gentle numbers in the Dublin volume:[179]

> For lo! the man whom all mankind admir'd,
> By every grace adorn'd, and every mus[e] inspir'd,
>   Is now triumphantly retir'd.
>   The mighty Cowley this hath done,
> And over thee[180] a Parthian conquest won:
>   Which future ages shall adore,
>   And which in this subdues thee more
> Then either Greeke or Roman ever could before.[181]

Philips imitates the irregular rhymed Pindarics that Cowley had pioneered in his 1656 collection of odes, and she plays with the inversion of Pindaric heroism that had characterized Jonson's Cary and Morison ode as well as Cowley's experiments.[182] Indeed, she perceptively detects an affinity between Cowley's prosodic attraction to loose but rhymed verse and his account of the attractions of private liberty in the country. This affinity would become more apparent when Cowley developed a full-fledged, autobiographical account of the retired life in his *Several Discourses by way of Essays, in Verse and Prose.*

According to Royal Society historian Thomas Sprat, who served as Cowley's literary executor, the essays in verse and prose are "the last Pieces that we have from his hand."[183] The essays are the products of Cowley's efforts to live his theory of retirement. As he notes in the eighth essay, agricultural life proved less idyllic than he expected, and he "perceived quickly, by infallible demonstrations, that [he] was still in old *England*, and not in *Arcadia*, or *La Forrest*" (*Essays*, 203). Indeed, in Sprat's semihagiographic account, Cowley died a martyr to his cause after a few years in the country. "His death was occasion'd by his very delight in the Country and the Fields" since he died after being "taken with a violent Defluxion, and Stoppage in his Breast, and Throat," apparently from "staying too long amongst his Laborers in the Medows" during the hottest part of the year.[184]

Despite Cowley's disenchantment and the tragic conclusion of his experiment with retirement, Cowley's literary experiment proved much more successful and enduring. His essays have long been recognized as exemplars of seventeenth-century prose, though they have rarely been examined in detail. As the precise title suggests, the genre and form of the essays are fundamental to their project: offering a unified if unsystematic account of private liberty. The eleven pieces contained in the work are "Discourses," logical but casually conversational treatises, yet they are discourses written in a particular manner, "by way of Essays, in Verse and Prose." Montaigne's influence ensured that the word "essays" implied incompleteness or "fragments of . . . conceits," as Bacon puts it, and that they were associated with a retired life dedicated to the examination of one's private "conditions and humours."[185] Cowley modifies the form by augmenting each prose essay with a collection of poems, including paraphrases of classical poems and original lyrics that often reproduce the argument and the structure of the prose essay. The paraphrases of poems by Martial, Virgil, and Horace seem to serve the same function as the extensive footnotes that Cowley includes in other works: they provide a record of the expansive reading that led to his principles and lend authority to his arguments by producing the appearance of a poetic consensus about the wisdom of the retired life. But Cowley's insistence on repeating his prose arguments in original poems suggests that the concluding verse serves another function. As he reveals in a final autobiographical essay, Cowley believes that the sound and numerical structure of verse make it more effective and enduring than any prose narrative and that lyric poetry is uniquely adapted to instill the affections and habits that incline one to the private life. Cowley's essays, then, are an experiment in persuasion and an exploration of the link between the lyric mode and a new vision of human happiness through complete dedication to one's own property and person.

Like Jonson, and Herrick and Philips after him, Cowley presents the life of liberty as one that is circumscribed within itself. He announces at the opening of "Of Liberty" that his subject is "private Liberty," and as he sketches his vision of the ideal retired life over the course of his eleven essays, Cowley depicts this form of liberty as a third way, distinct from the public duty of the old aristocratic life and from the business of the new life of trade (*Essays*, 108). Drawing on the same Roman satirical and Stoical traditions that inspired the couplet satirists and Jonson, Cowley catalogues the various ways in which the "great Dealers in this world," who may be divided into "the Ambitious, the Covetous, and the Voluptuous[,] . . . sell themselves to be Slaves" (*Essays*, 109). He dedicates the majority of the essay to the ambitious man, using his dialectic style to address the arguments of imaginary interlocutors who insist that the pursuit of greatness can be reconciled with virtue and liberty. Those who endeavor to navigate the "narrow, thorney, and little-trodden paths" to greatness by "vertuous industry" may be able to retain their "Honesty," he insists, but not their "Liberty" (*Essays*, 113–14). He argues that the qualities necessary for such a laborious ascent are by definition low: "Thou'rt careful, frugal, painful; we commend a Servant so, but not a Friend" (*Essays*, 114). By the late seventeenth century, "honesty" had largely lost its association with the noble "honor" and was instead used to describe the plain, humble virtue of the bourgeoisie.[186] Cowley uses the term in the condescending manner Joshua Scodel and William Empson both describe in their detailed analyses of the word, that is, to imply that an individual lacked "some more distinguished virtue" or, as Empson puts it, "could not be praised for anything else."[187] Cowley's disdain for honest industry not only challenges the emerging ethical principles of an increasingly commercial England but distinguishes his vision of the good life from Donne's account of the struggle for truth in "Satire III." Though Cowley's satire of the slavishness of civilized life and his focus on individual liberty is in many ways in line with the radical naturalism of the Elizabethan couplet poets, Cowley follows Jonson in viewing liberty as a static rather than a wandering virtue, a result of leisure rather than of action.

Cowley's rejection of the supposed virtues of those who strive does not, however, amount to a ratification of the aristocratic life. Those at the top of the hierarchy are equally alienated from liberty. From morning until night, the "Great man" is "besieged by two or three hundred Suitors," and there is "alwais, and every where, some restraint upon him. He's guarded with Crowds, and shackled with Formalities" (*Essays*, 115–17). In a biting passage that mocks the pretensions of the great man's table, Cowley goes so far as to deflate the ceremonies of hospitality that were seen as the markers of gentlemanly and aristocratic beneficence: "But every body pays him great respect, everybody commends his Meat, that is, his Mony; every body admires the exquisite dressing & ordering of it, that is, his Clark of the kitchin, or his Cook; every body loves his Hospitality, that is, his Vanity" (*Essays*, 116). Pulling away the veil that separated the banquet hall from the kitchen, Cowley reveals that money and labor are the foundations of hospitality as they are of professions typically considered "mean" (*Essays*, 117). Cowley wonders why the "honest In-keeper" should be considered meaner than this great man who keeps a magnificent table since "both sell, though for different things, the one for plain Mony, the other for I know not what Jewels, whose value is in Custom and in Fancy" (*Essays*,

116–17). In dismissing hospitality as a mercantile and vain pursuit, Cowley takes on one of the most sanctified symbols not only of the English gentry and aristocracy but of European political life more generally. Moreover, Cowley's criticism of the great man's table signals a decided break from poetic convention, not only from the Jonsonian country house tradition of celebrating conviviality and the open table but from the entire epic tradition, in which the host's table is depicted as the foundation of civilized life, and its defilement—as in *Beowulf* or the *Odyssey*, for example—is the original sin that initiates heroic action.[188] Cowley replaces the open table with the circumscribed plot of ground, holding up privacy and property as the only foundations of a contented life.

In "Of My self," the autobiographical essay that concludes his collection and his career as a writer, Cowley draws together the form and the argument of his essays by linking his pursuit of private liberty with his proclivity for verse. He begins the account of himself by tracing back his distaste for the public life to his earliest memories:

> As far as my Memory can return back into my past Life, before I knew, or was capable of guessing what the world, or glories, or business of it were, the natural affections of my soul gave me a secret bent of aversion from them, as some Plants are said to turn away from others, by an Antipathy imperceptible to themselves, and inscrutable to mans Understanding. Even when I was a very young Boy at School, instead of running about on Holy-daies, and playing with my fellows; I was wont to steal from them, and walk into the fields, either alone with a Book, or with some one Companion, if I could find any of the same temper. (*Essays*, 216)

In one of the few extended treatments of Cowley's essays, Alan De Gooyer calls attention to the distinctiveness and the prescience of Cowley's moral argument in this autobiographical essay. He argues that Cowley anticipates "new modes of interiority" that emphasized the insufficiency of reason as a basis for ethics, which must instead be grounded on natural affection.[189] But Cowley's account of the natural affections of his soul builds on existing royalist interest in those aspects of the human psyche that overreach reason or, in Cowley's phrase, are "inscrutable to mans Understanding." Cowley also represents the transcendent power of natural affections at the level of the structure of the essays themselves. Just as each individual essay moves from the linear argumentation of prose to the charming order of verse, the essays as a whole move from logic to affection, beginning with a definition of liberty and concluding with stories of Cowley's early childhood. Cowley presents the prerational affections of his youth as absolutely fundamental to the life of seclusion that he has depicted as the happiest throughout the essays. And he makes the case that these affections are best formed by an early exposure to the charms of verse.

After offering a sample of an ode written when he was thirteen as evidence of his early attachment to "Books" over "Business," Cowley wonders whether "perhaps" it was the "immature and immoderate love" of poets that "stampt first, or rather engraved these Characters in me: they were like the Letters cut into the Bark of a young Tree, which with the Tree still grow proportionally" (*Essays*, 218). With his second botanical metaphor, Cowley modifies his account of his dedication to retirement, attributing it to an extrinsic rather than an intrinsic cause. While a few sentences before he likened his aversion to the world and its business to the inscrutable natural antipathies of a plant, here he describes his proclivity for solitary life as the product of art forcefully imposing itself on nature, "stamp[ing]" and "engrav[ing]" characters on the tree that will never be effaced, but enlarged, as the tree grows.

Not content to conclude his intellectual origin story by attributing his affection for seclusion to the classical poets, Cowley goes further back and offers yet another anecdote of his youth to explain how his love of verse began (I quote at length once more since the particular manner of telling the story is inseparable from the argument of Cowley's essays):

> I believe I can tell the particular little chance that filled my head first with such Chimes of Verse, as have never since left ringing there: For I remember when I began to read, and to take some pleasure in it, there was wont to lie in my Mothers Parlour (I know not by what accident, for she her self never in her life read any Book but of Devotion) but there was wont to lie *Spencers* Works; this I happen'd to fall upon, and was infinitely delighted with the Stories of the Knights, and Giants, and Monsters, and brave Houses, which I found every where there: (Tho' my Understanding had little to do with all this) and by degrees with the tinckling of the Rhyme and Dance of the Numbers, so that I think I had read him all over before I was twelve years old, and was thus made a Poet as irremediably as a Child is made an Eunuch. (*Essays*, 218)

By situating his poetic origin story in a transitional moment on the verge of adolescence, Cowley gives primacy to the delightful and enchanting aspects of verse.[190] Admitting that his understanding had little to do with his admiration for *The Faerie Queene*, Cowley attributes his calling as a poet to the thrills of Spenser's tales of romance and chivalry and, even more, to the charming sounds of Spenser's verses, the "tinckling of the Rhyme" and the stately "Dance of the Numbers." Even more than Daniel, he embraces Campion's charge that rhyme is a "childish titillation."[191] Rhyme's ability to appeal to the affections before the understanding is fully formed gives it the power to shape minds and make poets. Like Beaumont, Cowley connects the "Chime" of rhyme with its ability to linger in the mind, but for Cowley the impression of rhyme is carved in wood instead of pressed in wax. It does not simply work on the memory, but through the power of habit actually shapes the mind and character of the listener. The chimes have "never since left ringing" in Cowley's head and, more dramatically, they have made him a poet "as irremediably as a Child is made an Eunuch." The unsettling comparison underscores the drastic effects of the features of verse that seem most innocuous and even trivial. Tinkling rhymes and dancing numbers do not simply tickle the ears but transmute the heart as irrevocably as castration does the body. And with this decisive metaphor Cowley concludes his account of the formation of his mind. The next sentence begins a new chapter of his life, "With these affections of mind, and my heart wholly set upon Letters, I went to the University," and the remainder of the essay explains how "that violent Publick storm" alienated him from his deepest affections for two decades (*Essays*, 218). Cowley's autobiographical narrative depicts politics and war, the stuff of epic, as a mere interruption and a distraction from his pursuit of seclusion and leisure. For Cowley, this longing for private life is rooted in the sound of verse. The tinkling rhymes and dancing numbers formed his affections and decided his fate before he was old enough to make a rational choice.

In the final strophe of his "Ode. Upon Liberty," which concludes the essay "Of Liberty," Cowley expands on his own association of life and verse by turning Ben Jonson's loose comparison between the upright lives of Cary and Morison and the measure, numbers, and syllables of verse into a full-fledged conceit:

> If Life should a well-order'd Poem be
> (In which he only hits the white
> Who joyns true Profit with the best Delight)
> The more Heroique strain let others take,
> Mine the Pindarique way I'le make.
> The Matter shall be Grave, the Numbers loose and free.
> It shall not keep one setled pace of Time,
> In the same Tune it shall not always Chime,
> Nor shall each day just to his Neighbour Rhime,
> A thousand Liberties it shall dispense,
> And yet shall mannage all without offence;
> Or to the sweetness of the Sound, or greatness of the Sence.
> (*Essays*, 128)

Cowley's declaration that he will take "A thousand Liberties" with rhyme and meter, leaving his "Numbers loose and free," seems to align with Donne and Marston's rejection of measure and burdensome "riming lawes" in favor of a "free-bred poesie" that allowed room for "boundless discursive apprehension."[192] Indeed, David Trotter has read the irregularity of Cowley's Pindaric odes as representative of his adherence to Hobbes's "radical psychology" in which the succession of thoughts is often arbitrary or loosely associative, and in a stunning reading of the odes Nathaniel Stogdill has argued that the formlessness and the digressions of Cowley's Pindarics "frustrate attempts to stabilize meaning, challenging the utility of reason as a means of making sense of the shifting multiplicities of Interregnum culture."[193] Cowley certainly saw his Pindaric experiment as a way of testing poetic and intellectual laws. Like the Elizabethan couplet poets, Cowley willingly embraces rhyme while identifying metrical regularity, or the "servile Law of . . . settled pace," as he puts it in "The Resurrection," as an instrument of poetic tyranny.[194] Indeed, though he occasionally intersperses triplets or rhymes at a distance in order to break up the regular rhyme scheme of a strophe, Cowley's ode is by and large a couplet poem. Yet, for all these resemblances to the young Elizabethans, Cowley's aim in rejecting settled pace is distinct from, and perhaps even antithetical to, that of Donne and Marston.

Cowley's declared resolution to take the "Pindarique way" in verse and life signals that the "Ode. Upon Liberty" extends the formal project of Cowley's *Pindarique Odes Written in the Style & Maner of the Odes of Pindar*, first published in his 1656 collection of poems. In the preface to these odes, Cowley explains that his aim is not so much to "let the Reader know precisely what [Pindar] spoke, as what was his *way* and *manner* of speaking; which has not been yet (that I know of) introduced into *English*)" (*Essays*, 20). The essence of Pindar's way and manner, Cowley maintains, is the "Musick of his *Numbers*, which sometimes (especially in *Songs* and *Odes*) almost without any thing else, makes an excellent *Poet*" (*Essays*, 18). Since our ears are "strangers" to Pindaric numbers, he endeavors to dress them in "an English habit" by inventing a new form of English verse that rhymes but does not adhere to a single metrical scheme (*Essays*, 18, 20). Cowley's irregularity in his odes, then, is not a Donne-like attempt to elevate reason over measure but an effort to imitate a rapturous Pindaric music that is still based on "*Numbers*," however strange and mysterious they may be. In both his translations and his imitations of Pindar, Cowley continues to associate the Greek lyricist with a sublime wildness that imitates a higher harmony.[195]

It is this kind of transcendent lyric irregularity that Cowley celebrates throughout the "Ode. Upon Liberty" rather than the irregularity of intellectual struggle that Donne represents in "Satire III." Cowley begins the strophe by accepting the Jonsonian premise that life should in fact be a "well-order'd Poem" (*Essays*, 128). And he does not, like Donne, insist that liberty of thought requires one to sacrifice measure or poetic sweetness. Equally intent on upholding both halves of the Horatian injunction to join "true Profit with the best Delight," he promises that the liberties he takes with rhyme and meter will give no "offence"

> Or to the sweetness of the Sound, or greatness of the Sence. (*Essays*, 128)

Though the fourteen-syllable line exceeds any other in the poem and does not adhere to a strict iambic pattern, the line nevertheless has a strict internal order. The syntactical and metrical parallelism between the two halves of the line, in combination with Cowley's use of alliteration to bridge the caesura, reinforces the idea that sound and sense not only have equal weight, but are actually parallels or analogues of one another. The balance of the line, which is characteristic of this poem and of all of Cowley's odes in the "Pindarick way," signals his distance from the rough, jolting verse of Elizabethan poets and his affinity for Jonson's measured syntax. Whereas Donne and Marston used irregularity to disrupt the expected sweetness and orderliness of verse, Cowley maintains that his liberties actually contribute to the sweet sound and ordered structure of his ode. Indeed, Cowley does quite the opposite of trying to disrupt his reader with harsh irregularity; as Thomas Ward has argued, Cowley imagines a collaboration with a skilled reader with "active prosodic discernment" in order to "realiz[e the] poetic meter."[196] In his preface, Cowley insists that the numbers may "*seem* harsh and uncouth" but only "if the just measures and cadencies be not observed in the pronunciation. So that almost all their *Sweetness* and *Numerosity* (which is to be found in the roughest, if rightly repeated) lies in a manner wholly at the *Mercy* of the *Reader*."[197] Measure and harmony in Cowley's odes are mysterious, demanding, and dependent on the labors of careful readers, but they are nonetheless worth pursuing since sweetness and numerosity are central to poetry's purpose. Cowley rejects facile harmony in his Pindarics but not the pursuit of a more strenuous sonic concord.

This dedication to enhancing the sweet sounds of verse through irregularity is visible in Cowley's treatment of the couplet in this strophe. When he declares that his life

> shall not keep one setled pace of Time,
> In the same Tune it shall not always Chime,
> Nor shall each day just to his Neighbour Rhime,

he appears to turn away from midcentury theories of verse that venerated the charming sound of the couplet's end rhymes and its power to linger in the mind (*Essays*, 128). But, upon closer inspection, it becomes apparent that Cowley is not opposed to the chime of rhyme itself but to the obligation to rhyme repeatedly "in the same Tune." The vague musical word could describe any aspect of verse—the meter, rhyme scheme, line length, or all three together—but Cowley's poetic practice demonstrates that his rejection of uniformity of tune does not entail a repudiation of rhyme. Indeed, the primary liberty that Cowley takes with rhyme is not to limit but to enhance the effects of rhyme's chime by extending couplets into triplets as he does here.[198] And, for all the metrical looseness of his odes, Cowley consistently works to make his rhymes more prominent by pausing at the end of the line and using precise, monosyllabic rhymes.

By combining the wildness of Pindaric numbers with the charming ring of rhyme, Cowley hopes to produce a higher music that transcends reason but that also feels familiar and homely, Pindar in an "English habit" (*Essays*, 20).

For, the intended effect of these soaring flights of lyric poetry, and of his experiment with persuasion in the essays as whole, is to convince himself and his listeners that they should content themselves with the liberty that comes from a life dedicated to private ties. In many ways, Cowley's "last Pieces," written in the years of retreat leading up to his death in July 1667, represent the culmination of the long and gradual lyricization of English verse that occurred over the course of the seventeenth century.[199] Cowley was buried alongside Chaucer and Spenser in Westminster Abbey on August 3, 1667, under a monument styling him *"Anglorum Pindarus, Flaccus, Maro, Deliciae, Decus, Desiderium aevi sui,"* the Pindar, Horace, and Virgil of the English, the darling, glory, and desire of his age.[200] On August 31, Royal Society fellow John Beale wondered in a letter to John Evelyn whether Milton could be persuaded to take Cowley's place: "Since we have lost Cowley, I wish we had a way to engage Milton upon some honest argument. For though he be old & blind, he wilbe doing mischiefe if he be not engagd better, & he was long agoe an excellent Pindariste: Good at all, But best at that straine, & too full of ye Devill."[201] Beale seems not to have known that less than two weeks before Samuel Symmons had entered "a booke or copie intituled *Paradise lost A Poem in Tenne bookes* by J.M." into the Stationers' Register.[202] Too full of the devil indeed! As it turned out, Beale was disappointed with Milton's performance in *Paradise Lost*, arguing that Milton's "first Inspirations" were "purer & brighter" than his epic, but he did appreciate the fact that without the "check of rhyme" Milton is able to overgo even the blank verse dramatists in "the measure of this flowing grace."[203] While Beale saw in Milton's youthful verse the potential to carry on the irregular Pindaric sublimity of Cowley, Milton inverted Cowley's Pindarics in his heroic blank verse, exchanging Cowley's rhymed but irregular numbers for the rhymeless but regular measures of *Paradise Lost*. Beale appreciated the combination of free flow and measure in Milton's prosody, but he was affronted by what he saw as the poem's "plea for Original right."[204] Milton, however, saw his poetical and political pleas as inseparable: his return to ancient measure was fundamental to his case for original right and against customary affection.

CHAPTER FIVE

Milton and the Known Rules of Ancient Liberty

DURING HIS TIME AT CAMBRIDGE (Lewalski posits it was at the end of his third year, in 1628) Milton was tasked with offering a brief Latin prelude to a daylong disputation on the music of the spheres in the public schools.[1] In defending the music of the spheres and its advocates Pythagoras and Plato, Milton chides their "aemulus & perpetuus Calumniator" Aristotle for his literal-minded debunking of the myth.[2] In a clever turn, Milton pulls back the curtain of Aristotelian cosmology and claims that music must be the motive force behind its order: "I can scarcely believe that your intelligences could have borne that sedentary labor of rotating the heavens for so many ages if that ineffable song of the stars had not prevented them from departing and had not swayed them to delay through the drawing out of harmonies [*modulationes delinimento*]. Truly if you deprived heaven of that [harmony], you would plainly give over those beautiful little intelligences and ministering gods to drudgery [*in Pistrinum*] and damn them to the grinding mill."[3] While Milton's depiction of weary celestial agents begrudgingly performing their Aristotelian tasks is mostly intended to elicit learned laughter, it contains an intriguing idea to which Milton would return throughout his career: the mere addition of song can prevent the maintenance of order from being servile drudgery. For the music of the spheres is a Pythagorean way of explaining, as Milton argues at the beginning of the prolusion, "amicissimos orbium complexus," the most loving embraces of the spheres.[4] M.N.K. Mander has pointed out the humor of the fact that Milton purports to explain the meaning behind the Pythagorean metaphor of the music of the spheres but does so by offering yet another metaphor.[5] But what both metaphors do—and what Milton charges Aristotle with failing to do—is make order voluntary and animated. The dancing or embracing orbs of Pythagoras are eager participants in a divine pattern, while Aristotle's soundless intelligences are simply acting on orders from above.

Milton returned insistently to the "measur'd motion" of celestial harmony in his early verse because it offered him a way of reconciling principles of measure and freedom that he held equally dear and that he was struggling to balance in his verse.[6] And until *Paradise Lost*, rhyme was an essential component of this pursuit of a flexible and harmonious measure. This chapter endeavors to take a fresh look at Milton's famous renunciation of rhyme by reading his turn to blank verse in light of both the long history of debate about the politics of rhyme and Milton's career-long struggle with rhyme. Although in his preface to *Paradise Lost* Milton depicts himself as a poetic revolutionary offering the first example in English of ancient poetic liberty, he draws on arguments that Donne, Hall, and Marston had marshalled decades before in defense of the libertine couplet. In fact, Milton's understanding of poetic liberty is in many ways less radical and less disruptive than that of his Elizabethan predecessors.[7] In his effort to craft a style distinct from the affective lyrics of the Royalists, Milton fuses the metrical discipline of Jonson with the flowing enjambment of Donne. The result is a peculiarly Miltonic prosodic style in which dedication to liberty of expression is accompanied by a painstaking attention to the rules of poetic measure.

In order to understand how Milton's poetic style was shaped by his engagement with royalist poetic theory, it is useful to attend to contemporary reactions to the dramatic political language contained in the preface to *Paradise Lost*. Though critics and defenders of Milton's blank verse referred to the note throughout the Restoration, Milton's most dogged interlocutor on questions of rhyme was John Dryden.[8] In his 1693 preface to an edition of Juvenal's satires, Dryden offers a revealing—if decidedly unsympathetic—interpretation of Milton's turn to blank verse. The nominal subject of the preface is the theory of satire, but, knowing that this is the "last time [he] will commit the Crime of Prefaces; or trouble the World with [his] Notions of any thing that relates to Verse," Dryden cannot resist embarking on a "digression from Satire to Heroique Poetry" in which he observes the "Failings of many great Wits amongst the Moderns, who have attempted to write an *Epique* Poem."[9] The chief among them, unsurprisingly, is "Mr. *Milton*," whom Dryden begrudgingly acknowledges "we all admire with so much Justice." After criticizing Milton for his tragic subject and his obsolete words, Dryden concludes with a final sally in the now decades-old battle over rhyme:

> Neither will I Justifie *Milton* for his Blank Verse, tho' I may excuse him, by the Example of *Hannibal Caro*, and other *Italians*, who have us'd it: For whatever Causes he alledges for the abolishing of Rhyme (which I have not now the leisure to examine) his own particular Reason is

plainly this, that Rhyme was not his Talent; he had neither the Ease of doing it, nor the Graces of it; which is manifest in his *Juvenilia*, or Verses written in his Youth: Where his Rhyme is always constrain'd and forc'd, and comes hardly from him at an Age when the Soul is most pliant; and the Passion of Love, makes almost every Man a Rhymer, tho' not a Poet.[10]

Dryden dismisses Milton's lofty arguments about the wider import of his prosodic decision as elaborate covers for a plain matter of poetic skill: Milton, he claims, simply did not have the "Talent" for rhyme. Though the justness of Dryden's assessment of Milton's rhymed juvenilia is certainly debatable, the particular manner in which Dryden attacks Milton's prowess as a rhymer is revealing. He depicts Milton's poetic deficiency as a symptom of a more significant flaw in Milton's character and understanding of verse. Just as Cowley traces back the "natural affections of [his] soul" to a youthful encounter with Spenser's "tinckling" rhymes, Dryden looks to Milton's youth for signs of his poetical disposition (*Essays*, 216). To Dryden's critical eye, the lines of Milton's juvenilia reveal that the poet's lack of ease and grace in rhyming is a congenital defect. Perhaps obliquely alluding to Milton's youthful declarations of celibacy, Dryden suggests that at an age when "almost every Man" is made a "Rhymer" by the first stirrings of the "Passion of Love," only a cold and unyielding soul like Milton's could produce such strained rhymes. He counters Milton's argument that rhyme is a modern affectation, favored only by poets who are "carried away by custom," by linking rhyme with the earliest and most natural human affections (*CPMP*, 210). Milton erroneously claimed that rhyme acts as "vexation, hindrance, and constraint" to the poet (*CPMP*, 210). Rather, cold poets like Milton produce "constrain'd and forc'd" rhymes. In associating Milton's failings as a rhymer with his estrangement from the natural passions of youth, Dryden depicts rhyme as an inherent and elemental component of verse instead of an ornamental appendage or "tag" that poets hang on the end of the line.[11] The chime of rhyme does not simply appeal to deep-rooted natural affections; it is a spontaneous outpouring of those affections into language.

Dryden's assessment of Milton's abilities as a rhymer reveals that the argument over rhyme is, at least in part, an argument over the role that the passions should play in verse. Despite Dryden's suggestion that Milton was constitutionally incapable of both passion and rhyme, Milton maintained throughout his career that poetry is powerful and laudable precisely because it is "more simple, sensuous, and passionate" than prose.[12] But from his youthful lyrics to *Samson Agonistes*, Milton works to distinguish the passion of his verse from the Anacreontic ecstasies celebrated by poets like Herrick. In "Elegia sexta," which he sent to Charles Diodati in 1629, he acknowledges that wine and merriment can fuel verse making: "Song loves Bacchus and Bacchus loves songs" (*CPMP*, 14). Yet he labors to separate himself and his epic ambitions from

those who write light elegy (*Elegia levis*) (*CPMP*, 49). Elegiac writers, led by a
host of gods associated with love and revelry—Liber, Erato, Ceres, Venus, and
Cupid—are permitted to partake of lavish banquets (*convivia larga*) and old
wine (*veteri . . . mero*) (*CPMP*, 51, 53, 54). The epic poet who wishes to sing of
wars and heroes, in contrast, must drink only the purest water, hold to the
most rigid moral laws, and remain completely chaste (*CPMP*, 55–64). Though
in "Elegia sexta" Milton presents the elegiac mode, with its celebrations of wine
and women, as a viable, if inferior, poetic path, in *The Reason of Church-
government* he expresses utter disdain for poetry "rays'd from the heat of youth,
or the vapours of wine, like that which flows at wast from the pen of some
vulgar Amorist, or the trencher fury of a riming parasite."[13] With the memo-
rable phrase "trencher fury," Milton ridicules the royalist effort to link high and
low, the transcendent powers of verse with the sensual pleasures of the table.
He charges that verse that flows from transitory passions for wine and women
can never transcend its sensual origins. Such poets may pretend to divine
furor, but their fury is a tempest in a teapot—or rather, in a trencher. It is as
shallow and fleeting as the trenchers of food and flagons of wine that feed their
muses. When the food provided by their hosts dries up and youthful heat no
longer flows in their veins, such parasites cease to rhyme. Milton agrees with
Dryden that the passion of love makes almost every man a rhymer in his youth,
but even in his youth he scorns poetry that flows naturally from such sensual
delights in favor of pursuing a more laborious but, he believes, ultimately more
rewarding poetic path.

Sacred and Home-Felt Delight:
Comus and the Charms of Rhyme

Milton's early effort to distinguish his austere, water-drinking muse from the
trencher fury of rhyming parasites did not immediately lead him to reject
rhyme. Indeed, his 1645 volume *Poems of Mr. John Milton*, like Jonson's *The
Forrest* and the formally and thematically heterogenous royalist volumes it
inspired, displays Milton's mastery of a variety of rhymed forms, from the
rhyme royal introduction to "On the Morning of Christ's Nativity" to the com-
plex and inventive rhyme patterns of "Arcades" and "Lycidas."[14] Though the
formal variety of the volume is undeniable, two forms dominate Milton's
youthful experiments: Italian sonnets and the tetrameter and pentameter
couplets that were also favored by Milton's royalist contemporaries. I will turn
to Milton's enduring interest in the Italian sonnet in the third section of this
chapter, but I would like to begin with the Miltonic couplet. Many of the cou-
plet poems in the 1645 volume—including "Epitaph on the Marchioness of
Winchester," "Song. On May Morning," "On the University Carrier," and "An-
other on the Same"—are some of the least discussed poems in Milton's corpus
and are easy to dismiss as occasional poems dashed off without much thought

during his years at Cambridge. But in "L'Allegro," "Il Penseroso," and the songs of *A Masque Presented at Ludlow Castle*, Milton engages seriously with the Jonsonian couplet and the ways it had been reinterpreted by the sons of Ben. The *Masque* in particular, placed in the final position in the 1645 volume, looks back over the collection and attempts to reckon with the powerful charms of rhyme.

The moment of first contact between Comus and the Lady encapsulates the poetic and moral contest that is the central drama of Milton's masque. Their initial encounter is based on the effects of sound as the Lady's harmonious sounds twice drive out wayward sounds associated with Comus and his mother.[15] When the Lady first enters, Comus has just bid his crew to "knit hands, and beat the ground, / In a light fantastic round" (*Masque*, 143–44).[16] But when he "feel[s] the different pace, / Of some chaste footing" approaching, he hurriedly orders his associates to "Break off, break off" their light "*Measure*" and hide themselves so that he can set to work on the Lady with his "charms" (*Masque*, 145–46, 145, 150). The idea that Comus can discern the Lady's character by her pace recalls Jonson's belief that the gait confesses the temperament of the individual. In fact, this is the second instance in the masque in which character is discerned through gait. When Comus enters the scene just moments before, the Attendant Spirit breaks off his own speech and hides himself because he "hear[s] the tread / Of hateful steps" (*Masque*, 90–92).[17] Comus subsequently attempts to disrupt this continuity between inward state and outward sign by using his charms to deceive the lady with "blear illusion" and "false presentments" (*Masque*, 155, 156). But here he himself admits that sound is a reliable indicator of character, that the even pace of a virtuous lady can be distinguished from the primitive ground beating of his riotous crew.

Comus's initial judgment about the chaste sound of the Lady's step is reinforced in the subsequent scene when he overhears the Lady's song to Echo. Her song, which begins with an interwoven rhyme scheme that is then resolved into couplets, reminds Comus of his original childhood encounter with music: hearing the heady songs of his "mother *Circe* with the Sirens three" (*Masque*, 253).[18] But he immediately distinguishes this primitive experience with song from the "Divine enchanting ravishment" of the Lady's rhymes (*Masque*, 245).[19] Comus is not capable of making distinctions about the nature of the music or the character of its makers, but he has a visceral understanding that the two songs have very different effects on his mind.[20] His mother's songs, like the "Potent herbs and baleful drugs" she prepares for unwitting visitors to her island, are pleasurable—in fact, they have the power to "take the prison'd soul, / And lap it in *Elysium*" (*Masque*, 255, 256–57). And "Yet," Comus seems to recognize for the first time, the delight of Circe's songs was enervating: it "lull'd the sense" "in pleasing slumber" and "in sweet madness robb'd it of itself" (*Masque*, 261, 261, 261, 262). In contrast, the Lady's song offers Comus an unfamiliar kind of pleasure, a "sacred and home-felt delight" and "sober

certainty of waking bliss" (*Masque*, 263, 264). Comus's pair of adjectives, "sa-
cred and home-felt," suggests that like his royalist contemporaries and his Ro-
mantic descendants, Milton believed that the transcendent appeals of verse
allowed it to unite what Wordsworth would later call the "kindred points of
heaven and home."[21] But unlike Cowley and Wordsworth, who hold up their
childhood experiences as the origins of their affinities for verse, Milton sug-
gests that an appreciation for the highest kind of verse requires a definitive
break from primitive experience. Comus first encounters delight that is "home-
felt"—a Miltonic coinage meaning felt intimately and intensely, to one's very
core—at the precise moment when he feels alienated from his mother and his
natural home on Circe's island.[22] The adjective registers a paradox in Milton's
understanding not only of verse, but of postlapsarian experience more gener-
ally. Building on a paradox that runs through the Hebraic and Christian tradi-
tion from Abraham's calling to leave his "country," "kindred," and "father's
house" to Jesus's declaration that he came to "set a man at variance against his
father, and the daughter against her mother," Milton repeatedly suggests that
the faithful must leave home in order to find it (Genesis 12:1, Matthew 10:35).
This paradox is at the heart of Milton's disagreement with royalist poetic the-
ory. Where the royalist poets endeavor to use the transcendent power of verse
to strengthen affective bonds to hearth and home, here Milton uses the sacred
delights of verse to shake loose more primitive desires in Comus.

Though Milton's deceptive sorcerer easily distinguishes between the Lady's
song and his mother's, the task is more difficult for the upright protagonists in
Milton's masque since Comus's charms upset the straightforward correlation
between sound and character. Milton dramatizes the struggle to distinguish
sacred and sensual verse by presenting Comus as a double of the Attendant
Spirit and, later, of the river nymph Sabrina. Both Comus and the Attendant
Spirit use their supernatural powers to disguise themselves as humble labor-
ers—the Attendant Spirit presents himself to the brothers "*habited like*" their
"father's Shepherd" Thyrsis, and Comus uses magic dust to make himself "ap-
pear some harmless Villager / Whom thrift keeps up about his Country gear"
(*Masque*, 489, 493, 167–68). The layers of disguises and the superficial resem-
blances between the two supernatural creatures recalls Spenser's tendency to
populate his romance with pairs of true and false versions of characters. And,
like the "sage and serious poet Spenser," Milton uses this doubling to encourage
the "warfaring Christian" to be to be vigilant since good and evil are interwoven
"in so many cunning resemblances hardly to be discern'd."[23]

More important than the physical resemblances between Comus and the
Attendant Spirit are the formal resemblances between their songs. Victoria
Kahn draws attention to the fact that Sabrina and Comus "speak the same
quadrimeter verse," arguing that the metrical similarities between these two
"creatures of *virtù*" underscore the fact that "rhetoric is a thing indifferent that
can be used well or badly."[24] The songs of Comus, the Attendant Spirit, and

Sabrina are all written in what I have described elsewhere as Anacreontic couplets—couplets of seven or eight syllables that were often used to render Anacreon's seven-syllable lines or to express sentiments associated with the Greek lyricist but that were also used in drama for the charms of supernatural creature. Kahn hints at this when she identifies Comus's songs as the "cadences of Shakespeare's Puck and Ariel."[25] Milton uses the short couplet in his masque much as Herrick would later use it in *Hesperides*: to mark verse at its most affective and effective.

Though the blank verse debates between the younger and elder brother and the Lady and Comus constitute the central drama of the masque and seem to represent the kind of rational exercise Milton values most, both result in a standstill. All the rhymed verse in the play, in contrast, moves listeners to immediate feeling and action: Comus's opening rhymes call the darker denizens of the forest to revelry, the Lady's echo song enchants Comus, the Attendant Spirit's verses call up Sabrina from the waters of the Severn, and Sabrina's charms undo the "charmed band" and unglue the Lady from her seat (*Masque*, 904). By framing his masque with the couplet songs of Comus and the benevolent spirits, Milton reinforces the idea that although rhyme's charm is transcendently powerful, more often than not it produces "a charm of powerful trouble."[26]

With its depiction of charms and countercharms, Milton's masque raises questions about the purpose of rhyme that it does not resolve. Comus's immediate recognition of the Lady's chaste step and of the difference between his mother's songs and the Lady's suggests that there is some connection between form and character, but the remainder of the play unsettles Jonsonian principles of personal style by showing how easy it is for Comus to imitate the harmonies of the upright. Though the 1645 volume ends with this skepticism about how to distinguish the proper use of rhyme from its abuse, other poems in the volume reveal that Milton continued to explore whether he could shape the binding and charming powers of rhyme to fit his understanding of devout verse making.

Repairing Rhymes in "Lycidas"

Comus was written and performed in 1634, two years after Milton retired to his parents' house in Hammersmith in 1632.[27] For three years after the performance of his *Masque*, Milton wrote no poetry, or at least no poetry that survives.[28] Then, in 1637, just a year before his six-year period of study came to an end when he went abroad, Milton broke his poetic silence with "Lycidas." The poem makes it abundantly clear that one of the problems Milton was meditating on during his years of study was the problem of rhyme's charms raised in the *Masque*. In "Lycidas," Milton responds to his own misgivings with a stunning display of the harmonious and logical uses of the charming bands of rhyme. Ants Oras and F. T. Prince have unraveled some of the elaborate principles of Milton's rhyme in "Lycidas" and have made it clear that Milton draws extensively—if innovatively—on the Italian canzone and madrigal traditions.[29] Prince draws out the ways in which Milton plays the "rhetoric of rhyme" with and against "the more usual rhetoric of sentence structure."[30] He draws particular attention to Milton's use of the Italian *chiave*, a rhyme that links lines in different syntactic units, and to the way that Milton's six-syllable lines always rhyme with a prior line, usually forming a couplet with the previous line.[31] It is noteworthy that these are both prominent features of Spenser's *Epithalamion* and *Prothalamion*. David Norbrook has noted that Edward King died in the same year as Ben Jonson and that Milton remained silent about the death of the poet as he crafted his ode for King.[32] It is telling that Milton overleaps Jonson's couplets in order to look back to the elaborate rhyming of Spenser and the Italian poets of the sixteenth century.[33] But Norbrook may go too far in arguing that the aim of Milton's complex rhymes in "Lycidas" is to build up "expectations of formal completion which are then disrupted" and to expose all attempts at ritual and closure "as a vain attempt to obscure the truth by specious beauty."[34] The poem certainly disrupts specious rituals and facile closure, but it endeavors to replace them with what Milton sees as loftier and more rational links.

As the biblical echo in the first line of "Lycidas" suggests, the poem is undoubtedly an attempt to reveal the truth through disruption. The opening phrase "Yet once more" echoes a verse in Hebrews that interprets an apocalyptic passage from Haggai: "but now he hath promised, saying, Yet once more I shake not the earth only, but also heaven. And this word, Yet once more, signifieth the removing of those things that are shaken, as of things that are made, that those things which cannot be shaken may remain" (Hebrews 12:26–27; see also Haggai 2:6). "Lycidas" shakes the earth, but it is in order to see what solid things remain unshaken. The first line of the poem is one of the ten supposedly unrhymed lines that John Crowe Ransom saw as "a gesture of [Milton's] rebellion against the formalism of his art," of his "lordly contempt for [poetry's] tedious formalities."[35] In fact, as Joseph Wittreich observed in a 1969 article, when the rhyme scheme of the whole poem is considered (and not just of a single paragraph), the opening line, "Yet once more, O ye laurels, and once more," is not an unrhymed gesture of rebellion but the beginning of a chain of rhymes that links together the poem and marks some of its most striking attempts at consolation ("Lycidas," 1).[36]

Indeed, rhyme in "Lycidas" is used not only to disrupt but, in Spenserian fashion, to bind together. When the A rhyme at length returns in line 58, it is in the midst of the darkest moment of the poem, the dismemberment of Orpheus:

What could the Muse herself that *Orpheus* <u>bore</u>,
The Muse herself, for her enchanting son
Whom Universal nature did lament,
When by the rout that made the hideous <u>roar</u>,
His <u>gory</u> visage down the stream was sent,
Down the swift *Hebrus* to the *Lesbian* <u>shore</u>? ("Lycidas," 58–63,
    underlining mine)

Far from bringing order, the rhymes here are almost parodic, driving home the hideous truth that Calliope is powerless to protect even the son she "bore" against the "roar" of the "rout" that ripped his "gory visage" from his body and sent it floating down "to the *Lesbian* shore." Here, Milton's horror at the natural forces of disorder that brought about Edward King's watery death and about the fact that his body has been left to "welter" under the "whelming tide" rather than rest in the grave is fused together with his fear that poetry is bootless against the more nefarious "roar" of human disorder ("Lycidas," 13, 157, 61). If the story—and the rhyme—ended here, "Lycidas" would be an exclusively disruptive poem.

But the *-ore* rhyme appears in two more places in the poem. First, in perhaps the most debated couplet:

But that two-handed engine at the door
Stands ready to smite once, and smite no more. ("Lycidas," 130–31)

Rhyme here is emphatically an instrument of closure. But, like the shaking of "Yet once more," the apocalyptic finality of the two-handed engine is promised rather than realized. Milton wants all the blind mouths to know that the mysterious engine hangs over their heads "ready to smite"—that is, that there is a time of judgment and closure to come—but the promise of a future day of reckoning does not conclude the poem. The continuation of the poem after the apocalyptic couplet does not mean that Milton is repudiating its promise of closure, just that he sees a need, or at least a desire, for more proximate and human consolation.

The penultimate verse paragraph offers several attempts at such a consolation. And it interweaves the *-ore* rhyme that has run through the monody into a complex rhyme scheme:

Weep no <u>more</u>, woeful Shepherds, weep no <u>more</u>,
For *Lycidas* your sorrow is not dead,
Sunk though he be beneath the wat'ry <u>floor</u>,
So sinks the day-star in the Ocean bed,
And yet anon repairs his drooping head,
And tricks his beams, and with new-spangled <u>Ore</u>,
Flames in the forehead of the morning sky:
So *Lycidas*, sunk low, but mounted high,

Through the dear might of him that walk'd the waves,
Where other groves, and other streams along,
With *Nectar* pure his oozy Locks he laves,
And hears the unexpressive nuptial Song,
In the blest Kingdoms meek of joy and love.
There entertain him all the Saints above,
In solemn troops, and sweet Societies
That sing, and singing in their glory move,
And wipe the tears for ever from his eyes.
Now *Lycidas*, the Shepherds weep no <u>more</u>,
Henceforth though art the Genius of the <u>shore</u>,
In thy large recompense, and shalt be good,
To all that wander in that perilous flood. ("Lycidas," 165–85,
    underlining mine)

There are no unrhymed lines in this verse paragraph (and no short lines), and the complex interwoven rhyme scheme resolves itself into a pair of couplets as do many of the stanzas of Spenser's *Epithalamion* and *Prothalamion*.[37] One notable difference between Spenser's odes and Milton's poem, however, is that "Lycidas" does not have the refrains or linking verses that bind together Spenser's variable stanzas.[38] Spenser's repeated turns to the woods in *Epithalamion* are part of his marriage poem's effort to make a community through ceremonial poetry. Milton is not opposed to linking, but, in spite of several lines addressing "the Shepherds" in general, Milton's focus in the final verse paragraph is not on repairing or building a community but on repairing the intellectual despair of the poem. Instead of using sonic links to form a web of social connections as Spenser does in *Epithalamion*, Milton uses rhyme to form a web of intellectual connections: the -*ore* rhymes in the penultimate verse paragraph point to the poem's responses to the woes and fears expressed in the prior -*ore* rhymes. In answer to a disconsolate "Yet once more, O ye laurels, yet once more," we hear, "Weep no more, woeful shepherds, weep no more" ("Lycidas," 1, 165). The promise that Lycidas will be resurrected from "beneath the wat'ry floor" just as the daystar "repairs his drooping head" each morn and rises with "new-spangled Ore" responds to, or rather, "repairs" the Orphic decapitation by that "rout" with the horrifying "roar" ("Lycidas," 167, 169, 170, 169, 61, 61). But the most powerful retort provided by the rhymes is Milton's effort to wrest back the word "shore." In answer to the idea that the ineffectual poet will float helplessly downstream to the "*Lesbian* shore," Milton makes Lycidas the "Genius of the shore" ("Lycidas," 63, 183). This seems like a paltry consolation after the promises of resurrection that precede it, but I think it is a crucial consolation for Milton and the one that allows him to end the mazy poem at last. By calling Lycidas the genius of the shore, Milton responds to two fears that are central to the poem: that Edward King will remain placeless, and that he will be nameless. In spite of the fact that King's body still welters in the ocean and that he was cut off before he could make a name for himself as a poet or a priest, Milton poetically offers the young man "a local habitation and a name."[39] The apocalyptic justice offered in the poem may hinge on the couplet rhyme of "door" and "no more," but the elegy draws to a close with the imaginative act of making the shore—the border between the chaotic, fatal sea and the pastoral land—into a place of comfort where Lycidas will be "good" to all who "wander in that perilous flood" ("Lycidas," 130, 131, 184, 185).[40]

Milton's rhyming in "Lycidas" disrupts many of our expectations, but he is not a reckless rhymer flouting all rules like Marston purported to be in his satires. Rather, he takes the lessons of Spenser's interwoven rhyme schemes several steps further, endeavoring to show how difficult it is to bind up the forces of social and natural disorder that seem to hold sway over the earth. He does seem to think that rhyme has a role to play in the restoration of order. And, after drawing his penultimate stanza to a close with two couplets, he offers a stanza in ottava rima in which he promises that the piping shepherd will proceed "Tomorrow to fresh wood and pastures new" ("Lycidas," 193). This conclusion, with its winking allusions to the Virgilian *rota*, may suggest that in 1637 Milton's planned epic was to be written in ottava rima, in the heroic form of Boiardo, Ariosto, and Tasso, and of their English translators Fairfax and Harington.[41] Ottava rima offers a condensed version of the complex interweaving that at length resolves into closure that Milton plays with in "Lycidas." Indeed, Michael Drayton described it in precisely this way when he related in 1603 that he had rewritten *Barron's Wars* to change it from a seven-line stanza to ottava rima because his seven-line stanza had two couplets and the "often harmonie thereof softned the verse more than the maiestie of the subiect would permit." He concludes that "Ariostos stanza" consisting of "six interwoven, and a couplet in base," has "maiestie, perfection, & soliditie."[42] The choice of ottava rima would have allowed Milton to avoid "often harmonie" while still allowing for some closure. And it would have been very much in line with his tendency to look to Italian and Spenserian models as he made prosodic decisions. He may have had an ottava rima epic in mind as he embarked on his travels to Italy in 1638. Perhaps his discussions during this journey convinced him to follow another Italian epic model—the model of *versi sciolti* or blank verse—or perhaps his decision to write in blank verse was not made until he began *Paradise Lost* two decades later.[43] In the meantime, Milton's epic intentions were interrupted by his entrance into the public arena. When he returned from the continent, he seems to have intended to embark on his epic. He suggests in *Epitaphium Damonis*, which he wrote shortly after his return in 1639, that he had made efforts to write an Arthurian epic, but no evidence about the prosody of the poem remains. Between 1639 and 1641, Milton continued his studies, focusing primarily on English histories, but in May 1641, shortly after the execution of Strafford, he became a prose controversialist when *Of Refor-*

mation was published anonymously.[44] In the prayer that concludes *Of Refor-mation*, Milton predicts that the "Warlike Nation" will be "instructed and inur'd to the Continual practice of truth and righteousness" when "amidst the *Hymns* and *Halleluiahs* of *Saints*, some one" is "heard offering at high *strains* in new and lofty *Measures*."[45] But from 1641 until he began work on *Paradise Lost*, likely around 1658, Milton did not offer at new and lofty measures but instead turned back to the old and middling measures of the Petrarchan sonnet.[46]

Measuring Life: Defining Liberty in the Sonnets

The Trinity manuscript of Milton's poems includes two drafts of a 1633 letter Milton sent to an unknown friend, in which he enclosed his well-known seventh sonnet, "How soone hath Time, the suttle theefe of youth."[47] In the second draft of the letter, Milton introduces his sonnet as "some of my nightward thoughts some while since . . . made up in a Petrarchian stanza."[48] The phrase is intriguing because it acknowledges a gap between thought and verse: Milton describes the thoughts as something that preexisted in his nocturnal mind before they were "made up in" Petrarch's stanza form. But an examination of the first draft of the letter makes the phrase even more fascinating since Milton seems to have revised the verb he used to describe the act of versifying not once, but twice. In the first draft, Milton originally described his thoughts as "made up in a Petrarchian stanza" but then crossed out "made" and replaced it with "pack't." He then crossed out "pack't" as well, presumably because he had decided to return to the word "made" as he does in the second draft.[49] The humbler and less euphonious "pack't up" gives us an almost comical image of Milton bundling up his nightward thoughts into a pack or stuffing them into a trunk so that they can more easily be conveyed to his friend. Milton was likely drawn to the image precisely because (fulfilling Cleanth Brooks's worst fears) it reduces form to a container for thought. For Milton was contending against a seventeenth-century poetic theory that he felt elevated form, sound, and passion above rational engagement with verse. He states firmly in the opening summary of his pedagogical principles in "Of Education" that "language is but the instrument convaying to us things usefull to be known."[50] Like Sidney and other sixteenth-century theorists, Milton insists on a dichotomy between the idea or fore-conceit and the verse itself and elevates the conceit above the language that conveys it. Milton's night-ward thoughts about ripeness and divine providence are the real gift to his friend; Petrarch's stanza is just so much packing material.

But Milton had second thoughts about the packing metaphor. His first—and his final—verb, "made up," connects his sonnet writing with the tradition of the poet as a "maker" who imitates divine creation. Since the divine maker lavished so much attention on formal arrangements, on the measure, number, and weight of the cosmos, they must not be entirely indifferent matters. In the vision of the poet as a maker rather than an idea packer, there is a seed of Milton's later monism. Just as body is on a continuum with spirit, form is on a continuum with thought.[51] But, at this early moment in his poetic career, Milton is unsure whether it is more consonant with his exalted vision of the poetic enterprise to imagine versification as packing or making. The same wavering about the status of form that is visible in Milton's manuscript revisions of his letter can be seen in his sonnets themselves. The "Petrarchian" sonnet was not simply a passing vehicle for Milton's night-ward thoughts about his inward ripeness, but a form to which he returned again and again over the course of three decades. In this section, I explore why Milton repeatedly chose to make up his thoughts in what seems like the quintessential troublesome and modern form and how his Petrarchan experiments reveal his fundamental poetic principles and his ambivalence about rhyme.

Milton wrote his first group of sonnets, one in English and five in Italian, during his final years at Cambridge in the late 1620s. After writing only the seventh sonnet in the 1630s, Milton returned to the sonnet after the outbreak of the First English Civil War and the collapse of his marriage to Mary Powell in 1642. Between 1642 and 1658, while he worked as a schoolmaster and prose controversialist and then as secretary for foreign tongues for the Commonwealth government, Milton wrote seventeen sonnets, many of them praise poems in the vein of Ben Jonson. The only other poems he produced during this period were two sets of translations of the Psalms. Though Milton's interest in the sonnet has often been explained in terms of his general love for Italianate forms, it has not been sufficiently explained why he sought out the sonnet at this particular moment in his career. At the same time as Milton positioned himself as a public advocate of political, religious, and domestic liberty against the tyranny of custom, he displayed a preference for a fixed, customary form that sonneteers from Petrarch to Sidney had used to describe the tribulations of a captive will. And Milton was certainly not ignorant of the sonnet's associations with the "footstep of lost liberty."[52] His first youthful sonnet, "O Nightingale, that on yon bloomy Spray," concludes with conventional language of courtly service as Milton informs the bird, "Whether the Muse, or Love call thee his mate, / Both them I serve, and of their train am I" (Sonnet 1.13–14).[53] And the five Italian sonnets also written in 1629–30 tell a familiar story of a stubborn youth who disdained love and laughed at its snares before becoming entangled in them himself.[54]

At least since Wordsworth, critics have endeavored to rescue the poet of liberty from the restrictions of the sonnet form by emphasizing the fact that his unorthodox overflowing of lines and sections in the sonnets presages his practice of "variously" drawing out the sense "from one Verse into another" in *Paradise Lost* (*CPMP*, 210).[55] But even this contravention of poetic boundaries was an Italian tradition by the time Milton wrote, and, more importantly, these attempts to redeem Milton's poetic radicalism explain only how he accommodated the sonnet form to his purposes, not why he chose the genre in the first place.[56] Milton fashioned unique, intricate rhyme schemes for each of the lyric poems he produced during his years of private study at his parents' homes in Hammersmith and Horton in the 1630s: "Arcades," "At a Solemn Music," "On Time," "Upon the Circumcision," and "Lycidas." If his primary goal was to find a flexible form to maximize freedom of expression, he could have continued his experiments with open-ended, interwoven lyrics. Instead he turned to the sonnet and continued to experiment with the form for fifteen years, never returning to the elaborate and inventive rhyme patterns of his early career. The persistence of Milton's fascination with the sonnet suggests that there was something about the form that was congenial to Milton's thinking and his public aims at this critical juncture in the political history of England.

Although Milton's sonnets do not form a coherent sequence, they do share certain preoccupations that illuminate his motivations for making up his thoughts in a traditional Italian form. From the tributes to Protestant ladies to the poems on restrained merriment, Milton's mature sonnets consistently strive to teach readers how "To measure life," as he puts it in the sonnet on mirth to Cyriack Skinner (Sonnet 21.9). In the sonnets, the Jonsonian idea of measuring life entails both living temperately and making ethical distinctions such as those between patience and sloth, the spiritual sword and the civil, license and liberty. In his account of seventeenth-century symposiastic lyrics in *Excess and the Mean*, Joshua Scodel explores one crucial piece of Milton's understanding of the measured life. In detailed readings of Milton's two "convivial sonnets," Sonnets 20 and 21, Scodel argues that the sonnets respond to the excesses of cavalier drinking poetry, and of the Anacreontic and Horatian tradition of symposiastic lyric more generally, by "promoting a moderate pleasure that complements Puritan-Parliamentarian religious and political reformation."[57] Scodel's use of the word "reformation" is particularly apt since it highlights the continuity between ethical reform and poetic form in Milton's sonnets. Like Jonson, Milton attempts to craft a poetic style that can offer "to mankind a certain rule and pattern of living well and happily."[58]

But, characteristically, Milton does not accept Jonson's understanding of the correlation between character and style without alteration. He endeavors to reform Jonsonian formalism, which had been co-opted by royalist poets who focused on the affective powers of Jonson's ringing couplets and even rhythm. Though Milton had written in continuous couplets throughout the first half of his career, after the *Masque* at Ludlow he turned away from couplets and never returned to them. Instead, he took up the form that Jonson eschewed because its fixed length and rhyme scheme required him to stretch and maim his thoughts like the victims of Procrustes's bed.[59] Milton selected the sonnet in order to distinguish his poetic project from the lyric style and theory of poetry favored by the Royalists. Rejecting the English sonnet and its concluding couplet, Milton once again overlooked the recent, native poetic tradition in favor of a more established continental tradition. In the Italian sonnet, Milton found a form that incorporates couplets into a more intricate and continuous pattern of rhyme.[60] In other words, Milton did not reject rhyme's chime but worked to contain it.

This effort to use the sonnet form to harness the affective power of rhyme is consonant with Milton's oft-quoted statement about the purpose of verse in *The Reason of Church-government*, published in 1642, the same year in which Milton returned to the sonnet. After noting that scripture offers examples of poetry that are "incomparable" not only in their "divine argument" but also in "the very critical art of composition," Milton declares that poetic abilities are of "power beside the office of a pulpit, to imbreed and cherish in a great people the seeds of vertu, and publick civility, to allay the perturbations of the mind, and set the affections in right tune."[61] Milton goes on to describe more spiritual purposes of the poetic office, but he begins with the poet's earthly power to cultivate civility in nations and in individual minds. Though he shares the Royalists' conviction that verse has influence over the passions, Milton's declaration that poetry fosters "public civility" suggests a resistance to the private turn in contemporary lyric. Indeed, Milton's political sonnets of the 1640s and 1650s are a direct rebuke to the Royalists' efforts to center both lyric poetry and virtuous living in the personal realm. Milton focuses on individual character and experience in his sonnets, and his sonnet subjects have usually "shunn'd the broad way and the green" like Jonson's lyric heroes, but they are nonetheless politically engaged (Sonnet 9.2). As Anna Nardo notes, Milton's sonnets hold "together, perhaps for the last time, both the lyric intensity of private and the historical consciousness of public poetry."[62] In his controversial prose of the 1640s, Milton frequently makes the case that domestic, political, and religious liberty cannot be disentangled from one another. In the sonnets, Milton uses the lyric form most associated with private reflection and intimate allegiances to advance his argument for a continuity between personal and public liberty.

Though questions of liberty and measure run through all of Milton's sonnets, two sonnets composed at a critical moment in Milton's career provide insight into his reasons for returning to the form throughout the 1640s and 1650s. Written in the mid-1640s in response to critics of his divorce treatises, Sonnets 11 and 12 draw together two aspects of Milton's vocation and self-image: his role as a poet and his role as a prose controversialist dedicated to defending domestic and political liberty. Milton's first divorce tract, *The Doctrine and Discipline of Divorce: Restored to the Good of Both Sexes, From the bondage of Canon Law, and other mistakes, to Christian freedom, guided by the Rule of Charity*, was published in August 1643, and the revised and augmented edition appeared in February 1644.[63] Although, as his title indicates, Milton tried to establish himself as a defender of a thoughtful and disciplined liberty of divorcing, the tract quickly elicited charges of libertinism from political opponents and supposed allies alike. In a sermon preached to Parliament in 1644, Herbert Palmer condemned the "wicked book" for the dangerously licentious potential of its arguments for liberty of conscience: "Or what *Bounds* or *Limits* can there be set to men *any Way*, if this opinion of *Liberty of Conscience*, as it is pleaded for, shall be admitted?"[64] And, in a book published at the end of the decade, in 1649, Bishop Joseph Hall (erstwhile licentious rhymer who grew up to be a defender of episcopacy and regular opponent of Milton in the 1640s) looks back and condemns Milton's "licentious pamphlet" (it's unclear which of Milton's tracts he was reading) with its "too-well-penned" defense of a "Libertinism" that "Even modest Heathens would hisse ... off the stage."[65] Milton responded to his critics in a series of pamphlets published after *Doctrine of Discipline of Divorce*: *The Judgment of Martin Bucer* in August 1644 and *Tetrachordon* and *Colasterion* in March 1645.[66] But in his sonnets he endeavors to articulate and defend the nature of his liberty in form as well as word. His central contention is that his liberty is indeed bounded, but that the boundaries are rational rather than conventional. In the opening line of Sonnet 12, which Milton likely wrote before Sonnet 11, he wastes no time with poetic throat clearing but launches straight into a spirited defense of his divorce tracts: "I did but prompt the age to quit their clogs," he asserts in indignant monosyllables that recall the forthright style and iconoclastic arguments of the Elizabethan satirists much more than the sweetness of the sonneteers (Sonnet 12.1).[67] Indeed, Milton's argument here and in the divorce tracts themselves has much in common with the radical naturalism of the couplet satirists; like them, he bids his listeners to throw off the fetters of custom in order to return to "ancient liberty."[68] In particular, he attempts to understand the "prime institution of Matrimony" by "enquir[ing], as our Saviours direction is, how it was in the beginning," that is, by scrutinizing the verses in Genesis that describe the divinely officiated marriage between Adam and Eve.[69]

But, for all his affinity for the natural liberty arguments of Donne, Hall, and Marston, Milton's formal decisions in the sonnet align him with Jonson's reformation of the Elizabethan discursive mode. His indignation is not the free-running, meter-disrupting rage of the satirical school but is reined in by the even pace of the iambic line. Even his overflowing of line endings, so often cited as an early sign of Milton's resistance to conventional poetic bonds, resembles Jonson's controlled enjambment. Like Jonson's, his enjambment reinforces rather than disrupts syntax. Milton's opening line, "I did but prompt the age to quit their clogs," is a complete independent clause. The second line adds a dependent clause that expands on the initial claim: "By the known rules of ancient liberty." The enjambment allows Milton to supplement his initial call to cast off fetters with a more measured claim about the standards that inform his pursuit of liberty. Though Milton, like Donne, encourages readers to disregard the arbitrary and modern laws that burden love, he does so in order to impose another set of rules that he believes is not only knowable but long since "known." The ancient past that Milton appeals to in the divorce treatises is not a golden age of free love in which natural desire reigned, but a theocratic age in which God oversaw marriage directly in the Garden of Eden and then indirectly in the Deuteronomic law.

The distance between Milton's "ancient liberty" and the radical naturalism of Donne becomes more apparent as he proceeds to compare his detractors to a slew of wild animals, including an earsplitting assembly "Of Owls and Cuckoos, Asses, Apes and Dogs," who respond to his regulated account of ancient liberty with nothing but "barbarous noise" (Sonnet 12.2, 4, 3). In the second quatrain, Milton goes on to compare his opponents to another group of obstreperous animals—the Lycian "Hinds," or peasants, who were "transform'd to Frogs" for railing at "Latona's twin-born progenie," Apollo and Diana (Sonnet 12.5, 5, 6). At first glance the simile seems simply to suggest that the great and good are always reviled, since even the most illustrious of creatures, the divine twins who "after held the sun and moon in fee," had to endure raillery while their mother attempted to drink from a stream (Sonnet 12.7). But Milton, as usual, has selected his allusion with care. The Lycian peasants are perhaps the most reprehensible in a series of foolish humans who crossed Latona and her children; the Lycians attempted to deny Latona water, the most basic of human necessities. In Ovid's account, their crime is claiming something as their own (*proprium*) that nature designed for common use.[70] In Milton's view, opponents of divorce have similarly refused to offer a thirsty soul the most basic spiritual necessity, the "pure and more inbred desire of joyning to itself in conjugall fellowship a fit conversing soul (which desire is properly call'd love)"; this desire, Milton contends, quoting the Song of Solomon, "*is stronger than death*, as the Spouse of Christ thought, *many waters cannot quench it, neither can the floods drown* it."[71] Only opponents as ungenerous and beastly as the hinds of Lycia could deny their fellows the most basic necessity, the remedy for this "rationall burning."[72]

Though Milton's allusion imports these Ovidian implications, his simile does not focus on Latona's thirst or on the Lycians' attempt to restrict a common good. Instead, he highlights the fact that the inhospitable Lycian peasants "Raild" at the gods who would later regulate the movements of the sun and the moon (Sonnet 12.6). In comparing himself to Apollo and Diana, Milton aligns his work in the divorce treatises with the emblems of regulated nature and "measur'd motion."[73] Indeed, the story of Apollo and Diana's birth is in many ways an account of law and order triumphing over raw energy and mutability: the wandering island of Delos was fixed in place, and the sun and moon were established in their daily course, when the children of Jove superseded the Titans. Apollo's reign as the god of lyric poetry also represents the supersession of a more primitive and sensual kind of poetry. In the story that immediately follows the story of the Lycian hinds in book 6 of Ovid's *Metamorphoses*, Apollo defeats the panpipes of the satyr Marsyas with a flute made by Minerva.[74] Milton uses the simile of the divine twins and Lycian frogs to position himself on the side of celestial and lyric harmony and his opponents on the side of bestial noise.

The distinction between brute nature and rational nature is essential to his argument in the divorce treatises. Though he appeals to the idea of natural liberty in making his case for divorce, he argues that the liberty he advocates is disciplined while the conventional limitations his opponents defend are dissolute. By allowing divorce only in cases of frigidity and adultery, he claims, modern law reduces marriage to an "animal or beastish meeting."[75] The "Owls and Cuckoos, Asses, Apes, and Dogs" object to Milton's attempt to restore ancient liberty because his strict freedom does not appeal to their sensual desires (Sonnet 12.4). They may make a show of admiring liberty, but this "bawl[ing]" admiration for freedom is based on whim and affect, on "senseless mood," rather than a steady dedication to the "known rules" of liberty (Sonnet 12.9, 9, 2).

Milton manipulates the rhyme pattern of the sonnet to bolster his argument that his attempt to restore ancient liberty is consonant with the strictest adherence to measure. Indeed, the rhymes of the sonnet suggest that liberty can contain the barbarous impulses that his opponents have loosed.

> I did but prompt the age to quit their clogs
> > By the known rules of ancient liberty,
> > When straight a barbarous noise environs me
> > Of Owls and Cuckoos, Asses, Apes and Dogs.
> As when those Hinds that were transform'd to Frogs
> > Rail'd at *Latona's* twin-born progeny
> > Which after held the Sun and Moon in fee.
> > But this is got by casting Pearl to Hogs,
> That bawl for freedom in their senseless mood,
> > And still revolt when truth would set them free.
> > License they mean when they cry liberty;
> For who loves that, must first be wise and good;
> > But from that mark how far they rove we see,
> > For all this waste of wealth and loss of blood.

While the A rhyme links the "clogs" of traditional marriage law with the beasts who support them—"Dogs," "Frogs," and "Hogs"—in the B rhyme Milton rhymes the word "liberty" with the individuals who endure the raillery of the animals: "me" and Latona's "progeny," who hold the sun and moon in "fee." Milton's rhymes in this sonnet seem to tame his unruly opponents. For all their barbarous noise, the dogs, frogs, and hogs can be incorporated into the poet's orderly pattern of sound. In fact, in this sonnet about the distinction between license and liberty, Milton works to heighten, rather than to relax, the connective function of rhyme. Instead of beginning an entirely new group of rhymes in the sestet, Milton carries over the B rhyme from the first two quatrains, rhyming "free," "liberty," and "see." As a result, the rhyme appears in every section of the sonnet and binds together the entire poem in a way that is reminiscent of Spenser's entertangled sonnet schemes.

Milton's use of rhyme as a connective force in this sonnet complicates the traditional account of his enjambment between lines and sections of the sonnet form. Milton's sonnets do anticipate his argument in the preface to *Paradise Lost* that true musical delight consists in the "sense variously drawn out from one verse to another," but in the sonnets the drawing out of the sense from one line to the next is paired with a rhyme scheme that weaves the whole together (*CPMP*, 210). The result of this combination is a controlled freedom of movement; his thoughts may wind over line endings and section breaks, but, like the music in "L'Allegro," Milton's sonnets are composed of "many a winding bout / Of *linked* sweetness long drawn out" (*CPMP*, lines 139–40). Both the drawing out of the enjambment and the linking of the rhymes contribute to the unity of the sonnet, which Wordsworth saw as the defining characteristic of Milton's sonnets. In an 1833 letter to Alexander Dyce, Wordsworth argues that Milton refused to "submit" to the traditional division between the octet and the sestet because his aim was to emphasize the unity of the sonnet rather than its partitioned structure:

> Now it has struck me, that this is not done merely to gratify the ear by variety and freedom of sound, but also to aid in giving that pervading sense of intense Unity in which the excellence of the Sonnet has always seemed to me mainly to consist. Instead of looking at this composition as a piece of architecture, making a whole out of three parts, I have been much in the habit of preferring the image of an orbicular body,—a sphere—or a dew-drop. All this will appear to you a little fanciful.[76]

Wordsworth's image of the dewdrop or sphere captures something about the argument of the Miltonic sonnet as well as its form. In his praise poetry, Ben Jonson uses the image of the sphere or circle to express his ideal of the "gathered self," who is "round within himself," that is, the individual whose moral probity gives him complete autonomy and liberates him from dependence on fortune.[77] In his account of self-esteem in *The Reason of Church-government*, Milton adopts but modifies the Jonsonian image along with the Jonsonian ethics of integrity. After describing self-esteem as "the radical moisture and fountain head, whence every laudable and worthy enterprize issues forth," Milton pauses to qualify his metaphor: "although I have giv'n it the name of a liquid thing, yet is it not incontinent to bound it self, as humid things are, but hath in it a most restraining and powerfull abstinence to start back, and glob it self upward from the mixture of any ungenerous and unbeseeming motion, or any soile wherewith it may peril to stain it self."[78] Milton's "liquid thing" has the purity and restraint of Jonson's gathered self, combined with the fluidity and liberty of movement prized by Donne and Marston. And his sonnets are likewise "dew-drops" of verse that combine the fluidity of enjambment with the unity produced by the restraints of a traditional rhyme scheme and a regular iambic meter.

Wordsworth's idea of the Miltonic sonnet as a dewdrop dovetails not only with Milton's general view of measured liberty but with the particular argument of this sonnet. After charging that his opponents "revolt" from freedom because they do not grasp the distinction between license and liberty, Milton clarifies his understanding of liberty in one of the most Jonsonian lines in Milton's verse: "For who loves that must first be wise and good" (Sonnet 12.10, 12). With its plain English monosyllables and its emphasis on adjectives, the line sounds as if it could have been plucked from one of Jonson's praise poems. But, more importantly, the ethical argument of the line is Jonsonian in spirit because it makes character primary.[79] While for Donne, discursive liberty is a necessary precursor to the pursuit of wisdom and goodness, for Milton, at least in this instance, wisdom and goodness are necessary precursors to a devotion to liberty. And just as Jonson's focus on character leads him to favor metaphors of fixity, Milton describes being wise and good as a "mark" from which his licentious critics "rove" (Sonnet 12.13). Without a foundation of fixed character, Milton argues, all love of liberty is bawling for freedom, and all action, even action undertaken in the name of liberty, is nothing but a "waste of wealth and loss of blood" (Sonnet 12.14).

While Sonnet 12 offers a vision of what internal liberty, concord, and self-restraint might look like, Milton's other sonnet in response to opponents of the divorce treatises, Sonnet 11, lampoons those who falsely usurp the name of concord. When the two sonnets are read side by side, it becomes clear that Milton sees rhyme as he did in his masque: as a powerful instrument that can represent both true and false harmony. The opening two lines of the sonnet present Milton's third divorce treatise as a paragon of true concord: "A book was writ of late call'd *Tetrachordon*, / And wov'n close, both matter, form, and style" (Sonnet 11.1–2). As the title page of *Tetrachordon* suggests, the book is named after an ancient four-stringed instrument or four-note scale because it attempts to harmonize the "foure chief places in Scripture, which treat of Marriage."[80] The second line of Sonnet 11 indicates that this act of biblical harmonizing required thoughtful attention to form as well as argument; it is important for Milton to note that he did not simply organize the "matter" of his treatise, but ensured that its "form and style" were likewise "wov'n close."[81]

Milton's closely woven writing stands in contrast to the "stall-reader[s]" who inspect the title-page of the book in the second quatrain (Sonnet 11.5).

"Bless us!" they cry out in consternation, "what a word on / a title page is this!" (Sonnet 11.5, 5–6). Milton's disdain for unlearned readers who stand gaping at the Greek word is evident, but his complaint is as much about the way these readers assimilate the unfamiliar into their lives as about their ignorance of Greek. Milton asks the stall readers why they had less trouble incorporating the rugged names (and perhaps the royalist politics) of Scottish warriors like "Gordon, / Colkitto, or Macdonnel, or Galasp" into their English vocabulary (Sonnet 11.8–9). In the Trinity manuscript, Milton first describes these names as "barbarous" and then as "rough-hewn" before settling on "rugged."[82] The final adjective allows Milton to develop a metaphor for the process of becoming accustomed. These rocky names become "sleek" to English mouths because those mouths are "like" the names—that is, equally rugged (Sonnet 11.10). It's as if the rough, abrasive mouths of the stall readers polish the Scottish names until they become agreeably smooth. The likeness between rugged mouths and rugged names produces a superficial concord that covers over a deep political divide.

Sonnet 11 therefore extends an argument that is central to the divorce treatises themselves: that "Custome" has long been the foremost guide in religion and manners because "her method is so glib and easie," and that "work[ing] off the inveterate blots and obscurities wrought upon our mindes by the suttle insinuating of Error and Custome" will require the utmost exertion of "study and true labour."[83] This is, of course, also the argument Milton raises about rhyme in the preface to *Paradise Lost*. And in this sonnet, Milton anticipates his later association of rhyme with the false concord produced by custom. For the Scottish names Milton mentions are "rugged" partly because they disrupt the metrical regularity of the poem: the line "Colkitto, or Macdonnel, or Galasp" could perhaps be scanned as an iambic pentameter line, but it requires some prosodic ingenuity to make the names fit into the metrical pattern (Sonnet 11.9, 10). Yet these "rugged" names do manage to fit neatly into the rhyme scheme of the poem: "Gordon" rhymes tidily, and comically, with "Tetrachordon," "por'd on," and "word on" while "Galasp" rhymes with "gasp" and "Asp." Rhyme in this sonnet serves as emblem of the kind of glib and superficial harmony achieved through custom rather than labor. Rugged mouths may be able to make rugged names seem "sleek," but achieving true harmony or measure is a much more difficult enterprise. And, as Milton argues in the preface to *Paradise Lost*, obvious concord like rhyme can be used "to set off" or disguise the deeper cacophony of "wretched matter and lame Meter" (*CPMP*, 210). Milton's two sonnets, then, reveal an early division within Milton's thinking about rhyme and its place in measured verse that resembles Jonson's stance in "A Fit of Rhyme against Rhyme." While rhyme may be an instrument of concord in the hands of a judicious poet, it can also become a customary crutch for poets unwilling to take on the laborious task of closely weaving matter, form, and style.

Solemn Planetary Wheelings: The Measured Motion of Paradise Lost

In "The Printer to the Reader," added to the 1668 reissued first edition of *Paradise Lost*, Samuel Simmons indicates that he "procured" the arguments to each book along with "a reason of that which stumbled many others, why the poem Rimes not" (*CPMP*, 210). It is delightful to imagine Simmons going to "procure" a "reason" for Milton's blank verse and being met with an indignant poet who had long prepared for this particular battle: "The stumblers want a reason? I'll give them a reason." This is pure fantasy, of course, but Milton's preface does read like a spontaneous and truculent articulation of the prosodic principles that Milton had been formulating for decades. The preface continues the argument for measured liberty and against custom that he makes not only in rhyme, but through rhyme, in Sonnets 11 and 12. The preface rejects rhyme as a product of "Custom" and an unnatural "vexation, hindrance, and constraint" to expression, but it grounds this rejection on the fact that rhyme interferes with more praiseworthy forms of self-restraint (*CPMP*, 210). Even as Milton declares himself free from one kind of poetic restraint, he imposes other prosodic obligations on his poem, announcing that he will vigilantly observe "apt Numbers" and "fit quantity of syllables" (*CPMP*, 210). The shift from the "Petrarchian stanza" to blank verse, then, simply marks a change in Milton's understanding of what constitutes well-measured liberty, not a complete revolution in his stance on poetic license and liberty. As we have seen, Milton had been suspicious since at least 1634, when he wrote his *Masque*, of rhyme's association with the primitive and the customary, but his more definitive opposition to rhyme in *Paradise Lost* was brought about by the shift in its meaning during the Civil War and Protectorate. Though the movement toward a personal, affective understanding of lyric and rhyme had begun when Milton was still a schoolchild, affective poetics had become more dominant, and more politically charged, in the 1650s and 1660s as poets like Katherine Philips and Abraham Cowley reckoned with the consequences of royalist defeat and restoration. In his sonnets, Milton worked to distinguish himself formally from royalist poetry by weaving rhyme's chime into a more intricate pattern of sound and wielding it satirically to mock adherents of custom. But, by 1668, when Milton wrote the preface to *Paradise Lost*, rhyme had become so fraught with the baggage of royalist poetic theory that Milton decided to eliminate it altogether in order to clear the way for a renewed focus on the measure of his numbers and syllables.

Milton's preface to *Paradise Lost*, with its disdain for "vulgar readers" who will not understand the "neglect of rhyme," takes a belligerent approach to defending his poetic liberty, but printer Samuel Simmons added another prefatory text to the 1674 second edition of the poem to aid those who "stumbled" over the blank verse (*CPMP*, 210). Andrew Marvell's well-known response to

the poem and its prosody in "On Mr. Milton's Paradise Lost," printed just be-
fore Milton's preface, reveals how the most sympathetic couplet writer of Mil-
ton's age came to terms with Miltonic blank verse by detecting measure within
its prosodic rebellion.[84] Indeed, the poem makes the case that John Creaser
makes in his deft comparison of Marvell and Milton's prosody: that in spite of
the fact that "freedom is foregrounded" in Milton's prosody, the two poets are
"less distinct . . . than might appear, since both exploit prosodic discipline in
the cause of freedom."[85] Andrew Shifflett and Nigel Smith have shown that
Marvell's poem draws on Jonson's prefatory poem to Tom May's Lucan, in
which Jonson sees the number, measure, and harmony of Lucan's verse as a
way of containing the passionate forces of Pompey, Caesar, Cato, and Brutus.[86]
As Shifflett argues, both poems begin with doubt and proceed by "straining
praise through the sieve of doubt."[87] In particular, both poets "doubt" (i.e., fear)
that the towering ambitions of the poets will result in devastating destruction:
in Jonson's poem, that the "general Engine" will "cracke," and, in Marvell's, that
the poet will, like a spiteful Samson pulling down the temple posts, "ruin (for
I saw him strong) / The sacred truths to fable and old song."[88] Marvell's Lati-
nate verb of destruction, "ruin," echoes his description of Cromwell in the
Horatian ode as one who "Could by industrious valour climb / To ruin the great
work of time / And cast the kingdoms old / Into another mold."[89] In spite of
his wonder at Cromwell's energetic force and Milton's bold vastness, Marvell
distrusts their grand designs and fears that they may bring all the work of time
tumbling to the ground without building anything in its place.[90] Milton, who
like Marvell's Cromwell seems to be opposed to being "inclose[d]"—prosodi-
cally or thematically—eventually succeeds in allaying Marvell's fears.[91] For as
Marvell reads on in *Paradise Lost*, he discovers that the epic poet can in fact
"span"—a word that means both to reach across and to measure—"so infinite"
a "work."[92] Marvell suggests that Milton's ability to span the infinite derives as
much from the equanimity as from the magnitude of his mind. Nigel Smith's
edition of Marvell draws attention to the many echoes of *Paradise Lost* in the
poem, many of which seem intended to show that measure is present in the
most threateningly sublime moments of Milton's epic. Echoing Milton's own
description of his soaring song in book 1, lines 12–16, Marvell writes, "And
above human flight dost soar aloft / With plume so strong, so equal, and so
soft."[93] The lines are almost a gentle reminder to the adventurous Milton: re-
member that your free soaring is made possible by the fact that your wings are
"strong," "equal," and "soft." Shifflett sees Marvell's allusions to Jonson's com-
mendatory poem as evidence that he is praising Milton as a Stoic, Jonsonian
hero.[94] Marvell's choice of the word "equal" to describe the bird's plumage
bolsters Shifflett's argument; the word, and the way that Marvell balances
"strong" and "soft" on either side of "equal," points to the Horatian idea of *ae-
quus animus*.[95] Milton's soaring, his transcendence of human laws, is made
possible by the balance and measure built into his own mind. Marvell depicts

Milton's republican boundary breaking as a precarious and potentially ruinous enterprise in which Milton succeeds only because he internalizes the measures that were once extrinsic in the political and poetic "work[s] of time."[96] Birds without equal plumes should not venture on this task.[97]

The first forty-four lines of Marvell's poem ostensibly focus on his fears about the divine "theme" of Milton's poem, but Milton's prosodic rebellion lurks behind Marvell's account of his doubts and conversion. In the final section of the poem, Marvell at length overtly addresses the stumbling block of blank verse: "Well mightst thou scorn thy readers to allure / With tinkling rhyme, of thine own sense secure."[98] Drawing on Milton's own use of the word "sense" in the preface and on the old distinction between sound and sense, rhyme and reason, Marvell depicts rhyme, with all its "allur[ing]" affective appeal, as a way for poets who are not secure of their sense to seduce readers with sound. In the following couplet, Marvell joins Milton in mocking the chimes and bells that Beaumont and Cowley thought left such an enduring impression on the mind:

> While the town-Bayes writes all the while and spells,
> And like a pack-horse tires without his bells.[99]

In depicting Dryden and his ilk as poetic drudges who can persevere in churning out one uninspired verse after another only if they are rewarded for their labors with a bit of jingling at the end of each line, Marvell contradicts the idea that the ringing of rhyme appeals to the deepest and loftiest desires of the heart.[100] Rhyme is a not a magical charm but a mere carrot for tired packhorse poets. In the penultimate couplet, Marvell brings together the contentions he has raised against rhyme—that it is superficial, sensual, and base—by comparing it to the tassels added to hose fastenings for the sake of "fashion."[101] Translating Milton's complaint in the prefatory note that rhyme has been "graced" by "some famous modern Poets, carried away by Custom," Marvell confesses himself to be one of those guilty moderns who "transported by the mode offend, / And while I meant to praise thee must commend."[102] The lines are certainly self-deprecatory, but they also seem to poke at Milton a bit for his sweeping characterization of his fellow rhymers. Sharon Achinstein has argued that these lines, and the poem in general, make rhyme a "thing indifferent" and defend Milton's "political ideology of rational choice and individual agency."[103] If this is the case, then Marvell is defending Milton's ideology of choice against Milton himself, since Milton had made the distinction between rhyme and blank verse sound like anything but a thing indifferent in the preface to *Paradise Lost*. Marvell may be correcting the pugnacious Milton of the note, reminding him that it is his *modus*, his measure, not his "mode" that matters. For Marvell concludes the poem by returning to the idea that measure undergirds Miltonic sublimity. Drawing on the same verse from the Book of Wisdom that was marshalled by advocates of measure like Puttenham and Jonson, Marvell argues that because Milton's "verse" is "created like [his] theme sublime / In number, weight, and measure" it "needs not rhyme."[104] Royalist poets like Philips and Cowley had made the case that rhyme's chime contributes to the sublimity of lyric, appealing to the mind on a level that is both above and below reason. Marvell may hint at his sympathy with this position by ending with a rhyme between *sublime* and *rhyme*, but he also makes it clear that Miltonic sublimity is of a different kind.[105] Milton's verse, "created . . . In number, weight, and measure," is instead an imitation a rational and geometric creator who in book 7 "circumscribe[s] / This Universe and all created things" and sets the "bounds" of the world with his "golden Compasses" (*PL*, 7.226–27, 230, 225). Marvell recognizes that for all of Milton's breaking of customary bonds like rhyme and the line ending, the epic poet's ultimate project is to "recover" not only the ancient liberty but the ancient measure of Homer, Virgil, and the compass-wielding creator of Genesis. While Milton's preface emphasizes the poet's liberation from customary bonds, Marvell's prefatory poem draws out the sublime restraint built into Miltonic freedom.

As Marvell's doubts about Milton's infinite ambitions suggest, Milton is much more confident than the licentious rhymers of the 1590s that his verse can resemble the divine laws and not just the messy struggle to find them. The blank verse of *Paradise Lost*, with its fusion of enjambment and metrical regularity, owes as much to Spenser and Jonson's defenses of measure as it does to Donne's liberation of sense. This fusion of metrical regularity with syntactical elongation explains how celebrations of the fluidity and freedom of Milton's verse can exist alongside complaints about the uniformity of his epic style like F. R. Leavis's famously tetchy assessment in "Milton's Verse." In his 1933 article, Leavis maintains that claims about the "variety" of "Milton's Grand Style" do not stand up to "an honest interrogation of experience." The real experience of the verse of *Paradise Lost*, he insists, is one of unbearable monotony:

> In the end we find ourselves protesting—protesting against the routine gesture, the heavy fall, of the verse, flinching from the foreseen thud that comes so inevitably, and, at last, irresistibly: for reading Paradise Lost is a matter of resisting, of standing up against, the verse-movement, of subduing it into something tolerably like sensitiveness, and in the end our resistance is worn down; we surrender at last to the inescapable monotony of the ritual.[106]

Though Leavis is deliberately provocative in his effort to challenge the prevailing view of Milton's prosody, his complaint does draw attention to a quality of Milton's verse that is just as central to the poetic project of *Paradise Lost* as its famed liberty of movement. It is the same quality that has led more charitable readers to describe the poem as incantatory, solemn, processional, and grand.[107] Generic expectations and Miltonic diction partly account for such ritualistic experiences of the poem, but Milton's "measure" also plays an important role.

Drawing on Derek Attridge's prosodic theories, John Creaser compared a sample of Milton's verse in *Paradise Lost* to the blank verse of Surrey, Gascoigne, and Marlowe.[108] He found that Milton employed "promotion" (when weak syllables carry a metrical beat) at nearly double the rate of these sixteenth-century practitioners (an average of fifty-seven per two hundred lines, versus an average of thirty-seven per two hundred lines for the others); the effect, he suggests, is to make *Paradise Lost* more "light and fleet than its predecessors."[109] Creaser found that Milton also uses "demotion" more liberally than Surrey and Gascoigne, but at nearly half the rate he uses promotion, and far less than the emphatic verse of Marlowe's Lucan translation.[110] Creaser's analysis supports the more experiential sense that Milton's rhythm is flexible and that irregularity is most often in the service of movement, of "variously draw[ing] out" the sense from one line to another. Indeed, I would argue that not only sense and syntax but also prosody is drawn out in Milton's verse paragraphs. Milton plays rhythmical variety against the iambic norm of the poem in order to delay resolution and push onward.[111]

But for all of Milton's liberal play with rhythm, he is strict in his observation of prosodic limits in a variety of ways. Creaser notes that, in sharp contrast with Shakespeare, Milton rarely departs from the norm of five metrical beats and ten metrical syllables.[112] He also observes Milton's respect for the line boundary: in 95.75 percent of the twelve hundred lines from across the epic Creaser examined, "the fifth beat falls either on a stressed monosyllable or a disyllable with second-syllable stress (usually the former)."[113] Milton's firm (and predominately monosyllabic) final stresses make the bound of the line audible without the aid of rhyme.[114] In *Paradise Lost*, regularity is less insistent than it is in Spenser or Jonson because it is elongated. But the play of variety in the midst of the line is balanced by the reminder of measure at the close of the line. This practice of accommodating flexibility but then resolving it into measure is also visible on a larger scale in the epic: Milton often concludes verse paragraphs with strictly iambic (and often monosyllabic) lines without the promotions or demotions Creaser detects elsewhere. For example, the syntactical, theological, and prosodic complexity of the opening lines of the epic and their account of the fall come to a close in a regular and predominately monosyllabic line that announces Milton's theodicy:

And justify the ways of God to men. (*PL*, 1.26)

At the end of the verse paragraph, prosodic justness bears witness to Milton's ability to translate human disobedience into divine justice. And in the unforgettable pair of lines (I dare not call it a couplet) that concludes Milton's epic, there seems to be some subtle comfort about the fate of the wandering pair contained within the prosody:

> They hand in hand with wand'ring steps and slow,
> Through *Eden* took thir solitary way. (*PL*, 12.648–49)

Adam and Eve may take their way with "slow" and "wand'ring" steps, but the poet's step is even and unfaltering. As in Spenser's stanza about Mercy's firm up-bearing of Redcrosse Knight, here measure provides assurance that Adam and Eve are attended on their open-ended and seemingly solitary "way" by the divine "guide" of "Providence" (*PL*, 12.649, 647, 647). This practice of resolving the midline and midparagraph flexibility into closing regularity recalls Milton's use of rhyme in "Lycidas." There, he defers closing his rhymes hastily or merely for the sake of sound, instead drawing out the bands of rhyme to link his poetic consolations to his Orphic fears. As he stretches the bands of rhyme to (and perhaps beyond) their limits in "Lycidas," here he elongates the measure of English verse so that its regularity is ever present without being insistent.

In Tasso's account of epic style, which Milton cites approvingly in "Of Education," Tasso describes the kind of elongation that Milton cultivates metrically and syntactically as a key component of epic "*magnificenza*"; indeed, he justifies his preference for the ottava rima stanza over tercets by arguing that the stanza allows for longer, and therefore more magnificent, clauses and periods.[115] The lengthened epic period is designed to accommodate the grand scale of the "*concetti*"—conceits or subjects—that Tasso sees as appropriate to epic, which include "God, the world, heroes, land and sea battles, and the like."[116] Such subjects are not only grand but intricate. Epic poets therefore require a style elongated and complex enough to map out the web of ties that bind an epic hero. The need for elongation to encompass an epic argument is apparent from the opening lines. Virgil does not simply sing of "*virum*," a man, or even of "*Arma virumque*," arms and a man, but piles on phrases and clauses that draw out his links to the fallen walls of Troy and the unbuilt walls of Rome, to a wrathful Juno and his household gods.[117] The sixteen-line opening sentence of *Paradise Lost*, with its dizzying time shifts from the fall to the redemption and then back to Moses and David, makes it abundantly clear that justifying the "ways of God to men" requires even more elaborate and elongated syntax than singing of the founding of Rome (*PL*, 1.26). Milton internalizes epic, but he does not sacrifice the epic web of connections in order to focus strictly on the inner life of his heroes. *Paradise Lost* is not Herbert's *Temple* or Donne's *Holy Sonnets*, which are absorbed in an inward conversation between a single human voice and a divine interlocutor. Milton does not concentrate his attention on a single bond, between God and humanity, or Adam and Eve, or Satan and God, or Satan and humanity, but endeavors to give a comprehensive image of the world in which these figures live and move. Whereas Jonson found the couplet congenial to his ethics because he viewed the ideal life as round within itself and guarded from the world of strife, Milton heaps layer upon layer of elaboration onto his account of the upright and pure heart because his upright heart is living and making free choices within a mazy world. The elongated scale of Milton's syntax and measure allows him to span the infinite argument of his poem.

In an 1848 essay on Charles Lamb, Thomas De Quincey offers a metaphor for Milton's prosodic style that reconciles measure with mobility, arguing that Lamb did not have the taste for "the solemn planetary wheelings of *Paradise Lost*."[118] The metaphor is a "happy one," as turn-of-the-century critic Walter Raleigh argued, because "the verse revolves on its axis at every line, but it always has another motion, and is related to a more distant centre."[119] The metaphor conveys the sense of order on a grand scale that I have attributed to *Paradise Lost* and captures the way that the poem is both energetic and processional. But the metaphor is also particularly appropriate to Milton because it draws on Milton's own image of regulated freedom in *Paradise Lost*, the solemn planet-like wheelings of the angels in book 5. This scene of spontaneous heavenly art provides insight into how Milton might conceive of his own efforts to combine the fluidity of enjambed, unrhymed lines with the regularity of apt numbers and fit quantity of syllables:

> So spake th' Omnipotent, and with his words
> All seem'd well pleas'd, all seem'd, but were not all.
> That day, as other solemn days, they spent
> In song and dance about the sacred Hill,
> Mystical dance, which yonder starry Sphere
> Of Planets and of fixt in all her Wheels
> Resembles nearest, mazes intricate,
> Eccentric, intervolv'd, yet regular
> Then most, when most irregular they seem:
> And in thir motions harmony Divine
> So smooths her charming tones, that God's own ear
> Listens delighted. Ev'ning now approach'd
> (For wee have also our Ev'ning and our Morn,
> Wee ours for change delectable, not need)
> Forthwith from dance to sweet repast they turn
> Desirous; all in Circles as they stood,
> Tables are set, and on a sudden pil'd
> With Angels' Food, and rubied Nectar flows
> In Pearl, in Diamond, and massy Gold,
> Fruit of delicious Vines, the growth of Heav'n.

On flow'rs repos'd, and with fresh flow'rets crown'd,
They eat, they drink, and in communion sweet
Quaff immortality and joy, secure
Of surfeit where full measure only bounds
Excess, before th' all bounteous King, who show'r'd
With copious hand, rejoicing in thir joy. (*PL*, 5.616–41)

The scene follows God's "Decree" that he has begotten and ordained the Son
on the "holy Hill" of heaven (*PL*, 5.602, 604). The elevation of the Son seems
to be a singular event that radically disrupts the undifferentiated flow of heav-
enly time. But the angels' response to this remarkable turn of events is to re-
turn to their routine. While God begins his proclamation with "This day," Ra-
phael begins his account of the angelic dancing with "That day, as other solemn
days" (*PL*, 5.603, 618). It's unclear whether the angelic liturgical calendar in-
cludes ordinary days as well as solemn days or whether every day is a solemn
day in heaven, but it is clear that the angels have spent their days in song and
dance before and will do so again. The description of the dance that follows
embraces the repetition and regularity of a solemn ritual without forgoing
variety and flexibility.

In drawing out the resemblance between the mystical dance and the move-
ments of the spheres, Milton works to accommodate complexity, eccentricity,
and change. The angels resemble not only the "fixt" stars but also the wander-
ing stars or "Planets" that pursue apparently erratic paths across the sky (*PL*,
5.621, 621). Indeed, the angels seem to be given remarkable latitude in their
individual maneuvers, meandering in "mazes intricate." At this moment in
Raphael's account of heavenly events, Milton's syntax becomes particularly
mazy as he repeatedly doubles back to further explicate his image of planetary
and angelic motion. This interest in accommodating complex and nonlinear
thought and speech resembles Donne's efforts to adapt his verse to the rough
and winding path to truth. When Milton argues that the movements of the
spheres are "Eccentric, intervolv'd, yet regular / Then most, when most irregu-
lar they seem," he could be arguing, in a Donnean vein, that we must forgo
earthly rules of regularity in order to adhere to a higher but invisible divine law
(*PL*, 5.623–24). But there is something of a prosodic joke in the fact that Mil-
ton's trisyllabic words capturing the idiosyncrasies of the angelic movements—
"Eccentric, intervolv'd"—fit into the iambic pattern. Milton seems to offer a
view of regularity that situates him somewhere between the advocates of dis-
cursive liberty and the defenders of rhyme's bands. The dance of the angels and
the movements of the spheres are regular, but their regularity cannot be seen
at a glance. The elaborate regularity of their dance can be discovered only with
careful study.

This principle of hidden order applies as much to Milton's verse as to the
dance of the angels. Milton uses enjambment liberally and at times even breaks

lines between subjects and verbs ("God's own ear / Listens delighted") (*PL*, 5.626–27). But, for the most part, Milton breaks lines between prepositional phrases and the nouns or verbs they modify ("yonder starry Sphere / Of Planets"; and "With Angels' Food, and rubied Nectar flows: / In Pearl, in Diamond, and massy Gold") (*PL*, 5.620–21, 634–35). Whereas Donne frequently uses line breaks to disrupt, Milton generally uses them to elaborate, to draw out his description and to carry listeners along through the winding but smooth paths of his verse. Milton's verse displays the same qualities that he prizes in this angelic dance: it is "intricate" and "intervolv'd," words that seem more characteristic of Spenserian entertangle rhyme than Donnean discursive verse (*PL*, 5.622, 623). The result of this intricacy is not the energetic roughness of Donne's satires, but a liquid harmony that "smooths her charming tones" (*PL*, 5.626).

In the final clause of the winding, inverted sentence that describes the angelic dance, Milton reveals that the sonic charms of angelic and planetary harmony have an effect on the divine audience: the angels' eccentric motions produce a "harmony Divine" that "So smooths her charming tones that God's own ear / Listens delighted" (*PL*, 5.625, 626–27). And yet, even as Milton reintroduces the idea of musical or poetic charm celebrated by the Royalists, he works to contain it. In order to understand what distinguishes Milton's account of charming harmony from that of the Royalists, it is illuminating to trace his use of the word "charm" through other parts of the epic. Throughout *Paradise Lost*, Milton uses the verb and noun forms of the word "charm" only in connection with the devils and with Eve. He uses the word six times in the first two books to describe the devils' pursuits in hell.[120] In book 1, music of the "*Dorian* mood" serves as a source of both music and comfort for the defeated devils as they "Breathing united force with fixed thought / Mov'd on in silence to soft Pipes that charm'd / Thir painful steps o'er the burnt soil" (*PL*, 1.550, 560–62). This idea of salving the pains of Hell with the charms of language appears again when Satan bids the devils to "render Hell / More tolerable" in his absence, "if there be cure or charm / To respite or deceive, or slack the pain / Of this ill Mansion," and later when the devils carry out his order by engaging in eloquent discourse that "with a pleasing sorcery could charm / Pain for a while or anguish, and excite / Fallacious hope, or arm th' obdured breast / With stubborn patience as with triple steel" (*PL*, 2.459–60, 461–62, 566–69). The pleasing but deceptive sorcery of the devils' infernal music recalls Circe's soul-robbing songs in Milton's *Masque*. And, as he does in his masque, in the opening books of his epic Milton associates "charm" with the questionable supernatural forces that inhabit the earth. In his chilling description of Sin and Death, he speaks of the "charms" of "*Lapland* Witches" who fuel their spells with "infant blood" (*PL*, 2.666, 665, 664). And in the famous simile in which Milton compares the devils to "Faery Elves" whom "some belated Peasant sees, / Or dreams he sees," the music of the elves "charm[s]" the "ear" of the late wanderer and makes his "heart reboun[d]" (*PL*, 1.781, 783–84, 787, 787, 787). The charms of the opening books have undeniable power to overreach reason and move the ear and the heart. But, for Milton, acquiescing to such charms is a transgressive abdication of reason rather than a transcendent surrender to natural affections.

The hellish charms of the first two books serve as a warning to the reader—if not to Adam—to be wary of what the narrator calls "Female charm" in his account of Adam's fall (*PL*, 9.999). While Adam is never characterized as a charmer, after Eve's account of her awakening in book 4, the narrator takes note of Adam's delight in her "Beauty and submissive Charms" (*PL*, 4.4998). In conversation with Raphael in book 8, Adam elaborates on his response to Eve's beauty and charms, distinguishing the "delight" he takes in "Taste, Sight, Smell, Herbs, Fruits, and Flow'rs"—which "works in the mind no change"—from the "passion" he first felt when he saw Eve, a "Commotion strange" that "transport[s]" him (*PL*, 8.524, 527, 525, 530, 531, 529). In "all enjoyments else" Adam sees himself as a proper Virgilian hero—"superior and unmov'd"—but he is "here only weak / Against the charm of Beauty's powerful glance" (*PL*, 8.531, 532, 532–33). In his response, Raphael appeals to Adam's "self-esteem," enjoining him to recognize his rational superiority, to disdain outward adornments, and to distinguish between passion and love:

> In loving though dost well, in passion not,
> Wherein true Love consists not; Love refines
> The thoughts, and heart enlarges, hath his seat
> In Reason, and is judicious, is the scale
> By which to heav'nly Love thou mayst ascend. (*PL*, 8.572, 588–92)

Though the royalist poets, particularly those of a Platonic bent like Philips, would hardly disagree with the idea of a higher love, they often endeavor to incorporate the passions into their vision of higher love and even to build upward from the most natural and primitive passions. Indeed, Tom Luxon has recently compared the interplay between Adam and Eve in Dryden's 1674 libretto for a rhymed operatic version of Milton's epic, *State of Innocence*, to Milton's own account of the unfallen pair. Luxon concludes that Dryden sees the marriage between Adam and Eve as "an ongoing negotiation between masculine reason and feminine charms" in which "sovereignty and obedience are more complicated" than in Milton's unequivocal pronouncement that reason should rule.[121] Dryden's Raphael sums up the balance of power in a set of couplets:

> An equal, yet thy subject, is design'd,
> For thy soft hours, and to unbend thy mind.
> Thy stronger soul shall her weak reason sway;
> And thou, through love, her beauty shalt obey;

Thou shalt secure her helpless sex from harms;
And she thy cares shall sweeten, with her charms.[122]

The rhymes of "sway" and "obey," "harms" and "charms" draw attention to the mutual subjection of Dryden's first pair: she obeys his reason, and he her beauty. Dryden's Eve may be Adam's "subject," but he need not worry about subjecting his passion for her to his reason; he can simply "obey" her "beauty" and enjoy the fruits of her "charms." The passage speaks to a distinction between the poets on the idea of divine design and human liberty in paradise: Dryden's pair are "design'd" in a perfect balance so Adam does not need to strive to keep his mind in right tune as Milton's Adam does. But it is also clear that Dryden's vision of the rightly tuned mind incorporates the commotion and love of outsides that Milton's Raphael rules out for Adam.

Milton's unfallen Adam responds to Raphael's correction "half abash't" but just as a Miltonic hero should: he affirms that he is not "foil'd" by what he "feels" but that he meets "with various objects, from the sense / Variously representing; yet still free / Approve the best, and follow what [he] approve[s]" (8.595, 608, 609–11). Yet there is a hint of potential vulnerability in his apparently right-minded response to Raphael's warning about the passions. He does not open by saying that he will follow reason over passion, but by denying that the "Commotion" he feels for Eve has to do with her outsides or with animal appetite: "Neither her out-side form'd so fair, nor aught / In procreation common to all kinds" delights him so much as "Those thousand decencies that daily flow / From all her words and actions" (*PL*, 8.531, 596–97, 601–2). Adam thinks he is correcting the record and proving himself less attracted to her outsides than to a matrimonial "Harmony" between them, but he also shows himself susceptible to being transported by precisely the kind of passions that the Royalists believed were most deeply rooted and powerful: the passionate ties built out of personal, daily connections to one's own land and mistress (*PL*, 8.605). Milton certainly acknowledges the power of these daily decencies, and he does not reject them if they are part of a rational hierarchy of loves. But he suspects that a retreat into the pleasures of daily life like the one Herrick celebrates in "His content in the Country" could easily slide into the slavish "domestic ease" Dalila offers in *Samson Agonistes*; "domestic *Adam*" is particularly vulnerable to the temptation (*SA*, 917; *PL*, 9.318).[123]

In his exchange with Raphael, Adam submits his longings to the rule of reason, but after Eve's fall in book 9 the pull of passion proves too much for him as he is "fondly overcome by Female charm" (*PL*, 9.999). In his final words before joining Eve in eating the apple, Adam describes the irresistible power of affective ties in a way that echoes royalist celebrations of rooted natural bonds: "So forcible within my heart I feel / The Bond of Nature draw me to my own" (*PL*, 9.955–56).[124] While Eve transgresses by attempting to fly beyond the bounds of human knowledge, Adam lapses by contracting the human sphere, by heeding the royalist call to seek fulfillment in the circumscribed freedom of enjoying one's "own" spouse, land, and intimate friends. In his discussion with Raphael, Adam had expressed his awe at the fact that Eve seemed "so absolute" and "in her self complete, so well to know / Her own" (*PL*, 8.547, 548–49). In book 9, he cedes to the romantic temptation to see Eve, and the passion he feels for her, as all in all. Milton mistrusts the bonds of passion for the same reason he denounces the bands of rhyme: both offer an illusory feeling of closure and completeness that can lead away from what Milton sees as the lasting pleasures of measured verse and measured living.

While "charms" successfully move ears and hearts in Hell and Paradise, Milton's angels and his God are never connected with the verb or noun forms of the word "charm" but only with the adjective "charming."[125] The significance of this decision becomes apparent if we return to the tortuous grammatical construction Milton uses to describe God's enjoyment of the angelic singing and dancing: "in thir motions harmony Divine / So smooths her charming tones, that God's own ear / Listens delighted" (*PL*, 5.625–27). The construction allows Milton to make "God's ear" a subject rather than a direct object of musical charming. Unlike the passive ears of royalist poetic theory, which are passionately swayed by the powerful charms of rhyme, God's ear consciously "Listens," then exercises judgment and decides that it is "delighted." Just as the angelic dance provides a model of art making that reconciles regularity with liberty, God's ear is a model of the ideal listener, who recognizes the transcendent charms of poetry's patterns and sounds without forgoing autonomous judgment.

Milton's desire to preserve some room for reason to work between the charming tones and the delighted ear has a corollary in the account of poetic composition he offers in the invocation to book 3. After describing his nightly visits to Sion and recalling the blind prophets of old, he abruptly begins a new sentence: "Then feed on thoughts that voluntary move / Harmonious numbers" (*PL*, 3.37–38). I would posit that the subject of "feed" is the "I" from line 32, though Milton could also be addressing the holy light once again. Either way, the lines deliberately open up a gap between thoughts and poetic numbers. Thoughts are undeniably prior to numbers, and Milton goes out of his way to insert an element of deliberation and choice between thinking and verse. Thoughts do not inevitably flow into harmonious verse. They "voluntar[il]y" move numbers. But, unlike in his youthful account of packing or making up his night-ward thoughts into a Petrarchan sonnet, here Milton maintains a sense of the mysterious and sensual aspects of verse making. His use of the word "feed" is striking since it makes thoughts seem like the fuel rather than the primary agents of the poetic enterprise. Milton does not make it clear who or what is feeding on these thoughts. Moreover, thought does not produce or even instill order on numbers but simply "move[s]" them. This enigmatic phrasing suggests that harmonious numbers have a life and order of their own. Thought can only prod them. With their complex vision of composition, these nine words from the invocation encapsulate Milton's understanding of freedom and form, passion and reason in *Paradise Lost*. Form is voluntary, deliberate, and a product of reason, but it is also sensual, mobile, and musical. Milton quarrels with poets whose verse is raised from the vapors of wine or the heat of passion and who desire to work directly on the passions of their listeners. He is careful to insert deliberation and volition into verse making and listening. But, in the end, he insists, this deliberate and rational verse has more sublime and mysterious harmony than verse that is the product of unpurified affections.

Ever Best Found in the Close: Rhyme and Resolution in Samson Agonistes

Though the solemn wheelings of Milton's blank verse in *Paradise Lost* seem like a satisfying solution to his career-long effort to reconcile measure with flexibility of thought, the preface to *Paradise Lost* was not Milton's final word on the subject of rhyme. Critics have long noted that the "jingling sound" of internal and end rhyme finds its way into *Paradise Lost* in spite of Milton's protestations.[126] And, more significantly, Milton seems to have come to terms with rhyme at the end of his poetic career since he uses it liberally in the choruses of *Samson Agonistes*, which was published with *Paradise Regained* in 1671.[127] He indicates in the preface to his tragedy that the "measure of Verse" in the choruses is "of all sorts, call'd by the Greeks *Monostrophic*, or rather *Apolelymenon*," a term for irregular meter that derives from a verb meaning to be freed, released, or loosed (*CPMP*, 550).[128] Though Milton does not tie himself to a particular rhyme pattern in the choruses, shifting between couplets and alternating rhyme and blank verse at will, he does appear to reconcile himself to the idea that the bands of rhyme have a significant role to play even in loosened verse.[129]

One possible explanation for this is that the incorporation of rhyme in the choruses is meant to highlight the limitations of the Chorus as interpreters of the actions of the play. The Chorus, which consists of Samson's fellow Danites, often offers counsel that is difficult to reconcile with Milton's previous positions on divine justice and human reason. Moreover, the members of the tribe of Dan rely too heavily on conventional wisdom to be seen as the authoritative voices of a Miltonic tragedy. Rhyme often marks the moments when they attempt to distill their experiential knowledge into epigrammatic sayings, the *sententiae* that were an expected feature of neoclassical tragedy, such as when they reflect on the enigmatic ways of women after Samson's verbal battle with Dalilah:

It is not virtue, wisdom, valor, wit,
Strength, comeliness of shape, or amplest merit
That woman's love can win or long inherit;
But what it is, hard is to say,
Harder to hit,
(Which way soever men refer it)
Much like thy riddle, *Samson*, in one day
Or seven, though one should musing sit. (*SA*, 1010–17)

The recurrence of the same rhyme throughout this speech—the Chorus returns to the "-it" rhyme six times—has an almost comical effect and makes the Chorus's reflections on the ways of womankind seem just a bit too pat. These rhyming Danites are representatives of ordinary Israelites who have access to God through the law but are not "solemnly elected" like Samson: neither vicious nor saintly, neither foolish nor exceptionally wise, they use custom to supplement reason and revelation (*SA*, 678). In an earlier Miltonic text, the conventional thinking of the Chorus might have inspired more scorn, but in the "Irrecoverably dark" world of *Samson Agonistes*, their approximation of truth is depicted as superior to that of the "common rout / That wand'ring loose about / Grow up and perish, as the summer fly" (*SA*, 81, 674–76). And their concern with convention and obedience makes them important interlocutors for the lawbreaking, impulse-following Samson. Their tendency to incorporate rhyme into their songs is a sign of their reliance on custom as an imperfect but useful guide. Milton's restoration of rhyme in the choruses of *Samson Agonistes* may be a concession to the customary, affective power of rhyme. Rhyme may be "no necessary Adjunct . . . of a Poem or good Verse," but it is perhaps an adjunct nonetheless (*CPMP*, 210).

In the final chorus of the play, it becomes clear that the reintroduction of rhyme in *Samson Agonistes* is related to Milton's exploration of the kind of closure provided by Aristotelian catharsis:

All is best, though we oft doubt,
What th' unsearchable dispose
Of highest wisdom brings about,
And ever best found in the close.
Oft he seems to hide his face,
But unexpectedly returns
And to his faithful Champion hath in place
Bore witness gloriously; whence *Gaza* mourns
And all that band them to resist
His uncontrollable intent;
His servants he with new acquist
Of true experience from this great event

With peace and consolation hath dismist,
And calm of mind, all passion spent. (*SA*, 1745–58)

The regularity of the alternating rhyme scheme contrasts with the Chorus's loose and haphazard use of rhyme in the majority of the play. This final chorus is not only a return to rhyme but a partial return to Milton's preferred lyric form: the sonnet. In his brief examination of rhyme in *Samson Agonistes*, Michael Cohen notes that the final chorus comprises fourteen lines and that the ABABCDCDEFEFEF rhyme scheme breaks the speech into an octave and a sestet. Cohen argues that Milton uses rhyme in this final sonnet and in other choruses throughout the play to "approximate in speech the musical effects of choral passages in classical tragedy."[130] In other words, Milton reconciles himself to rhyme in *Samson Agonistes* for the same reason that Jonson uses rhyme in the Cary and Morison ode: he sees it as a way of compensating for the loss of the music and dancing that would have heightened the ceremony and order of the ancient chorus. But Milton's return to the sonnet in particular suggests that he is once more considering rhyme's role as an instrument of measure and closure.

Indeed, the rhyme between "dispose" and "close" in the first section of the chorus suggests that the return of regular rhyme in the final moments of the play is linked to Milton's struggle to reconcile individual conscience with divine order in the tragedy. "Dispose" and its derivatives is a key word for divine providence in *Samson Agonistes*. After his first lament, the Chorus tells Samson to "Tax not divine disposal," and he in turn enjoins his father Manoa to "Appoint not heavenly disposition" (*SA*, 210, 373). Manoa later uses the verb to counsel his son not to act but "th' execution leave to high disposal" (*SA*, 506). But Samson disregards his father's advice because he believes he is an agent of the divine plan when he "begin[s] to feel / Some rouzing motions in [him] which dispose / To something extraordinary [his] thoughts" (*SA*, 1381–83). As these examples indicate, Milton is playing with the ambivalence of the words "dispose" and "disposition," which on the one hand can describe a personal inclination or individual temperament and the other can refer to an orderly (and often divine) arrangement or the action of setting things in order. Russ Leo's work has drawn attention to the fact that "dispositio" (along with "constitutio") was also the word for the orderly arrangement of a tragic plot in commentaries on Aristotle's *Poetics*; Milton uses the term in this way when he defines plot as "nothing indeed but such economy, or disposition of the fable as may stand best with verisimilitude and decorum" (*CPMP*, 550).[131] The double meaning of the term highlights a central question that runs through the play about how to determine whether the "intimate impulse[s]" Samson uses to direct his violent and amorous exploits are from "providence or instinct of nature" (*SA*, 223, 1545).[132] Are Samson's internal "motions" like the seemingly irregular "motions" of the angels in *Paradise Lost* that contribute to divine harmony, or are they just the idiosyncratic, unregulated passions that Cowley feared the Civil War and nonconformist religion unleashed in England? In its final lines, the Chorus attempts to reconcile the two senses of "disposition" by assuring its audience that individual passion can be incorporated into the divine pattern, even when that pattern is not entirely searchable or even visible. The divine "dispose," they argue, will be found to be "ever best" in the "close."[133]

So much of the Chorus's final speech seems to run counter to Milton's deepest allegiances that it is tempting to dismiss it as a model of the wrong way to engage with the "experience" of Samson's death. Victoria Kahn sees the "antinomian complacency" of the Chorus's calm minds and spent passions as antithetical to the tragedy's invitation to "move from passion to action."[134] And, in a reading of the prosodic subtleties of Samson, Janel Mueller sees the unmetrical first line paired with the "banal jauntiness and sing-song regularity of the following lines" as signs of the Chorus's failure to produce lyric, and to understand God's ways.[135] But Ryan Netzley has recently invited a reconsideration of the idea that "the unreliable, jingoistic Chorus" is offering "an ironic promise of order."[136] Pointing out how the seemingly passive and "spent" state of the Chorus in their sonnet echoes Milton's own standing, waiting service in "When I consider how my light is spent," Netzley maintains that passion, in Milton's sonnets, can itself be a thoughtful "event" rather than a "passive state."[137] In order to adjudicate between these understandings of the Chorus's spent passions, it is necessary to return to Milton's account of the purpose of tragedy in his preface on "that sort of dramatic poem which is call'd tragedy":

> Tragedy, as it was anciently compos'd, hath been ever held the gravest, moralest, and most profitable of all other Poems: therefore said by *Aristotle* to be of power by raising pity and fear, or terror, to purge the mind of those and such like passions, that is to temper and reduce them to just measure with a kind of delight, stirr'd up by reading or seeing those passions well imitated. Nor is Nature wanting in her own effects to make good his assertion: for so in Physic things of melancholic hue and quality are us'd against melancholy, sour against sour, salt to remove salt humors. (*CPMP*, 549)

Milton uses several metaphors to render the concept of catharsis: he begins with an image of the passions being utterly purged from the mind but then restates the idea in a different way, arguing that stirring up delight through imitation "temper[s] or reduce[s]" the passions "to just measure."[138] Appealing to the Aristotelian theory of catharsis and the medical theory that like drives out like allows Milton to have his passion and temper it too. Poetry does overreach reason by raising the passions, but its powers can also be used to countercharm the passions and subject them to the just measures dictated by reason.

I would argue that the cathartic closure experienced by the Chorus is neither the lyric apotheosis of the drama nor a sign of the Danites' doltish misunderstanding of the higher logic of the events that have transpired. For *Samson Agonistes* offers a hierarchy of ways to address the problem of unruly passions. Samson may—and the uncertain nature of his heroism is crucial to the play's argument about the necessity of suffering and debate—have brought order to his wild internal "motions" through internal resources alone, through "plain Heroic magnitude of mind / and celestial vigor" (*SA*, 1382, 1279–80). If so, the belated, passive purgation experienced by the Chorus is inferior to the mental and affective agon Samson experiences over the course of the play. But, while Milton clearly treats the Chorus and their rhyming customary knowledge with irony, it is a gentle irony that contrasts sharply with the indignant scorn he heaped on followers of custom in the rest of his corpus. *Samson Agonistes* contains perhaps the darkest political vision of any of Milton's works. Disheartened by the Restoration, which he had likened to the Israelites choosing captains to guide them back to captivity in Egypt in the second edition of *The Readie and Easie Way to establish a free Commonwealth* (April 1660), Milton retains very little confidence that anyone beyond a few individuals is capable of the strenuous liberty he had long striven to inculcate, or even of following leaders who are liberators rather than idolators.[139] And yet out of his dejection comes a willingness to consider a hierarchy of knowledge and revelation. The Chorus occupies a lower rung on the Miltonic ladder than does a successful Samson, but the end of the play holds out hope that the Chorus may draw closer to something like understanding. Janel Mueller suggests that the "metrical symbolics" of the play reveal that the Chorus is at its best—metrically and intellectually—when it is attempting to read Samson and his heroics rather than God's ways.[140] In other words, while they may not be capable of the free and rational political and theological engagement Milton desires, they can see, or rather feel, that something extraordinary has happened in and through Samson. To return to the language of Milton's account of poetry in his 1642 *Reason of Church-government*, by the late 1660s Milton has less confidence that poetry can serve its political purpose, "to imbreed and cherish in a great people the seeds of vertu," but it may still serve the ethical purpose, "to allay the perturbations of the mind, and set the affections in right tune."[141] Through their passionate response to Samson's tragedy, the Chorus gains a mediated, indistinct vision of the divine disposition. Though the "dispose / Of highest wisdom" remains largely "unsearchable" to their minds, the Chorus feels evidence of the restored order within their own hearts as their passions are raised and then calmed. And the Chorus's rhyme contributes to both stages of catharsis: it stirs up the passions with its charming sounds and then organizes them with its binding powers. Milton lets this theory of poetry stand without correction at the end of *Samson Agonistes* because the "measure" offered by catharsis and rhyme is an imitation—if a pale one—of the strict internal measure Milton desires to inbreed and cherish in the few.

Milton's accommodation of rhyme at the end of his tragedy suggests that his dedication to measure outweighed his antipathy to rhyme. Royalist theories about the couplet's magical power to restore affective ties had made rhyme a symbol of a vision of poetry and of the good life that Milton rejected from the beginning of his career. From Milton's perspective, the Royalists had chosen the soul-imprisoning songs of Circe over the divine, enchanting ravishment of the Lady. His rejection of rhyme in *Paradise Lost* was an attempt to free himself and his readers from the more familiar and sense-lulling pleasures of rhymed verse. He attempts to counter the "bondage with ease" of rhyme with the "strenuous liberty" of his free-flowing, carefully measured verse (*SA*, 271). But in the fallen world of *Samson Agonistes*, Milton reconciles himself once again to rhyme because he sees that, as "troublesome and modern" as its "bondage" may be, it has a role to play in tempering and reducing the passions to just measure ("The Verse," *CPMP*, 210). Thus, Milton's rejection of rhyme in *Paradise Lost* and his return to it in *Samson Agonistes* were both motivated by his career-long dedication to form as an instrument of measure.

Coda: In Strictest Measure Even

I would like to conclude by returning to that youthful sonnet that Milton either "made" or "pack't up" in a "Petrarchian stanza."[142] His sonnet about time's robbery of his youth meditates on forms of measurement in a way that makes it clear that he had already absorbed the debate between Spenser and Donne on binding and liberty and shaped his own distinctive version of measured liberty. The poem begins with a problem of disjunction between two kinds of measurement: the poet's inward state is out of joint with the measurement of "Time," which tells him that he has arrived at maturity and ripeness (Sonnet 7.1). We might expect Milton to respond to this disjunction with sovereign disdain for the measurements of something so earthly and base as time. Indeed, in another youthful poem, "On Time," Milton does in fact channel all the contempt that Donne expresses for Death in "Death be not proud," urging time to "Fly" because all that he devours is "what is false and vain, / and merely mortal dross."[143] He imagines a "long Eternity" in which his "heav'nly-guided soul" will sit "About the supreme Throne" "Triumphing over Death, and Chance, and thee / O Time."[144] Milton could easily answer the problem of his untimeliness in Sonnet 7 by contending, in a Donnean vein, that time is an earthly measurement and that such earthly measurements are mortal dross that distract from the higher measurement of heaven. Sonnet 7 does argue for a different standard of measurement, but in a quiet and even gaited—a measured—way:

> Yet be it less or more, or soon or slow,
>> It shall be still in strictest measure ev'n
>> To that same lot, however mean, or high,
> Toward which Time leads me, and the will of Heav'n;
>> All is, if I have grace to use it so,
>> As ever in my great task-Master's eye. (Sonnet 7.9–14)

Instead of triumphing over time and its drossy mortal allies, Milton softly if reluctantly resigns himself to his untimeliness and the possibility that he might be "less" fruitful than he hopes in one of his most exquisite monosyllabic lines: "Yet be it less or more, or soon or slow" (Sonnet 7.9). There is no touch of Donnean disdain here, and Milton is not loose with poetic measurement as he attempts to look toward higher standards of measure. In terms of its poetic measurements, Milton's ascent to his heavenly "lot" more closely resembles Redcrosse Knight's divinely aided journey than Donne's solitary struggle up the hill of truth. He adheres to the time-bound measurement of meter even as he makes the case for a divine perspective.

The kinship with Spenser extends beyond prosody. For the assurance that Milton offers himself still seems to hold on, if loosely, to earthly measure. In the final six lines, he does not simply tell himself that he will attain the allotted end and that he can therefore disregard the messiness of the path to that end. Rather, in some of his richest and knottiest lines, he may in fact draw together human and divine measurement: "It shall be still in strictest measure ev'n / To that same lot" (Sonnet 7.10–11). The phrase "ev'n / To" could mean "all the way to" as in Shakespeare's "bears it out even to the edge of doom."[145] But the enjambment makes it tempting—at least for a moment—to read "ev'n" as an adjective rather than an adverb. Perhaps the vague human "It" (does it refer back to "ripeness"?) will turn out to be "ev'n" (that is, level, smooth, or straight) when it is weighed according to the strictest divine measurements. The equivocal "ev'n" speaks to the broader equivocality of the sonnet, and of Milton's career-long position on providence and human action. A conditional clause in the penultimate line of the sonnet unexpectedly suggests that Milton must (with the aid of "grace") "use" something ("it") in the right way ("so") in order to fulfill the apodosis: "All is . . . / As ever in my great task Master's eye" (Sonnet 7.13–14). I read the doubleness of "in strictest measure ev'n" in light of this closing conditional and its allusion to the parable of the talents. The sonnet consoles by assuring the untimely youth that there is a divine design and that even his laggard footsteps will carry him inevitably even to his preordained lot. But, as in the closing conditional, there is also a suggestion that Milton must not neglect his individual effort to be "in strictest measure ev'n" according to his own earthly standards of measurement. The hope, held out by the rhyme between "ev'n" and "Heav'n," is that his own strict measurement of evenness will turn out to "keep in tune with Heav'n."[146] Or perhaps heaven will stoop to make the human "ev'n" and the divine "Heav'n" accord, as Milton suggests in the final rhymes of Comus:

> Mortals that would follow me,
> Love virtue, she alone is free,
> She can teach ye how to climb
> Higher then the Sphery chime;
> Or if Virtue feeble were,
> Heav'n it self would stoop to her. (*Masque*, 1018–23)

The combination of disdain for earthly measurement and hope that it can in some way approximate divine measurement that is visible in Sonnet 7 captures the tension at the heart of the early modern debate about rhyme. Like Milton, most poets of the period were measuring their verse by the standards of other kinds of harmony. They disagreed among themselves about rhyme because they disagreed about precisely what kind of "ev'n"-ness was most likely to accord with "Heav'n." In working out the nature of rhyme, a feature of verse poised somewhere between sound and sense, custom and reason, liberty and measure, poets were also deliberating within and among themselves about how these forces could or should be balanced in earthly and heavenly structures.

NOTES

Introduction

1. See Kendrick, *Milton*, 83; Achinstein, "Milton's Spectre," 6. See also the lively, testy, and, in the end, versified exchange between David Norbrook and Craig Raine in the pages of the *London Review of Books* about whether Milton's preface to *Paradise Lost* is political or entirely aesthetic. The exchange began with Norbrook's review of *The Faber Book of Political Verse*, ed. Tom Paulin, in *London Review of Books* 8, no. 10 (1986), and it continued through 1987.

2. John Milton, "The Verse," in *The Complete Poems and Major Prose*, edited by Merritt Y. Hughes (Indianapolis: Hackett, 2003), 210. All references to this text are hereafter cited parenthetically and abbreviated *CPMP*. Poetry will be cited by line number and prose by page number.

3. Carew, *Poems*, H4v. The date is based on a 1636 note by Tom Killigrew. See Carew, *Poems and Masques*, 253.

4. Milton, "Of Reformation" (1641), in *Complete Prose Works of John Milton*, 1:585; Lilburne, *Englands Birth-Right Justified*. Lilburne became known as "Free-born John" as early as 1638. Gregg, *Free-Born John*, 63. Rachel Foxley notes that the phrase "free-born Englishmen" was rare before Lilburne and that he is intentionally replacing the phrase "free-born subject." Foxley, "John Lilburne," 852. See also Williams, *Milton's Leveller God*, 7. Quentin Skinner discusses the distinction between the terms "free-born" and "free-man" as they were used during the Civil War, particularly during the Putney Debates of 1647. He notes that many participants on both sides of the Putney Debates, including Cromwell, Ireton, and Levellers Thomas Reade and Maximilian Petty, agreed in seeing servants, apprentices, and alms takers as "free-born" individuals but not as "free-men" because the latter required being "freed from dependence" and not bound to the wills of others. Skinner, "Rethinking Political Liberty," 162.

5. Milton, "Areopagitica," in *Complete Prose Works of John Milton*, 2:528. On this tension in love poetry, see Strier, "Bondage and the Lyric," 73. Strier considers the (usually paradoxical) relation of freedom and constraint in the work of Petrarch, George Herbert, and Robert Frost. He argues that the rule-governed nature of lyric form makes lyric a "wonderful test case for exploring the will's need for artificial constraints." Strier, "Bondage and the Lyric," 74.

6. In his reading of Carew's Caroline verse, Kevin Sharpe argues that this poem "denies the polygamous mode of Platonic love" favored by Henrietta Maria and the Caroline court. Sharpe, *Criticism and Compliment*, 117. Sharpe sees the image of marriage as central to Carew's idea of politics as well as of love: it is a middle way in which the passions are neither cut off nor set loose but incorporated into an orderly union. Sharpe, *Criticism and Compliment*, 145.

7. Daniel, *A Defence of Ryme*, in G. Smith, *Elizabethan Critical Essays*, 2:363.

8. See Tschann, "Layout of 'Sir Thopas,'" 6, 7. See also Purdie, *Anglicising Romance*, 66–92. Tschann connects the scribal effort to guide the reader prosodically through the layout of the text with the ideas of *ordinatio* and *compilatio*. In an influential article, Malcolm Parkes argued that the layout and "scholarly apparatus which we take for granted—analytical table of contents, text disposed into books, chapters, and paragraphs, and accompanied by

footnotes and index—originated in the application of the notions of *ordinatio* and *compila-tio* by writers, scribes, and rubricators of the thirteenth, fourteenth, and fifteenth centuries." Parkes, "Influence of the Concepts of *Ordinatio* and *Compilatio* in the Development of the Book," 135.

9. Puttenham, *Arte of English Poesie* (London, 1589), M3r, M2v. All references to this text are hereafter cited parenthetically by page signature and abbreviated *Arte*.

10. For a brief note on the significance of these diagrams in Puttenham and Drayton and an effort to use them in his own scholarship, see G. Alexander, "On the Reuse of Poetic Form," 136–37.

11. On the language of binding in Shakespeare, see John Kerrigan, *Shakespeare's Binding Language*, especially the introductory discussion on pp. 9–32.

12. Wesling, *Chances of Rhyme*, ix. In his account of rhyme in Pope's verse, W. K. Wimsatt argues that the pleasurable surprise of rhyme "depends on some incongruity or unlikelihood inherent in the coupling"; "the greater the difference in meaning between rhyme words the more marked and the more appropriate will be the binding effect." Wimsatt, *Verbal Icon*, 164. John Hollander briefly notes the association of rhyme with bonds and fetters in *Vision and Resonance* and then expands on his observation in a chapter on bondage and freedom in Romantic poetry in *Melodious Guile*. Hollander, *Vision and Resonance*, 118; Hollander, *Melodious Guile*, 85–110. See also J. Hunter, "Seven Reasons for Rhyme," 186–89; Pinsky, *Sounds of Poetry*, 80.

13. Daniel, *A Defence of Ryme*, in G. Smith, *Elizabethan Critical Essays*, 2:360.

14. Manley, *Convention*, 69.

15. Wisdom of Solomon 11:20, in *The Bible: Authorized King James Version*, ed. Robert Carroll and Stephen Prickett (Oxford: Oxford University Press, 2008). Except where otherwise noted, all biblical quotations are hereafter cited parenthetically from this version. See Spitzer, *Classical and Christian Ideas of World Harmony*; Hollander, *Untuning of the Sky*; Pahlka, *Saint Augustine's Meter*. In her work on Shakespearean measure, Paula Blank connects the omnipresence of number, weight, and measure in early modern poetics with the "emergence of scientific thought" and a growing "early modern quantitative and empirical imagination." Blank, *Shakespeare and the Mismeasure*, 3, 4. S. K. Heninger, on the other hand, sees this way of thinking as a holdover from Pythagorean cosmology and Augustinian theology that early modern poets held onto in the teeth of the new science. Heninger, *Touches of Sweet Harmony*, 146–49. Henry S. Turner offers a compromise position in his study of geometry and the English stage, arguing that there was a "geometric turn" in sixteenth-century England but that it was "pre-scientific" and indebted to earlier humanist habits of thought. Turner, *English Renaissance Stage*, 12, 14.

16. This translation is from the 1546 English abridgment, Vergil, *Abridgement of the notable woorke of Polidore Vergile*. According to its modern editor, *De inventoribus Rerum* appeared in more than a hundred editions in eight languages from 1499 through the eighteenth century. Copenhaver, introduction to *On Discovery*, viii.

17. Samuel Daniel, "Musophilis," in *Works of Samuel Daniel*, C6r.

18. See Minear, *Reverberating Song*, 19–25, 42.

19. Abraham Cowley and Andrew Marvell both use the adjective "tinkling" to describe rhyme. Cowley, "Of My self," in Cowley, *The Essays and Other Prose Writings*, edited by Alfred B. Gough (Oxford: Oxford University Press, 1915), 218. All quotations from Cowley's essays and prose are hereafter cited parenthetically by page number and abbreviated *Essays*. Marvell, "On Mr. Milton's Paradise Lost," line 46, in *Poems of Andrew Marvell*. Milton uses the word "jingling" in his preface to *Paradise Lost*. CPMP, 210. John Beaumont explicitly compares rhyme's chime to that of a bell; Beaumont, "To his late Maiestie, concerning

the true forme of English Poetry," in Beaumont, *Bosworth-field*, H7r. See also Pope, "An Essay on Criticism," lines 348–49, in *Poetry and Prose of Alexander Pope*, 47.

20. Wesling, *Chances of Rhyme*, 3, 4, 4. See also Jarvis, "Why Rhyme Pleases."

21. Wesling, *Chances of Rhyme*, ix. On rhyme's irrationality and its binding of unlike words, see also Wimsatt, *Verbal Icon*, 164; Agamben, "End of the Poem," 431; J. Hunter, "Seven Reasons for Rhymes," 186–89.

22. Webbe, *A Discourse of English Poetrie*, in G. Smith, *Elizabethan Critical Essays*, 1:267.

23. W. Scott, *Model of Poesy*, 60. William Scott's manuscript treatise (written c. 1599) was rediscovered in 2003.

24. Daniel, *A Defence of Ryme*, in G. Smith, *Elizabethan Critical Essays*, 2:360.

25. Jonson, "A Fit of Rhyme Against Rhyme," line 46, in *The Cambridge Edition of the Works of Ben Jonson*, edited by David Bevington, Martin Butler, and Ian Donaldson (Cambridge: Cambridge University Press, 2012), 5:209. All references to Jonson's poetry are hereafter cited parenthetically by line number and abbreviated *Jonson*; Milton, "The Verse," in *CPMP*, 210. For the comparison of sonnets to a Procrustean bed, see Campion, *Observations in the Art of English Poesy*, in G. Smith, *Elizabethan Critical Essays*, 2:331; and Jonson, *Informations to William Drummond of Hawthornden*, in *Jonson*, 5:362. See also Drayton, *Barrons Wars*, A3v.

26. See Attridge, *Well-Weighed Syllables*; Woods, *Natural Emphasis*, 124–30.

27. See Attridge, *Well-Weighed Syllables*; Helgerson, *Forms of Nationhood*, 25–39; Thompson, *Founding of English Metre*, 128–38.

28. Daniel, *A Defence of Ryme*, in G. Smith, *Elizabethan Critical Essays*, 2:357.

29. Ascham, *Scholemaster*, in G. Smith, *Elizabethan Critical Essays*, 1:30.

30. Ascham, *Scholemaster*, in G. Smith, *Elizabethan Critical Essays*, 1:29.

31. Campion, *Observations in the Art of English Poesy*, in G. Smith, *Elizabethan Critical Essays*, 2:329.

32. Campion, *Observations in the Art of English Poesy*, in G. Smith, *Elizabethan Critical Essays*, 2:329.

33. Helgerson, *Forms of Nationhood*, 28–29.

34. B. Cummings, *Book of Common Prayer*, 248. See the debate between Luther and Erasmus on the bondage of the will. Erasmus, *De Libero Arbitrio*; Luther, *De Servo Arbitrio*.

35. On the desire to be artificial, see Attridge, *Well-Weighed Syllables*, 105–8; Wilson-Okamura, *Spenser's International Style*, 37–41. For an effort to "restore value to artifice," see Forrest-Thomson, *Poetic Artifice*, xi.

36. Spenser, "To My Long Approoued and Singular Good Friend, Master G.H." in G. Smith, *Elizabethan Critical Essays*, 1:99.

37. Campion, *Observations in the Art of English Poesy*, in G. Smith, *Elizabethan Critical Essays*, 2:331.

38. Sidney, *Apology for Poetry*, in G. Smith, *Elizabethan Critical Essays*, 1:180.

39. Philip Sidney notes in *An Apology for Poetry* that "all learned Hebricians agree" that the Psalms are "fully written in meeter, . . . although the rules be not yet fully found." Sidney, *Apology for Poetry*, in G. Smith, *Elizabethan Critical Essays*, 1:155. Jerome and many later scholars argued that Hebrew poetry obeyed the classical rules of quantity, but the idea that there was rhyme in Hebrew is less widespread. Israel Baroway, who wrote a series of articles on early modern understandings of Hebrew form, quotes an early sixteenth-century Italian Old Testament scholar, Agostino Steuco, who says that there is rhyme in Hebrew. Baroway "Accentual Theory of Hebrew Prosody," 124.

40. See also Webbe: "men were first withdrawne from a wylde and sauadge kinde of life to ciuillity and gentlenes and the right knowledge of humanity by the force of this measurable or tunable speaking." Webbe, *Of English Poetry*, in G. Smith, *Elizabethan Critical Essays*, 1:231.

41. Daniel, *A Defence of Ryme*, in G. Smith, *Elizabethan Critical Essays*, 2:357, 360–61.

42. Spenser, "To My Long Approoued and Singular Good Friend, Master G.H." in G. Smith, *Elizabethan Critical Essays*, 1:99; Campion, *Observations in the Art of English Poesy*, in G. Smith, *Elizabethan Critical Essays*, 2:331.

43. Daniel, *A Defence of Ryme*, in G. Smith, *Elizabethan Critical Essays*, 2:361.

44. Daniel, *A Defence of Ryme*, in G. Smith, *Elizabethan Critical Essays*, 2:362.

45. Sidney, *Apology for Poetry*, in G. Smith, *Elizabethan Critical Essays*, 1:204. See also Susan Stewart's statement that rhyme is often the "symptom or indication that the poem is quickening." Stewart, "Rhyme and Freedom," 29.

46. Daniel, *A Defence of Ryme*, in G. Smith, *Elizabethan Critical Essays*, 2:362. In describing rhyme as the "enargie" of verse and saying it stirs the heart, Daniel draws on the rhetorical concepts of *energeia* and *enargeia*. Though *energeia* referred to a dynamic, forcible style and *enargeia* meant vividness, the two were often conflated in Renaissance England. See Tuve, *Elizabethan and Metaphysical Imagery*, 29–32; and Heninger, *Sidney and Spenser*, 255.

47. Sidney also insists that the purpose of poetry is not just to "teach" but to "moue." Sidney, *Apology for Poetry*, in G. Smith, *Elizabethan Critical Essays*, 1:184.

48. Daniel, *A Defence of Ryme*, in G. Smith, *Elizabethan Critical Essays*, 2:362. Cf. T. S. Eliot's statement that "it is this contrast between fixity and flux, this unperceived evasion of monotony, which is the very life of verse." Eliot, "Reflections on Vers Libre," 185.

49. Rayna Kalas discusses the many uses of the word "frame" in early modern poetic treatises in Kalas, *Frame, Glass, Verse*, 54–81. See also Crane, *Framing Authority*.

50. Philip Sidney puns on these (and several other) meanings of touch in "Astrophil and Stella 9" ("Queen Virtue's court, which some call Stella's face"), in P. Sidney, *Major Works*, 156. Neil Rhodes sees "incounters of touch" as an articulation of an "idea of language rooted in the body" and connects it with a Chapman passage in which rhyme words "kiss." Rhodes, "Framing and Tuning," 41. For a similar idea of the corporality or sensuality of Daniel's idea of rhyme, see also Kalas, *Frame, Glass, Verse*, 59; and M. Healy, *Shakespeare, Alchemy, and the Creative Imagination*, 188.

51. Rosenfeld, "Artificial Life of Rhyme," 74.

52. Helgerson describes Daniel as an advocate of nature and custom against the artificial self-fashioning of the advocates of quantitative meter. While I agree that Daniel wants nature and custom to be the roots of politics and poetry, I would argue that he sees a certain amount of self-fashioning as natural. Helgerson, *Forms of Nationhood*, 36–40.

53. Daniel, *A Defence of Ryme*, in G. Smith, *Elizabethan Critical Essays*, 2:366.

54. Daniel, *A Defence of Ryme*, in G. Smith, *Elizabethan Critical Essays*, 2:366.

55. Levine, *Forms*, 25.

56. Levine, *Forms*, 39, 27, 33.

57. Levine, *Forms*, 24–48. See Blank, *Shakespeare and the Mismeasure*. On the idea of measure as moderation or pursuing the mean, see Scodel, *Excess and the Mean*.

58. Daniel, *A Defence of Ryme*, in G. Smith, *Elizabethan Critical Essays*, 2:359.

59. This useful (and nicely alliterative) term is from Cushman, *Fictions of Form*.

60. See, for example, I. Armstrong, *Victorian Poetry*; Wolfson, *Formal Charges*; M. Brown and Wolfson, *Reading for Form*; Dubrow, *Challenges of Orpheus*; Jason Hall, *Meter Matters*; Martin, *Rise and Fall of Meter*; Michael C. Cohen, *Social Lives of Poems*.

61. Butterfield, "Why Medieval Lyric?"

62. V. Jackson, *Dickinson's Misery*, 8, 85–108, 29.

63. For two thoughtful critiques of historical poetics along other lines, see Burt's review of *The Lyric Theory Reader*, "What Is This Thing Called Lyric?"; and Culler, *Theory of the Lyric*, 83–85.

64. V. Jackson, *Dickinson's Misery*, 85–108; Prins, "What Is Historical Poetics?"

65. Rasmussen, *Renaissance Literature and Its Formal Engagements*; S. Cohen, *Shakespeare and Historical Formalism*; Burton and Scott-Baumann, *Work of Form*.

66. S. Cohen, "Between Form and Culture," 32.

67. Clarke and Coolahan, "Gender, Reception, and Form," 145.

68. Scodel, "Allusions and Distinctions," 39; Bruster, "Shakespeare and the Composite Text." See also Bruster, *Quoting Shakespeare*.

69. Raphael Lyne, "Thinking in Stanzas," 88.

70. On humanist reading, see Grafton and Jardine, *From Humanism to the Humanities*; Eden, *Hermeneutics and the Rhetorical Tradition*; Wakelin, *Humanism, Reading, and English Literature*.

71. Foucault argues that Renaissance epistemology was governed by the belief in a "web of resemblances" between word and world, in the opening chapter of *The Order of Things*, 20. Joseph Anthony Mazzeo describes what he calls "a poetic of correspondences" in seventeenth-century poetry on the continent and in England and points to "the desire to discover cosmic affinities and to draw and develop universal correspondences and analogies" as the origin of metaphysical wit. Mazzeo, "Metaphysical Poetry," 230, 231. Victoria Kahn makes the case that humanists criticized the scholastic analogy between God and the created world but nevertheless transferred analogical thinking to ideas of ethical and literary decorum. Kahn, *Rhetoric, Prudence, and Skepticism*, 49.

72. Hieatt, *Short Time's Endless Monument*; A. Fowler, *Triumphal Forms*. See also Hopper, *Medieval Number Symbolism*; Patrides, "Numerological Approach"; Rostvig, "Hidden Sense."

73. Hollander, *Untuning of the Sky*, 333.

74. I have chosen to describe the way early modern poets connected art and cosmos as analogical, but it can also be seen as synecdochal. Playing with the word *kosmos*, which meant both general order and a particular sign of that order, Jeff Dolven discusses the "ancient idea of the synecdochic ornament." Dolven, *Senses of Style*, 35. Another word that early modern poetic theorists often use for this idea is "proportion." See G. Alexander, "Sidney, Scott, and the Proportions of Poetics."

75. Pythagoreans distinguished between arithmetic, which is the study of numbers without relationship to anything else, and music, which is about the ratios or proportions among numbers. Moxon, *Mathematicks made Easie*, B4v. Heninger, *Touches of Sweet Harmony*, 91.

76. The examples Alexander Pope offers in his dilation on the idea that the "*Sound* must seem an *Eccho* to the *Sense*" suggest that he is interested in something closer to arithmetical correspondence between local sound and local sense than early modern critics. After all, he prescribes that "when loud Surges lash the sounding Shore, / The *hoarse, rough verse* shou'd like the *Torrent* roar." It is noteworthy, however, that Pope's focus in this verse paragraph is on the "Numbers" of a poem; in other words, he is to a certain extent thinking about the patterns formed by many sounds and the ways that these patterns might represent the waves. Pope, "An Essay on Criticism," lines 365, 368–69, 337, in *Poetry and Prose of Alexander Pope*, 47.

77. Puttenham uses the word "analogy" as a synonym for the Latin *decorum*, which he translates as "decency." We tend to think of rhetorical decorum as a fit between style and

genre or between speech and the circumstances of time, place, and person, but Puttenham discusses every manner of proportionality in this concluding chapter of his book. Thomas Kranidas offers a thorough survey of classical and early modern passages on decorum in the opening chapter of his book on Milton's decorum. Kranidas, *Fierce Equation*, 13–48. See also G. Gregory Smith, introduction to G. Smith, *Elizabethan Critical Essays*, 1:xli–xlvi; Tuve, *Elizabethan and Metaphysical Imagery*, 192–247; Patterson, *Hermogenes and the Renaissance*, 3–43.

78. On the connection between decorum and prudence, see Kahn, *Rhetoric, Prudence, and Skepticism*, 30–54.

79. Paul Fussell argues in a chapter on the ethics of stress regularity in the eighteenth century that analogical thinking about form did not disappear in the "empirical age." It was, however, narrowed. He notes that only a few bold spirits "make an attempt to connect the order and regularity of conservative verse structure with a metaphysical theory of universal order." Instead, most "ground the conservative theory of prosody in what were conceived to be the truths of a universal morality and a universal psychology." Fussell, *Theory of Prosody*, 38.

80. Jarvis, "For a Poetics of Verse," 932. In her introduction to *Hearing Things*, Angela Leighton discusses Jarvis and other critics who have taken a cognitive approach to verse; she offers "listening" as an alternative. Leighton, *Hearing Things*, 13–17.

81. Jarvis, "Melodics," 612.

82. Jarvis, "Melodics," 612, 616.

83. In his understanding of this struggle, Jarvis is indebted to Adorno, who argues that art always "stood in opposition to social domination and its *mores*"; but Adorno also maintains that its "autonomy, its growing independence from society, was a function of the bourgeois consciousness of freedom that was itself bound up with the social structure." For Adorno, art becomes more social by opposing society. Adorno, *Aesthetic Theory*, 307. For accounts of the complexity and influence of theories of art's autonomy, see Leighton, *On Form*, 30–54; Goldstone, *Fictions of Autonomy*.

84. Davies, *Orchestra*, in *Poems of Sir John Davies*. See also the chapter "The Cosmic Dance," in Tillyard, *Elizabethan World Picture*, 101–6.

85. Woods, *Natural Emphasis*, 11.

86. Jarvis, "Melodics," 612.

87. Jarvis, "Melodics," 612.

88. See Cushman, "On Middlebrow Formalism."

89. Wallace Stevens, "Sunday Morning," in Stevens, *Harmonium*, 104.

90. C. Brooks, *Well-Wrought Urn*, 203. See also the critique of "message-hunting" in C. Brooks and Warren, "Introduction to *Understanding Poetry* (1938)," 185.

91. Wilson-Okamura, *Spenser's International Style*. See Harington, *A Briefe Apologie of Poetrie* (1591), in G. Smith, *Elizabethan Critical Essays*, 2:206; Sidney, *Apology for Poetry*, in G. Smith, *Elizabethan Critical Essays*, 1:160; W. Scott, *Model of Poesy*, 63; Edward Phillips, "Preface to *Theatrum Poetarum, or A Compleat Collection of the Poets*, 1675," in Spingarn, *Critical Essays of the Seventeenth Century*, 2:264. See also Wills, *De Re Poetica*, 50–51; Alexander, *Anacrisis: Or, A Censure of some Poets Ancient and Modern*, in Spingarn, *Critical Essays of the Seventeenth Century*, 1:182; Bede, *Libri II De Arte Metrica*, 168–69. On the garment of style, see Tuve, *Elizabethan and Metaphysical Imagery*, 61–78; Wilson-Okamura, *Spenser's International Style*, 150.

92. Daniel, *A Defence of Ryme*, in G. Smith, *Elizabethan Critical Essays*, 2:377–78.

93. John Harington explicitly divides poetry into two parts thrice in his treatise. The first time he says that the parts are "fiction and imitation" on the one hand and "verse" on the other; the second time he describes the parts as "Imitation" and "Verse," and the third

time as "inuention or imitation and verse." Harington, *Apologie of Poetrie*, in G. Smith, *Elizabethan Critical Essays*, 2:204, 206, 207; Samuel Daniel uses the words "inuentions" and "conceits" in contrast to rhyme in the passage where he argues that rhyme is not a "tyrannical bounding" quoted above. Daniel, *A Defence of Ryme*, in G. Smith, *Elizabethan Critical Essays*, 2:365–66. Gascoigne says that the "first and most necessarie point" in writing poetry is to "grounde it upon some fine inuention." Gascoigne, *Certayne Notes of Instruction Concerning the Making of Verse or Ryme in English*, in G. Smith, *Elizabethan Critical Essays*, 1:47. See also W. Scott, *Model of Poesy*, 38.

94. Sidney, *Apology for Poetry*, in G. Smith, *Elizabethan Critical Essays*, 1:157. The stages of composition in the classical rhetorical tradition were *inventio, dispositio* (arrangement or ordering), *elocutio, memoria,* and *pronunciatio.* See Vickers, *Classical Rhetoric*, 61–65; Dolven, *Scenes of Instruction*, 45. For a thirteenth-century version of this idea, see the opening of Geoffrey of Vinsauf, *Poetria Nova*, 17. Geoffrey compares the poet to an architect and advises that he construct an "archetypal" version of his poem in his "mind's citadel" before turning to the pen or the tongue.

95. W. Scott, *Model of Poesy*, 38.

96. See Sidney, *Apology for Poetry*, in G. Smith, *Elizabethan Critical Essays*, 1:157; Puttenham, *Arte*, C1r. Heninger traces this idea back to Landino, Scaliger, and, ultimately, Augustine. Heninger, *Sidney and Spenser*, 181–96.

97. Wilson-Okamura, *Spenser's International Style*, 152.

98. Wilson-Okamura, *Spenser's International Style*, 151.

99. W. Scott, *Model of Poesy*, 65.

100. C. Brooks, *Well-Wrought Urn*, 69.

101. It is also revealing, though, that Eliot, Brooks, and the New Critics prefer Donne, whose most elaborate patterns are often at the level of image and metaphor rather than form.

102. W. Scott, *Model of Poesy*, 32; C. Brooks, *Well-Wrought Urn*, 178, 202.

103. Greenblatt, *Renaissance Self-Fashioning*, 7.

104. Leighton, *Hearing Things*, 17.

105. Leighton, *Hearing Things*, 13–16.

106. Daniel, *A Defence of Rhyme*, in G. Smith, *Elizabethan Critical Essays*, 2:359.

107. Nicholson, *Uncommon Tongues*, 124–63. See also Hardison, *Prosody and Purpose*, 236–57.

108. Robert Greene, *Menaphon*, *2v.

109. Marlowe, *Tamburlaine the Great*, A3r.

110. Shakespeare, *Much Ado about Nothing*, 5.2.29, in *Norton Shakespeare*.

111. Marlowe's translation of Lucan into blank verse is an exception.

112. Italian critics complained that the blank verse used by Gian Giorgio Trissino in his 1548 epic might be appropriate for drama but that it was too close to common speech for an epic. See Wilson-Okamura, *Spenser's International Style*, 34–38.

113. On rhyme in Shakespeare, see Ness, *Use of Rhyme*; Attie, "Passion Turned to Prettiness."

114. A quincunx is an arrangement of five points with four in a square and the fifth in the center (the most familiar example is the arrangement of the five points on a die). In *The Garden of Cyrus* (1658), physician and natural philosopher Thomas Browne detects the quincunx figure in every aspect of nature and art. Browne concludes his treatise by declaring, "All things began in order, so shall they end, and so shall they begin again; according to the ordainer of order and mystical Mathematicks of the City of Heaven." Browne, *Hydrotaphia*, O5r.

Chapter One. Sweet Be the Bands:
Spenser and the Sonnet of Association

1. Coleridge, "To Thomas Poole, November 7th, 1796," in Coleridge, *Collected Letters*, 1:252. For an account of the circumstances that led Coleridge to produce this little pamphlet, see Fairer, "Coleridge's 'Sonnets from Various Authors.'"

2. Coleridge, *Complete Works*, number 16, volume 1, part 2, p. 1235.

3. The *OED* definition of "lyric" is remarkably similar to Coleridge's definition of the sonnet: "Now used as the name for short poems (whether or not intended to be sung), usually divided into stanzas or strophes, and directly expressing the poet's own thoughts and sentiments." The definition has not changed since 1953, when T. S. Eliot cited it in his lecture series "Three Voices of Poetry" and complained that "there is no necessary relation between brevity and expression of the poet's own thoughts and feelings." *Oxford Engish Dictionary*, s.v. "lyric"; Eliot, "The Three Voices of Poetry," in *On Poetry and Poets*, 105.

4. Coleridge, *Complete Works*, number 16, volume 1, part 2, p. 1235.

5. G. K. Hunter, "Spenser's *Amoretti*," 128–29.

6. T. Greene, *Light in Troy*, 100–101.

7. Petrarch, "Rime Sparse 35," lines 1, 13, in *Petrarch's Lyric Poems*, 95.

8. See Braden, "Unspeakable Love," 256; Braden, *Petrarchan Love*, 37–38.

9. Gordon Braden argues that Petrarch's *De vita solitaria* looks backward to the monastic tradition but also clears space for a more secular version of "autarkic individualism." Braden, *Petrarchan Love*, 3.

10. Northrop Frye argues that lyric must begin with some kind of "frustrating or blocking point" that leads the speaker to turn inward and thereby open "another world of experience." Frye, "Approaching the Lyric," 36.

11. Silliman et al., "Aesthetic Tendency and the Politics of Poetry," 263.

12. Spenser, *Amoretti*, Sonnet 5, line 14, in *Yale Edition of the Shorter Poems of Edmund Spenser*, edited by William A. Oram, Einar Bjorvand, Ronald Bond, Thomas H. Cain, Alexander Dunlop, and Richard Schell (New Haven, CT: Yale University Press, 1989). All references to this text are hereafter cited parenthetically and abbreviated *SP*. *Amoretti* will be cited by sonnet and line number and all other poems by line number.

13. Alastair Fowler notes the prevalence of couples in the *Faerie Queene* in his discussion of Spenser's Neoplatonism. A. Fowler, "Emanations of Glory," 54. In addition to using "doubleness" as a guiding principle in his analysis of the *Faerie Queene*, Bart Giamatti notes that Spenser plays with the word "pair" and its derivatives (despair, impair, and repair) throughout his corpus, "punning on the problems of paring/pairing—dividing and making whole" in order to underscore the destructive and unifying powers of language. Giamatti, *Play of Double Senses*, 103.

14. For readings of the lady as a stand-in for the queen and *Amoretti* as an allegory of Elizabethan politics, see Marotti, " 'Love Is Not Love' "; Bates, "Politics of Spenser's *Amoretti*"; Fleming, "View from the Bridge." For related readings of Sidney's *Astrophil and Stella*, see Jones and Stallybrass, "Politics of *Astrophil and Stella*"; Wilson, "Struggle for Sovereignty."

15. Spenser, *The Faerie Queene*, edited by A. C. Hamilton (New York: Longman, 2007), book 1, proem, stanza 1. All references to this text are hereafter cited parenthetically by book, canto, and stanza and abbreviated *FQ*; T. Smith, *De Republica Anglorum*, C2v. Andrew Hadfield includes a detailed account of Spenser's connections with Sir Thomas Smith in his recent biography of Spenser. Smith was Harvey's patron and is mentioned in both the Harvey-Spenser letters and the glosses to *The Shepheardes Calender*. Hadfield, *Edmund Spenser*, 56, 63–64. Elizabeth Fowler also sees Smith's position on the continuity between

marriage and society as similar to Spenser's. E. Fowler, *Literary Character*, 203. Citing La Primaudaye, James Nohrnberg makes the case that in the sixteenth century marriage was considered the "original of all social bonds." Nohrnberg, *Analogy of the "Faerie Queene,"* 601.

16. Aristotle, *Politics*, 1252a, in *Basic Works of Aristotle*, 1127–28.

17. T. Smith, *De Republica Anglorum*, C2v.

18. Quoted from the 1606 English translation, Bodin, *Six bookes of the common-weale*, B4v. For a meditation on Spenser's relation to Machiavelli, Bodin, and Smith, see Baker, "Spenser and Politics."

19. Bodin, *Six bookes of the common-weale*, B4v.

20. *Amoretti* does include three sonnets that address people outside of the relationship—Sonnet 33 to Lodowick Bryskett on *The Faerie Queene*, Sonnet 80 (also on *The Faerie Queene*), and Sonnet 86 to a "Venemous toung" that speaks ill of him—but these exceptional sonnets only draw attention to the fact that the majority of the sonnets focus on the pair of lovers. Elizabeth Fowler has highlighted a similar paring down to focus on the couple in the marriage of the Thames and the Medway; she argues that "the authority of [the Medway's] consent is further stressed by the absence of her parents." E. Fowler, *Literary Character*, 202.

21. P. Cummings, "Spenser's *Amoretti* as an Allegory of Love," 164; Alexander Dunlop also argues that "through the symbolic framework of *Amoretti* Spenser places the narrative-historical details in a universal context." Dunlop, "Drama of *Amoretti*," 107. On Elizabeth Boyle's family and Spenser's possible connections with them, see Hadfield, *Edmund Spenser*, 296–301.

22. E. Fowler, *Literary Character*, 204, 204, 205. In a 1579 letter to Gabriel Harvey, Spenser says that he will soon "set forth" a book in quantitative meter called "*Epithalamion Thamesis*." The connection between this project, which was never published, and the marriage of the Thames as it is described in *The Faerie Queene* is unknown. Edmund Spenser, *To My Long Aprooued and Singular Good Frende, Master G.H.*, in G. Smith, *Elizabethan Critical Essays*, 1:100.

23. Hooker, *Of the Lavves of Ecclesiasticall Politie*, H3r–v.

24. "Bond of Association" was also an alternative title for the 1584 "Instrument of Association for the Preservation of Her Majesty's Royal Person." The subjects who signed this document bound themselves to defend the queen against her enemies and to avenge her death. As in the Hooker passage, in this document there is a tension or interplay between consent and constraint—the document repeatedly stresses the fact that the signatories *voluntarily* bind themselves to defend the queen. PRO SP 12/174. Patrick Collinson has argued that the bond was "quasi-republican" because it "was in the form of a covenant," envisioned the death of the queen and its aftermath, and suggested that vengeance would be carried out by "no other authority than that residing in the body politic." Collinson, "Monarchical Republic of Queen Elizabeth I," 50. See also Cressy, "Binding the Nation."

25. Aristotle, *Aristotles Politiques*, D5r. Spenser's friend Lodowick Bryskett mentions the human inclination to society in his political treatise, noting that "this loue maketh one man courteous, gracious, and affable to another, if he degenerate not from his owne nature which hath framed him sociable." Bryskett, *Discourse of Ciuill Life*, Gg2r.

26. Rosenthal, *Crown under Law*, 83, 116.

27. The original ending to book 3 of *The Faerie Queene*, in which Amoret and Scudamour dwell in "long embracement" and become like "that faire *Hermaphodite*," is the most striking Spenserian image of this longing for complete union (*FQ*, 3.12.45,46).

28. Yeats, "Edmund Spenser," 4:266.

29. Particularly in Spenser, who displays a preoccupation with verse forms and a penchant for prosodic experimentation early in his career, the relationship between formal

choices and social theories is a two-way street: his views on poetry inform and modify his political thought as well as the other way around.

30. Dubrow, *Challenges of Orpheus*; Catherine Nicholson discusses the dual nature of Orpheus as emblem of civilization and of unruliness in Nicholson, *Uncommon Tongues*, 1–18.

31. Spenser, *To the Worshipful His Very Singular Good Friend, Maister G.H., Fellow of Trinitie Hall in Cambridge* in G. Smith, *Elizabethan Critical Essays*, 1:89; Spenser, *To My Long Approved and Singular Good Friend, Master G.H.*, in G. Smith, *Elizabethan Critical Essays*, 1:99; Gabriel Harvey, *A Gallant Familiar Letter, Containing An Answere to That of M. Immerito, with Sundry Proper Examples and Some Precepts of Our English Reformed Versifying*, in G. Smith, *Elizabethan Critical Essays*, 1:101. "Balductum" was a noun for hot curdled milk with wine that came to mean trash or nonsense. It was most commonly used to describe bad writing and doggerel verse: Abraham Fraunce speaks of "all our balductum and vncoherent pamphlets," and Gabriel Harvey's brother John complains of "gewgawes, pricked vp in rime dogrell, and balductum meter." *Oxford English Dictionary*, s.v. "balductum/balducta, n."; Fraunce, *Lawiers Logike*, Iir; J. Harvey, *Discoursiue Problem*, K1r.

32. Spenser, *To My Long Approved and Singular Good Friend*, in G. Smith, *Elizabethan Critical Essays*, 1:99. For a detailed analysis of this passage, see Atridge, *Well-Weighed Syllables*, 146–47.

33. Helgerson, *Forms of Nationhood*, 28, 3.

34. Gabriel Harvey, *A Gallant Familiar Letter*, in G. Smith, *Elizabethan Critical Essays*, 1:102.

35. On the different ways both Spenser and Harvey appeal to custom and the connection to Spenser's *View*, see Elsky, " 'Wonne with Custome.' "

36. David Scott Wilson-Okamura also argues that there is a continuity between Spenser's experiments with quantitative meter and his turn to stanzaic poetry, though he focuses on Spenser's pursuit of artificiality and elaborateness rather than his interest in restraint. Wilson-Okamura, *Spenser's International Style*, 37–42.

37. Spenser, argument to "October," in *SP*, 170.

38. The phrase "looselie scattered abroad" is from the printer's letter that prefaces Spenser, *Complaints*, A2r.

39. On the Spenser's engagements with the strange and the rude in the *Shepheardes Calender*, see Nicholson, *Uncommon Tongues*, 100–123; Harrison, "Rude Poet."

40. Hadfield, *Edmund Spenser's Irish Experience*, 17. Lord Grey was recalled in 1582, but Spenser lived in Ireland until he fled to Westminster in 1599.

41. I will not discuss Spenser's cosmic philosophy in any detail in this chapter, but the idea of *discordia concors*, which is patently related to the interweaving of like and unlike sounds in the rhyme patterns that Spenser prefers, has been discussed in Berger, "Spenserian Dynamics"; Wolfe, "Spenser, Homer, and the Mythography of Strife"; and Nicholson, *Uncommon Tongues*, 100–123.

42. See "Terms used by the Brick-layer" in *Academy of Armory*, Kk3r-v. On Puttenham's interest in practical geometric arts, see Turner, *English Renaissance Stage*, 118–27.

43. The use of alphabetical notation seems to have arisen with critical commentary on the sonnet. The earliest use of such notation that I have discovered is in a discussion of the Petrarchan sonnet in Italian critic Antonio Sebastian Minturno's dialogue *De Poeta, Libri Sex* (Venice, 1559). The earliest English work I have found that uses this notation is Robert Fletcher Housman, *Collection of English Sonnets* (London, 1835).

44. Cicero, *De Inventione* 1.2.2.

45. Machiavelli, *Discorsi*, libro I, cap. II, p. 20.

46. Machiavelli, *Discourses*, in *"The Prince" and the "Discourses,"* 118.

47. Spenser, *A View of the Present State of Ireland*, in *Works of Edmund Spenser*, 10:43, 146–47.

48. Spenser, *A View of the Present State of Ireland*, in *Works of Edmund Spenser*, 10:43, 43, 54, 125.

49. Spenser, *A View of the Present State of Ireland*, in *Works of Edmund Spenser*, 10:49.

50. Hamilton, *Calendar of the State Papers*, 247.

51. Andrew Hadfield weighs the two claims in *Edmund Spenser*, 202–6. See also Herron, "Colonialism and Irish Plantation."

52. Spenser, "To My Long Approoued and Singular Good Friend, Master G.H." in G. Smith, *Elizabethan Critical Essays*, 1:99.

53. Webbe, *A Discourse of English Poetrie*, in G. Smith, *Elizabethan Critical Essays*, 1:270.

54. Webbe, *A Discourse of English Poetrie*, in G. Smith, *Elizabethan Critical Essays*, 1:270.

55. Webbe, *A Discourse of English Poetrie*, in G. Smith, *Elizabethan Critical Essays*, 1:271.

56. Matthew Harrison offers a thoughtful reading of the "lay" in "April" in which he argues that "the moment of binding adorns the rude rhythms of the native tradition, transmuting them into something more graceful" but also notes that something is "left loose" about the stanza. Harrison, "Rude Poet," 254–55.

57. Spenser, "The generall argument of the whole booke," in *SP*, 23.

58. Kinney, *Strategies of Poetic Narrative*, 70; Dolven, "Method of Spenser's Stanza," 20–22. For further analysis of the Spenserian stanza, see also Woods, *Natural Emphasis*, 148; Addison, "Little Boxes."

59. Dolven, "Method of Spenser's Stanza," 20–22.

60. On the "jarring" effect of Spenser's use of similar connective words to link stanzas in *The Faerie Queene*, see Kinney, *Strategies of Poetic Narrative*, 7.

61. Barolini, "Making of a Lyric Sequence." For an account of *Amoretti* as a narrative "dramatization" of the steps of courtship, see Dunlop, "Drama of *Amoretti*."

62. The lovers are alienated from the opening sonnet, but the sonnets that specifically depict one or both of them as warriors or wild beasts are 10, 11, 12, 14, 20, 31, 36, 38, 41, 42, 47, 49, 52, 53, and 57.

63. Consent had been a defining characteristic of marriage since at least the twelfth century. Harrington, *Reordering Marriage and Society*. In the sixteenth century, the idea of marriage as a contract became even more influential because of the rise of covenantal theology in Reformed circles. In his influential treatise on marriage, which was printed in English in 1542, Heinrich Bullinger compares marriage to the covenants of the new and old testaments. Bullinger, *Golden boke of christen matrimonye*. In their account of marriage in Shakespeare, B. J. and Mary Sokol point out that the word "contract" is used almost exclusively for spousal contracts in Shakespeare's corpus. My searches for the term in *Early English Books Online* indicate that a majority of the hits prior to 1600 relate to marriage. Sokol and Sokol, *Shakespeare, Law and Marriage*, 19.

64. Buchanan, *Dialogue on the Law of Kingship among the Scots*.

65. On the relationship between the marriage contract and the social contract in the seventeenth century, see Kahn, *Wayward Contracts*, 57–80 and 174–76; Shanley, "Marriage Contract."

66. Petrarch, "Rime Sparse 21" in *Petrarch's Lyric Poems*. Spenser's warrior and wild beast sonnets are 10, 11, 12, 14, 20, 31, 36, 38, 41, 42, 47, 49, 52, 53, and 57. In her reading of *Amoretti*, Cynthia N. Nazarian draws attention to the violence of Spenser's sequence and to its focus on sovereignty and abjection. Nazarian, *Love's Wounds*, 183–84.

67. Lever, *Elizabethan Love Sonnet*, 99–100.

68. Martz, "*Amoretti*: Most Goodly Temperature," 154–56; Dunlop, "Drama of *Amoretti*," 108. For the latter interpretation, see also P. Cummings, "Spenser's *Amoretti* as an Allegory of Love," 168–69; Dasenbrock, "Petrarchan Context," 39. Lisa M. Klein argues that the love-as-war trope is rejected after Sonnet 14, Klein, "'Let Us Love,'" 113. A notable exception is Ruth Kaplan's recent article on pity in *Amoretti*, which takes the war images seriously and sees Spenser as rejecting the sonnet paradigm in which the poet triumphs if his lady pities him. Spenser, she argues, transcends the tragic logic of pitying in favor of the comic logic of loving. Kaplan, "Problem of Pity."

69. T. Smith, *De Republica Anglorum*, C2v.

70. Philip Sidney, "Astrophil and Stella 1," lines 12, 14, in P. Sidney, *Major Works*, 151.

71. Milton, *Paradise Lost*, 2.648–870, in *CPMP*, hereafter cited as *PL*.

72. See Loewenstein, "Note on the Structure of Spenser's *Amoretti*," 312.

73. Regional and temporal variations in pronunciation make it difficult to make definitive claims about imperfect rhymes in sixteenth-century poetry. There is, however, some evidence to suggest that "proud" and "food" are not perfect rhymes here: (1) The two words are listed under separate categories in Peter Levens's rhyming dictionary, *Manipulus Vocabulorum* (London, 1570). (2) Spenser uses the word *proud* as a rhyme word two other times in *Amoretti and Epithalamion* and six times in *The Faerie Queene*; in these instances, the word never rhymes with words ending in *-ood*, but always rhymes with words ending in *-oud* or *-owd*: cloud, shroud, aloud, avow'd, vow'd, alow'd, crowd, and loud. (3) I have done an extensive survey of late sixteenth-century poetry and have not uncovered a single instance in which proud rhymes with a word ending in *-od* or *-ood*. In the works surveyed, it always rhymes with words ending in *-oud* or *-owd*, including cloud, allow'd, loud, avow'd, aloud, crowd, and bow'd. (4) The fact that proud is often spelled prowd or prowde both in Elizabethan poetry more generally and in Spenser's poetry (especially when he uses it as a rhyme word) suggests that it was pronounced praud, as it is today.

74. Hollander, "Romantic Verse Form."

75. For an extensive analysis of pride in the sequence, see Braden, "Pride, Humility, and the Petrarchan Happy Ending." See also Nazarian, *Love's Wounds*, 192–95.

76. *Second Tome of Homelyes*, Lll2v.

77. *Oxford English Dictionary*, s.v. "term, n."

78. Hooker, *Of the Lavves of Ecclesiasticall Politie*, H3r–v.

79. Joseph Loewenstein draws attention to this ambiguity and also suggests that the lady's condition "cannot honestly be described except as a kind of bondage." Loewenstein, "Note on the Structure of Spenser's *Amoretti*," 315.

80. *Oxford English Dictionary*, s.v. "mew, n. 2."

81. In his article on Spenserian pastoral and *Amoretti*, John D. Bernard also uses this poem to demonstrate that a cage can be an oasis and refuge. Bernard is one of only a few critics who sees "liberating bondage" as a central trope of the sequence. Bernard, "Spenserian Pastoral."

82. W. Johnson, "Gender Fashioning," 508. See also Klein, "'Let Us Love,'" 129–32. Loewenstein discusses the "limits of [Spenser's] momentous feminism." Loewenstein, "Note on the Structure of Spenser's *Amoretti*," 320.

83. Bell, *Elizabethan Women*, 183.

84. Pointing to these images of violence and abjection, Nazarian likewise argues that the betrothal sonnet and the last third of the sonnet sequence do not figure "consent and mutuality." She makes the case that the postbetrothal sonnets simply reverse the tyrant and the victim in the sequence. I argue instead that both lady and poet have yielded themselves to captivity by the end of the sequence. Nazarian, *Love's Wounds*, 231.

85. Fleming, "View from the Bridge," 151–52; Bell, *Elizabethan Women*, 175, 177; P. Cummings, "Spenser's *Amoretti* as an Allegory of Love," 173.

86. Keats's 1817 *Poems* begins with an epigraph from Spenser's "Muiopotmos, or the Fate of the Butterflie" and includes numerous poems that either imitate or allude to Spenser. It is intriguing that in the epigraph and the poems within the volume, Keats repeatedly associates Spenser with liberty. Keats, *Poems*. See Kucich, *Keats, Shelley, and Romantic Spenserianism*.

87. Keats, *Letters of John Keats*, 2:108.

88. Spenser, "Letter of the Authors," in *FQ*, 714.

89. *SP*, 42, underlining mine.

90. Milton's play with the word *yield* and with Eve's willingness in book 4 of *Paradise Lost* may owe something to this line and Spenser's other uses of the word yield. Milton, *PL*, 4.309–10, in *CPMP*.

91. See Sonnets 27, 52, and 42. Sidney also uses "pain" frequently as a rhyme word, but he prefers to rhyme it with a word that Spenser does not use a single time in *Amoretti and Epithalamion*: "brain."

92. Larsen, note to sonnet 65, *Edmund Spenser's "Amoretti and Epithalamion,"* 195. *Holie. Bible. conteyning the olde Testament and the newe.* Naseeb Shaheen's study of Spenser's use of the bible in *The Faerie Queene* indicates that he used a mixture of the Geneva, Vulgate, and Bishops' versions. I have chosen to quote from the Bishops' Bible here because Spenser's address to his "deare loue" seems to echo the address to "Dearely beloved" in the Bishops' version. In the Geneva, the verses simply begin "Beloued." *Bible and Holy Scriptures conteyned in the Olde and Newe Testament*; Shaheen, *Biblical References*, 34.

93. *Second Tome of Homelyes*, Lll5v.

94. *Holie. Bible. conteyning the olde Testament and the newe.*

95. Fleming, "View from the Bridge," 152; Cummings, "Spenser's *Amoretti* as an Allegory of Love," 173; Villeponteaux, "'With Her Own Will Beguyld,'" 30. Lisa M. Klein likewise argues that there is a paradoxical logic of freedom in bondage in the *Amoretti* but thinks that the cage image must be replaced by the image of a bower or enclosed garden. I argue that Spenser pushes his reader to address and come to terms with the cage image rather than reject it. Klein, "'Let Us Love,'" 127.

96. Bell, *Elizabethan Women*, 175.

97. Ilona Bell argues that in this poem the speaker becomes caught in his own rhetoric and irony. Bell, *Elizabethan Women*, 177.

98. *Oxford Engish Dictionary*, s.v. "gentle, adj. and n."

99. Rousseau, *Discourses, and Other Early Political Writings*, 6.

100. Daniel, *Delia*, H1r.

101. See W. Johnson, "Spenser's *Amoretti* and the Art of the Liturgy." R. L. Kesler argues that the sonnet, particularly in contrast to medieval romances, is "isolating and analytical, dissolving the integration of their represented world in favor of the integrity of their analysis." Kesler, "Formalism and the Problem of History," 179–80.

102. Thomas Greene notes that, although Spenser's lengthy stanza is related to the Italian canzone, no poem has been found in an identical pattern. T. Greene, "Spenser and the Epithalamic Convention," 224.

103. Dubrow, "Epithalamium"; Dubrow also discusses the ways that later poets imitated and adapted Spenser's refrain in Dubrow, *Happier Eden*, 101–4.

104. Webbe, *A Discourse of English Poetrie*, in G. Smith, *Elizabethan Critical Essays*, 1:270.

105. For comments that indicate the term was commonly associated with marriage

poetry, see Scaliger, *Poetices Libri Septem*, 3.101.151; Jonson, marginal note to "Epithalamion," *Hymenaei*, line 397, in *Jonson*, 2:710; A. Jackson, *Annotations Upon The five Books*, 7T1r.

106. Servius, *Servii Grammatici*, 3:95. Translation mine.

107. Hieatt, *Short Time's Endless Monument*.

108. Hieatt, *Short Time's Endless Monument*, 80.

109. The other use is in book 6 of *The Faerie Queene* where Serena is also brought before an "altar" and "priest" but for a very different kind of rite—the "diuelish ceremonies" of the "Saluages" who wish to sacrifice the virgin's blood to their god (FQ, 6.8.45). The sacrificial logic of Amoretti makes the resemblance between the two scenes more than superficial. The lady of *Epithalamion* is also, in a way, being sacrificed. Collating the two scenes draws attention to the proximity of superstition and religion, nature and high artifice.

110. It is arguable whether any marriages are actually realized "on stage," so to speak, in *The Faerie Queene*. Though Spenser describes the marriage procession of the rivers in remarkable detail, he does not describe the marriage ceremony itself or even the marriage banquet since he instead follows Marinell—who, being half mortal, is not invited to the banquet—in his wanderings (*FQ*, 4.11–12). David Norbrook notes that *The Faerie Queene* "is full of prophesies of future ceremonies which will resolve all contradiction, most notably the marriage of Arthur and Gloriana. But these ceremonies are always deferred, and the emphasis is on the difficulty of completing the quests and the dangers of complacency." Norbrook, *Poetry and Politics*, 110.

111. Max Wickert also highlights the centrality of this word and its implications for the efficacy of ceremony in Wickert, "Structure and Ceremony," 138. Cf. *FQ*, 2.4.22. Elizabeth B. Tribble discusses Elizabethan ambivalence about ceremony, particularly in relation to the Lord's Supper, in Tribble, "Partial Sign."

112. T. Smith, *De Republica Anglorum*, C2v.

113. From E.K.'s epistle "To the most excellent and leaned both Orator and Poete, Mayster Gabriell Harvey," Spenser, *SP*, 17.

114. Howard, *Spencer Redivivus*, A3v.

115. Warton, *Observations on the Fairy Queen of Spenser (1762)*, 55.

Chapter Two. Licentious Rhymers: Donne and the Late Elizabethan Couplet Revival

1. In "Sleeping Beauties," J. Paul Hunter explains how the "couplet's bad reputation" as a "carrier" of imperialist ideologies derives from critiques of the Enlightenment raised by Horkheimer and Adorno. Reading poems by Denham and Pope, Hunter works to show that the couplet was more "subtle, flexible, and supple" than criticism has allowed. J. Hunter, "Sleeping Beauties," 3, 7. It should be noted, however, that the Romantics attributed political implications to the Augustan couplet. William Keach discusses Keats's early efforts to flout the Augustans, who, Keats claims in "Sleep and Poetry," "were closely wed / To musty laws lined out with wretched rule / And compass vile." Keats, "Sleep and Poetry," lines 194–96, in Keats, *Poems of John Keats*, 77. Keach argues that Keats's loose, enjambed "Cockney couplets" were an important part of this effort. Keach's reading of the complex "politics of style" during this period shows that, in many ways, the Romantics replayed the debates about liberty and rule I consider in this chapter; Keach, "Cockney Couplets."

2. Philip J. Finkelpearl provides an illuminating account of the social background that informed this school's literary endeavors in Finkelpearl, *John Marston of the Middle Temple*. Richard Helgerson's distinction between amateurs and laureates captures one aspect

of the distinction between these two schools. Helgerson, *Self-Crowned Laureates*, 32–34. On the Ovidian vogue, see Stapleton, *Harmful Eloquence*; A. Armstrong, "Apprenticeship of John Donne"; G. Brown, "Gender and Voice," 151–52; G. Brown, *Redefining Elizabethan Literature*, 36–52; James, "Poet's Toys"; Moss, *Ovidian Vogue*.

3. Marlowe, *All Ovids Elegies*, book 2, elegy 1, line 4, in *Complete Works of Christopher Marlowe*, 1:36.

4. A notable exception is Arnold Stein's insightful article on Donne's couplet art, which delineates the ways in which Donne cultivates variety by avoiding precise rhymes in his couplets. He sees this as a revolt against the smooth verse of Spenser and the sonneteers. Stein, "Donne and the Couplet."

5. W. B. Piper mentions Donne's preference for the couplet in Piper, *Heroic Couplet*, 4–5. He argues that Donne and other Elizabethans adopted the couplet as a way of reproducing the Latin elegiac distich. Since the couplet was used to translate a variety of classical genres and verse forms, the Ovidian influence does not entirely account for the renewal of the couplet in the 1590s.

6. The three late Elizabethan works whose title pages announce that they are written "in English heroical verse" are translations of Italian poems into English ottava rima. Harington, *Orlando Furioso in English Heroical Verse*; Tofte, *Orlando Inamorato*; Fairfax, *Godfrey of Bulloigne*.

7. Scholars once thought that early modern poets misread the meter of *The Canterbury Tales* because they did not know that the final *e* was pronounced. Joseph T. Shipley carefully considers the evidence for this Elizabethan ignorance and convincingly demonstrates that, despite an imperfect understanding of pronunciation, Elizabethans did in fact recognize that the Chaucerian line was iambic and decasyllabic, though Dryden did not. Shipley, "Spenserian Prosody."

8. Gascoigne, *Posies*, U2v; Puttenham, *Arte*, M2v. See Mannyng, *Story of England*, lines 1–144. In his consideration of Spenser's stanzas, David Scott Wilson-Okamura notes that the couplet was associated with light verse in Elizabethan England. Wilson-Okamura, *Spenser's International Style*, 43–44, 63–64.

9. On Heywood's efforts to present "'homely' native proverbial wisdom rather than classical wisdom" in "a deliberately rough, vernacular verse form," see Crane, "*Intret Cato*," 177, 178.

10. Guilpin, *Skialetheia*, D7v.

11. Joseph Hall, *Virgidemiarum, Sixe Bookes. First three Bookes*, E3v, E4r; Marlowe, *Hero and Leander*, lines 385–484, in *Complete Works of Christopher Marlowe*, 1:198–201.

12. Joseph Hall, *Virgidemiarum, Sixe Bookes. First three Bookes*, D8v.

13. Chapman, *Achilles Shield*, B3r.

14. Marston, *Scourge of Villanie. Three Bookes of Satyres* (London, 1598), E8v. All references to this text are hereafter cited parenthetically by page signature and abbreviated *Scourge*.

15. P. Sidney, *Countesse of Pembrokes Arcadia*, M6r.

16. The first two terms are from Puttenham, *Arte*, K1v; "cooples" from Gascoigne, *Posies*, U2v; "geminels" from Drayton, *Barrons Wars*, A3r; "riding rhyme" from Gascoigne, *Posies*, U2v, and Puttenham, *Arte*, I1v; the final phrase from W. Scott, *Model of Poesy*, 78.

17. Gascoigne, *Posies*, U2v.

18. Gascoigne, *Posies*, U2v.

19. Geoffrey Chaucer, *The House of Fame*, lines 1096, 1099, 1100, 1100, in Chaucer, *Riverside Chaucer*.

20. Mannyng, *Story of England*, lines 118, 74, 84, 123–24.

21. Mannyng, *Story of England*, lines 112, 89, 85–86. "fordon" means done in, doomed, or frustrated.

22. Mannyng, *Story of England*, lines 143–44. See Coleman, "Strange Rhyme."

23. Mannyng, *Story of England*, line 3.

24. Robert Matz argues that Puttenham equates poetic competence with courtly linguistic competence. Matz, "Poetry, Politics, and Discursive Forms," 200–203. See also Javitch, *Poetry and Courtliness*.

25. Tessa Watt breaks down this passage in her discussion of the printing and performance of ballads in sixteenth-century England. Watt, *Cheap Print*, 11–38.

26. The heading of this section is quoted from Marston, *Scourge*, B2r. On Puttenham, see Rebhorn and Whigham, introduction to *The Art of English Poesy*, by George Puttenham, 15.

27. The rhyme between "poetrie" and "liberty" could be described as "double promotion." William Harmon uses the word "liberty" as his example when he notes that promotion occurs "when a word of three or more syllables that normally ends as a dactyl is so changed—with stress added to the final syllable and the vowel quality altered correspondingly—that it forms a rhyme with a regularly stressed syllable. 'Thee' and 'liberty' make up what is probably the most familiar instance for Americans." Harmon, "Rhyme in English Verse," 377.

28. Jonson, *Poetaster* 5.3.462, in *Jonson*, 2:162; "Prologue to Volpone," line 21, in *Jonson*, 3:44.

29. Dekker, *If It Be Not Good*, C4r.

30. See also Marston, *Scourge*, D2v, F3r, G4r, G8v.

31. Marston, *Scourge of Villanie, Corrected*, H8v.

32. Marston, *Scourge of Villanie, Corrected*, H8v.

33. *Oxford English Dictionary*, s.v. "discursive, adj."

34. See, for example, Puttenham, *Arte*, M3r; Jonson, "Why I Write Not of Love," in *Jonson*, 5:209.

35. At least one early modern reader shared this view of couplets. See Daniel, *A Defence of Ryme*, in G. Smith, *Elizabethan Critical Essays*, 2:282.

36. Beaumont, "To his late Maiesty, concerning the true forme of English Poetry," in Beaumont, *Bosworth-field*, H7r.

37. Jonson, *Informations to William Drummond of Hawthornden*, in *Jonson*, 5:359.

38. In her analysis in the section headed "The Rhymed Couplet," Barbara Herrnstein Smith argues that continuous couplets can have much "the same effect as the iambic stress pattern" or any other pattern of repetition: "each couplet creates the expectation of another" and therefore can be as much a "force for continuation" as a "force for closure." B. Smith, *Poetic Closure*, 72, 72, 71, 71.

39. Wilson-Okamura, *Spenser's International Style*, 147.

40. Joseph Hall, *Virgidemiarum, The Three Last Bookes*, F4v.

41. Joseph Hall, *Virgidemiarum, Sixe Bookes. First three Bookes*, D7r, D8v.

42. Joseph Hall, *Virgidemiarum, Sixe Bookes. First three Bookes*, D7r, D8v.

43. Jonson, *Cynthia's Revels (Q)*, 2.3.66–67, in *Jonson*, 1:479.

44. Joseph Hall, *Virgidemiarum, Sixe Bookes. First three Bookes*, B2r. "dight" could mean ordered, arranged, clothed, or adorned.

45. Joseph Hall, *Virgidemiarum, Sixe Bookes. First three Bookes*, B8r.

46. Daniel, *A Defence of Ryme*, in G. Smith, *Elizabethan Critical Essays*, 2:378, 377–78, 362, 362.

47. Marston, *Metamorphosis of Pigmalions Image*, C1r.

48. Marotti, *John Donne, Coterie Poet*, 39. Donne, "Satyre 1," lines 1, 31, 31–32, in *The*

Variorum Edition of the Poetry of John Donne, edited by Gary A. Stringer et al., vol. 3, *The Satyres*, edited by Jeffrey S. Johnson (Bloomington: Indiana University Press, 2016), 5 (hereafter *Satyres*).

49. Donne, "Satyre 1," lines 39, 40, 37, 41–48, *Satyres*, 6.

50. Donne, "Elegy 8. To his Mistress going to bed," lines 33–35, in *The Variorum Edition of the Poetry of John Donne*, vol. 2, *The Elegies*, ed. John R. Roberts et al. (Bloomington: Indiana University Press, 2000). All quotations from Donne's elegies are from this edition. All references to this text are hereafter cited parenthetically by line number and abbreviated *Elegies*.

51. Donne, "Satyre 1," lines 61, 61, 61, 62, *Satyres*, 6.

52. Marlowe, *Hero and Leander*, lines 207–8, in *Complete Works of Christopher Marlowe*, 1:194.

53. On the Ovidian libertinism of *Hero and Leander* as religiously iconoclastic, see Duncan, "'Headdie Riots.'"

54. Marlowe, *Hero and Leander*, lines 12, 51, in *Complete Works of Christopher Marlowe*, 1:189, 190. For a thoughtful reading of clothing in *Hero and Leander*, with the conclusion that Marlowe renders "the female body" strange, dangerous, and unsatisfying in the poem while Leander remains the "natural" erotic choice, see Carlson, "Clothing Naked Desire," 36, 38.

55. Marlowe, *Hero and Leander*, lines 319, 320, 726, 726, 726, in *Complete Works of Christopher Marlowe*, 1:207.

56. Marlowe, *Hero and Leander*, lines 801–10, in *Complete Works of Christopher Marlowe*, 1:209. On whether Hero and Leander is intentionally unfinished, see Campbell, "'Desunt Nonnulla.'"

57. Marlowe, *Hero and Leander*, 817–18, in *Complete Works of Christopher Marlowe*, 1:209. On Leander's gaze, see Miller, "Death of the Modern," 779–80; C. Summers, *"Hero and Leander,"* 146; Semler, "Marlovian Therapy," 179. For a counterargument to Miller's view of the ending and an argument that this moment does not represent the naked truth because Hero is reclothed in simile, see Haber, "'True-Loves Blood,'" 385. Gordon Braden argues for a softened reading of Leander's gaze, but the comparison to Dis does seem to suggest that Marlowe is darkening the picture of Hero's radiance. Braden, "Hero and Leander in Bed," 228.

58. Braden, "Hero and Leander in Bed," 228.

59. On the classical passages that lie behind the vision of fate in the poem, see Semler, "Marlovian Therapy."

60. Marlowe, *Hero and Leander*, line 772, in *Complete Works of Christopher Marlowe*, 1:208.

61. Braden, "Hero and Leander in Bed," 224. Marlowe, *All Ovids Elegies*, book 1, elegy 5, lines 17, 16, 16, in *Complete Works of Christopher Marlowe*, 1:19.

62. Riggs, *World of Christopher Marlowe*, 62, 97, 101. See also Kuriyama, *Christopher Marlowe*, 119, 69.

63. James, "Poet's Toys," 114.

64. James, "Poet's Toys," 111–15.

65. Marlowe, *All Ovids Elegies*, book 2, elegy 1, line 4, in *Complete Works of Christopher Marlowe*, 1:36; Ovid, *Amores* 1.2.4, in *Ovid I: Heroides and Amores*, 380. On softness in Marlowe's translation of Ovid, see Mann, "Marlowe's 'Slack Muse.'"

66. See Bieman, "Comic Rhyme."

67. For a cognitive approach to the sestains of *Venus and Adonis*, see Raphael Lyne, "Thinking in Stanzas."

68. See Gill, general introduction to *All Ovids Elegies*, in *Complete Works*, 4–5; Mann, "Marlowe's 'Slack Muse,' " 64.

69. Louis I. Bredvold discusses Donne's naturalism and skepticism in Bredvold, "Naturalism of Donne"; Robert Ornstein follows up his argument in Ornstein, "Donne, Montaigne, and Natural Law." In describing liberty as the central preoccupation of Donne's early work, I am building on the work of Richard Strier and Joshua Scodel, whose seminal essays on the satires aim to restore what Strier calls the "Empsonian sense" of Donne's radicalism. Strier, "Radical Donne," 283; Scodel, " 'None's Slave,' " 363. Strier refers to Empson's famous article "John Donne the Space Man." Annabel Patterson also contributes to this restoration of the Empsonian Donne by arguing that he was "never so simply the king's man as the newer historical criticism has asserted." Patterson, "John Donne, Kingsman?" All these critics are responding to the careerist version of Donne that dominated criticism in the wake of Carey, *John Donne*. More recently, James Kuzner has explored the question of liberty in *Biathanatos* and in the religious poetry of Donne, Herbert, and Vaughan in Kuzner, "Metaphysical Freedom"; and Kuzner, "Donne's *Biathanatos*."

70. For detailed and illuminating readings of the skepticism and libertinism of Donne's early elegies and their connection with the early modern use of the word "libertine" to describe a spiritual antinomian, see Guibbory, "Reconsidering Donne."

71. Donne, *Pseudo-Martyr*, 134.

72. Donne, *Pseudo-Martyr*, 138.

73. Donne, *Pseudo-Martyr*, 12–13.

74. Ferrabosco, *Ayres*, C2v. See Milgate, "Early References"; A. J. Smith, *John Donne*, 33–35.

75. Guilpin, *Skialetheia*, C2v; Joseph Hall, *Virgidemiarum, The Three Last Bookes*, C8v; Bennett, "John Donne and Everard Gilpin," 71; Hester, " 'All Are Players,' "; A. J. Smith, *John Donne*, 33–35.

76. Foster, *Register of Admissions to Gray's Inn*, 83. This quotation is from Davison's notes on loose sheets, British Library Harley manuscript 298, printed in Davison, *Davison's Poetical Rhapsody*, liii.

77. Davison, *Davison's Poetical Rhapsody*, liii. For an account of the demand for Donne's satires and their early circulation in fascicle format, see D. Smith, "Before (and after) the Miscellany."

78. Davison, *Davison's Poetical Rhapsody*, liii.

79. Jonson, "To Lucy, Countess of Bedford, with Master Donne's Satires," in *Jonson*, 5:160.

80. Jonson, *Informations to William Drummond of Hawthornden*, in *Jonson*, 5:365.

81. Jonson, *Informations to William Drummond of Hawthornden*, in *Jonson*, 5:359.

82. Gardner, introduction to *John Donne*, l; Marotti, *John Donne, Coterie Poet*, 16.

83. Gardner, *John Donne*, l.

84. Beaumont, "To his late Maiesty, concerning the true forme of English Poetry," in Beaumont, *Bosworth-field*, H7r.

85. Donne, "To Mr. T.W.," lines 1–6, in Donne, *The Variorum Edition of the Poetry of John Donne*, edited by Jeffrey S. Johnson, vol. 5, *The Verse Letters*, edited by Jeanne Shami et al. (Bloomington: Indiana University Press, 2019), 125. All references to this text are hereafter cited parenthetically by line number and abbreviated *Verse Letters*. For this verse letter, I have added the indentation as it was printed in the 1633 edition because it draws attention to the verse form of the poem. The editor of the 1633 edition appears to have attended to stanzaic forms when indenting the poems.

86. The poem has fourteen lines only in the Westmoreland manuscript (Berg Collec-

tion, New York Public Library, Shelf Locator: Berg Coll [Donne]) since the potentially blasphemous lines 5–6 were omitted from all other manuscripts and the printed editions. Even in the Westmoreland manuscript, the lines have been struck out, although they are still legible.

87. On sugar and sweetness, see the second chapter of Jacobson, *Barbarous Antiquity*. On harshness, see Stein, "Donne's Harshness."

88. Jonson, *Timber: Or, Discoveries*, lines 502–6, in *Jonson*, 7:523–24.

89. Jonson, *Timber: Or, Discoveries*, line 507, in *Jonson*, 7:524.

90. Donne, "To Sir Henry Wotton," lines 2, 2, 1, 1, in *Verse Letters*.

91. On the relationship between Donne's elegies and Petrarchan and courtly love poetry, see Young, "Elegy"; A. Armstrong, "Apprenticeship of John Donne"; Braden, "Classical Love Elegy"; Marotti, *John Donne, Coterie Poet*, 45–54; Eckhardt, *Manuscript Verse Collectors*, 33–66. For a specifically political interpretation of the elegies, see Guibbory, " 'Oh Let Me Not Serve So.' "

92. The phrase is from Carew's elegy on Donne, in Donne, *Poems by I.D.*, Dddıv.

93. For a brief survey of selected classical and Renaissance allusions to this myth, see Levy, "Vergil, Ovid, and Claudian."

94. Golding, *The. xv. Bookes of P. Ouidius Naso*, Cc8r.

95. On the connection between the raw, formless matter of Ovidian tradition and the idea of the "rude" poet, see Harrison, "Rude Poet," 252.

96. See Jacobs, *Marriage Contracts*, 2.

97. See Donne's "Confined Love" and "Metempsychosis," in *Complete Poems of John Donne*, 158–59, 422–62.

98. Gardner, note to lines 35–36, in *John Donne*, 137.

99. Rockett, "John Donne," 62.

100. For "Satyre 3," I have opted to use what the editors of the *Variorum* Donne describe as the "Original Version" of "Satyre 3," based on the Westmoreland manuscript, which is in the hand of Donne's friend Rowland Woodword. John Donne, "Satyre 3," lines 6, 5, *Satyres*, 91–93. All references to "Satyre 3" are hereafter cited parenthetically by line number and abbreviated as Satyre. For a summary of speculation about the date, see Donne, *Satyres*, 650–54.

101. Donne, *Sermons*, 5:104.

102. Donne, *Letters to Severall Persons of Honour*, 25.

103. Donne, *Sermons*, 5:104.

104. Though the 1633 edition of Donne's work includes a second "must" after "about," most manuscripts do not. Robin Robbins points out that there is no decisive authority for the variant and that the wrenched meter of the nine-syllable line would fit Donne's account of the struggle here. Robin Robbins, note to line 81, in Donne, *Complete Poems of John Donne*, 394.

105. See Strier, "Radical Donne," 303; Ryzhik, "Complaint and Satire," 123.

106. I am indebted to Ben Glaser for pointing out Donne's remarkable use of the metrical flexibility of the word "will" in these lines.

107. See Yulia Ryzhik's comparison of the two poets; she notes that Spenser is typically seen as a poet of complaint, which promotes "an ideal of the world as it should be," and Donne as a poet of satire, which attacks "the facts of the world as it is." She complicates those associations. Ryzhik, "Complaint and Satire," 110. In a more recent piece, she argues that Donne's "most consistent and systematic engagement is with Spenser." Ryzhik, "Spenser and Donne Go Fishing," 418.

Chapter Three. An Even and Unaltered Gait: Jonson and the Poetics of Character

1. Arber, *Transcript of the Registers*, 3:677.

2. For the satire and libel theory, see McCabe, "Elizabethan Satire"; and Clegg, *Press Censorship*, 198. For the sexual license theory, see Peter, *Complaint and Satire*, 148–50; Finkelpearl, *John Marston of the Middle Temple*, 116; B. Smith, *Homosexual Desire*, 164; Boose, "1599 Bishops' Ban."

3. The list appears to include only eight poetic volumes, but the first banned item, "Satyres tearmed Halls Satyres, viz' Virgidemiarum, or his toothless or biting Satyres," actually describes two volumes that were sometimes combined and given a new title page to form a single volume. The works in couplets include six collections of formal satire written in the 1590s, one Elizabethan translation of Ovid's elegies ("marlowes Elegyes"), and one early sixteenth-century translation of a French satire against women ("the xv ioyes of marriage"). As it turned out, Joseph Hall's satires, along with the rhyme royal poem *Caltha Poetarum*, were exempted from the bonfire and were only "staid." Arber, *Transcript of the Registers*, 3:678.

4. Jonson, *Informations to William Drummond of Hawthornden*, in *Jonson*, 5:365.

5. Jonson, *Informations to William Drummond of Hawthornden*, in *Jonson*, 5:359.

6. Jonson, *Informations to William Drummond of Hawthornden*, in *Jonson*, 5:359, 362.

7. Campion, *Observations in the Art of English Poesy*, in G. Smith, *Elizabethan Critical Essays*, 2:331.

8. It is noteworthy that "A Fit of Rhyme against Rhyme" follows one of Jonson's few sonnets, "A Sonnet: To the Noble Lady, the Lady Mary Wroth," in *The Underwood*, in *Cambridge Edition of the Works of Ben Jonson*, 7:142–43

9. See Flantz, "Authoritie of Truth," 60–61.

10. Jonson, *Timber: Or, Discoveries*, lines 1339–441, in *Jonson*, 5:567. On the "inseparability of good matter and good manner" in Jonson as a response to Baconian dualism, see Woods, "Context of Jonson's Formalism," 79.

11. See Woods, "Context of Jonson's Formalism," 85–86.

12. For an account of Jonson's skill at using quantitative measure in combination with accentual-syllabic measures, see Flantz, "Authoritie of Truth."

13. Donne, *Poems by I.D.*

14. On Jonsonian and Donnean style in Carew's elegy for Donne, see Scodel, *English Poetic Epitaph*, 12–39.

15. Norbrook, *Poetry and Politics*, 195–214; O'Callaghan, *"Shepheardes Nation,"* 1–25, 147–62.

16. Wither, *Abuses Stript*, B1r.

17. Wither, *Wither's Motto*, A3r.

18. Wither, *Wither's Motto*, A5r; Wither, *Faire-virtue*, C2v.

19. Wither, *Faire-virtue*, C2v, C3r.

20. Norbrook, *Poetry and Politics*, 218–19. See also Riggs, *Ben Jonson*, 274–76.

21. Pearl, "Jonson's Masques of 1620–5," 68–69.

22. "Prologus" to *Cynthia's Revels* (Q), in *Jonson*, 1:453.

23. O'Callaghan, *"Shepheardes Nation,"* 156. See also Calhoun, "George Wither."

24. Jonson, *Time Vindicated to Himself and To His Honours*, lines 85–86, in *Jonson*, 5:623.

25. See Gascoigne, *Posies*, U2v; Puttenham, *Arte*, I1v.

26. Jonson, *Timber: Or, Discoveries*, lines 680–87, in *Jonson*, 7:532.

27. On the continuity between bodily and moral characteristics in Jonson and the

Roman moralists, see Maus, *Jonson and the Roman Frame of Mind*, 24–29. She notes that it is primarily vices that have physical manifestations; virtue may not be so visible.

28. Aristotle, *Nicomachean Ethics*, book 4, chapter 3, section 34.

29. Virgil, *Aeneid*, 1:405, in *Virgil: Eclogues, Georgics, Aeneid 1–6*, 290.

30. Jeff Dolven discusses bodily metaphors for style, including the breath and the writer's hand, and suggests that the body is "solid, fixed, the stable site of nature and fate over against the mind's art and choice"; it is what "guarantees the idiosyncrasy of the artifact." Dolven, *Senses of Style*, 74–75.

31. See Pritchard, "George Wither," 224.

32. See John Taylor's later attack on Wither's character as revealed in his style in *Aqua-Musae* (London, 1645), B3v. Quoted in Loxley, *Royalism and Poetry*, 110.

33. Smythe, *Sir Thomas Smithes Voiage*, K1v. See Gavin Alexander, introduction to *The Model of Poesy*, by William Scott, xxiii–xxv. Alexander reports that William Scott went on the embassy with Smythe and that his only surviving letter, a letter to Robert Cecil that survives in the National Archives, indicates that Scott wrote an extensive account of the embassy. Alexander is not convinced that the passages on literature must be derived from Scott's account, but he does see many characteristic marks of Scott's style and interests.

34. *Oxford English Dictionary*, s.v. "elaborate, adj." Katharine Maus notes that Jonson uses the word "labored" as a term of praise, a sign of his affinity with Roman moralists like Cicero and Horace who viewed artistry as a result of sustained practice. Maus, *Jonson and the Roman Frame of Mind*, 12. See also Moul, *Jonson, Horace*, 2–3.

35. Nichols, *Poetry of Ben Jonson*, 31.

36. Smythe, *Sir Thomas Smithes Voiage*, K1v.

37. Jonson, *Timber: Or, Discoveries*, lines 1666–67, 1695–96, in *Jonson*, 7:578, 580.

38. Jonson, *Timber: Or, Discoveries*, line 1666, in *Jonson*, 7:578.

39. Jonson, *Timber: Or, Discoveries*, lines 1666, 1695, 1695, 1695, in *Jonson*, 7:578, 580.

40. Jonson, *Timber: Or, Discoveries*, lines 1666–67, in *Jonson*, 7:578.

41. Jonson, *Timber: Or, Discoveries*, line 1696, in *Jonson*, 7:580. Paul Fussell discusses a similar conception of the connection between prosody and ethics in the eighteenth century, including in Samuel Johnson. Fussell, *Theory of Prosody*, 37–56.

42. On Jonson as a middle ground between Spenser and Donne, see Parfitt, "Compromise Classicism," 117.

43. Donne, *Poems by I.D.*, Bbbb3r–Fff3r; Jasper Mayne, "To the Memory of Ben. Iohnson," in Duppa, *Ionsonus Virbivs*, E3r; John Beaumont, "To the Memory of him who can never be forgotten, Master Benjamin Johnson," in Duppa, *Ionsonus Virbivs*, C2r.

44. Sidney Godolphin, "The Muses fairest light in no darke time," in Duppa, *Ionsonus Virbius*, E2r.

45. See Schoenfeldt, "'Mysteries of Manners, Armes, and Arts.'"

46. Maus, *Jonson and the Roman Frame of Mind*, 24.

47. T. Greene, "Ben Jonson and the Centered Self."

48. George Parfitt describes the "poles of Jonson's art" as "ethics and realism." While the two are intermixed in all his work, his lyrics are more exclusively focused on ethics and often leave aside the realism of the plays. Parfitt, *Ben Jonson*, 147.

49. Barish, *Ben Jonson and the Language of Prose Comedy*; McDonald, "Jonson and Shakespeare and the Rhythm of Verse."

50. McDonald, "Jonson and Shakespeare and the Rhythm of Verse," 109, 114; Wesley Trimpi provides an important corrective to the idea that Jonson's style is baroque or Senecan by showing how Jonson, like Bacon, was as skeptical of the excesses of the Senecan style as he was of the Ciceronian style. Trimpi, *Ben Jonson's Poems*, 41–59.

51. Jonson, *Sejanus His Fall*, 1.1.56–66, in *Jonson*, 2:239.

52. McDonald, "Jonson and Shakespeare and the Rhythm of Verse," 115.

53. See Gardiner, *Craftsmanship in Context*, 54.

54. Jonson, "4. To King James" and "118. On Gut," in *Jonson*, 5:114, 181.

55. There are also three epigrams and one poem in *The Forrest* in triplets (*Jonson*, 5:209–48). Joshua Scodel discusses the prominence of the couplet in these two collections and argues that the indentation of the poems suggests that Jonson is presenting the couplet as an analogue of the Latin elegiac couplet. Scodel, "Allusions and Distinctions."

56. Jonson, "To the Great Example of Honour and Virtue, The Most Noble William, Earl of Pembroke, Lord Chamberlain, etc.," in *Jonson*, 5:111.

57. Doelman, *Epigram in England*, 51–56. See Guilpin, *Skialetheia*, C1r.

58. Jonson, "To My Book," lines 3–4, in *Jonson*, 5:113.

59. Winner, "Ben Jonson's Epigrammes," 62–63. See also Moul, *Jonson, Horace*, 65–67.

60. Joseph Hall, *Virgidemiarum, The Three Last Bookes*; Marston, *Scourge*, G7r, B1r, B8v, F4r; Bastard, *Chrestoleros*, D2v.

61. On the idea of "sales" or "salt" in the epigrammatic tradition, see Winner, "Ben Jonson's Epigrammes," 70–71; Doelman, *Epigram in England*, 31.

62. Nothing in this particular epigram identifies the playwright as Marston, but another epigram, "On Playwright," seems to allude to Jonson's fight with Marston, in which Jonson supposedly "beat" Marston and "took his pistol from him." *Informations to William Drummond of Hawthornden*, in *Jonson*, 5:367.

63. Joseph Hall, *Virgidemiarum, Sixe Bookes. First three Bookes*, H3v.

64. "Rheum" or "rhume" means watery or mucous secretions, but it is not entirely clear what Guilpin means by "salt rhume" here. The secondary meaning is an overflow of salt, that is, satirical wit.

65. Guilpin, *Skialetheia*, B6v.

66. See van den Berg, *Action of Ben Jonson's Poetry*, 90.

67. *Informations to William Drummond of Hawthornden*, in *Jonson*, 5:389.

68. Scodel, *English Poetic Epitaph*, 140–42. Empson, *Structure of Complex Words*, 185–249. The word, like the pejorative adjectives Jonson uses for the rough satirists, also has sexual implications, as Jonson revealed when he told Drummond his wife was "a shrew yet honest." *Informations to William Drummond of Hawthornden*, in *Jonson*, 5:372.

69. "98. To Sir Thomas Roe," line 3, in *Jonson*, 5:165.

70. Jonson, *Timber: Or, Discoveries*, lines 1439, 1518–21, in *Jonson*, 7:567, 572.

71. Jonson, *Timber: Or, Discoveries*, lines 1516–18, in *Jonson*, 7:572.

72. Ben Jonson, *Cynthia's Revels*, "Prologus," line 20, in *Jonson*, 1:453. For a brief overview of Jonson's engagement with the classical "*res et verba* controversy," see Mulryan, "Jonson's Classicism," 167–68. See also Trimpi, *Ben Jonson's Poems*, 42, 235.

73. Ben Jonson, "Epistle" to *Volpone*, in *Jonson*, 3:27.

74. Ovid, *Amores* 1:1, line 1, in *Ovid I: Heroides and Amores*, 318. See Helgerson, *Self-Crowned Laureates*, 110; Scodel, "Allusions and Distinctions," 50.

75. Ovid, *Amores* 1:1, line 19, in *Ovid I: Heroides and Amores*, 319.

76. Sara van den Berg contrasts Petrarchan and Erasmian humanism, discusses Jonson's debts to both figures, and concludes that his humanism is ultimately more Erasmian, in van den Berg, *Action of Ben Jonson's Poetry*, 36–62.

77. Cowley, *Poems*, B1r. "The Mistress" was originally published in 1647.

78. Duncan-Jones, "Was the 1609 'Shake-Speares Sonnets' Really Unauthorized?," 168–69; J. Kerrigan, introduction to *The Sonnets and a Lover's Complaint*, 13–15.

79. Neely, "Structure of English Renaissance Sonnet Sequences," 378–80.

80. Ovid, *Amores* 1:2, lines 30, 8, 35, in *Ovid I: Heroides and Amores*, 322–24.

81. Petrarch, "Rime Sparse 2," "Rime Sparse 3" in *Petrarch's Lyric Poems*.

82. Watson, *Hekatompathia*, A1r. See also Barnes, *Parthenophil and Parthenope*, A3r–v; G. Fletcher, *Licia*, B4v; Percy, *Sonnets to the Fairest Coelia*, A3v.

83. Sidney, "Astrophil and Stella 2," lines 9–10, in P. Sidney, *Major Works*, 153.

84. Robert Sidney, "2 Sonnet. 12," lines 5–6, in R. Sidney, *Poems of Robert Sidney*, 17. This sonnet is the second poem in Robert's incomplete crown of sonnets. The second sonnet of his main sequence also concerns the "Blest . . . bands" of love, "Sonnet 2," line 7, in R. Sidney, *Poems of Robert Sidney*, 134.

85. Wroth, *Pamphilia to Amphilanthus* 14, lines 4, 10, 14, in *Poems of Lady Mary Wroth*, 95.

86. On Jonson and the Sidneys, see van den Berg, *Action of Ben Jonson's Poetry*, 114–42; Wayne, "Jonson's Sidney"; Waller, *Sidney Family Romance*, 116–19.

87. *Informations to William Drummond of Hawthornden*, in *Jonson*, 5:377.

88. In an illuminating account of the moral psychology that underlies Jonson's drama, Katharine Maus makes the case that Jonson refuses to provide the kind of romantic plots expected by readers because he does not adhere to the Platonic and Augustinian idea that desire is fundamental and that the goal is to direct it to the proper object. The Roman moralists, and Jonson after them, reject this "strategy of abasement" because it undermines the independence required for true happiness. Maus, *Jonson and the Roman Frame of Mind*, 77–82.

89. See Achilleos, "'Ile Bring Thee *Herrick* to *Anacreon*,'" 206–7.

90. McPherson, "Ben Jonson's Library," 77. McPherson notes that Jonson marks the Latin translation rather than the Greek text of Pindar's poems. Jonson's copy is now owned by the Isabella Stuart Gardener Museum.

91. In the *Old Arcadia*, Sir Philip Sidney describes Cleophila's song in book 2 as "Anacreon's kind of verse." The poem is heptasyllabic, and he scans it ∪ – ∪ – ∪ – –. It's telling that Sidney describes the song as an outburst of passion: "as if her long-restrained conceits did now burst out of prison, she thus . . . threw down the burden of her mind in Anacreon's kind of verse." P. Sidney, *Countess of Pembroke's Arcadia: The Old Arcadia*, 163.

92. Stanley, *Poems*; Cowley, *Poems*, Aaa1r.

93. Breton, "A farewell to loue," in Breton, *Melancholike humours*, D2v. The songs were omitted from the Elizabethan quartos of Lyly, but are printed in Edward Blount's Caroline edition; see Lyly, *Sixe Court Comedies*, N8v.

94. "Greenes ode, of the vanitie of wanton writings," in Robert Greene, *Greenes Vision*, B1r.

95. Robert Greene, *Mamillia*, I3r, L4r. Francis Meres includes the latter passage under "Loue" in *Palladis Tamia*, T5v.

96. G. Fletcher, *Licia*, I1r–v; Lodge, *Phillis*, H3v; Barnfield, *Cynthia*, C8r–D2v.

97. Jonson, "To Sir Robert Wroth," in *Jonson*, 5:215–20; Virgil, *Georgics*, book 2, lines 490–542, in *Virgil: Eclogues, Georgics, Aeneid 1–6*, 170–75; Horace, "Epode 2," in Horace, *Odes and Epodes*, 272–77; Jonson, "The Praises of the Country Life," in *Jonson*, 7:279.

98. British Library Harley manuscript 4064.

99. Thomas Greene observes that throughout Jonson's verse virtues are "transcribed by nouns and adjectives" while vice is described in the "livelier poetry of verbs." T. Greene, "Ben Jonson and the Centered Self," 332.

100. On standing and fixity in Jonson, see Peterson, *Imitation and Praise*, 35–90; and T. Greene, "Ben Jonson and the Centered Self," 330. See also Creaser, "Milton," 163–64.

101. Juvenal, satire 10, line 356, in Juvenal and Perseus, *Juvenal and Perseus*, 396.

102. Don Wayne discusses the emergence of a new aristocracy under the Tudors that continued to use the imagery of chivalry but served primarily in administrative roles. He

sees in these aristocrats many of the seeds of a "bourgeois ideology" long before its triumph. Wayne, *Penshurst*, 24–25. On Jonson's preference for peaceful activities over Protestant militancy, see also Norbrook, *Poetry and Politics*, 184.

103. For a contrast between these two poems, see van den Berg, *Action of Ben Jonson's Poetry*, 128–38.

104. Jonson, *Informations*, line 278, in *Jonson*, 5:377.

105. Jonson, *Informations*, lines 159–60, in *Jonson*, 5:370; Donaldson, *Ben Jonson*, 291–93.

106. Donaldson, *Ben Jonson*, 182–86. See also Riggs, *Ben Jonson*, 191–92.

107. Donaldson, *Ben Jonson*, 206–13.

108. Van den Berg, *Action of Ben Jonson's Poetry*, 136.

109. Maus, "Womb of His Own," 95.

110. Donne also wrote verse epistles to aristocratic patronesses, but not until nearly a decade after Jonson wrote the "Epistle to Elizabeth, Countess of Rutland" in 1600. Donne's verse epistles to ladies were probably written between 1609 and 1615, the same period when Jonson wrote the epistle to Lady Aubigny. Since most of Donne's epistles were addressed to the Countess of Bedford, who was also Jonson's patroness, Jonson may have had access to these poems in manuscript.

111. John Donne, "Epigrams, 1.," in *Variorum Edition of the Poetry of John Donne*, vol. 8, *The Epigrams, Epithalamions, Epitaphs, Inscriptions, and Miscellaneous Poems*, 5.

112. Marlowe, *Hero and Leander*, lines 167–68, 175–76, in *Complete Works of Christopher Marlowe*, 1:193. Like other Elizabethan and Jacobean dramatists, Jonson at times uses the couplet to set off sententious wisdom in his drama. In a 1951 article surveying Jonson's dramatic uses of the couplet, Alexander Sackton draws attention to a scene in *Poetaster* in which Caesar, Virgil, and Horace offer dueling aphorisms in closed couplets. Sackton, "Rhymed Couplet," 92.

113. McDonald, "Jonson and Shakespeare and the Rhythm of Verse."

114. See Moul, *Jonson, Horace*, 109.

115. Gascoigne recommends the use of monosyllables because "the most auncient English wordes are of one sillable, so that the more monasyllables that you vse the truer Englishman you shall seeme, and the lesse you shall smell of the Inkehorne: Also wordes of many syllables do cloye a verse and make it vnpleasant, whereas woordes of one syllable will more easily fall to be shorte or long as occasion requireth, or wilbe adapted to become circumflexe or of an indifferent sounde." Gascoigne, *Posies*, T4r.

116. Puttenham, *Arte*, L1r; W. Scott, *Model of Poesy*, 63.

117. *Informations to William Drummond of Hawthornden*, in *Jonson*, 5:361. See Gardiner, *Craftsmanship in Context*, 17.

118. Trimpi, *Ben Jonson's Poems*, 115–35; Cicero, *Orator* 81–83, in Cicero, *Brutus, Orator*, 363.

119. *Informations to William Drummond of Hawthornden*, in *Jonson*, 5:361.

120. Cf. Milton, "Il Penseroso," lines 37–38, "Come, but keep thy wonted state, / With ev'n step and musing gait," in Milton, *CPMP*.

121. Peterson, *Imitation and Praise*, 199. See also Revard, "Pindar and Jonson's Cary-Morison Ode." David Trotter notes the mismatch but sees Jonson's rejection of Pindaric inconstancy as a failure to "follow through" on his efforts to imitate Pindar rather than as a deliberate contrast. Trotter, *Poetry of Abraham Cowley*, 111. On Jonson's early engagements with Pindar and the tensions between Horatian and Pindaric tones in his odes, see Moul, *Jonson, Horace*, 13–48.

122. Jasper Mayne, "To the Memory of Ben. Iohnson," in Duppa, *Ionsonus Virbius*, E3r.

123. Horace, ode 4.2, lines 5–12, in Horace, *Odes and Epodes*, 220–22.

124. Quintilian, *Institutio Oratoria*, book 10, chapter 1, section 61, in *Institutio Oratoria of Quintilian*, 4:34.

125. Cowley, "The Praise of Pindar," in Cowley, *Poems*, Dddıv–Ddd2r.

126. Cowley, "The Resurrection," lines 54, 57–61, in Cowley, *Poems*, Ddd3v.

127. See, for example, Erasmus, *Seconde tome*, cc4r; Parsons, *Christian Directorie*, O2r; Worseley, *A most godly and vvorthy Treatis of holy Signes*, C3v; Darcie, *Originall of Idolatries*, D4v.

128. Pindar, Nemean 5, lines 1–4, in Pindar, *Pindar*, 2:47.

129. Pindar, Nemean 5, lines 19–20, in Pindar, *Pindar*, 2:49. William Fitzgerald discusses this passage in his account of the Pindaric agon between order and disorder. Fitzgerald, *Agonistic Poetry*, 140.

130. Fry, *Poet's Calling*, 25.

131. Jonson, *Timber: Or, Discoveries*, line 1411, in *Jonson*, 7:566. On the connection between this passage and one in Scaliger, see Trimpi, *Ben Jonson's Poems*, 49.

132. See Moul, *Jonson, Horace*, 51–52.

133. Riggs, *Ben Jonson*, 312–13.

134. Lucius Cary, "An Elegie on the death of my dearest (and allmost only) freind Syr Henry Moryson," lines 131–38, reproduced in Murdock, "Elegy on Sir Henry Morison, by Lucius Cary."

135. See Hankins, "Jonson's 'Ode on Morison,'"; Peterson, *Imitation and Praise*.

136. See Oates, "Jonson's 'Ode Pindarick' and the Doctrine of Imitation," 145.

137. Scaliger, *Poetices Libri Septem*, 40; Annabel Patterson has a detailed discussion of Jonson's Cary and Morison ode and Renaissance theories of the Pindaric ode and cosmic harmony in Patterson, *Hermogenes and the Renaissance*, 88–89. See also Peterson, *Imitation and Praise*, 200–201.

138. See Ravelhofer, "Dance."

139. On the "choric art" of the ode, see Blanchard, "Ut Encyclopedia Poesis."

140. Jonson, *Mercury Vindicated from the Alchemists at Court*, lines 183–88, in *Jonson*, 4:442.

141. See Woods, "Ben Jonson's Cary-Morison Ode," 61.

142. Ben Jonson's copy of Puttenham's treatise was used for the Scolar Press Facsimile Series. George Puttenham, *The Arte of English Poesie* (Menston, England: Scolar, 1969), 33.

143. Drayton, *Poemes Lyrick and pastorall*, A3v.

144. This heading is from the seventeenth-century edition of Pliny. Pliny, *Historie of the World*, P1r; Pliny, *Natural History*, book 7, chapter 3, section 35, in *Pliny: Natural History in Ten Volumes*, 2:530.

145. Pliny, *Natural History*, book 7, chapter 3, section 35, in *Pliny: Natural History in Ten Volumes*, 2:530.

146. Peterson argues that the Scipios are the "hidden heroes" of the opening stanzas, but they are never mentioned or alluded to in the ode; Peterson, *Imitation and Praise*, 206.

147. Livy, *Ab Urbe Condita*, 21.2, in Livy, *Livy in Fourteen Volumes*, 5:6.

148. Peterson, *Imitation and Praise*, 204. See also Fry, *Poet's Calling*, 18–19; R. Jackson, "Ben Jonson," 198–200.

149. See Woods, "Ben Jonson's Cary-Morison Ode," 61.

150. This impulse to contain short lines was characteristic of Jonson—his odes to Sir William Sidney and to James, Earl of Desmond have a similar pinched structure.

151. Seneca, epistle 93.4, in Seneca, *Epistles 93–124*.

152. Jonson, *Timber: Or, Discoveries*, lines 1666–67, 1695–96, in *Jonson*, 7:578, 580.

153. *Oxford English Dictionary*, s.v. "answer, v."

154. See Woods, "Ben Jonson's Cary-Morison Ode," 69.

155. Peterson, *Imitation and Praise*, 221. See also Woods, *Natural Emphasis*, 209; Trotter, *Poetry of Abraham Cowley*, 110–11.

156. See J. Tuck, "'Thou Fall'st, My Tongue,'" 88.

157. Marston, *Iacke Drums Entertainment*, I3r. See Patterson, *Censorship and Interpretation*, 143; R. Evans, *Ben Jonson and the Poetics of Patronage*, 212.

158. Jonson, *Timber: Or, Discoveries*, lines 1695–96, in *Jonson*, 7:580.

159. *Informations to William Drummond of Hawthornden*, lines 1–3, in *Jonson* 5:359.

160. Jane Hedley has pointed out that Jonson's lyric poems of praise celebrate heroes in a way that befits his emphasis on individual virtue over collective piety. Hedley, *Power in Verse*, 168.

Chapter Four. Rhyme Oft Times Overreaches Reason: Measure and Passion after the Civil War

1. On the couplets of Waller and Denham as forces of containment, see Nevo, *Dial of Virtue*, 30–38; Norbrook, *Writing the English Republic*, 71–79, 134–35. On Cowley's couplets, see MacLean, *Time's Witness*, 180–81.

2. Nethercot, *Muse's Hannibal*, 58–60, 80–81; Allan Pritchard, introduction to *The Civil War*, by Abraham Cowley, 12–13.

3. Jonson, "To my chosen Friend, The learned Translator of LUCAN, THOMAS MAY, Esquire," in May, *Lucan's Pharsalia*, A8r. Quoted in MacLean, *Time's Witness*, 32. Jonson's celebration hardly does justice to the episodic formlessness and hyperbolic carnage of Lucan's poem. See Quint, *Epic and Empire*, 131–57; N. Smith, *Literature and Revolution*, 205. On May's translation of Lucan as a "gesture of support for an international anti-absolutist alliance," see Norbrook, *Writing the English Republic*, 43. On Cowley's reinterpretation of Lucan, see Norbrook, *Writing the English Republic*, 83–92; and N. Smith, *Literature and Revolution*, 203–12.

4. Allan Pritchard, introduction to *The Civil War*, by Abraham Cowley, 15; Trotter, *Poetry of Abraham Cowley*, 7.

5. Cowley, *Poems*, a4r.

6. Allan Pritchard, introduction to *The Civil War*, by Abraham Cowley, 3.

7. Cowley, *Civil War*, 1:1–8.

8. On the ways this opening departs from epic convention, see MacLean, *Time's Witness*, 184.

9. See Kilburn and Milton, "Public Context of the Trial and Execution of Strafford," 234. See also MacLean, *Time's Witness*, 195; Wilcher, *Writing of Royalism*, 40–66; Griffin, "'Twixt Treason and Convenience.'"

10. Cowley, *Civil War*, 1:140, 143–48.

11. See Welch, *Renaissance Epic and the Oral Past*, 111–12.

12. Cowley, "Ode 1. On the Prayse of Poetry," in *Poeticall Blossomes*, F4r.

13. Golding, *The. xv. Bookes of P. Ovidius Naso*, S7v.

14. Golding, *The. xv. Bookes of P. Ovidius Naso*, S8r.

15. Milton, "Lycidas," lines 61, 62, in *CPMP*, 122. For other royalist uses of the Orpheus myth, see N. Smith, *Literature and Revolution*, 101, 290.

16. Cowley, *Civil War*, 3:291, 293.

17. Cowley, *Civil War*, 3:525–28.

18. See Trotter, *Poetry of Abraham Cowley*, 19.

19. Cowley, *Civil War*, 3:529–30.

20. Shakespeare, *A Midsummer Night's Dream*, 4.1.200–209, in *Norton Shakespeare*.

21. Cowley, *Civil War*, 3:539–50.

22. Cowley, *Davideis*, note 46 to book 3, in Cowley, *Poems*, Pppp3r.

23. Tasso, *Discorsi*, H3r. Translation from Tasso, *Genesis of Tasso's Narrative Theory*, 146–47.

24. Donne, "The Good Morrow," lines 10, 10, 11; "A Nocturnal Upon Saint Lucy's Day," lines 15, 15, 29, 29, in *Complete Poems of John Donne*.

25. Jonson, *Informations*, lines 31–33, in *Jonson*, 5:361.

26. Puttenham, *Arte*, Y2r.

27. Jonson, *Discoveries*, line 1350, in *Jonson*, 7:562.

28. Cowley, *Civil War*, 3:563–68.

29. In his two elegies in his 1636 *Poetical Blossomes*, "An Elegie on the Death of Mrs. Anne Whitfield" and "An Elegy on the Death of Iohn Littleton," Cowley balances the pathetic fallacy and the passions with restrained Jonsonian reflections on the upright characters of the deceased. Cowley, *Poeticall Blossomes*, E8r–F1v.

30. Cowley, *Civil War*, 3:572–76.

31. See Trotter, *Poetry of Abraham Cowley*, 20.

32. MacLean, *Time's Witness*, 207; N. Smith, *Literature and Revolution*, 208; Trotter, *Poetry of Abraham Cowley*, 21. See also Anselment, *Loyalist Resolve*, 161; Loxley, *Royalism and Poetry*, 86–88; Wilcher, *Writing of Royalism*, 183–92.

33. Power, "'Teares Break Off My Verse,'" 145. The title of Power's essay is one of Cowley's hemistichs; Power shrewdly notes that the hemistich in which verse is supposedly broken off by emotion rhymes with the line before.

34. Anthony Welch detects a similar intermixing of genres in *Davideis* and quotes Restoration critic Thomas Rymer's complaints about the fact that Cowley not only mixes lyrical matters into his epic poem, but uses lyric measures. Welch, *Renaissance Epic and the Oral Past*, 118–19.

35. Cowley, *Civil War*, 3:9, 13, 17, 17–18. See Norbrook, *Writing the English Republic*, 84.

36. Thomas Sprat, "Account of the Life and Writings of Mr Abraham Cowley," claimed that Cowley wrote most of *Davideis* while at Cambridge, but Frank Kermode has convincingly argued that all or most of the poem was written between 1650 and 1654. Kermode, "Date of Cowley's *Davideis*."

37. Cowley, *Poems*, Aaaa2v.

38. Cowley, *Poems*, Ffff3r, b1v. For a different account of the friction between the Virgilian model and biblical theme of the poem, see Dykstal, "Epic Reticence of Abraham Cowley."

39. Cowley, *Poems*, b2r, b2v.

40. Cowley, *Poems*, b3v.

41. D'Addario, "Abraham Cowley and the Ends of Poetry," 124–25.

42. Cowley, *Civil War*, 1:144, 143.

43. Joshua Scodel includes Cowley in a group of late seventeenth-century English Neo-epicureans who, following Montaigne, doubted that reason could moderate the passions. Scodel, "Cowleyan Pindaric Ode," 182–83.

44. Angela Leighton discusses how eighteenth- and nineteenth-century philosophers worried over form's entanglement with charm and emotion. Leighton, *On Form*, 4–12.

45. Victoria Kahn has considered how political theorists like Hobbes and royalist prose romance writers of the 1650s responded to the problem of the passions in the wake of the Civil War. The political argument she detects in three prose romances—that the "passions [for older aristocratic values of love and honor] may become the basis of a new political order" and that "artistic craft and aesthetic interest could contribute to the hoped-for Restoration of Charles II"—has much in common with the positions of royalist lyric poets. The

lyric poets of the period, however, are much less apt than the romance writers Kahn discusses to incorporate Hobbesian self-interest into their accounts of the ideal community or ideal life. Kahn, *Wayward Contracts*, 215.

46. McDowell, *Poetry and Allegiance*, 2–6, 13–24. See also McDowell, "Classical Liberty and Cavalier Poetics"; McDowell, "Towards Redefinition of Cavalier Poetics"; Norbrook, *Writing the English Republic*, 159.

47. McDowell, *Poetry and Allegiance*, 20. See also N. Smith, *Literature and Revolution*, 255–56.

48. For an extensive account of Brome's work, see Anselment, *Loyalist Resolve*, 127–54. See also Hirst, "Politics of Literature."

49. A concluding note attributes the verses to "Rob. Napeir E medio Templo," probably the "Robert Napper, son and heir of Robert N., of the Middle Temple" who was admitted to the Middle Temple in 1655 and was called to the bar in February 1659/60. Sturgess, *Register of Admissions to the Honourable Society of the Middle Temple*, 1:156.

50. Robert Napeir, "To the Ingenious Author Mr. A.B.," in Brome, *Songs and Other Poems*, A6v.

51. See Major, *Writings of Exile*, 118.

52. On associations between King David and the monarch, see Potter, *Secret Rites*, 160–62; Corns, *Uncloistered Virtue*, 88–91; Major, *Writings of Exile*, 36–37. Major also notes that Independents and Calvinists were also able to interpret the Psalms to defend their own causes.

53. Cowley, *Poems*, Bbbb3r.

54. Cowley, *Poems*, Bbbb3r. On Cowley and harmony in Davideis, see Welch, *Renaissance Epic and the Oral Past*, 115–16.

55. Sandys, *Ovid's Metamorphosis Englished*, Tt2v.

56. Hollander, *Untuning of the Sky*, 172–73.

57. It is also important to note how continental influences were at work alongside classical influences. See McDowell, "Towards Redefinition of Cavalier Poetics"; N. Smith, "Cross-Channel Cavaliers."

58. Drayton, *Poemes Lyrick and pastorall*, B1r.

59. Marotti, *Manuscript*, 247.

60. Marotti, *Manuscript*, 259–65.

61. N. Smith, *Literature and Revolution*, 203. See also Welch, *Renaissance Epic and the Oral Past*, 117–18.

62. See Roland Greene, *Post-Petrarchism*, 5–7.

63. Roland Greene, "Lyric"; V. Jackson, "Lyric." See also Patterson, *Censorship and Interpretation*, 123–25; Lindley, " 'Words for Music, Perhaps,' " 10–12; T. Healy, " 'Trewly Wrote,' " 53–54.

64. W. Scott, *Model of Poesy*, 25.

65. *Oxford English Dictionary*, s.v. "lyric, n."

66. See Abrams, *Mirror and The Lamp*, 98–99; see also Culler, "Introduction: Critical Paradigms."

67. On the shift away from this idea of common sense, see Arendt, *Human Condition*, 280–84.

68. Tom Cain and Ruth Connolly, introduction to Herrick, *Complete Poetry*, 1:lv.

69. John Creaser argues that the "oeuvre is spread fairly evenly over forty years" and provides a helpful table of datable poems. Creaser, " 'Times Trans-shifting.' "178.

70. Herrick, "665. What Kind of Mistresse He Would Have," line 8, in Herrick, *Complete Poetry*, 1:220.

71. Herrick, *Complete Poetry*, 1:1–320. This count does not include the religious verse

in *His Noble Numbers*, where the percentage of couplet poems is even higher—about 95 percent. Herrick, *Complete Poetry*, 1:321–88.

72. Watts, *Works*, 4:xx. Robin Leaver, following Nicholas Temperley, has argued that the ballad meter Sternhold adopted was not widely used at the time and that it became "common" and popular only as a result of Sternhold and Hopkins. Leaver, *Goostly Psalmes and Spirituall Songes*, 119–20; Temperley, *Music of the English Parish Church*, 1:26.

73. See Thomas Blount's 1656 definition: "*Anacreontic Verse* (so called from *Anacreon*, a *Lyrick* Poet, who was the first inventor of it) consists of seven syllables, which as I take it, are not tied to any certain Law of quantity." Blount, *Glossographia*, C5v–C6r. As mentioned in the previous chapter, tetrameter couplets were also frequently used to translate and imitate Anacreon.

74. Herrick, like Jonson, seems to have drawn on Henri Estienne's anthology of the nine lyric poets, *Carminum Poetarum novem, lyricae poesieos principum fragmentum*. See Achilleos, "'Ile Bring Thee *Herrick* to *Anacreon*,'" 196.

75. Drayton, *Poemes Lyrick and Pastorall*, A4r.

76. Herrick, "544. An Ode to Sir Clipsebie Crew," line 9, and "1017. The Vision," line 14, in Herrick, *Complete Poetry*, 1:187, 298. See Braden, *Classics*, 214; Achilleos, "'Ile Bring Thee *Herrick* to *Anacreon*.'"

77. Herrick, "889. Another," lines 5–6, in Herrick, *Complete Poetry*, 1:270. See also "888. Charmes" and "891. Another Charme for Stables," in Herrick, *Complete Poetry*, 1:270.

78. Shakespeare, *Macbeth*, 1.3.30–35, in *Norton Shakespeare*.

79. Jonson, *Masque of Queens*, lines 35–43, in *Jonson*, 3:307.

80. Shakespeare, *A Midsummer Night's Dream*, 2.2.84–89, in *Norton Shakespeare*.

81. J. Fletcher, *Faithfvll Shepherdesse*, F3r–v.

82. Like Herrick's fairy poems and his poems celebrating traditional rural festivals, the charm poems can be seen as part of a larger royalist effort to revive old rituals and pastimes that Leah Marcus argues was intended to broaden "the scope of Anglican 'liberty'" in the hopes that controlled license would "shore up a traditional system against the inroads of newer forms." Marcus, *Politics of Mirth*, 145. Peter Stallybrass draws attention to the fact that these supposed revivals of old holiday calendars and pastimes were often new inventions for the purpose of allowing the controlled release of passions. Stallybrass, "'We Feaste in Our Defense.'"

83. Corns, *Uncloistered Virtue*, 99.

84. For some samples of cavalier invective in couplets, see Nevo, *Dial of Virtue*, 52–73. On Civil War satire, see N. Smith, *Literature and Revolution*, 295–319; Loxley, *Royalism and Poetry*, 96–123. On drollery, see Raylor, *Cavaliers, Clubs, and Literary Culture*.

85. Norbrook, *Writing the English Republic*, 140, 143.

86. Wither, *Campo-Musae*, A3r.

87. Wither, *Campo-Musae*, A1v.

88. Harris, *Mercurius Militaris, or the Armies scout*, no. 4 (October 31–November 9, 1648): D1r. Quoted in N. Smith, *Literature and Revolution*, 61.

89. On the war of the theaters and satire, see Dutton, "Jonson's Satiric Styles," 64.

90. Brainford, *Levellers and the English Revolution*, 210–12; Heinemann, *Puritanism and Theatre*, 252–54; N. Smith, *Literature and Revolution*, 65.

91. Ed. May, "On the deceased Authour, Master Thomas Beedom, and his Poems," in Beedome, *Poems, Divine, and Humane*, A2v.

92. Beedome, "Epigram 4," in Beedome, *Poems, Divine, and Humane*, G1v, F5r. On the little that is known about Beedome, see Shaver, "Thomas Beedome." One of the commendatory poems in the volume is by Henry Glapthorne, a friend of Richard Lovelace's. On Glapthorne's poem to Lovelace, see McDowell, *Poetry and Allegiance*, 189–90.

93. See McDowell, *Poetry and Allegiance*, 45–46.

94. Dudley Posthumus Lovelace, "To my much honored Cozen Mr. Stanley, Upon his Poems set by Mr. JOHN GAMBLE," in Gamble, *Ayres and Dialogues*, a4r.

95. Alexander Brome, "To his Friend THOMAS STANLEY, Esq; On his Odes Set and Published by Mr. JOHN GAMBLE," in Gamble, *Ayres and Dialogues*, a4v. The volume also contains a dedicatory poem by Richard Lovelace that compares Stanley to Amphion and declares that his harmonies, which echo the music of the spheres, ravish listeners and raise them to heaven. Richard Lovelace, "To my much honored Cozen Mr. Stanley, Upon his Poems set by Mr. JOHN GAMBLE," in Gamble, *Ayres and Dialogues*, a3r.

96. On Beaumont's life and ties to Buckingham, see Sell, introduction to Sell, *Shorter Poems of Sir John Beaumont*, 3–22.

97. John Beaumont, "To his late Maiesty, concerning the true forme of English Poetry," in Beaumont, *Bosworth-field*, H7r.

98. See, for example, John Davies, "Nosce Teipsum," lines 958–60, in *Poems of Sir John Davies*, 36. The metaphor derives from Aristotle, *On the Soul*, 424a, in Aristotle, *Basic Works of Aristotle*, 580.

99. See Restoration playwright Edward Howard's statement that he has "closed some Scenes, and all my Acts likewise with [rhyme], which places have ever been allowed most proper for it, because they are Period in which the Audience may best expect a weighty and sententious close." Howard, *Womens Conquest*, a1r.

100. In fact, one of Marston's favorite strategies for disrupting the end of the line is to pair a polysyllable with a monosyllable in his rhymes, directly contradicting Beaumont's argument about "Saxon shortnesse."

101. Beaumont, "To his late Maiesty, concerning the true forme of English Poetry," in Beaumont, *Bosworth-field*, H7r; Marston, *Scourge of Villanie, Corrected*, K8v.

102. Herrick, "869. To His Honour'd Friend, Sir Thomas Heale," in Herrick, *Complete Poetry*, 1:266.

103. Herrick, "8. When He Would Have His Verses Read," in Herrick, *Complete Poetry*, 1:9.

104. Richard Lovelace, "A Vintage to the Dungeon. A Song. Set by Mr. William Lawes," in Lovelace, *Lucasta*, D7r.

105. *Cassell's New Latin Dictionary* (1959), s.v. "canto."

106. Herrick, "106. A Country life: To his Brother, M. Tho. Herrick," line 106, in Herrick, *Complete Poetry*, 1:34. Jonson uses the phrase "private Lares" in an "Entertainment" performed before the king and queen at Theobalds in 1607. The directions for performance include a description of the "glorious place, figuring the Lararium, or seat of the household gods, where both the Lares and Penates were painted in copper colours." Jonson, "An Entertainment at Theobalds," in *Jonson*, 3:209.

107. Miner, *Cavalier Mode*, 3.

108. Marcus, *Politics of Mirth*; Sharpe, *Criticism and Compliment*; Potter, *Secret Rites*.

109. Raylor, *Cavaliers, Clubs, and Literary Culture*, 197.

110. Burlinson, "'Finest Gossamer,'" 459.

111. Miner, *Cavalier Mode*, 3.

112. Miner, *Cavalier Mode*, 41.

113. Hammond, *Fleeting Things*. See also Maus, "Why Read Herrick?," 28, 37–38.

114. Ullrich Langer argues that "attentiveness to the extreme particular—*you and no other, this and nothing else*" is the central preoccupation of Petrarch's poetry. Langer, *Lyric in the Renaissance*, 8. While the poets I consider in this chapter are deeply indebted to the dedication to particularity visible in the Petrarchan tradition, they turn it in a new direction

by situating the love for a single individual among a variety of other links to things, places, and people that they consider their "own."

115. Connolly, "Bestiaries of Feeling," 474.

116. Connolly, "Bestiaries of Feeling," 486.

117. Drayton, *Poemes Lyrick and pastorall*, B1r.

118. Swann, *Curiosities and Texts*, 189.

119. Poliziano, *Oratio super Fabio Quintiliano et Statii Sylvis*, 872.

120. On the disruption of time and narrative sequence in Petrarch, see Barolini, "Making of a Lyric Sequence."

121. See Rostvig, *Happy Man*, 1:121; Miner, *Cavalier Mode*, 179; Summers, "Herrick, Vaughan and the Poetry of Anglican Survivalism"; Chernaik, "Books as Memorials."

122. Firth and Rait, *Acts and Ordinances of the Interregnum*, 2:349. On the "five-mile tether," see Major, *Writings of Exile*, 105. Major notes in his chapter on internal exile that while banishment abroad was rare, "blanket exclusions from London were applied at various times to every 'delinquent', often irrespective of whether they had sought an accommodation with the new regime by compounding for their estates. The volume of measures taken to remove Royalists and Catholics from the capital is significantly high: in response to intelligence on planned royalist uprisings between 1646 and 1660, no fewer than 18 acts, ordinances and proclamations were passed to this effect by parliament, the Council of State, or the Lord Protector." Major, *Writings of Exile*, 101. See Steele, *Bibliography of Royal Proclamations of the Tudor and Stuart Sovereigns*, 1:323–93. Lovelace and Fane were actually confined to London for short periods of time. Major, *Writings of Exile*, 133–37.

123. On the idea of Stoic self-rule and contentment in the country in the Caroline era, particularly in the works of Thomas Carew, William Cartwright, and George Daniel, see Anselment, *Loyalist Resolve*.

124. A. Fowler, introduction to *The Country House Poem*, 20.

125. Herrick, "1. The Argument of his Book," line 9, in Herrick, *Complete Poetry*, 1:7.

126. Herrick, "377. A Panegyrick to Sir Lewis Pemberton," line 15, in Herrick, *Complete Poetry*, 1:138. The editors of the 2013 Oxford edition date this poem to 1617–19. John Creaser dates it to 1621–22. Creaser, " 'Times Trans-shifting,' " 185–87.

127. Herrick, "2. To his muse," lines 2, 4, in Herrick, *Complete Poetry*, 1:7.

128. Herrick, "552. His content in the Country," in Herrick, *Complete Poetry*, 1:189. On the dating of this poem, see Creaser, " 'Times Trans-shifting,' " 193.

129. Cf. Jonson's praise of Sir Robert Wroth's "unbought provision"; Jonson, "To Sir Robert Wroth," line 14, in *Jonson*, 5:216.

130. A rejection of trade and emphasis on the sufficiency of the land owner are evident in Herrick's early country poem "The Country life," where Herrick celebrates the confinement of Endymion Porter's economic concerns within his "own dear bounds"; he contrasts Porter's thoughts about the "fleece" produced by his sheep or "how to pay [his] Hinds" with the economic ambition of those who plow "the Oceans foame / To seek, and bring rough Pepper home" or to bring "home the Ingot from the West." Herrick, "662. The Country life, to the honoured M. End. Porter, Groome of the Bed-Chamber to His Maj." lines 15, 12, 13, 5–6, 10, in Herrick, *Complete Poetry*, 1:217.

131. Herrick, "377. A Panegyric to Sir Lewis Pemberton," line 15, in Herrick, *Complete Poetry*, 1:138; Carew, "To Saxham," line 54, in Chaplin and Rumrich, *Seventeenth Century British Poetry*, 301; Jonson, "To Penshurst, line 48, in *Jonson*, 5:212; Herrick, "377. A Panegyric to Sir Lewis Pemberton," line 11, in Herrick, *Complete Poetry*, 1:138; Jonson, "To Penshurst," lines 48, 27, in *Jonson*, 5:211–12. On the open door motif, see Heal, *Hospitality*, 108.

132. Tom Cain and Ruth Connolly, introduction to Herrick, *Complete Poetry*, lvi.

133. Tom Cain and Ruth Connolly, introduction to Herrick, *Complete Poetry*, 1:lix; Major, *Writings of Exile*, 101–2, 127–28.

134. Corns, *Uncloistered Virtue*, 89–91; Rudrum, "Royalist Lyric," 183. As Katharine Maus suggests, one suspects "that his royalist views follow from his sensibility, rather than creating it." Maus, "Why Read Herrick?," 35.

135. Line Cottegnies has emphasized the continuities between the poetic projects of Herrick and Katherine Philips, making the case that both poets "evince a new understanding of the role of poetry halfway between the private and the public spheres and as a paradoxical medium for performing semi-private rituals in a public arena, with a similar attention to their own literary fame." Cottegnies, " 'Leaves of Fame,' " 134.

136. See Hageman, "Making a Good Impression."

137. Gardiner, "To my dear Friend Mr. Samuel Woodford, upon his Paraphrase of the Psalms," in Woodford, *Paraphrase upon the Psalms of David*, d1v; Francis Bernard, "To My Dear Friend Mr. Thomas Flatman upon the publication of his Poems. Pindarique Ode," in Flatman, *Poems and Songs*, a8r. Both names are invoked repeatedly in the volumes of Henry Vaughan, Aphra Behn, John Oldham, and Jane Barker, among others. Vaughan, *Thalia Redivivas*; Behn, *Poems upon Several Occasions*; Oldham, *Some New Pieces*; Barker, *Poetical Recreations*.

138. Scott-Baumann, *Forms of Engagement*, 81–112.

139. See Faderman, *Surpassing the Love of Men*, 68–71; Libertin, "Female Friendship"; Andreadis, "Sapphic-Platonics"; Stiebel, "Not since Sappho."

140. Barash, *English Women's Poetry*; Gray, "Katherine Philips and the Post-courtly Coterie"; Chalmers, *Royalist Women Writers*, 56–104; Anderson, *Friendship's Shadow*, 69–103, 153–81. Though she brings the two together, Anderson is interested in the ways that Philips's friendship poetry challenge her political and Stoic writing. For an intriguing account of how we can see connections between the political absolutism and the absolute individualism of another seventeenth-century royalist poet, Margaret Cavendish, see Gallagher, "Embracing the Absolute."

141. Philips, "57. Friendship," lines 7–8, and "70. Submission," line 46, in *Collected Works of Katherine Philips*, 1:150, 1:180

142. The manuscript of Powell's poem was located by Elizabeth H. Hageman and Andrea Sununu and reproduced in Hageman and Sununu, " 'More Copies,' " 128–30. For an account of Powell's publications and his post-Restoration imprisonments, as well as a reading of the rough rhyme and enjambment in his *Lamentations of Jeremiah*, see Achinstein, *Literature and Dissent*, 76–78.

143. G. Wright, *Producing Women's Poetry*, 112–13.

144. Philips, "Upon the double murther of K. Charles, in answer to the libellous rime made by V.P.," lines 1–8, in *Collected Works of Katherine Philips*, 1:69.

145. Ross, *Women, Poetry, and Politics*, 1; see also Loxley, "Unfettered Organs," 243.

146. Philips, "A Retir'd Frienship, To Ardelia," line 20; Philips, "An ode upon retirement, made upon occasion of Mr. Cowley's on that subject," line 44, in *Collected Works of Katherine Philips*, 1:98, 1:194.

147. Herodotus, *The famous hystory of Herodotus*, C2r. The story is frequently cited, particularly in sermons and devotional works of the seventeenth century.

148. James I, *Workes of the Most High and Mightie Prince Iames*, R2r. See, among others, Goldberg, "Fatherly Authority"; R. Tuck, *Philosophy and Government*, 260–63; Ng, *Literature and the Politics of Family*; Sharpe, *Image Wars*, 22–23.

149. On marriage and love as the defining images of the Caroline monarchy, see Pat-

terson, *Censorship and Interpretation*, 167–76; Sharpe, *Criticism and Compliment*; Kahn, *Wayward Contracts*, 13; Sharpe, *Image Wars*, 260–66.

150. D. Scott, "Counsel and Cabal," 131–33. See also Underdown, *Royalist Conspiracy*, 10–12.

151. Philips, "Upon the double murther of K. Charles, in answer to the libellous rime made by V.P.," lines 10, 10, 10, 16, 16, in *Collected Works of Katherine Philips*, 1:69.

152. Philips, "Upon the double murther of K. Charles, in answer to the libellous rime made by V.P.," line 34, in *Collected Works of Katherine Philips*, 1:70.

153. Philips, "Upon the double murther of K. Charles, in answer to the libellous rime made by V.P.," lines 33, 12, 13, 13–14, in *Collected Works of Katherine Philips*, 1:70, 69.

154. Philips, "Upon the double murther of K. Charles, in answer to the libellous rime made by V.P.," lines 17, 17, 18, in *Collected Works of Katherine Philips*, 1:69. See R. Evans, "Paradox in Poetry and Politics," 181.

155. Philips, "Upon the double murther of K. Charles, in answer to the libellous rime made by V.P.," line 26, in *Collected Works of Katherine Philips*, 1:70.

156. Philips, "Upon the double murther of K. Charles, in answer to the libellous rime made by V.P.," line 27, 28, in *Collected Works of Katherine Philips*, 1:70.

157. Philips, "Upon the double murther of K. Charles, in answer to the libellous rime made by V.P.," line 1, in *Collected Works of Katherine Philips*, 1:70.

158. See Kuzner, "Friendship, Sovereignty, and Sexuality."

159. Philips, "17. Friendship's Mysterys, to my dearest Lucasia. (set by Mr. H. Lawes)," lines 2, 2, 3, 3, in *Collected Works of Katherine Philips*, 1:90.

160. Philips, "17. Friendship's Mysterys, to my dearest Lucasia. (set by Mr. H. Lawes)," lines 6, 7, 8, 10, 9, in *Collected Works of Katherine Philips*, 1:90.

161. Philips, "57. Friendship," line 24, in *Collected Works of Katherine Philips*, 1:150.

162. Philips, "43. To my Lucasia," line 10, in *Collected Works of Katherine Philips*, 1:129. See also Philips, "64. A Friend," lines 25–30, in *Collected Works of Katherine Philips*, 1:166. On Donne and Philips, see Andreadis, "Sapphic-Platonics"; Loscocco, "Inventing the English Sappho"; Scott-Baumann, *Forms of Engagement*, 116–25.

163. Spenser, *Amoretti* 71, lines 11, 12, in *SP*.

164. Philips, "17. Friendship's Mysterys, to my dearest Lucasia. (set by Mr. H. Lawes)," lines 19, 19, 20, 20, in *Collected Works of Katherine Philips*, 1:91. Catharine Gray also compares Spenser's view of fetters to Philips's in Gray, "Katherine Philips and the Post-courtly Coterie," 446.

165. La Primaudaye, *French Academie*, N2r. La Primaudaye is quoted in Miller, *Poem's Two Bodies*, 30. See Dolven, *Senses of Style*, 35.

166. Philips, "70. Submission," lines 5, 9, 29, 31, 37, in *Collected Works of Katherine Philips*, 1:179.

167. Philips, "70. Submission," lines 1–4, in *Collected Works of Katherine Philips*, 1:178.

168. John Donne, "Divine Meditation 2," lines 1–2, in *Variorum Edition of the Poetry of John Donne*, vol. 7.1, *The Holy Sonnets*, 5.

169. Philips, "70. Submission," lines 15–16, in *Collected Works of Katherine Philips*, 1:179.

170. Philips, "72. The World," line 59, in *Collected Works of Katherine Philips*, 1:184.

171. Philips, "70. Submission," lines 17, 19, 19, in *Collected Works of Katherine Philips*, 1:179.

172. Philips, "70. Submission," lines 21–24, in *Collected Works of Katherine Philips*, 1:179.

173. Philips, "70. Submission," line 77, in *Collected Works of Katherine Philips*, 1:180.

174. Philips, "70. Submission," line 21, in *Collected Works of Katherine Philips*, 1:179.

175. Saintsbury, *History of English Prosody*, 2:394.

176. Cowley, "On Orinda's Poems. Ode," in *Poems, by Several Persons*, F2r. Some early versions of this poem have "fancies high" instead of "passions high."

177. Nethercot, *Muse's Hannibal*, 90–91, 196–216.

178. Cowley, "The Complaint," in Cowley, *Verses, Written Upon Several Occasions*, D7r. Nethercot discovered evidence that Henrietta Maria conveyed some lands to Cowley before he retired to Barn Elms in 1663. No other evidence indicates that he lived there. Nethercot, *Muse's Hannibal*, 209, 212.

179. See Philips, "Upon the engraving. K:P: on a Tree in the short walke at Barn=Elms," in *Collected Works of Katherine Philips*, 1:208.

180. "Thee" here refers to "the world."

181. Philips, "An ode upon retirement, made upon occasion of Mr. Cowley's on that subject," lines 73–80, in *Collected Works of Katherine Philips*, 1:195.

182. See Scott-Baumann, *Forms of Engagement*, 99–103. On heroism in Cowley's odes, see Scodel, "Cowleyan Pindaric Ode," 186–94, 199. On the political engagements and evasions of the Pindarick Odes, especially the Brutus ode, see Nevo, *Dial of Virtue*, 199–227; Allan Pritchard, introduction to *The Civil War*, by Abraham Cowley, 31; Langley, "Abraham Cowley's 'Brutus'"; Keough, "Cowley's Brutus Ode"; Patterson, *Censorship and Interpretation*, 146–58; Revard, *Politics, Poetics, and the Pindaric Ode*, 125–52; D'Addario, "Abraham Cowley and the Ends of Poetry," 125–32.

183. Sprat, "Account of the Life and Writings of Mr Abraham Cowley," d1v.

184. Sprat, "Account of the Life and Writings of Mr Abraham Cowley," e2r.

185. The first quote is from Bacon, *Essayes*, A3r; the second from Montaigne, *Essayes Or Morall, Politike, and Millitarie Discourses*, A6v.

186. Scodel, *English Poetic Epitaph*, 140–62; Empson, *Structure of Complex Words*, 185–250.

187. Scodel, *English Poetic Epitaph*, 141; Empson, *Structure of Complex Words*, 187.

188. See A. Fowler, introduction to *The Country House Poem*, 8. David Hill Radcliffe contrasts Cowley's essays with Jonson's *Forrest*, both of which he characterizes as *sylvae*, in Radcliffe, "Sylvan States."

189. De Gooyer, "Sensibility and Solitude," 7.

190. In his Pindaric ode "Destinie," Cowley traces his poetic nature further back: "Me from the *womb* the *Midwife Muse* did take: / She cut my *Navel, washt me*, and mine *Head* / With her own *Hands* she *Fashioned*." Cowley, *Poems*, Ee4r.

191. Campion, *Observations in the Art of English Poesy*, in G. Smith, *Elizabethan Critical Essays*, 2:331.

192. Marston, *Scourge*, E1r, E8v. The final quote is from the expanded and corrected version of Marston's satires, Marston, *Scourge*, K8v.

193. Trotter, *Poetry of Abraham Cowley*, 115; Stogdill, "Abraham Cowley's 'Pindaric Way,'" 501.

194. Cowley, "The Resurrection," line 60, in Cowley, *Poems*, Ddd3v.

195. See Hinman, *Abraham Cowley's World of Order*, 88–90.

196. Ward, "Abraham Cowley's Odes 'Rightly Repeated,'" 50, 44.

197. Cowley, *Poems*, b1v (emphasis mine).

198. For a different reading of the effects of rhyme in Cowley's Pindarics, see Jarvis, "Hyper-Pindaric."

199. Sprat, "Account of the Life and Writings of Mr Abraham Cowley," d1v.

200. Lindsay, "Cowley, Abraham (1618–1667)," in *Oxford Dictionary of National Biog-*

raphy, ed. H.C.G. Matthew and Brian Harrison (Oxford: Oxford University Press, 2004), http://www.oxforddnb.com/themes/theme.jsp?articleid=92747 (accessed May 27, 2016).

201. Quoted in Poole, "Two Early Readers," 79.

202. Eyre, *Transcript of the Registers of the Worshipful Company of Stationers*, 2:381.

203. Quoted in Poole, "Two Early Readers," 80.

204. Quoted in Poole, "Two Early Readers," 81.

Chapter Five. Milton and the Known Rules of Ancient Liberty

1. Lewalski, *Life of John Milton*, 29.

2. Translation mine, from Milton, *Prolusion 2: "In Scholis Publicis: De Sphaerarum Concentu,"* in Milton, *Works of John Milton*, 12:152.

3. On the idea of the "Pistrinum," the mill, a metaphor for servile drudgery that Milton returns to again and again and that becomes literal in *Samson Agonistes*, see Dzelzianis, "'In Power of Others,'" 288–89.

4. Milton, *Prolusion 2: "In Scholis Publicis: De Sphaerarum Concentu,"* in Milton, *Works of John Milton*, 12:150.

5. Mander, "Milton and the Music of the Spheres," 63.

6. Milton, "Arcades," line 71, in *CPMP*. See Minear, *Reverberating Song*, 183–95; Welch, *Renaissance Epic and the Oral Past*, 140–62.

7. Two recent books on Miltonic liberty have clarified both the overlaps and the tensions between modern concepts of liberty and Milton's. See Woods, *Milton and the Poetics of Freedom*; Chernaik, *Milton and the Burden of Freedom*. Woods considers how Milton builds what she calls a "poetics of choice" into every aspect of his verse. She argues that Milton's indeterminate language invites readers to navigate the process of judging and making choices as they read his verse. Chernaik shares Woods's focus on ambivalence: he highlights the contradictions in Milton's theological and political views on liberty, often by reading the poet's works alongside Reformation theology and Civil War political writings. Both Woods and Chernaik present nuanced accounts of freedom in Milton by reading across his theology, politics, and poetry and bringing new contexts to bear on his thought.

8. See Freedman, "Milton and Dryden on Rhyme"; Zwicker, "John Dryden Meets, Rhymes, and Says Farewell to John Milton."

9. Dryden, *Satires*, C1r.

10. Dryden, *Satires*, C1r.

11. The most famous use of this term for rhyme is Aubrey's report that Dryden went to Milton "to have leave to putt his Paradise Lost into a drama in rhyme. Mr. Milton received him civilly, and told him he would give him leave to tagge his verses." Aubrey, *Brief Lives*, 203. Marvell also uses the verb in his commendatory poem. Andrew Marvell, "On Mr Milton's Paradise Lost," line 50, in *Poems of Andrew Marvell*, 184. On tagged points in cavalier dress and their reputation, see Burlinson, "'Finest Gossamer.'"

12. Milton, "Of Education," in *Complete Prose Works of John Milton*, 2:403.

13. Milton, *The Reason of Church-government Urg'd against Prelaty*, in *Complete Prose Works of John Milton*, 1:820.

14. On the 1645 volume, see Martz, "Rising Poet, 1645"; Corns, "Milton's Quest for Respectability"; R. Johnson, "Politics of Publication"; Revard, *Milton and the Tangles of Naera's Hair*. On Moseley, see Kastan, "Invention of English Literature."

15. On music in the *Masque* and the ways in which Milton's masque engages with Shakespeare and the dramatic tradition of music, see Minear, *Reverberating Song*.

16. All quotations from *A Masque Presented at Ludlow Castle* are from *CPMP*. All references to the masque are hereafter cited parenthetically by line number and abbreviated *Masque*.

17. See Friedman, "'Comus' and the Truth of the Ear," 129–30.

18. On the polyphony of Circe's song and the Lady's monody, see Buhler, "Counterpoint and Controversy," 26.

19. For a psychological interpretation of Comus's appreciation of the Lady's music over his mothers, see W. Kerrigan, *Sacred Complex*, 52. John Rumrich responds with a different reading of motherhood in the masque in Rumrich, *Milton Unbound*, 70–93. See also Minear, *Reverberating Song*, 210.

20. See Friedman, "'Comus' and the Truth of the Ear," 130.

21. Wordsworth, "To a Skylark," line 12, in Wordsworth, *Selected Poems*, 300.

22. *Oxford English Dictionary*, s.v. "home-felt, adj."

23. Milton, "Areopagitica," in *Complete Prose Works of John Milton*, 2:513, 514.

24. Kahn, *Machiavellian Rhetoric*, 202, 207. See also Larson, "'Blest Pair of Sirens.'"

25. Kahn, *Machiavellian Rhetoric*, 194.

26. Shakespeare, *Macbeth*, 4.1.18, in *Norton Shakespeare*.

27. Lewalski, *Life of John Milton*, 63.

28. Lewalski, *Life of John Milton*, 64, 73–74.

29. Oras, "Milton's Early Rhyme Schemes"; Prince, *Italian Element*, 71–88. See also MacKenzie, "Rethinking Rhyme."

30. Prince, *Italian Element*, 85.

31. Prince, *Italian Element*, 84, 87.

32. Norbrook, *Poetry and Politics*, 269.

33. It is unclear whether Milton would have had access to the Cary and Morison ode in manuscript, but it was not published until the second folio collection of Jonson's works was published in 1640. In any case, he was certainly familiar with the couplet poetry of the 1615 *Works*.

34. Norbrook, *Poetry and Politics*, 271, 270.

35. Ransom, "Poem Nearly Anonymous," 74.

36. Wittreich, "Milton's 'Destin'd Urn,'" 63–64. Anthony Low responded to the piece by arguing that the "extra-stanzaic rhymes in *Lycidas* are instances of random repetition." Low, "Circular Rhymes in 'Lycidas'?," 1032. While Low is right to emphasize the fact that no reader could hear such distant rhyme connections and that poets do repeat rhymes inadvertently, there are thematic connections among many of the rhyming lines that Wittreich cites that suggest planning is at work here. Wittreich defends his article and the idea of "'intellectual' patterning" in rhyme that cannot be heard in his reply in the same number of *PMLA*. Wittreich, "Circular Rhymes in 'Lycidas'?," 1033. James Rutherford presents manuscript evidence that the repetition of the *-ore* rhyme is related to the opening line, in Rutherford, "Experimental Form," 27.

37. For a comparison of Spenser's odes to Milton's monody, see Saintsbury, *History of English Prosody*, 2:219–20.

38. Milton does use a refrain in his "Epitaphium Damonis" (*CPMP*, 132–39), written only two years later after his return from the continent.

39. Shakespeare, *A Midsummer Night's Dream* 5.1.17, in *Norton Shakespeare*.

40. On Milton's interest in gods of boundaries in the 1645 volume, see Burrow, "Poems 1645," 67.

41. See J. M. Evans, "Lycidas," 52.

42. Drayton, *Barrons Wars*, A3r.

43. Prince, *Italian Element*, 109–12.

44. Lewalski, *Life of John Milton*, 129.

45. Milton, *Of Reformation*, in *Complete Prose Works of John Milton*, 1:616.

46. Lewalski, *Life of John Milton*, 351.

47. For more on the "Letter to a Friend," see Fallon, *Milton's Peculiar Grace*, 14–20.

48. Trinity College, Cambridge ms. R.3.4, p. 7.

49. Trinity College, Cambridge ms. R.3.4, p. 6.

50. Milton, "Of Education," in *Complete Prose Works of John Milton*, 2:369.

51. On Milton's transition to monism, see Fallon, *Milton among the Philosophers*.

52. Sidney, "Astrophil and Stella 2," line 9, in P. Sidney, *Major Works*, 153.

53. All references to Milton's sonnets are from *CPMP*; all quotations are hereafter cited parenthetically by sonnet and line number and abbreviated Sonnet.

54. "Diodati, e te 'l dirò con maraviglia, / Quel ritroso io, ch' Amor spreggiar soléa / E de' suoi lacci spesso mi ridéa / Già caddi, ov' uom dabben talor s' impiglia" (Sonnet 4.1–4).

55. See Wordsworth, "W. W. to Alexander Dyce (c. 22 Apr. 1833)," in Wordsworth, *Collected Letters of the Wordsworths*, 5:804. On Milton's enjambment as a sign of his pursuit of liberty and an anticipation of the drawn-out blank verse of *Paradise Lost*, see Smart, introduction to *The Sonnets of Milton*, 27–28; Prince, *Italian Element*, 89; Fussell, *Poetic Meter*, 117; Nardo, *Milton's Sonnets*, 162.

56. On the Italian tradition of enjambment, see Prince, *Italian Element*, 100–101.

57. Scodel, *Excess and the Mean*, 236.

58. Jonson, *Timber: Or, Discoveries*, lines 1695–96, in *Jonson*, 7:580.

59. *Informations to William Drummond of Hawthornden*, in *Jonson*, 5:362.

60. See Creaser, "Fear of Change," 177. For an argument that Milton's sonnets defy both the Italian and English strategies of sonnet resolution, see Netzley, *Lyric Apocalypse*, 73–75.

61. Milton, *The Reason of Church-government Urg'd against Prelaty*, in *Complete Prose Works of John Milton*, 1:816, 816, 816–17.

62. Nardo, *Milton's Sonnets*, 178.

63. Lewalski, *Life of John Milton*, 164, 169. For more on the context of the tracts, see van den Berg and Howard, introduction to their *Divorce Tracts John Milton*, 1–35.

64. Palmer, *Glasse of Gods Providence*, I1r.

65. Joseph Hall, *Resolutions and Decisions*, S3r, S4r, S6v–S7r.

66. Lewalski, *Life of John Milton*, 175, 182.

67. In the Trinity manuscript, what we now number "Sonnet 12" appears before "Sonnet 11."

68. See Hill, *Milton and the English Revolution*, 108–9.

69. Milton, *Tetrachordon*, in *Complete Prose Works of John Milton*, 2:586–87.

70. Ovid, *Metamorphoses*, book 6, line 350.

71. Milton, *The Doctrine and Discipline of Divorce*, in *Complete Prose Works of John Milton*, 2:251.

72. Milton, *The Doctrine and Discipline of Divorce*, in *Complete Prose Works of John Milton*, 2:251.

73. The phrase "measur'd motion" is from Milton's "Arcades," line 71, *CPMP*, 79.

74. Ovid, *Metamorphoses*, book 6, lines 382–400.

75. Milton, *The Doctrine and Discipline of Divorce*, in *Complete Prose Works of John Milton*, 2:275.

76. Wordsworth, "W. W. to Alexander Dyce (c. 22 Apr. 1833)," in Wordsworth, *Collected Letters of the Wordsworths*, 5:804.

77. Jonson, "98. To Sir Thomas Roe," lines 9, 3, in *Cambridge Edition of the Complete*

Works of Ben Jonson. On the image of the circle and the gathered self, see T. Greene, "Ben Jonson and the Centered Self."

78. Milton, *The Reason of Church-government Urg'd against Prelaty*, in *Complete Prose Works of John Milton*, 1:841, 841–42.

79. On Milton and Jonson's shared emphasis on the character of the poet, see Helgerson, *Self-Crowned Laureates*.

80. Milton, *Tetrachordon: Expositions*.

81. Matter, form, and style seem to be Milton's translations of *inventio, dispositio*, and *elocutio*. See Vickers, *Classical Rhetoric*, 61–65.

82. Trinity College, Cambridge ms. R.3.4, p. 47.

83. Milton, *The Doctrine and Discipline of Divorce*, in *Complete Prose Works of John Milton*, 2:222, 222, 223–24, 224.

84. Sharon Achinstein emphasizes the way Marvell's poem offers an account of the experience of reading the epic. Achinstein, "Milton's Spectre," 19.

85. Creaser, "Prosodic Style and Conceptions of Liberty," 10.

86. Shifflett, "'By Lucan Driv'n About'"; N. Smith, "Andrew Marvell and Ben Jonson," 175.

87. Shifflett, "'By Lucan Driv'n About,'" 807–8.

88. Ben Jonson, "To my chosen Friend, The learned Translator of LUCAN, THOMAS MAY, Esquire," in May, *Lucan's Pharsalia*, A8r; Marvell, "On Mr Milton's Paradise Lost," lines 78, in *Poems of Andrew Marvell*.

89. Marvell, "An Horatian Ode upon Cromwell's Return from Ireland," lines 33–36, in *Poems of Andrew Marvell*.

90. Nigel Smith points out that the words "vast" and "design" are associated with Satan in Paradise Lost. Nigel Smith, note to line 2, "On Mr. Milton's Paradise Lost," in Marvell, *Poems of Andrew Marvell* (ed. N. Smith).

91. Marvell, "An Horatian Ode upon Cromwell's Return from Ireland," line 19, in *Poems of Andrew Marvell*.

92. Marvell, "On Mr Milton's Paradise Lost," line 17, in *Poems of Andrew Marvell. OED* s.v. "span, v." Cf. Milton, "Sonnet 13," line 2, in *CPMP*.

93. Marvell, "On Mr Milton's Paradise Lost," lines 37–38, in Marvell, *Poems of Andrew Marvell* (ed. N. Smith).

94. Shifflett, "'By Lucan Driv'n About.'"

95. See Horace, *Epistles* 1.11, line 30, in Horace, *Satires, Epistles, Ars Poetica*, 324.

96. Marvell, "An Horatian Ode upon Cromwell's Return from Ireland," line 34, in *Poems of Andrew Marvell*.

97. On the connection of Marvell's image to Milton's own association of birds and divine inspiration, see Benet, "Genius of the Wood," 242.

98. Marvell, "On Mr Milton's *Paradise Lost*," lines 45–46, in *Poems of Andrew Marvell*.

99. Marvell, "On Mr Milton's *Paradise Lost*," lines 47–48, in *Poems of Andrew Marvell*.

100. On the connection of Marvell's literary critique of Dryden to the toleration debate, see Achinstein, "Milton's Spectre," 11. On whether Town-Bays is Dryden specifically or hack poets generally, see Lippencott, "Marvell's 'On Paradise Lost,'" 272; Wittreich, "Perplexing the Explanation," 289.

101. N. Smith, note to lines 49–50, "On Mr Milton's *Paradise Lost*," in *Poems of Andrew Marvell*.

102. Milton, *CPMP*, 210; Marvell, "On Mr Milton's *Paradise Lost*," lines 51–52, in *Poems of Andrew Marvell*. On the connection of "transported" to Restoration debates about enthusiasm, see Achinstein, "Milton's Spectre," 27.

103. Achinstein, "Milton's Spectre," 27, 28.

104. Marvell, "On Mr Milton's *Paradise Lost*," lines 53, 53, 54, in *Poems of Andrew Marvell*.

105. See McWilliams, "Milton and Marvell's Literary Friendship," 172.

106. Leavis, "Milton's Verse," 124.

107. De Quincey, *Style and Rhetoric*, 41. C. S. Lewis describes the styles of Milton and Virgil as "ritualistic" and "incantatory." He attributes the grandeur of Virgil's and Milton's epic styles to their efforts to compensate for the loss of "all those external aids to solemnity" that Homer "enjoyed. There is no robed and garlanded *aoiodos*, no altar, not even a feast in a hall—only a private person reading a book in an armchair." Lewis, *Preface to "Paradise Lost,"* 40. See also Ricks, *Milton's Grand Style*.

108. Creaser, "Service Is Perfect Freedom," 295.

109. Creaser, "Service Is Perfect Freedom," 295; Creaser, "Prosodic Style and Conceptions of Liberty," 3.

110. Creaser, "Service Is Perfect Freedom," 295.

111. On rhythm, see Attridge, *Poetic Rhythm*; Culler and Glaser, *Critical Rhythm*.

112. Creaser, "Service Is Perfect Freedom," 288–90.

113. Creaser, "Service Is Perfect Freedom," 294.

114. See Prince, *Italian Element*, 135, 165.

115. Milton, "Of Education," in *Complete Prose Works of John Milton*, 2:404; Tasso, *Discorsi*, G3v. For the English translation, see Tasso, *Genesis of Tasso's Narrative Theory*, 140. See also Prince, *Italian Element*, 108.

116. Tasso, *Discorsi*, G2r. Translation from Tasso, *Genesis of Tasso's Narrative Theory*, 138.

117. Virgil, *Aeneid*, line 1, in *Virgil: Eclogues, Georgics, Aeneid 1–6*, 262.

118. De Quincey, "Charles Lamb, 450. Quoted in Ricks, *Milton's Grand Style*, 36.

119. Raleigh, *Milton*, 192.

120. In addition to the passages cited in this paragraph, see *PL*, 2.555.

121. Luxon, "Heroic Restorations," 216.

122. Dryden, *The State of Innocence*, act 2, scene 1, lines 64–69, in *Works of John Dryden*, 12:107.

123. *Samson Agonistes*, in *CPMP*, hereafter cited as *SA*.

124. See Lobis, *Virtue of Sympathy*, 150–53.

125. See *PL*, 3.368, 8.2.

126. Diekhoff, "Rhyme in Paradise Lost."

127. I am convinced by those who have made the case that *Samson Agonistes* is a Restoration work, likely written after 1667. See Hill, "Appendix 2," in *Milton and the English Revolution*; Mary Ann Radzinowicz, "Appendix E," in Radzinowicz, *Toward "Samson Agonistes"*; Worden, "Milton, *Samson Agonistes*, and the Restoration." The argument for an earlier date was brought forward in Parker, *Milton: A Biography*.

128. *A Greek-English Lexicon, compiled by Henry George Liddell and Robert Scott*. 9th ed. (Oxford: Clarendon Press, 1940), s.v. "ἀπολύω." Perseus digital library (accessed January 2014).

129. The meter of *Samson Agonistes* has challenged many talented prosodists. See, for example, Bridges, *Milton's Prosody*; Sprott, *Milton's Art of Prosody*, 129–33; Hardison, *Prosody and Purpose*; J. Mueller, "Just Measures?"

130. Michael Cohen, "Rhyme in *Samson Agonistes*," 5.

131. Leo, "Milton's Aristotelian Experiments."

132. See Shore, *Milton and the Art of Rhetoric*, 159–60.

133. For a thoughtful reading of the Chorus's sonnet, especially of the meaning of "passions spent," see Netzley, *Lyric Apocalypse*, 103–11.

134. Kahn, *Wayward Contracts*, 237.

135. J. Mueller, "Just Measures?," 78.

136. Netzley, *Lyric Apocalypse*, 105.

137. Netzley, *Lyric Apocalypse*, 108, 110, 111.

138. On Milton's reinterpretation of catharsis and his relation to other critics of Aristotle's *Poetics*, see Leo, "Milton's Aristotelian Experiments."

139. Milton, *Readie and Easie Way (Second Edition)*, in *Complete Prose Works of John Milton*, 7:463.

140. J. Mueller, "Just Measures?," 79.

141. Milton, *The Reason of Church-government Urg'd against Prelaty*, in *Complete Prose Works of John Milton*, 1:816, 816, 816–17.

142. Trinity College, Cambridge ms. R.3.4, pp. 6–7.

143. Milton, "On Time," lines 1, 5–6, in *CPMP*.

144. Milton, "On Time," lines 11, 19, 17, 22–23, in *CPMP*.

145. Shakespeare, "Sonnet 116," line 12, in *Norton Shakespeare*.

146. Milton, "At a Solemn Music," line 26, in *CPMP*.

BIBLIOGRAPHY

Primary

MANUSCRIPT

British Library Harley manuscript 298.

British Library Harley manuscript 4064.

PRO SP 12 / 174.

Trinity College, Cambridge manuscript R.3.4.

Westmoreland manuscript of the poems of John Donne, Berg Collection, New York Public Library, Shelf Locator: Berg Coll (Donne)

PRINT

The Academy of Armory, or, A Store House of Armory & Blazon, Containing all thinges Borne in Coates of Armes Both Forraign and Domestick. With the termes of Art used in each Science. London, 1688.

Arber, Edward, ed. *A Transcript of the Registers of the Company of Stationers of London.* London, 1876.

Aristotle. *Aristotles Politiques, or Discourses of Government. Translated out of Greeke into French, with Expositions taken out of the best Authours.* Translated by John Dickenson. London, 1598.

———. *The Basic Works of Aristotle.* Edited by Richard McKeon. New York: Modern Library, 2001.

———. *The Nicomachean Ethics.* Translated by H. Rackham. Cambridge, MA: Harvard University Press, 1994.

Aubrey, John. *Brief Lives.* Edited by O. L. Dick. New York: Penguin, 1962.

Bacon, Francis. *Essayes. Religious Meditations. Places of perswasion and disswasion.* London, 1597.

Barker, Jane. *Poetical Recreations: Consisting of Original Poems, Songs, Odes, &c. With several New Translations.* London, 1688.

Barnes, Barnabe. *Parthenophil and Parthenope.* London, 1593.

Barnfield, Richard. *Cynthia. With Certaine Sonnets, and the Legend of Cassandra.* London, 1595.

Bastard, Thomas. *Chrestoleros. Seuen bookes of Epigrams written by TB.* London, 1598.

Beaumont, John. *Bosworth-field: With A Taste Of The Variety Of Other Poems.* London, 1629.

Bede. *Libri II De Arte Metrica et De Schematibus et Tropis,* trans. Calvin B. Kendall. Saarbrucken, Germany: AQ-Verlag, 1991.

Beedome, Thomas. *Poems, Divine, and Humane.* London, 1641.

Behn, Aphra. *Poems upon Several Occasions: with a Voyage to the Island of Love.* London, 1684.

The Bible and Holy Scriptures conteyned in the Olde and Newe Testament. Geneva, 1561.

Blount, Thomas. *Glossographia: Or a Dictionary of Hard Words.* London, 1656.

Bodin, Jean. *The six bookes of the common-weale. Written by I. Bodin a famous lawyer, and a man of great experience in matters of state.* London, 1606.

Breton, Nicholas. *Melancholike humours, in verses of diuerse natures, set down by Nich: Breton, Gent.* London, 1600.

Brome, Alexander. *Songs and Other Poems. By Alex. Brome, Gent.* London, 1661.

Browne, Thomas. *Hydrotaphia, Urne-Buriall, Or, A Discourse of the Sepulchrall Urnes lately found in Norfolk. Together with The Garden of Cyrus, or the Quincunciall, Lozenge, or Net-work Plantations of the Ancients, Artificially, Naturally, Mystically Considered.* London, 1658.

Bryskett, Lodowick. *A Discourse of Ciuill Life: Containing the Ethike part of Morall Philosophie. Fit for the instructing of a Gentleman in the course of a vertuous life.* London, 1606.

Buchanan, George. *A Dialogue on the Law of Kingship among the Scots.* Translated by Robert A. Mason and Martin S. Smith. Burlington, VT: Ashgate, 2004.

Bullinger, Heinrich. *The golden boke of christen matrimonye, moost necessary [and] profitable for all them, that entend to liue quietly and godlye in the Christen state of holy wedlock newly set forthe in English by Theodore Basille.* London, 1542.

Campion, Thomas. *Obseruations in the Art of English Poesie.* London, 1602.

Carew, Thomas. *The Poems and Masques of Thomas Carew.* Edited by Joseph Woodfall Ebsworth. London: Reeves and Turner, 1893.

———. *Poems By Thomas Carevv Esquire. One of the Gentlemen of the Privie-Chamber, and Sewer in Ordinary to His Majesty.* London, 1640.

Chaplin, Gregory, and John P. Rumrich, eds. *Seventeenth Century British Poetry, 1603–1660.* New York: Norton, 2006.

Chapman, George. *Achilles Shield.* London, 1598.

Chaucer, Geoffrey. *The Riverside Chaucer.* Edited by Larry D. Benson. Boston: Houghton Mifflin, 1987.

Cicero. *Brutus, Orator.* Translated by G. L. Hendrickson and H. M. Hubbell. Cambridge, MA: Harvard University Press, 2007.

———. *De Inventione, De Optimo Genere Oratorum, Topica.* Translated by H. M. Hubbell. Cambridge, MA: Harvard University Press, 1976.

Coleridge, Samuel Taylor. *Collected Letters.* Edited by Earl Leslie Griggs. Oxford: Clarendon, 1956.

———. *The Complete Works of Samuel Taylor Coleridge.* Edited by J.C.C. Mays. Princeton, NJ: Princeton University Press, 2001.

Cowley, Abraham. *The Civil War.* Edited by Allan Pritchard. Toronto: University of Toronto Press, 1973.

———. *The Essays and Other Prose Writings.* Edited by Alfred B. Gough. Oxford: Oxford University Press, 1915.

———. *Poems: Viz., I. Miscellanies, II. The Mistress, or, Love Verses, III. Pindarique Odes, And IV. Davideis, or, a Sacred Poem of the Troubles of David. Written by A. Cowley.* London, 1656.

———. *Poeticall Blossomes. The Second Edition enlarged by the Author.* London, 1636.

———. *Verses, Written Upon Several Occasions, By Abraham Cowley.* London, 1663.

Cummings, Brian, ed. *The Book of Common Prayer: The Texts of 1549, 1559, and 1662.* Oxford: Oxford University Press, 2011.

Daniel, Samuel. *Delia. Contayning certayne Sonnets: with the complaint of Rosamond.* London, 1592.

———. *The Works of Samuel Daniel, Newly augmented.* London, 1601.

Darcie, Abraham. *The Originall of Idolatries: Or, the Birth of Heresies.* London, 1624.

Davies, John. *The Poems of Sir John Davies.* Edited by Robert Krueger and Ruby Nemser. Oxford: Oxford University Press, 1975.

Davison, Francis. *Davison's Poetical Rhapsody*. Edited by A. H. Bullen. London, 1890.

Dekker, Thomas. *If It Be Not Good, The Diuel is in it. A New Play*. London, 1612.

Donne, John. *The Complete Poems of John Donne*. Edited by Robin Robbins. New York: Longman, 2010.

———. *Letters to Severall Persons of Honour*. Edited by Charles Edmund Merill. New York: Sturgis and Walton, 1910.

———. *Poems by I.D.* London, 1633.

———. *Pseudo-Martyr*. Edited by Anthony Raspa. Montreal: McGill-Queen's University Press, 1993.

———. *The Satires, Epigrams and Verse Letters*. Edited by W. Milgate. Oxford: Clarendon, 1967.

———. *The Sermons of John Donne*. Edited by George Potter and Evelyn Simpson. Berkeley: University of California Press, 1984.

———. *The Variorum Edition of the Poetry of John Donne*. Edited by Gary A. Stringer and Jeffrey S. Johnson. Vols. 2, 3, 7.1, and 8. Bloomington: Indiana University Press, 1995–2016.

Drayton, Michael. *The Barrons Wars in the raigne of Edward the second. With Englands Heroicall Epistles*. London, 1603.

———. *Poemes Lyrick and pastorall*. London, 1606.

Dryden, John. *Of Dramatick Poesie, An Essay*. London, 1668.

———. *The Satires of Decimus Junius Juvenalis. Translated into English Verse. By Mr. Dryden, and Several other Eminent Hands. Together with the Satires of Aulus Persius Flaccus. Made English by Mr. Dryden*. London, 1693.

———. *The Works of John Dryden*. Edited by Vinton A. Dearing. Berkeley: University of California Press, 1994.

Duppa, Brian, ed. *Ionsonus Virbivs: Or, The Memorie of Ben: Iohnson Revived By the Friends of the Muses*. London, 1638.

Erasmus, Desiderius. *De Libero Arbitrio diatribe, sive collatio, D. Eras. Rot.* Basel, 1524.

———. *The seconde tome or volume of the Paraphrase of Erasmus vpon the newe testament*. London, 1549.

Eyre, G.E.B., ed. *A Transcript of the Registers of the Worshipful Company of Stationers; from 1640–1708 A.D.* London, 1913.

Fairfax, Edward. *Godfrey of Bulloigne, or The Recouerie of Ierusalem. Done into English Heroicall verse, by Edward Fairefax Gent*. London, 1600.

Ferrabosco, Alfonso. *Ayres: by Alfonso Ferrabosco*. London, 1609.

Firth, C. H., and R. S. Rait, eds. *Acts and Ordinances of the Interregnum*. London: H.M.S.O., 1911.

Flatman, Thomas. *Poems and Songs*. London, 1674.

Fletcher, Giles. *Licia, or Poemes of Love*. London, 1593.

Fletcher, John. *The Faithfvll Shepherdesse*. London, 1610.

Foster, Joseph, ed. *The Register of Admissions to Gray's Inn, 1521–1889*. London, 1889.

Fraunce, Abraham. *The Lawiers Logike, exemplifying the praecepts of Logike by the practise of the common Lawe*. London, 1588.

Gamble, John. *Ayres and Dialogues (To be Sung to the Theorbo-Lute or Bass-Viol)*. London, 1656.

Gascoigne, George. *The Posies of George Gascoigne, Esquire*. London, 1575.

Golding, Arthur. *The. xv. Bookes of P. Ouidius Naso, entytuled Metamorphosis, translated out of Latin into English meeter, by Arthur Golding Gentleman, A worke very pleasant and delectable*. London, 1567.

Greene, Robert. *Greenes Vision: Written at the instant of his death.* London, 1592.

———. *Mamillia. A Mirrour or looking-glasse for the Ladies of Englande.* London, 1583.

———. *Menaphon: Camillas alarum to slumbering Euphues, in his melancholie Cell at Silexdra.* London, 1589.

Guilpin, Everard. *Skialetheia. Or, A shadowe of Truth, in certaine Epigrams and Satyres.* London, 1598.

Hall, Joseph. *Resolutions and Decisions of Divers Practical Cases of Conscience in continuall Use amongst men, Very necessary for their Information and Direction.* London, 1649.

———. *Virgidemiarum, Sixe Bookes. First three Bookes. Of tooth-lesse Satyrs.* London, 1597.

———. *Virgidemiarum, The Three Last Bookes, Of byting Satyres.* London, 1598.

Hamilton, Hans Claude, ed. *Calendar of the State Papers, Relating to Ireland, of the Reign of Elizabeth, 1588, August–1592, September.* Nendeln: Kraus, 1974.

Harington, John. *Orlando Furioso in English Heroical Verse, by Iohn Harington.* London, 1591.

Harris, John. *Mercurius Militaris, or the Armies scout.* London, 1648.

Harvey, Gabriel, and Edmund Spenser. *Three Proper, and wittie, familiar Letters: lately passed betweene tvvo Vniuersitie men: touching the Earthquake in Aprill Last, and our English refourmed Versifying.* London, 1580.

Harvey, John. *A Discoursiue Probleme concerning Prophesies, How far they are to be valued, or credited, according to the surest rules, and directions in Diuinitie, Philosophie, Astrologie, and other learning.* London, 1588.

Herodotus. *The famous hystory of Herodotus Conteyning the discourse of dyuers countreys, the succession of theyr kyngs: the actes and exploytes atchieued by them: the lavves and customes of euery nation: with the true description and antiquitie of the same. Deuided into nine bookes, entituled vvith the names of the nine Muses.* London, 1584.

Herrick, Robert. *The Complete Poetry of Robert Herrick.* Edited by Tom Cain and Ruth Connolly. Oxford: Oxford University Press, 2013.

The. holie. Bible. conteyning the olde Testament and the newe. London, 1568.

Hooker, Richard. *Of the Lavves of Ecclesiasticall Politie.* London, 1593.

Horace. *Odes and Epodes.* Translated by Niall Rudd. Cambridge, MA: Harvard University Press, 2004.

———. *Satires, Epistles, Ars Poetica.* Translated by H. Rushton Fairclough. Cambridge, MA: Harvard University Press, 1926.

Housman, Robert Fletcher. *A Collection of English Sonnets.* London, 1835.

Howard, Edward. *Spencer Redivivus, Containing the First Book of the Fairy Queen, His Essential Design preserv'd, but his obsolete Language and manner of Verse totally laid aside. Deliver'd in Heroick Numbers, By a Person of Quality.* London, 1687.

———. *The Womens Conquest: A Tragi-Comedy.* London, 1671.

Jackson, Arthur. *Annotations Upon The five Books, immediately following the Historicall Part of the Old Testament.* London, 1658.

James I. *The Workes of the Most High and Mightie Prince Iames.* London, 1616.

Jonson, Ben. *The Cambridge Edition of the Works of Ben Jonson.* Edited by David Bevington, Martin Butler, and Ian Donaldson. Cambridge: Cambridge University Press, 2012.

Juvenal and Perseus. *Juvenal and Perseus.* Translated by Susanna Morton Braund. Cambridge, MA: Harvard University Press, 2004.

Keats, John. *The Letters of John Keats.* Edited by Hyder Edward Rollins. Cambridge, MA: Harvard University Press, 1958.

———. *Poems.* London, 1817.

———. *The Poems of John Keats.* Edited by Miriam Allott. New York: Longman, 1977.

La Primaudaye, Pierre de. *The French Academie.* London, 1586.

Levens, Peter. *Manipulus Vocabulorum*. London, 1570.

Lilburne, John. *Englands Birth-Right Justified Against all Arbitrary Usurpation, whether Regall or Parliamentary, or under what Vizor soever, With divers Queries, Observations, and Grievances of the People*. London, 1645.

Livy. *Livy in Fourteen Volumes*. Translated by B. O. Forster. Cambridge, MA: Harvard University Press, 1982.

Lodge, Thomas. *Phillis: Honoured with Pastorall Sonnets, Elegies, and amorous delights. Where-vnto is annexed, the tragicall complaynt of Elstred*. London, 1593.

Lovelace, Richard. *Lucasta: Epodes, Odes, Sonnets, Songs, &c. To which is added Aramantha, A Pastorall*. London, 1649.

Luther, Martin. *De Servo Arbitrio Mar. Lutheri ad D. Erasmum Roterodamum*. Wittenberg, 1525.

Lyly, John. *Sixe Court Comedies*. London, 1632.

Machiavelli, Niccolò. *Discorsi Sopra La Prima Deca di Tito Livio*. Edited by Francesco Bausi. Rome: Salerno, 2001.

———. *"The Prince" and the "Discourses."* Translated by Luigi Ricci and Christian E. Detmold. New York: Random House, 1950.

Mannyng, Robert. *The Story of England*. Edited by Frederick J. Furnivall. London: Longman, 1887.

Marlowe, Christopher. *The Complete Works of Christopher Marlowe*. Edited by Roma Gill. Oxford: Clarendon, 1987.

———. *Tamburlaine the Great. Who, from a Scythian Shephearde, by his rare and woonderfull Conquests, became a most puissant and mightye Monarque. And (for his tyranny, and terrour in Warre) was tearmed, The Scourge of God*. London, 1590.

Marston, John. *Iacke Drums Entertainment: Or The Comedie of Pasquill and Katherine*. London, 1601.

———. *The Metamorphosis of Pigmalions Image. And Certaine Satyres*. London, 1598.

———. *The Scourge of Villanie, Corrected, with the addition of newe Satyres*. London, 1599.

———. *The Scourge of Villanie. Three Bookes of Satyres*. London, 1598.

Marvell, Andrew. *The Poems of Andrew Marvell*. Edited by Nigel Smith. New York: Longman, 2013.

May, Thomas. *Lucan's Pharsalia: Or The Civill Warres of Rome, betweene Pompey the great, and Iulius Caesar*. London, 1627.

Meres, Francis. *Palladis Tamia*. London, 1598.

Milton, John. *The Complete Poems and Major Prose*. Edited by Merritt Y. Hughes. Indianapolis: Hackett, 2003.

———. *Complete Prose Works of John Milton*. Edited by Douglas Bush, John S. Deikhoff, J. Milton French, Herbert Grierson, Merritt Y. Hughes, Maurice Kelley, Alexander M. Witherspoon, Don M. Wolfe, and A. S. P. Woodhouse. New Haven, CT: Yale University Press, 1953.

———. *Milton's Paradise Lost. A New Edition, by Richard Bentley, D.D*. Edited by Richard Bentley. London, 1732.

———. *Paradise lost. A Poem Written in Ten Books*. London, 1667.

———. *Tetrachordon: Expositions Upon The foure chief places of Scripture, which treat of Mariage, or nullities in Mariage*. London, 1645.

———. *The Works of John Milton*. Edited by Frank Allan Patterson, Allan Abbott, Harry Morgan Ayres, Donald Lemen Clark, John Erskine, William Haller, George Philip Krapp, and W. P. Trent. New York: Columbia University Press, 1936.

Minturno, Antonio Sebastian. *De Poeta, Libri Sex*. Venice, 1559.

Montaigne, Michel de. *The Essayes Or Morall, Politike, and Millitarie Discourses*. Translated by John Florio. London, 1603.

Moxon, James. *Mathematicks made Easie: Or, a Mathematical Dictionary*. London, 1679.

Oldham, John. *Some New Pieces Never Before Publish'd: By the Author of the Satires upon the Jesuites*. London, 1684.

Ovid. *Ovid I: Heroides and Amores*. Translated by Grant Showerman. Cambridge, MA: Harvard University Press, 2002.

———. *Metamorphoses*. Translated by Frank Justus Miller. Cambridge, MA: Harvard University Press, 1956.

Palmer, Herbert. *The Glasse of Gods Providence Towards His Faithful Ones*. London, 1644.

Parsons, Robert. *A Christian Directorie Gviding Men to Their Salvation*. London, 1585.

Percy, William. *Sonnets to the Fairest Coelia*. London, 1594.

Petrarch, Francis. *Petrarch's Lyric Poems: The Rime Sparse and Other Lyrics*. Translated by Robert M. Durling. Cambridge, MA: Harvard University Press, 1976.

Philips, Katherine. *The Collected Works of Katherine Philips*. Edited by Patrick Thomas. Essex: Stump Cross Books, 1990.

Pindar. *Pindar*. Translated by William H. Race. Cambridge, MA: Harvard University Press, 1997.

Pliny. *The Historie of the World, Commonly called, The Naturall Historie of C. Plinius Secvndus*. London, 1601.

———. *Pliny: Natural History in Ten Volumes*. Translated by H. Rackham. Cambridge, MA: Harvard University Press, 1989.

Poems, by Several Persons. Dublin, 1663.

Poliziano, Angelo. *Oratio super Fabio Quintiliano et Statii Sylvis*. In *Prosatori latini del Quattrocento*, edited by Eugenio Garin, 869–85. Milan: R. Ricciardi, 1952.

Pope, Alexander. *Poetry and Prose of Alexander Pope*. Edited by Aubrey Williams. Boston: Houghton Mifflin, 1969.

The Psalms of King David Paraphrased, And turned into English Verse, according to the common Metre, As they are usually sung in Parish Churches. London, 1664.

Puttenham, George. *The Arte of English Poesie*. London, 1589.

———. *The Arte of English Poesie*. Menston, England: Scolar, 1969.

Quintilian. *The Institutio Oratoria of Quintilian in Four Volumes*. Translated by H. E. Butler. Cambridge, MA: Harvard University Press, 1979.

The Retvrne from Parnassus: Or, The Scourge of Simony. London, 1606.

Rousseau, Jean-Jacques. *The Discourses, and Other Early Political Writings*. Translated by Victor Gourevitch. Cambridge: Cambridge University Press, 2013.

Sandys, George. *Ovid's Metamorphosis Englished, Mythologiz'd, And Represented in figures*. London, 1632.

Scaliger, Julius Caesar. *Poetices Libri Septem*. Stuttgart: F. Frommann, 1987.

The Second Tome of Homelyes. London, 1563.

Seneca. *Epistles 93–124*. Translated by Richard M. Gunmere. Cambridge, MA: Harvard University Press, 1925.

Servius. *Servii Grammatici qui feruntur in Vergilii Carmina Commentarii*. Edited by George Thilo and Hermann Hagen. Leipzig: B. G. Teubner, 1887.

Scott, William. *The Model of Poesy*. Edited by Gavin Alexander. Cambridge: Cambridge University Press, 2013.

Shakespeare, William. *The Norton Shakespeare*. Edited by Walter Cohen, Stephen Greenblatt, Jean E. Howard, and Katharine Eisaman Maus. New York: Norton, 2008.

Sidney, Philip. *The Countesse of Pembrokes Arcadia*. London, 1590.

———. *The Countess of Pembroke's Arcadia: The Old Arcadia*. Edited by Jean Robertson. Oxford: Oxford University Press, 1973.

———. *The Defence of Poesie*. London, 1595.

———. *The Major Works*. Edited by Katherine Duncan-Jones. Oxford: Oxford University Press, 2008.

Sidney, Robert. *The Poems of Robert Sidney*. Edited by P. J. Croft. Oxford: Oxford University Press, 1984.

Smith, Thomas. *De Republica Anglorum. The maner of Gouernement or policie of the Realme of England*. London, 1583.

Smythe, Thomas. *Sir Thomas Smithes Voiage and Entertainment in Rushia*. London, 1605.

Spenser, Edmund. *Complaints. Containing sundrie small Poemes of the Worlds Vanitie*. London, 1591.

———. *The Faerie Queene*. Edited by A. C. Hamilton. New York: Longman, 2007.

———. *The Works of Edmund Spenser: A Variorum Edition*. Edited by Edwin Greenlaw, Charles Grosvener Osgood, Frederick Morgan Padelford, and Ray Heffner. Baltimore: Johns Hopkins University Press, 1949.

———. *The Yale Edition of the Shorter Poems of Edmund Spenser*. Edited by William A. Oram, Einar Bjorvand, Ronald Bond, Thomas H. Cain, Alexander Dunlop, and Richard Schell. New Haven, CT: Yale University, 1989.

Spingarn, J. E., ed. *Critical Essays of the Seventeenth Century*. Oxford: Clarendon, 1908.

Sprat, Thomas. "An Account of the Life and Writings of Mr Abraham Cowley." In *The Works of Mr Abraham Cowley*, by Abraham Cowley, A1r–e2v. London, 1668.

Stanley, Thomas. *Poems, by Thomas Stanley Esquire*. London, 1651.

Steele, Robert R., ed. *A Bibliography of Royal Proclamations of the Tudor and Stuart Sovereigns, and others published under authority, 1495–1714*. Oxford: Clarendon, 1910.

Stevens, Wallace. *Harmonium*. New York: Knopf, 1923.

Sturgess, H.A.C., ed. *Register of Admissions to the Honourable Society of the Middle Temple*. London: Butterworth, 1949.

Tasso, Torquato. *Discorsi Del Signor Torquato Tasso. Dell'Arte Poetica; Et in particolare del Poema Heroico*. Venice, 1587.

———. *The Genesis of Tasso's Narrative Theory: English Translations of the Early Poetics and a Comparative Study of Their Significance*. Translated by Lawrence F. Rhu. Detroit: Wayne State University Press, 1993.

Taylor, John. *Aqua-Musae: Or Cacafogo, Cacadaemon, Captain George Wither Wrung in the Withers*. London, 1645.

Tofte, Robert. *Orlando Inamorato, The three first Bookes of that famous Noble Gentleman and learned Poet, Mathew Maria Boiardo Earle of Scandiano in Lombardie. Done into English Heroicall Verse, by R.T. Gentleman*. London, 1598.

Vaughan, Henry. *Thalia Rediviuas: The Pass-Times and Diversions of a Countrey-Muse, in Choice Poems on several Occasions*. London, 1678.

Vergil, Polydore. *An Abridgement of the notable woorke of Polidore Vergile conteygning the devisers and first finders out aswell of Artes, Ministries, Feastes, & civill ordinances, as of Rites, and Ceremonies, commonly vsed in the churche: and the original beginnyng of the same. Compendiously gathered by Thomas Langley*. London, 1546.

Vinsauf, Geoffrey of. *Poetria Nova*. Translated by Margaret F. Nims. Toronto: Pontifical Institute of Medieval Studies, 1967.

Virgil. *Virgil: Eclogues, Georgics, Aeneid 1–6*. Translated by H. R. Fairclough. Cambridge, MA: Harvard University Press, 2004.

Warton, Thomas. *Observations on the Fairy Queen of Spenser (1762)*. In *Spenser's Critics: Changing Currents in Literary Taste*, edited by William R. Mueller, 44–66. Syracuse, NY: Syracuse University Press, 1959.

Watson, Thomas. *The Hekatompathia or Passionate Centurie of Loue*. London, 1582.

Watts, Isaac. *The Works of the Late Reverend and Learned Isaac Watts, D.D.* London, 1753.

Webbe, William. *A Discourse of English Poetrie*. London, 1586.

Wills, Richard. *De Re Poetica*. Edited by A.D.S. Fowler. Oxford: Basil Blackwell, 1958.

Wither, George. *Abuses Stript, and Whipt. Or Satirical Essayes*. London, 1613.

———. *Campo-Musae, or Field-Musings of Captain George Wither, touching his Military Ingagement for the King ann Parliament*. London, 1643.

———. *Faire-virtue, the mistresse of Phil'arete*. London, 1622.

———. *A Satyre: Dedicated to His Most Excellent Majestie*. London, 1614.

———. *Wither's Motto: Nec habeo, nec Careo, nec Curo*. London, 1621.

Wordsworth, William. *The Collected Letters of the Wordsworths*. Edited by Alan G. Hill. Oxford: Clarendon, 1979.

———. *Poems in Two Volumes*. Edited by Helen Darbyshire. Oxford: Clarendon, 1952.

———. *Selected Poems*. Edited by John O. Hayden. New York: Penguin Books, 1994.

Worseley, Edward. *A most godly and vvorthy Treatis of holy Signes, Sacrifices, and Sacraments instituted of God, euen since the beginning of the world*. London, 1609.

Woodford, Samuel. *A Paraphrase upon the Psalms of David*. London, 1667.

Wright, Abraham, ed. *Parnassus Biceps. Or Severall Choice Pieces of Poetry, Composed by the best Wits that were in both the Universities Before their Dissolution*. London, 1656.

Wroth, Mary. *The Poems of Lady Mary Wroth*. Edited by Josephine A. Roberts. Baton Rouge: Louisiana State University Press, 1983.

Secondary

Abrams, M. H. *The Mirror and The Lamp: Romantic Theory and the Critical Tradition*. Oxford: Oxford University Press, 1953.

Achilleos, Stella. "'Ile Bring Thee *Herrick* to *Anacreon*': Robert Herrick's Anacreontics and the Politics of Conviviality in *Hesperides*." In *"Lords of Wine and Oile": Community and Conviviality in the Poetry of Robert Herrick*, edited by Ruth Connolly and Tom Cain, 191–219. Oxford: Oxford University Press, 2011.

Achinstein, Sharon. *Literature and Dissent in Milton's England*. Cambridge: Cambridge University Press, 2003.

———. "Milton's Spectre in the Restoration: Marvell, Dryden, and Literary Enthusiasm." *Huntington Library Quarterly* 59, no. 1 (1996): 1–29.

Addison, Catherine. "Little Boxes: The Effects of the Stanza on Poetic Narrative." *Style* 37, no. 3 (Summer 2003): 124–43.

Adorno, Theodor W. *Aesthetic Theory*. Translated by Robert Hullot-Kentor. New York: Bloomsbury, 2013.

Agamben, Giorgio. "The End of the Poem." Translated by Daniel Heller-Roazen. In *The Lyric Theory Reader: A Critical Anthology*, edited by Virginia Jackson and Yopie Prins, 430–33. Baltimore: Johns Hopkins University Press, 2014.

Alexander, Gavin. "On the Reuse of Poetic Form: The Ghost in the Shell." In *The Work of Form: Poetics and Materiality in Early Modern Culture*, edited by Ben Burton and Elizabeth Scott-Baumann, 123–43. Oxford: Oxford University Press, 2015.

———. "Sidney, Scott, and the Proportions of Poetics." *Sidney Journal* 33, no. 1 (January 2015): 7–28.

Alexander, J.J.G. and M. T. Gibson, eds. *Medieval Learning and Literature: Essays Presented to Richard William Hunt*. Oxford: Clarendon, 1976.

Allen, M.J.B., Dominic Baker-Smith, and Arthur F. Kinney, eds. *Sir Philip Sidney's Achievements*. New York: AMS, 1990.

Anderson, Penelope. *Friendship's Shadow: Women's Friendship and the Politics of Betrayal in England, 1640–1705*. Edinburgh: Edinburgh University Press, 2012.

Andreadis, Harriette. "The Sapphic-Platonics of Katherine Philips, 1632–1664." *Signs: Journal of Women in Culture and Society* 15, no. 1 (Autumn 1989): 34–60.

Anselment, Raymond. *Loyalist Resolve: Patient Fortitude in the English Civil War*. Newark: University of Delaware Press, 1988.

Archer, John Michael, and Richard Burt. *Enclosure Acts: Sexuality, Property, and Culture in Early Modern England*. Ithaca, NY: Cornell University Press, 1994.

Arendt, Hannah. *The Human Condition*. Chicago: University of Chicago Press, 1998.

Armstrong, Alan. "The Apprenticeship of John Donne: Ovid and the *Elegies*." *English Literary History* 44, no. 3 (Autumn 1977): 419–42.

Armstrong, Isobel. *Victorian Poetry: Poetry, Poetics, and Politics*. London: Routledge, 1993.

Attie, Katherine Bootle. "Passion Turned to Prettiness: Rhyme or Reason in *Hamlet*." *Shakespeare Quarterly* 63, no. 3 (Fall 2012): 393–423.

Attridge, Derek. *Poetic Rhythm: An Introduction*. Cambridge: Cambridge University Press, 1995.

———. *Well-Weighed Syllables: Elizabethan Verse in Classical Metres*. Cambridge: Cambridge University Press, 1974.

Baker, David J. "Spenser and Politics." In *The Oxford Handbook of Edmund Spenser*, edited by Richard A. McCabe, 48–64. Oxford: Oxford University Press, 2010.

Barash, Carol. *English Women's Poetry, 1649–1714: Politics, Community, Linguistic Authority*. Oxford: Clarendon, 1996.

Barish, Jonas A. *Ben Jonson and the Language of Prose Comedy*. Cambridge, MA: Harvard University Press, 1960.

Barolini, Teodolinda. "The Making of a Lyric Sequence: Time and Narrative in Petrarch's *Rerum vulgarium fragmenta*." *Modern Language Notes* 104, no. 1 (January 1989): 1–38.

Baroway, Israel. "The Accentual Theory of Hebrew Prosody: A Further Study in Interpretation of Renaissance Form." *English Literary History* 17, no. 2 (June 1950): 115–35.

Bates, Catherine. "The Politics of Spenser's *Amoretti*." *Criticism* 33, no. 1 (Winter 1991): 73–89.

Bell, Ilona. *Elizabethan Women and the Poetry of Courtship*. Cambridge: Cambridge University Press, 1998.

Benet, Diana Treviño. "The Genius of the Wood and the Prelate of the Grove: Milton and Marvell." In *Heirs of Fame: Milton and Writers of the English Renaissance*, edited by Margo Swiss and David A. Kent, 230–46. Lewisburg, PA: Bucknell University Press, 1995.

Bennett, R. E. "John Donne and Everard Gilpin." *Review of English Studies* 15, no. 57 (January 1939): 66–72.

Berger, Harry, Jr. "The Spenserian Dynamics." *Studies in English Literature* 8, no. 1 (Winter 1968): 1–18.

Bernard, John D. "Spenserian Pastoral and the *Amoretti*." *English Literary History* 47, no. 3 (Autumn 1980): 419–32.

Bieman, Elizabeth. "Comic Rhyme in Marlowe's 'Hero and Leander.'" *English Literary Renaissance* 9, no. 1 (Winter 1979): 69–77.

Blanchard, W. Scott. "Ut Encyclopedia Poesis: Ben Jonson's Cary-Morison Ode and the 'Sphaere' of 'Humanitie.'" *Studies in Philology* 87, no. 2 (1990): 194–220.

Blank, Paula. *Shakespeare and the Mismeasure of Renaissance Man*. Ithaca, NY: Cornell University Press, 2006.

Boose, Lynda. "The 1599 Bishops' Ban, Elizabethan Pornography, and the Sexualization of the Jacobean State." In *Enclosure Acts: Sexuality, Property, and Culture in Early Modern England*, edited by Richard Burt and John Michael Archer, 185–200. Ithaca, NY: Cornell University Press, 1994.

Braden, Gordon. "Classical Love Elegy in the Renaissance (and after)." In *The Oxford Hand-book of the Elegy*, edited by Karen Weisman, 153–69. Oxford: Oxford University Press, 2010.

———. *The Classics and English Renaissance Poetry: Three Case Studies*. New Haven, CT: Yale University Press, 1978.

———. "Hero and Leander in Bed (and the Morning After)." *English Literary Renaissance* 45, no. 2 (2015): 205–30.

———. *Petrarchan Love and the Continental Renaissance*. New Haven, CT: Yale University Press, 1999.

———. "Pride, Humility, and the Petrarchan Happy Ending." *Spenser Studies* 18 (2003): 123–42.

———. "Unspeakable Love: Petrarch to Herbert." In *Soliciting Interpretation: Literary Theory and Seventeenth-Century English Poetry*, edited by Elizabeth D. Harvey and Katharine Eisaman Maus, 253–72. Chicago: University of Chicago Press, 1990.

Brainford, H. N. *The Levellers and the English Revolution*. Edited by Christopher Hill. Stanford, CA: Stanford University Press, 1961.

Bredvold, Louis I. "The Naturalism of Donne in Relation to Some Renaissance Traditions." *Journal of English and Germanic Philology* 22, no. 4 (October 1923): 471–502.

Bridges, Robert. *Milton's Prosody: An Examination of the Rules of the Blank Verse in Milton's Later Poems, with an Account of the Versification in "Samson Agonistes," and General Notes*. Oxford: Clarendon, 1894.

Brooks, Cleanth. *The Well-Wrought Urn: Studies in the Structure of Poetry*. New York: Harcourt and Brace, 1947.

Brooks, Cleanth, and Robert Penn Warren. "Introduction to *Understanding Poetry* (1938)." In *The Lyric Theory Reader: A Critical Anthology*, edited by Virginia Jackson and Yopie Prins, 177–91. Baltimore: Johns Hopkins University Press, 2014.

Brooks, Douglas A., ed. *Printing and Parenting in Early Modern England*. Burlington, VT: Ashgate, 2005.

Brown, Georgia. "Gender and Voice in Hero and Leander." In *Constructing Christopher Marlowe*, edited by J. A. Downie and J. T. Parnell, 148–63. Cambridge: Cambridge University Press, 2000.

———. *Redefining Elizabethan Literature*. Cambridge: Cambridge University Press, 2002.

Brown, Marshall, and Susan Wolfson, eds. *Reading for Form*. Seattle: University of Washington Press, 2006.

Bruce, Yvonne, ed. *Images of Matter: Essays on British Literature of the Middle Ages and Renaissance*. Newark: University of Delaware Press, 2010.

Bruster, Douglas. *Quoting Shakespeare: Form and Culture in Early Modern Drama*. Lincoln: University of Nebraska Press, 2000.

———. "Shakespeare and the Composite Text." In *Renaissance Literature and Its Formal Engagements*, edited by Mark David Rasmussen, 43–66. New York: Palgrave, 2002.

Buhler, Stephen M. "Counterpoint and Controversy: Milton and the Critiques of Polyphonic Music." *Milton Studies* 36 (1998): 18–40.

Burchmore, D. W. "The Image of the Centre in 'Colin Clouts Come Home Againe.'" *Review of English Studies* 28 (1977): 393–406.

Burckhardt, Jacob. *The Civilization of the Renaissance in Italy*. New York: Penguin, 1990.

Burlinson, Christopher. "'Finest Gossamer': Cavalier Materials and Fragile Metaphors." *Seventeenth Century* 32, no. 4 (2017): 455–71.

Burrow, Colin. "Poems 1645: The Future Poet. In *The Cambridge Companion to Milton*, edited by Dennis Danielson, 54–69. Cambridge: Cambridge University Press, 1999.

Burt, Steph. "What Is This Thing Called Lyric?" *Modern Philology* 113, no. 3 (February 2016): 422–40.

Burton, Ben, and Elizabeth Scott-Baumann, eds. *The Work of Form: Poetics and Materiality in Early Modern Culture*. Oxford: Oxford University Press, 2015.

Butterfield, Ardis. "Why Medieval Lyric?" *English Literary History* 82, no. 2 (Summer 2015): 319–43.

Calhoun, Thomas O. "George Wither: Origins and Consequences of a Loose Poetics." *Texas Studies in Literature and Language* 16, no. 2 (Summer 1974): 263–79.

Campbell, Marion. "'Desunt Nonnulla': The Construction of Marlowe's *Hero and Leander* as an Unfinished Poem." *English Literary History* 51, no. 2 (Summer 1984): 241–68.

Carey, John. *John Donne: Life, Mind, and Art*. Oxford: Oxford University Press, 1981.

Carlson, Cindy. "Clothing Naked Desire in Marlowe's *Hero and Leander*." In *Gender Reconstructions: Pornography and Perversions in Literature and Culture*, edited by Cindy L. Carlson, Robert L. Mazzola, and Susan M. Bernardo, 25–41. Burlington, VT: Ashgate, 2002.

Carroll, Robert, and Stephen Prickett, eds. *The Bible: Authorized King James Version*. Oxford: Oxford University Press, 2008.

Cavanagh, Clare, Stephen Cushman, Roland Greene, Jahan Ramazani, and Paul Rouzer, eds. *The Princeton Encyclopedia of Poetry and Poetics*. 4th ed. Princeton, NJ: Princeton University Press, 2002.

Chalmers, Hero. *Royalist Women Writers, 1650–1689*. Oxford: Oxford University Press, 2004.

Chandler, James, and Maureen McLane, eds. *The Cambridge Companion to British Romantic Poetry*. Cambridge: Cambridge University Press, 2008.

Chernaik, Warren. "Books as Memorials: The Politics of Consolation." *Yearbook of English Studies* 21 (1991): 207–17.

———. *Milton and the Burden of Freedom*. Cambridge: Cambridge University Press, 2017.

Clarke, Danielle, and Elizabeth Clarke, eds. *"This Double Voice": Gendered Writing in Early Modern England*. London: Macmillan, 2000.

Clarke, Danielle, and Marie-Louise Coolahan. "Gender, Reception, and Form: Early Modern Women and the Making of Verse." In *The Work of Form: Poetics and Materiality in Early Modern Culture*, edited by Ben Burton and Elizabeth Scott-Baumann, 144–61. Oxford: Oxford University Press, 2015.

Clegg, Cyndia Susan. *Press Censorship in Elizabethan England*. Cambridge: Cambridge University Press, 1997.

Cohen, Michael. "Rhyme in *Samson Agonistes*." *Milton Quarterly* 8, no. 1 (March 1974): 4–6.

Cohen, Michael C. *The Social Lives of Poems in Nineteenth-Century America*. Philadelphia: University of Pennsylvania Press, 2015.

Cohen, Stephen. "Between Form and Culture." In *Renaissance Literature and Its Formal Engagements*, edited by Mark David Rasmussen, 17–41. New York: Palgrave, 2002.

———, ed. *Shakespeare and Historical Formalism*. Burlington, VT: Ashgate, 2007.

Coiro, Ann Baynes. *Robert Herrick and the Epigram Book Tradition*. Baltimore: Johns Hopkins University Press, 1988.

Coiro, Ann Baynes, and Blair Hoxby, eds. *Milton in the Long Restoration*. Oxford: Oxford University Press, 2016.

Coleman, Joyce. "Strange Rhyme: Prosody and Nationhood in Robert Mannyng's 'Story of England.'" *Speculum* 78, no. 4 (October 2003): 1214–38.

Collinson, Patrick. "The Monarchical Republic of Queen Elizabeth I." In *Elizabethan Essays*, 31–58. London: Hambledon, 1994.

Connolly, Ruth. "Bestiaries of Feeling: Flies, Snails, Toads and Spiders in Richard Lovelace's *Lucasta: Posthume Poems* (1659)." *Seventeenth Century* 32, no. 4 (2017): 473–91.

Connolly, Ruth, and Tom Cain, eds. *"Lords of Wine and Oile": Community and Conviviality in the Poetry of Robert Herrick*. Oxford: Oxford University Press, 2011.

Copenhaver, Brian P. Introduction to *On Discovery*, by Polydore Vergil, vi–xxix. Cambridge, MA: Harvard University Press, 2002.

Copley, Frank Olin. "*Servitium amoris* in the Roman Elegists." *Transactions and Proceedings of the American Philological Association* 78 (1947): 285–300.

Corns, Thomas N. "Milton's Quest for Respectability." *Modern Language Review* 77, no. 4 (October 1982): 769–79.

———. *Uncloistered Virtue: English Political Literature, 1640–1660*. Oxford: Clarendon, 1992.

Cottegnies, Line. " 'Leaves of Fame': Katherine Philips and Robert Herrick's Shared Community." In *'Lords of Wine and Oile': Community and Conviviality in the Poetry of Robert Herrick*, edited by Ruth Connolly and Tom Cain, 127–52. Oxford: Oxford University Press, 2011.

Crane, Mary Thomas. *Framing Authority: Sayings, Self, and Society in Sixteenth-Century England*. Princeton, NJ: Princeton University Press, 1993.

———. "*Intret Cato*: Authority and Epigram in Sixteenth-Century England." In *Renaissance Genres: Essays on Theory, History, and Interpretation*, edited by Barbara Kiefer Lewalski, 158–88. Cambridge, MA: Harvard University Press, 1986.

Creaser, John. "Fear of Change: Closed Minds and Open Forms in Milton." *Milton Quarterly* 42, no. 3 (September 2008): 161–82.

———. "Milton: The Truest of the Sons of Ben." In *Heirs of Fame: Milton and the Writers of the English Renaissance*, edited by David A. Kent and Margo Swiss, 158–83. Lewisburg, PA: Bucknell University Press, 1995.

———. "Prosodic Style and Conceptions of Liberty in Milton and Marvell." *Milton Quarterly* 24, no. 1 (March 2000): 1–13.

———. "Service Is Perfect Freedom: Paradox and Prosodic Style in *Paradise Lost*." *Review of English Studies* 58, no. 235 (June 2007): 268–315.

———. " 'Times Trans-shifting': Chronology and the Misshaping of Herrick." *English Literary Renaissance* 39, no. 1 (February 2009): 163–96.

Cressy, David. "Binding the Nation: The Bonds of Association, 1584 and 1696." In *Tudor Rule and Revolution: Essays for G. R. Elton from His American Friends*, edited by DeLloyd J. Guth and John W. McKenna, 217–34. Cambridge: Cambridge University Press, 1982.

Culler, Jonathan. "Introduction: Critical Paradigms." *PMLA* 125, no. 4 (October 2010): 905–15.

———. *Theory of the Lyric*. Cambridge, MA: Harvard University Press, 2015.

Culler, Jonathan, and Ben Glaser, eds. *Critical Rhythm: The Poetics of a Literary Life Form*. Fordham, NY: Fordham University Press, 2019.

Cummings, Peter. "Spenser's *Amoretti* as an Allegory of Love." *Texas Studies in Literature and Language* 12, no. 2 (Summer 1970): 163–79.

Cushman, Stephen. *Fictions of Form in American Poetry*. Princeton, NJ: Princeton University Press, 1993.

———. "On Middlebrow Formalism, or the Fallacy of Imitative Form Revisited." *Southwest Review* 99, no. 4 (2014): 507–30.

D'Addario, Christopher. "Abraham Cowley and the Ends of Poetry." In *Literatures of Exile in the English Revolution and Its Aftermath, 1640–1690*, edited by Philip Major, 119–32. Burlington, VT: Ashgate, 2010.

Danielson, Dennis, ed. *The Cambridge Companion to Milton*. Cambridge: Cambridge University Press, 1999.

Dasenbrock, Reed Way. "The Petrarchan Context of Spenser's *Amoretti.*" *PMLA* 100, no. 1 (January 1985): 38–50.

De Gooyer, Alan. "Sensibility and Solitude in Cowley's Familiar Essays." *Restoration: Studies in English Literary Culture, 1660–1700* 25, no. 1 (Spring 2001): 1–18.

De Quincey, Thomas. "Charles Lamb." In *De Quincey as Critic*, edited by John E. Jordan, 448–57. London: Routledge, 1973.

———. *Style and Rhetoric, and Other Papers.* Edinburgh: Adam and Charles Black, 1862.

Diekhoff, John S. "Rhyme in Paradise Lost." *PMLA* 49, no. 2 (June 1934): 539–43.

Doelman, James. *The Epigram in England: 1590–1640.* Manchester: Manchester University Press, 2016.

Dolven, Jeff. "The Method of Spenser's Stanza." *Spenser Studies* 19 (2004): 17–25.

———. *Scenes of Instruction in Renaissance Romance.* Chicago: University of Chicago Press, 2007.

———. *Senses of Style: Poetry before Interpretation.* Chicago: University of Chicago Press, 2017.

Donaldson, Ian. *Ben Jonson: A Life.* Oxford: Oxford University Press, 2012.

Downie, J. A., and J. T. Parnell, eds. *Constructing Christopher Marlowe.* Cambridge: Cambridge University Press, 2000.

Dubrow, Heather. *The Challenges of Orpheus: Lyric Poetry and Early Modern England.* Baltimore: Johns Hopkins University Press, 2008.

———. "Epithalamium." In *Princeton Encyclopedia of Poetry and Poetics*, 4th ed., edited by Clare Cavanagh, Stephen Cushman, Roland Greene, Jahan Ramazani, and Paul Rouzer, 452–53. Princeton, NJ: Princeton University Press, 2002.

———. *A Happier Eden: The Politics of Marriage in the Stuart Epithalamium.* Ithaca, NY: Cornell University Press, 1990.

Duncan, Helga. "'Headdie Ryots' as Reformations: Marlowe's Libertine Poetics." *Early Modern Literary Studies* 12, no. 2 (September 2006): 1–38.

Duncan-Jones, Katherine. "Was the 1609 'Shake-Speares Sonnets' Really Unauthorized?" *Review of English Studies* 34, no. 134 (May 1983): 151–71.

Dunlop, Alexander. "The Drama of *Amoretti.*" *Spenser Studies* 1 (1980): 107–20.

Dutton, Richard. "Jonson's Satiric Styles." In *The Cambridge Companion to Ben Jonson*, edited by Richard Harp and Stanley Stewart, 58–71. Cambridge: Cambridge University Press, 2000.

Dykstal, Timothy. "The Epic Reticence of Abraham Cowley." *Studies in English Literature* 31, no. 1 (Winter 1991): 95–115.

Dzelzianis, Martin. "'In Power of Others, Never in My Own': The Meaning of Slavery in *Samson Agonistes.*" In *Milton in the Long Restoration*, edited by Blair Hoxby and Ann Baynes Coiro, 285–301. Oxford: Oxford University Press, 2016.

Eckhardt, Joshua. *Manuscript Verse Collectors and the Politics of Anti-Courtly Love Poetry.* Oxford: Oxford University Press, 2009.

Eckhardt, Joshua, and Daniel Starza-Smith, eds. *Manuscript Miscellanies in Early Modern England.* Burlington, VT: Ashgate, 2014.

Eden, Kathy. *Hermeneutics and the Rhetorical Tradition: Chapters in the Ancient Legacy and Its Humanist Reception.* New Haven, CT: Yale University Press, 1997.

Eliot, T. S. *On Poetry and Poets.* New York: Farrar, Strauss, and Giroux, 2009.

———. "Reflections on Vers Libre." In *To Criticize the Critic, and Other Writings*, 183–89. Lincoln: University of Nebraska Press, 1965.

Elmore, A. E. "Herrick and the Poetry of Song." In *"Trust to Good Verses": Herrick Tercentenary Essays*, edited by Roger B. Rollin and J. Max Patrick, 65–75. Pittsburgh: University of Pittsburgh Press, 1978.

Elsky, Stephanie. "'Wonne with Custome': Conquest and Etymology in the Spenser-Harvey *Letters* and *A View of the Present State of Ireland*." *Spenser Studies* 28 (2013): 165–92.

Empson, William. "John Donne the Space Man." *Kenyon Review* 19, no. 3 (Summer 1957): 337–99.

———. *Seven Types of Ambiguity*. New York: New Directions, 1966.

———. *The Structure of Complex Words*. London: Chattto and Windus, 1951.

Evans, J. Martin. "Lycidas." In *The Cambridge Companion to Milton*, edited by Dennis Danielson, 39–53. Cambridge: Cambridge University Press, 1999.

Evans, Robert C. *Ben Jonson and the Poetics of Patronage*. Lewisburg, PA: Bucknell University Press, 1989.

———. "Paradox in Poetry and Politics: Katherine Philips in the Interregnum." In *The English Civil Wars in the Literary Imagination*, edited by Claude J. Summers and Ted-Larry Pebworth, 174–85. Columbia: University of Missouri Press, 1999.

Faderman, Lillian. *Surpassing the Love of Men: Romantic Friendship and Love between Women from the Renaissance to the Present*. New York: William Morrow, 1981.

Fairer, David. "Coleridge's 'Sonnets from Various Authors' (1796): A Lost Conversation Poem?" *Studies in Romanticism* 41, no. 4 (Winter 2002): 585–604.

Fallon, Stephen M. *Milton among the Philosophers: Poetry and Materialism in Seventeenth-Century England*. Ithaca, NY: Cornell University Press, 1993.

———. *Milton's Peculiar Grace: Self-Representation and Authority*. Ithaca, NY: Cornell University Press, 2007.

Finkelpearl, Philip J. *John Marston of the Middle Temple: An Elizabethan Dramatist and His Social Setting*. Cambridge, MA: Harvard University Press, 1969.

Fitzgerald, William. *Agonistic Poetry: The Pindaric Mode in Pindar, Horace, Holderin, and the English Ode*. Berkeley: University of California Press, 1987.

Flantz, Richard. "The Authoritie of Truth: Jonson's Mastery of Measure and the Founding of the Modern Plain-Style Lyric." In *Classic and Cavalier: Essays on Jonson and the Sons of Ben*, edited by Claude J. Summers and Ted-Larry Pebworth, 59–75. Pittsburgh: University of Pittsburgh Press, 1982.

Fleming, James. "A View from the Bridge: Ireland and Violence in Spenser's *Amoretti*." *Spenser Studies* 15 (2001): 135–64.

Flynn, Dennis, M. Thomas Hester, and Jeanne Shami, eds. *The Oxford Handbook of John Donne*. Oxford: Oxford University Press, 2011.

Forrest-Thomson, Veronica. *Poetic Artifice: A Theory of Twentieth-Century Poetry*. New York: St. Martin's, 1978.

Foucault, Michel. *The Order of Things: An Archeology of the Human Sciences*. New York: Routledge, 2002.

Fowler, Alastair, ed. *The Country House Poem: A Cabinet of Seventeenth-Century Estate Poems and Related Items*. Edinburgh: Edinburgh University Press, 1994.

———. "Emanations of Glory: Neoplatonic Order in Spenser's *Faerie Queene*." In *Theatre for Spenserians*, edited by Judith M. Kennedy and James A. Reither, 53–82. Toronto: University of Toronto Press, 1973.

———. *Triumphal Forms: Structural Patterns in Elizabethan Poetry*. Cambridge: Cambridge University Press, 1970.

Fowler, Elizabeth. *Literary Character: The Human Figure in Early English Writing*. Ithaca, NY: Cornell University Press, 2003.

Foxley, Rachel. "John Lilburne and the Citizenship of 'Free-Born Englishmen.'" *Historical Journal* 47, no. 4 (2004): 849–74.

Freedman, Morris. "Milton and Dryden on Rhyme." *Huntington Library Quarterly* 24 (1961): 337–44.

Friedman, Donald M. "'Comus' and the Truth of the Ear." In *"The Muses Common-Weale": Poetry and Politics in the Seventeenth Century*, edited by Claude J. Summers and Ted-Larry Pebworth, 119–34. Columbia: University of Missouri Press, 1988.

Fry, Paul H. *The Poet's Calling in the English Ode*. New Haven, CT: Yale University Press, 1980.

Frye, Northrop. "Approaching the Lyric." In *Lyric Poetry: Beyond New Criticism*, edited by Chaviva Hošek and Patricia Parker, 31–37. Ithaca, NY: Cornell University Press, 1985.

Fussell, Paul, Jr. *Poetic Meter and Poetic Form*. New York: Random House, 1965.

———. *Theory of Prosody in Eighteenth-Century England*. New London: Connecticut College, 1966.

Gallagher, Catherine. "Embracing the Absolute: Margaret Cavendish and the Politics of the Female Subject in Seventeenth-Century England." In *Early Women Writers: 1600–1720*, edited by Anita Pacheco, 133–46. New York: Longman, 1998.

Gardiner, Judith Keegan. *Craftsmanship in Context: The Development of Ben Jonson's Poetry*. The Hague: Mouton, 1975.

Gardner, Helen. *John Donne: "The Elegies" and the "Songs and Sonnets."* Oxford: Oxford University Press, 1965.

Giamatti, A. Bartlett. *Play of Double Senses: Spenser's "Faerie Queene,"* Englewood Cliffs, NJ: Prentice Hall, 1975.

Grafton, Anthony, and Lisa Jardine. *From Humanism to the Humanities: Education and the Liberal Arts in Fifteenth- and Sixteenth-Century Europe*. Cambridge, MA: Harvard University Press, 1986.

Gray, Catharine. "Katherine Philips and the Post-courtly Coterie." *English Literary Renaissance* 32 (2002): 426–51.

Goldberg, Jonathan. "Fatherly Authority: The Politics of Stuart Family Images." In *Rewriting the Renaissance: The Discourse of Sexual Difference in Early Modern Europe*, edited by Margaret W. Ferguson, Maureen Quilligan, and Nancy J. Vickers, 3–32. Chicago: University of Chicago Press, 1986.

Goldstone, Andrew. *Fictions of Autonomy: Modernism from Wilde to de Man*. Oxford: Oxford University Press, 2013.

Greenblatt, Stephen. *Renaissance Self-Fashioning from More to Shakespeare*. Chicago: University of Chicago Press, 1980.

Greene, Roland. "The Lyric." In *The Cambridge History of Literary Criticism*, edited by Glyn P. Norton, 3:216–28. Cambridge: Cambridge University Press, 1999.

———. *Post-Petrarchism: Origins and Innovations of the Western Lyric Sequence*. Princeton, NJ: Princeton University Press, 1991.

Greene, Thomas M. "Ben Jonson and the Centered Self." *Studies in English Literature* 10, no. 2 (Spring 1970): 325–48.

———. *The Light in Troy: Imitation and Discover in Renaissance Poetry*. New Haven, CT: Yale University Press, 1982.

———. "Spenser and the Epithalamic Convention." *Comparative Literature* 9, no. 3 (Summer 1957): 215–28.

Gregg, Pauline. *Free-Born John: A Biography of John Lilburne*. London: George G. Harrap, 1961.

Griffin, Julia B. "'Twixt Treason and Convenience': Some Images of Thomas Wentworth, Earl of Strafford." In *Images of Matter: Essays on British Literature of the Middle Ages and Renaissance*, edited by Yvonne Bruce, 153–82. Newark: University of Delaware Press, 2010.

Guibbory, Achsah. "'Oh Let Me Not Serve So': The Politics of Love in Donne's Elegies." *English Literary History* 57, no. 4 (Winter 1990): 811–33.

Guibbory, Achsah. "Reconsidering Donne: From Libertine Poetry to Arminian Sermons." *Studies in Philology* 114, no. 3 (Summer 2017): 561–90.

Haber, Judith. " 'True-Loves Blood': Narrative and Desire in *Hero and Leander*." *English Literary Renaissance* 28, no. 3 (1998): 372–86.

Hadfield, Andrew. *Edmund Spenser: A Life*. Oxford: Oxford University Press, 2012.

———. *Edmund Spenser's Irish Experience: Wilde Fruit and Salvage Soyl*. Oxford: Clarendon, 1997.

Hageman, Elizabeth H. "Making a Good Impression: Early Texts of Poems and Letters by Katherine Philips, the 'Matchless Orinda.'" *South Central Review* 11 (1994): 39–65.

Hageman, Elizabeth H., and Andrea Sununu. " 'More Copies of It Abroad Than I Could Have Imagin'd': Further Manuscript Texts of Katherine Philips, 'the Matchless Orinda.'" *English Manuscript Studies 1100–1700* 5 (1995): 128–31.

Hall, Jason David, ed. *Meter Matters: Verse Cultures of the Long Nineteenth Century*. Athens: Ohio University Press, 2011.

Hammond, Gerald. *Fleeting Things: English Poets and Poems*. Cambridge, MA: Harvard University Press, 1990.

Hankins, John E. "Jonson's 'Ode on Morison' and Seneca's *Epistulae Morales*." *Modern Language Notes* 51, no. 8 (December 1936): 518–20.

Hardison, O. B., Jr. *Prosody and Purpose in the English Renaissance*. Baltimore: Johns Hopkins University Press, 1989.

Harmon, William. "Rhyme in English Verse: History, Structures, Functions." *Studies in Philology* 84, no. 4 (Autumn 1987): 365–93.

Harp, Richard, and Stanley Stewart, eds. *The Cambridge Companion to Ben Jonson*. Cambridge: Cambridge University Press, 2000.

Harrington, Joel. *Reordering Marriage and Society in Reformation Germany*. Cambridge: Cambridge University Press, 1995.

Harrison, Matthew. "The Rude Poet Presents Himself: Breton, Spenser, and Bad Poetry." *Spenser Studies* 29 (2014): 239–62.

Harvey, Elizabeth D., and Katharine Eisaman Maus, eds. *Soliciting Interpretation: Literary Theory and Seventeenth-Century English Poetry*. Chicago: University of Chicago Press, 1990.

Heal, Felicity. *Hospitality in Early Modern England*. Oxford: Oxford University Press, 1990.

Healy, Margaret. *Shakespeare, Alchemy, and the Creative Imagination: The Sonnets and a Lover's Complaint*. Cambridge: Cambridge University Press, 2011.

Healy, Margaret, and Thomas Healy, eds. *Renaissance Transformations: The Making of English Writing, 1500–1650*. Edinburgh: Edinburgh University Press, 2009.

Healy, Thomas. " 'Trewly Wrote': Manuscript, Print, and the Lyric." In *The Lyric Poem: Formations and Transformation*, edited by Marion Thain, 51–70. Cambridge: Cambridge University Press, 2013.

Hedley, Jane. *Power in Verse: Metaphor and Metonymy in Renaissance Lyric*. University Park: Pennsylvania State University Press, 1988.

Heinemann, Margot. *Puritanism and Theatre: Thomas Middleton and Opposition Drama under the Early Stuarts*. Cambridge: Cambridge University Press, 1980.

Helgerson, Richard. *Forms of Nationhood: The Elizabethan Writing of England*. Chicago: University of Chicago Press, 1995.

———. *Self-Crowned Laureates: Spenser, Jonson, Milton and the Literary System*. Berkeley: University of California Press, 1983.

Heninger, S. K. *Sidney and Spenser: The Poet as Maker*. University Park: Pennsylvania State University Press, 1989.

———. *Touches of Sweet Harmony: Pythagorean Cosmology and Renaissance Poetics*. San Marino, CA: Huntington Library, 1974.

Herron, Thomas. "Colonialism and Irish Plantation." In *Edmund Spenser in Context*, edited by Andrew Escobedo, 72–82. Cambridge: Cambridge University Press, 2017.

Hester, M. Thomas. "'All Are Players': Guilpin and 'Prester Iohn' Donne." *South Atlantic Review* 49, no. 1 (January 1984): 3–17.

Hieatt, A. Kent. *Short Time's Endless Monument*. New York: Columbia University Press, 1960.

Hill, Christopher. *Milton and the English Revolution*. London: Faber and Faber, 1977.

Hinman, Robert B. *Abraham Cowley's World of Order*. Oxford: Oxford University Press, 1960.

Hirst, Derek. "The Politics of Literature in the English Republic." *Seventeenth Century* 5, no. 2 (Autumn 1990): 135–36.

Hollander, John. *Melodious Guile: Fictive Pattern in Poetic Language*. New Haven, CT: Yale University Press, 1988.

———. "Romantic Verse Form and the Metrical Contract." In *Romanticism and Consciousness*, edited by Harold Bloom, 181–200. New York: W. W. Norton, 1970.

———. *The Untuning of the Sky: Ideas of Music in English Poetry, 1500–1700*. New York: Norton, 1970.

———. *Vision and Resonance: Two Senses of Poetic Form*. New Haven, CT: Yale University Press, 1985.

Hopper, Vincent F. *Medieval Number Symbolism*. New York: Columbia University Press, 1938.

Hošek, Chaviva, and Patricia Parker, eds. *Lyric Poetry: Beyond New Criticism*. Ithaca, NY: Cornell University Press, 1985.

Houston, Alan, and Steve Pincus, eds. *A Nation Transformed: England after the Restoration*. Cambridge: Cambridge University Press, 2001.

Hunter, G. K. "Spenser's *Amoretti* and the English Sonnet Tradition." In *A Theatre for Spenserians*, edited by Judith M. Kennedy and James A. Reither, 124–44. Toronto: University of Toronto Press, 1973.

Hunter, J. Paul. "Seven Reasons for Rhyme." In *Ritual, Routine, and Regime: Repetition in Early Modern British and European Cultures*, edited by Lorna Clymer, 172–98. Toronto: University of Toronto Press, 2006.

———. "Sleeping Beauties: Are Historical Aesthetics Worth Recovering?" *Eighteenth-Century Studies* 34, no. 1 (Fall 2000): 1–20.

Jackson, R. Mark. "Ben Jonson and the Senecan Paradox of Long Life: The Cary-Morison Ode." *Ben Jonson Journal* 18, no. 2 (2011): 188–211.

Jackson, Virginia. *Dickinson's Misery: A Theory of Lyric Reading*. Princeton, NJ: Princeton University Press, 2005.

———. "Lyric." In *The Princeton Encyclopedia of Poetry and Poetics*, 4th ed., edited by Clare Cavanagh, Stephen Cushman, Roland Greene, Jahan Ramazani, and Paul Rouzer, 826–34. Princeton, NJ: Princeton University Press, 2002

Jackson, Virginia, and Yopie Prins, eds. *The Lyric Theory Reader: A Critical Anthology*. Baltimore: Johns Hopkins University Press, 2014.

Jacobs, Kathryn Elisabeth. *Marriage Contracts from Chaucer to the Renaissance Stage*. Gainesville: University of Florida Press, 2001.

Jacobson, Miriam. *Barbarous Antiquity: Reorienting the Past in the Poetry of Early Modern England*. Philadelphia: University of Pennsylvania Press, 2014.

James, Heather. "The Poet's Toys: Christopher Marlowe and the Liberties of Erotic Elegy." *Modern Language Quarterly* 67, no. 1 (2006): 103–27.

Jarvis, Simon. "For a Poetics of Verse." *PMLA* 125, no. 4 (October 2010): 931–39.

——. "Hyper-Pindaric: The Greater Irregular Lyric from Abraham Cowley to Keston Sutherland." In *Active Romanticism: The Radical Impulse in Nineteenth-Century and Contemporary Poetic Practice*, edited by Julie Carr and Jeffrey C. Robinson, 132–35. Tuscaloosa: University of Alabama Press, 2015.

——. "The Melodics of Long Poems." *Textual Practice* 24, no. 4 (October 2010): 607–21.

——. "Thinking in Verse." In *The Cambridge Companion to British Romantic Poetry*, edited by James Chandler and Maureen McLane, 98–116. Cambridge: Cambridge University Press, 2008.

——. "Why Rhyme Pleases." In *The Lyric Theory Reader: A Critical Anthology*, edited by Virginia Jackson and Yopie Prins, 434–48. Baltimore: Johns Hopkins University Press, 2014.

Javitch, Daniel. *Poetry and Courtliness in Renaissance England*. Princeton, NJ: Princeton University Press, 1978.

Jeffreys, Mark. "Songs and Inscriptions: Brevity and the Idea of Lyric." *Texas Studies in Literature and Language* 36, no. 2 (Summer 1994): 117–34.

Jocoy, Stacey. " 'Touch but Thy Lire (My Harrie)': Henry Lawes and the Mirthful Music of *Hesperides*." In *"Lords of Wine and Oile": Community and Conviviality in the Poetry of Robert Herrick*, edited by Ruth Connolly and Tom Cain, 250–75. Oxford: Oxford University Press, 2011.

Johnson, Richard M. "The Politics of Publication: Misrepresentation in Milton's 1645 'Poems.'" *Criticism* 36, no. 1 (Winter 1994): 45–71.

Johnson, William C. "Gender Fashioning and the Dynamics of Mutuality in Spenser's *Amoretti*." *English Studies* 74, no. 6 (August 1993): 503–19.

——. "Spenser's *Amoretti* and the Art of the Liturgy." *Studies in English Literature* 14, no. 1 (Winter 1974): 47–61.

Jones, Ann Rosalind, and Peter Stallybrass. "The Politics of Astrophil and Stella." *Studies in English Literature* 24 (1984): 53–68.

Kahn, Victoria. *Machiavellian Rhetoric: From the Counter-Reformation to Milton*. Princeton, NJ: Princeton University Press, 1994.

——. *Rhetoric, Prudence, and Skepticism in the Renaissance*. Ithaca, NY: Cornell University Press, 1985.

——. *Wayward Contracts: The Crisis of Political Obligation in England, 1640–1674*. Princeton, NJ: Princeton University Press, 2004.

Kalas, Rayna. *Frame, Glass, Verse: The Technology of Poetic Invention*. Ithaca, NY: Cornell University Press, 2007.

Kaplan, Ruth. "The Problem of Pity in Spenser's *Ruines of Time* and *Amoretti*." *Spenser Studies* 29 (2014): 263–94.

Kastan, David Scott. "The Invention of English Literature." In *Agents of Change: Essays in Honor of Elizabeth L. Eisenstein*, edited by Sabrina Baron, Eric Lundquist, and Eleanor Shavlin, 105–24. Amherst: University of Massachusetts Press, 2007.

Keach, William. "Cockney Couplets: Keats and the Politics of Style." *Studies in Romanticism* 25, no. 2 (Summer 1986): 182–96.

Kendrick, Christopher. *Milton: A Study in Ideology and Form*. New York: Methuen, 1986.

Kennedy, Judith M., and James A. Reither, eds. *A Theatre for Spenserians*. Toronto: University of Toronto Press, 1973.

Kent, David A., and Margo Swiss, eds. *Heirs of Fame: Milton and the Writers of the English Renaissance*. Lewisburg, PA: Bucknell University Press, 1995.

Keough, James G. "Cowley's Brutus Ode: Historical Precepts and the Politics of Defeat." *Texas Studies in Literature and Language* 19, no. 3 (Fall 1977): 382–91.

Kermode, Frank. "The Date of Cowley's *Davideis*." *Review of English Studies* 25, no. 98 (April 1949): 154–58.

Kerrigan, John. Introduction to *The Sonnets and a Lover's Complaint*, by William Shakespeare, 7–64. New York: Penguin, 1986.

———. *Shakespeare's Binding Language*. Oxford: Oxford University Press, 2016.

Kerrigan, William. *The Sacred Complex: On the Psychogensis of "Paradise Lost."* Cambridge, MA: Harvard University Press, 1983.

Kesler, R. L. "Formalism and the Problem of History: Sonnets, Sequence, and the Relativity of Linear Time." In *Shakespeare and Historical Formalism*, edited by Stephen A. Cohen, 177–94. Burlington, VT: Ashgate, 2007.

Kilburn, Terence, and Anthony Milton. "The Public Context of the Trial and Execution of Strafford." In *The Political World of Thomas Wentworth, Earl of Strafford, 1621–1641*, edited by J. F. Merritt, 230–51. Cambridge: Cambridge University Press, 1996.

Kinney, Clare. *Strategies of Poetic Narrative: Chaucer, Spenser, Milton, Eliot*. Cambridge: Cambridge University Press, 1992.

Klein, Lisa M. " 'Let Us Love, Dear Love, Lyke as We Ought': Protestant Marriage and the Revision of Petrarchan Loving in Spenser's *Amoretti*." *Spenser Studies* 10 (1992): 109–37.

Kranidas, Thomas. *The Fierce Equation: A Study of Milton's Decorum*. London: Mouton, 1965.

Kucich, Greg. *Keats, Shelley, and Romantic Spenserianism*. University Park: Pennsylvania State University Press, 1991.

Kuriyama, Constance Brown. *Christopher Marlowe: A Renaissance Life*. Ithaca, NY: Cornell University Press, 2002.

Kuzner, James. "Donne's *Biathanatos* and the Public Sphere's Vexing Freedom." *English Literary History* 81, no. 1 (Spring 2014): 61–81.

———. "Friendship, Sovereignty, and Sexuality in Katherine Philips's Poetry." *Studies in English Literature* 58, no. 1 (Winter 2018): 123–44.

———. "Metaphysical Freedom." *Modern Language Quarterly* 74, no. 4 (December 2013): 465–92.

Langer, Ullrich. *Lyric in the Renaissance from Petrarch to Montaigne*. Cambridge: Cambridge University Press, 2015.

Langley, T. R. "Abraham Cowley's 'Brutus': Royalist or Republican?" *Yearbook of English Studies* 6 (1976): 41–52.

Larsen, Kenneth. *Edmund Spenser's "Amoretti and Epithalamion": A Critical Edition*. Tempe: Arizona Center for Medieval and Renaissance Studies, 1997.

Larson, Katherine R. " 'Blest Pair of Sirens . . . Voice and Verse': Milton's Rhetoric of Song." *Milton Studies* 54 (2013): 81–106.

Leaver, Robin A. *Goostly Psalmes and Spirituall Songes: English and Dutch Metrical Psalms from Coverdale to Utenhove, 1535–1566*. Oxford: Oxford University Press, 1991.

Leavis, F. R. "Milton's Verse." *Scrutiny* 2 (1933): 123–36.

Leighton, Angela. *Hearing Things: The Work of Sound in Literature*. Cambridge, MA: Harvard University Press, 2018.

———. *On Form: Poetry, Aestheticism, and the Legacy of a Word*. Oxford: Oxford University Press, 2007.

Leo, Russ. "Milton's Aristotelian Experiments: Tragedy, *Lustratio*, and 'Secret Refreshings' in *Samson Agonistes* (1671)." *Milton Studies* 52 (2011): 221–52.

Leonard, John. "Marlowe's Doric Music: Lust and Aggression in *Hero and Leander*." *English Literary Renaissance* 30, no. 1 (2008): 55–76.

Lever, J. W. *The Elizabethan Love Sonnet*. London: Methuen, 1956.

Levine, Caroline. *Forms: Whole, Rhythm, Hierarchy, Network*. Princeton, NJ: Princeton University Press, 2017.

Levy, Harry L. "Vergil, Ovid, and Claudian on 'Licking into Shape.'" *Classical Weekly* 40, no. 19 (April 1947): 150–51.

Lewalski, Barbara Kiefer. *The Life of John Milton: A Critical Biography*. Malden, MA: Blackwell, 2000.

———, ed. *Renaissance Genres: Essays on Theory, History, and Interpretation*. Harvard, MA: Harvard University Press, 1986.

Lewis, C. S. *A Preface to "Paradise Lost."* Oxford: Oxford University Press, 1961.

Libertin, Mary. "Female Friendship in Women's Verse: Toward a New Theory of Female Poetics." *Women's Studies* 9 (1982): 291–308.

Lindley, David, ed. *The Court Masque*. Manchester: Manchester University Press, 1984.

———. "'Words for Music, Perhaps': Early Modern Songs and Lyric." In *The Lyric Poem: Formations and Transformation*, edited by Marion Thain, 10–29. Cambridge: Cambridge University Press, 2013.

Lippencott, Henry F., Jr. "Marvell's 'On Paradise Lost.'" *English Language Notes* 9 (1972): 265–72.

Lobis, Seth. *The Virtue of Sympathy: Magic, Philosophy, and Literature in Seventeenth-Century England*. New Haven, CT: Yale University Press, 2015.

Loewenstein, Joseph. "A Note on the Structure of Spenser's *Amoretti*: Viper Thoughts." *Spenser Studies* 8 (1987): 311–23.

Loscocco, Paula. "Inventing the English Sappho: Katherine Philips's Donnean Poetry." *Journal of English and Germanic Philology* 102, no. 1 (2003): 59–87.

Low, Anthony. "Circular Rhymes in 'Lycidas'?" *PMLA* 86, no. 5 (October 1971): 1032–35.

Loxley, James. *Royalism and Poetry in the English Civil Wars: The Drawn Sword*. London: Macmillan, 1997.

———. "Unfettered Organs: The Polemical Voices of Katherine Philips." In *"This Double Voice": Gendered Writing in Early Modern England*, edited by Danielle Clarke and Elizabeth Clarke, 230–48. London: Macmillan, 2000.

Luxon, Thomas H. "Heroic Restorations: Dryden and Milton." *Milton Studies* 59 (2018): 199–230.

Lyne, Raphael. "Thinking in Stanzas: *Venus and Adonis* and *The Rape of Lucrece*." In *The Work of Form: Poetics and Materiality in Early Modern Culture*, edited by Ben Burton and Elizabeth Scott-Baumann, 88–103. Oxford: Oxford University Press, 2015.

Lyne, R.O.A.M. "Servitium Amoris." *Classical Quarterly* 29 (1979): 117–30.

MacKenzie, Raymond. "Rethinking Rhyme, Signifying Friendship: Milton's 'Lycidas' and *Epitaphium Damonis*." *Modern Philology* 106, no. 3 (February 2009): 530–54.

MacLean, Gerald M., ed. *Culture and Society in the Stuart Restoration: Literature, Drama*. Cambridge: Cambridge University Press, 1995.

———. *Time's Witness: Historical Representation in English Poetry, 1603–1660*. Madison: University of Wisconsin Press, 1990.

Major, Philip, ed. *Literatures of Exile in the English Revolution and Its Aftermath, 1640–1690*. Burlington, VT: Ashgate, 2010.

———. *Writings of Exile in the English Revolution and Restoration*. Burlington, VT: Ashgate, 2013.

Mander, M.N.K. "Milton and the Music of the Spheres." *Milton Quarterly* 24, no. 2 (May 1990): 63–71.

Manley, Lawrence. *Convention 1500–1750*. Cambridge, MA: Harvard University Press, 1980.

Mann, Jenny C. "Marlowe's 'Slack Muse': *All Ovids Elegies* and an English Poetics of Softness." *Modern Philology* 113, no. 1 (2015): 49–65.

Marcus, Leah. *The Politics of Mirth: Jonson, Herrick, Milton, Marvell, and the Defense of Old Holiday Pastimes*. Chicago: University of Chicago Press, 1986.

Martin, Meredith. *The Rise and Fall of Meter: Poetry and English National Culture, 1860–1930*. Princeton, NJ: Princeton University Press, 2012.

Marotti, Arthur F. *John Donne, Coterie Poet*. Madison: University of Wisconsin Press, 1985.

———. "'Love Is Not Love': Elizabethan Sonnet Sequences and the Social Order." *English Literary History* 49, no. 2 (Summer 1982): 396–428.

———. *Manuscript, Print, and the English Renaissance Lyric*. Ithaca, NY: Cornell University Press, 1995.

Martz, Louis L. "The *Amoretti*: 'Most Goodly Temperature.'" In *Form and Convention in the Poetry of Edmund Spenser*, edited by William Nelson, 146–68. New York: Columbia University Press, 1961.

———. "The Rising Poet, 1645." In *The Lyric and Dramatic Milton: Selected Papers from the English Institute*, edited by Joseph Summers, 3–34. New York: Columbia University Press, 1965.

Matz, Robert. "Poetry, Politics, and Discursive Forms: The Case of Puttenham's *Arte of English Poesie*." *Genre* 30 (1997): 195–214.

Maus, Katharine Eisaman. *Jonson and the Roman Frame of Mind*. Princeton, NJ: Princeton University Press, 1984.

———. "Why Read Herrick?" In *"Lords of Wine and Oile": Community and Conviviality in the Poetry of Robert Herrick*, edited by Ruth Connolly and Tom Cain, 25–38. Oxford: Oxford University Press, 2011.

———. "A Womb of His Own: Male Renaissance Poets in the Female Body." In *Printing and Parenting in Early Modern England*, edited by Douglas A. Brooks, 89–108. Burlington, VT, Ashgate: 2005.

Mazzeo, Joseph Anthony. "Metaphysical Poetry and the Poetic of Correspondence." *Journal of the History of Ideas* 14, no. 2 (April 1953): 221–34.

McCabe, Richard. "Elizabethan Satire and the Bishops' Ban of 1599." *Yearbook of English Studies* 11 (1981): 188–93.

———, ed. *The Oxford Handbook of Edmund Spenser*. Oxford: Oxford University Press, 2010.

McDonald, Russ. "Jonson and Shakespeare and the Rhythm of Verse." In *The Cambridge Companion to Ben Jonson*, edited by Richard Harp and Stanley Stewart, 103–18. Cambridge: Cambridge University Press, 2006.

McDowell, Nicholas. "Classical Liberty and Cavalier Poetics: The Politics of Literary Community in Caroline London from Jonson to Marvell." *Yearbook of English Studies* 44 (2014): 120–36.

———. *Poetry and Allegiance in the English Civil Wars: Marvell and the Cause of Wit*. Oxford: Oxford University Press, 2008.

———. "Towards Redefinition of Cavalier Poetics." *Seventeenth Century* 32, no. 4 (2017): 413–31.

McElligott, Jason, and David L. Smith. *Royalists and Royalism during the English Civil Wars*. Cambridge: Cambridge University Press, 2007.

McPherson, David. "Ben Jonson's Library and Marginalia: An Annotated Catalogue." *Studies in Philology* 71, no. 5 (December 1974): 1–106.

McWilliams, John. "Milton and Marvell's Literary Friendship Reconsidered." *Studies in English Literature* 46, no. 1 (Winter 2006): 155–77.

Merritt, J. F. *The Political World of Thomas Wentworth, Earl of Strafford, 1621–1641*. Cambridge: Cambridge University Press, 1996.

Milgate, W. "The Early References to John Donne." *Notes and Queries* 195 (May 1950): 229–31; (June 1950): 246–47.

Miller, David Lee. "The Death of the Modern: Gender and Desire in Marlowe's 'Hero and Leander.'" *South Atlantic Quarterly* 88, no. 4 (Fall 1989): 757–87.

———. *The Poem's Two Bodies: The Poetics of the 1590 "Faerie Queene."* Princeton, NJ: Princeton University Press, 1988.

Minear, Erin. *Reverberating Song in Shakespeare and Milton: Language, Memory, and Musical Representation.* Burlington, VT: Ashgate, 2011.

Miner, Earl. *The Cavalier Mode from Jonson to Cotton.* Princeton, NJ: Princeton University Press, 1971.

Moss, Daniel D. *The Ovidian Vogue: Literary Fashion and Imitative Practice in Late Elizabethan England.* Toronto: University of Toronto Press, 2014.

Moul, Victoria S. *Jonson, Horace and the Classical Tradition.* Cambridge: Cambridge University Press, 2010.

Mueller, Janel. "Just Measures? Versification in *Samson Agonistes.*" *Milton Studies* 33 (1996): 47–82.

Mueller, William R., ed. *Spenser's Critics: Changing Currents in Literary Taste.* Syracuse, NY: Syracuse University Press, 1959.

Mulryan, John. "Jonson's Classicism." In *The Cambridge Companion to Ben Jonson,* edited by Richard Harp and Stanley Stewart, 163–74. Cambridge: Cambridge University Press, 2000.

Murdock, Kenneth B. "An Elegy on Sir Henry Morison, by Lucius Cary, Viscount Falkland." *Harvard Studies and Notes in Philology and Literature* 20 (1938): 29–42.

Nardo, Anna K. *Milton's Sonnets and the Ideal Community.* Lincoln: University of Nebraska Press, 1979.

Nazarian, Cynthia N. *Love's Wounds: Violence and the Politics of Poetry in Early Modern Europe.* Ithaca, NY: Cornell University Press, 2016.

Neely, Carol Thomas. "The Structure of English Renaissance Sonnet Sequences." *English Literary History* 45, no. 3 (Autumn 1978): 359–89.

Ness, Frederic W. *The Use of Rhyme in Shakespeare's Plays.* New Haven, CT: Yale University Press, 1941.

Nethercot, Arthur H. *The Muse's Hannibal.* Oxford: Oxford University Press, 1931.

Netzley, Ryan. *Lyric Apocalypse: Milton, Marvell, and the Nature of Events.* New York: Fordham University Press, 2015.

Nevo, Ruth. *The Dial of Virtue: A Study of Poems on Affairs of State in the Seventeenth Century.* Princeton, NJ: Princeton University Press, 1963.

Ng, Su Fang. *Literature and the Politics of Family in Seventeenth-Century England.* Cambridge: Cambridge University Press, 2007.

Nichols, J. G. *The Poetry of Ben Jonson.* London: Routledge, 1969.

Nicholson, Catherine. *Uncommon Tongues: Eloquence and Eccentricity in the English Renaissance.* Philadelphia: University of Pennsylvania Press, 2013.

Nohrnberg, James. *The Analogy of "The Faerie Queene."* Princeton, NJ: Princeton University Press, 1976.

Norbrook, David. *Poetry and Politics in the English Renaissance.* Boston: Routledge and Kegan Paul, 1984.

———. *Writing the English Republic: Poetry, Rhetoric and Politics, 1627–1660.* Cambridge: Cambridge University Press, 1999.

Oates, Mary I. "Jonson's 'Ode Pindarick' and the Doctrine of Imitation." *Papers on Language and Literature* 11, no. 2 (Spring 1975): 126–48.

O'Callaghan, Michelle. *The "Shepheardes Nation": Jacobean Spenserians and Early Stuart Political Culture, 1612–1625.* Oxford: Clarendon, 2000.

Oras, Ants. "Milton's Early Rhyme Schemes and the Structure of 'Lycidas.'" *Modern Philology* 52, no. 1 (August 1954): 12–22.

Ornstein, R. "Donne, Montaigne, and Natural Law." *Journal of English and Germanic Philology* 55, no. 2 (April 1956): 213–29.

Pahlka, William H. *Saint Augustine's Meter and George Herbert's Will.* Kent, OH: Kent State University Press, 1987.

Parfitt, George. *Ben Jonson: Public Poet and Private Man.* London: J. M. Dent and Sons, 1976.

———. "Compromise Classicism: Language and Rhythm in Ben Jonson's Poetry." *Studies in English Literature* 11, no. 1 (Winter 1971): 109–23.

Parker, W. R. *Milton: A Biography.* Oxford: Clarendon, 1968.

Parkes, Malcolm Beckwith. "Influence of the Concepts of *Ordinatio* and *Compilatio* in the Development of the Book." In *Medieval Learning and Literature: Essays Presented to Richard William Hunt,* edited by J.J.G. Alexander and M. T. Gibson, 115–44. Oxford: Clarendon, 1976.

Patrides, C. A., ed. *Approaches to Marvell: The York Tercentenary Lectures.* London: Routledge and Kegan Paul, 1978.

———. *Milton's "Lycidas": The Tradition and the Poem.* Columbia: University of Missouri Press, 1983.

———. "The Numerological Approach to Cosmic Order during the English Renaissance." *Isis* 49, no. 4 (December 1958): 391–97.

Patterson, Annabel. *Censorship and Interpretation: The Conditions of Writing and Reading in Early Modern England.* Madison: University of Wisconsin Press, 1984.

———. *Hermogenes and the Renaissance: Seven Ideas of Style.* Princeton, NJ: Princeton University Press, 1970.

———. "John Donne, Kingsman?" In *The Mental World of the Jacobean Court,* edited by Linda Levy Peck, 251–72. Cambridge: Cambridge University Press, 1991.

Pearl, Sara. "Jonson's Masques of 1620–5." In *The Court Masque,* edited by David Lindley, 60–77. Manchester: Manchester University Press, 1984.

Peck, Linda Levy, ed. *The Mental World of the Jacobean Court.* Cambridge: Cambridge University Press, 1991.

Peter, John. *Complaint and Satire in Early English Literature.* Oxford: Oxford University Press, 1936.

Peterson, Richard. *Imitation and Praise in the Poems of Ben Jonson.* New Haven, CT: Yale University Press, 1981.

Pinsky, Robert. *The Sounds of Poetry: A Brief Guide.* New York: Farrar, Strauss, and Giroux, 1998.

Piper, W. B. *The Heroic Couplet.* Cleveland, OH: Case Western Reserve University Press, 1969.

Poole, William. "Two Early Readers of Milton: John Beale and Abraham Hill." *Milton Quarterly* 38, no. 2 (2004): 76–99.

Potter, Lois. *Secret Rites and Secret Writings: Royalist Literature 1641–1660.* Cambridge: Cambridge University Press, 1989.

Power, Henry. "'Teares Break Off My Verse': The Virgilian Incompleteness of Abraham Cowley's 'The Civil War.'" *Translation and Literature* 16, no. 2 (Autumn 2007): 141–59.

Prince, F. T. *The Italian Element in Milton's Verse.* Oxford: Clarendon, 1954.

Prins, Yopie. "What Is Historical Poetics?" *Modern Language Quarterly* 77, no. 1 (March 2016): 13–40.

Pritchard, Allan. "George Wither: The Prophet as Poet." *Studies in Philology* 59, no. 2, part 1 (April 1962): 211–30.

Purdie, Rhiannon. *Anglicising Romance: Tail-Rhyme and Genre in Medieval English Literature.* Cambridge, UK: D. S. Brewer, 2008.

Quint, David. *Epic and Empire: Politics and Generic Form from Virgil to Milton.* Princeton, NJ: Princeton University Press, 1993.

Quitslund, Beth. *The Reformation in Rhyme: Sternhold, Hopkins and the English Metrical Psalter, 1547–1603.* Burlington, VT: Ashgate, 2008.

Radcliffe, David Hill. "Sylvan States: Social and Literary Formations in Sylvae by Jonson and Cowley." *English Literary History* 55, no. 4 (Winter 1988): 797–809.

Radzinowicz, Mary Ann. *Toward "Samson Agonistes": The Growth of Milton's Mind.* Princeton, NJ: Princeton University Press, 1978.

Raleigh, Walter. *Milton.* London: Edward Arnold, 1900.

Ransom, John Crowe. "A Poem Nearly Anonymous." In *Milton's "Lycidas": The Tradition and the Poem,* edited by C. A. Patrides, 68–85. Columbia: University of Missouri Press, 1983.

Rasmussen, Mark David, ed. *Renaissance Literature and Its Formal Engagements.* New York: Palgrave, 2002.

Ravelhofer, Barbara. "Dance." In *Ben Jonson in Context,* edited by Julie Sanders, 171–80. Cambridge: Cambridge University Press, 2010.

Raylor, Timothy. *Cavaliers, Clubs, and Literary Culture: Sir John Mennes, James Smith, and the Order of the Fancy.* Newark: University of Delaware Press, 1994.

Rebhorn, Wayne, and Frank Whigham. Introduction to *The Art of English Poesy,* by George Puttenham, 1–72. Ithaca, NY: Cornell University Press, 2007.

Revard, Stella P. *Milton and the Tangles of Naera's Hair: The Making of the 1645 Poems.* Columbia: University of Missouri Press, 1997.

———. "Pindar and Jonson's Cary-Morison Ode." In *Classic and Cavalier: Essays on Jonson and the Sons of Ben,* edited by Claude J. Summers and Ted-Larry Pebworth, 17–30. Pittsburgh: University of Pittsburgh Press, 1982.

———. *Politics, Poetics, and the Pindaric Ode: 1450–1700.* Tempe: Arizona Center for Medieval and Renaissance Studies, 2009.

Rhodes, Neil. "Framing and Tuning in Renaissance English Verse." In *Renaissance Transformations: The Making of English Writing, 1500–1650,* edited by Margaret Healy and Thomas Healy, 32–47. Edinburgh: Edinburgh University Press, 2009.

Ricks, Christopher. *Milton's Grand Style.* Oxford: Clarendon, 1963.

Riggs, David. *Ben Jonson: A Life.* Cambridge, MA: Harvard University Press, 1989.

———. *The World of Christopher Marlowe.* London: Faber and Faber, 2004.

Roberts, John G., ed. *New Perspectives on the Seventeenth-Century English Religious Lyric.* Columbia: University of Missouri Press, 1994.

Rockett, William. "John Donne: The Ethical Argument of Elegy III." *Studies in English Literature* 15, no. 1 (Winter 1975): 57–69.

Rosenfeld, Colleen Ruth. "The Artificial Life of Rhyme." *English Literary History* 83, no. 1 (Spring 2016): 71–99.

Rosenthal, Alexander. *Crown under Law: Richard Hooker, John Locke, and the Ascent of Modern Constitutionalism.* Lanham, MD: Lexington Books, 2008.

Ross, Sarah C. E. *Women, Poetry, and Politics in Seventeenth-Century Britain.* Oxford: Oxford University Press, 2015.

Rostvig, Maren-Sofie. *The Happy Man: Studies in the Metamorphoses of a Classical Ideal.* Oslo: Norwegian Universities Press, 1962.

———. "The Hidden Sense: Milton and the Neoplatonic Method of Numerical Composition." In *The Hidden Sense, and Other Essays*, 1–112. Oslo: Universitetsforlaget, 1963.

Rudrum, Alan. "Royalist Lyric." In *The Cambridge Companion to Writing of the English Revolution*, edited by N. H. Keeble, 181–97. Cambridge: Cambridge University Press, 2001.

Rumrich, John. *Milton Unbound: Controversy and Reinterpretation.* Cambridge: Cambridge University Press, 1996.

Rutherford, James. "The Experimental Form of Lycidas." *Milton Studies* 53 (2012): 17–37.

Rutledge, Douglas F., ed. *Ceremony and Text in the Renaissance.* Newark: University of Delaware Press, 1996.

Ryzhik, Yulia. "Complaint and Satire in Spenser and Donne: Limits of Poetic Justice." *English Literary Renaissance* 47, no. 1 (Winter 2017): 110–35.

———. "Spenser and Donne Go Fishing." *Spenser Studies* 31–32 (2017 / 2018): 417–37.

Sackton, Alexander. "The Rhymed Couplet in Ben Jonson's Plays." *University of Texas Studies in English* 30 (1951): 86–106.

Saintsbury, George. *A History of English Prosody from the Twelfth Century to the Present Day.* New York: Russell and Russell, 1961.

Sanders, Julie, ed. *Ben Jonson in Context.* Cambridge: Cambridge University Press, 2010.

Schoenfeldt, Michael S. " 'The Mysteries of Manners, Armes, and Arts': 'Inviting a Friend to Supper' and 'To Penshurst.' " In *"The Muses Common-Weale": Poetry and Politics in the Seventeenth Century*, edited by Claude J. Summers and Ted-Larry Pebworth, 62–79. Columbia: University of Missouri Press, 1988.

Scodel, Joshua. "Allusions and Distinctions: Pentameter Couplets in Ben Jonson's *Epigrams* and *Forest.*" In *The Work of Form: Poetics and Materiality in Early Modern Culture*, edited by Ben Burton and Elizabeth Scott-Baumann, 39–55. Oxford: Oxford University Press, 2015.

———. "The Cowleyan Pindaric Ode and Sublime Diversions." In *A Nation Transformed: England after the Restoration*, edited by Alan Houston and Steve Pincus, 180–210. Cambridge: Cambridge University Press, 2001.

———. *The English Poetic Epitaph: Commemoration and Conflict from Jonson to Wordsworth.* Ithaca, NY: Cornell University Press, 1991.

———. *Excess and the Mean in Early Modern English Literature.* Princeton, NJ: Princeton University Press, 2002.

———. " 'None's Slave': Some Versions of Liberty in Donne's *Satires* 1 and 4." *English Literary History* 72, no. 2 (Summer 2005): 363–85.

Scott, David. "Counsel and Cabal in the King's Party, 1642–1646." In *Royalists and Royalism during the English Civil Wars*, ed. Jason McElligott and David L. Smith, 112–35. Cambridge: Cambridge University Press, 2007.

Scott-Baumann, Elizabeth. *Forms of Engagement: Women, Poetry, and Culture 1640–1680.* Oxford: Oxford University Press, 2013.

Sell, Roger D., ed. *The Shorter Poems of Sir John Beaumont.* Abo: Abo Akademi, 1974.

Semler, L. E. "Marlovian Therapy: The Chastisement of Ovid in *Hero and Leander.*" *English Literary Renaissance* 35, no. 2 (March 2005): 159–86.

Shaheen, Naseeb. *Biblical References in "The Faerie Queene,"* Memphis, TN: Memphis State University Press, 1976.

Shanley, Mary Lyndon. "Marriage Contract and Social Contract in Seventeenth Century English Political Thought." *Western Political Quarterly* 32, no. 1 (March 1979): 79–91.

Sharpe, Kevin. *Criticism and Compliment: The Politics of Literature in the England of Charles I*. Cambridge: Cambridge University Press, 1987.

——. *Image Wars: Promoting Kings and Commonwealths in England, 1603–1660*. New Haven, CT: Yale University Press, 2010.

Shaver, Chester Linn. "Thomas Beedome." *Modern Language Notes* 53, no. 6 (June 1938): 412–14.

Shifflett, Andrew. "'By Lucan Driv'n About': A Jonsonian Marvell's Lucanic Milton." *Renaissance Quarterly* 49, no. 4 (Winter 1996): 803–23.

Shipley, Joseph T. "Spenserian Prosody: The Couplet Forms." *Studies in Philology* 21, no. 4 (October 1924): 594–615.

Shore, Daniel. *Milton and the Art of Rhetoric*. Cambridge: Cambridge University Press, 2012.

Silliman, Ron, Carla Harryman, Lyn Hejinian, Steve Benson, Bob Perelman, and Barrett Watten. "Aesthetic Tendency and the Politics of Poetry: A Manifesto." *Social Text* 19 / 20 (Autumn 1988), 261–75.

Skinner, Quentin. "Rethinking Political Liberty." *History Workshop Journal* 61 (Spring 2006): 156–70.

Smart, J. S. Introduction to *The Sonnets of Milton*, by John Milton, 1–46. Glasgow: Maclehose, 1921.

Smith, A. J., ed. *John Donne: The Critical Heritage*. Boston: Routledge, 1975.

Smith, Barbara Herrnstein. *Poetic Closure: A Study of How Poems End*. Chicago: University of Chicago Press, 1968.

Smith, Bruce. *Homosexual Desire in Shakespeare's England*. Chicago: University of Chicago Press, 1991.

Smith, Daniel Starza. "Before (and after) the Miscellany: Reconstructing Donne's *Satyres* in the Conway Papers." In *Manuscript Miscellanies in Early Modern England*, edited by Joshua Eckhardt and Daniel Starza Smith, 17–38. Burlington, VT: Ashgate, 2014.

Smith, G. Gregory, ed. *Elizabethan Critical Essays*. Oxford: Oxford University Press, 1932.

Smith, Nigel. "Andrew Marvell and Ben Jonson: Personality and Prosody." *Ben Jonson Journal* 20, no. 2 (2013): 157–78.

——. "Cross-Channel Cavaliers." *Seventeenth Century* 32, no. 4 (2017): 433–53.

——. *Literature and Revolution in England, 1640–1660*. New Haven, CT: Yale University Press, 1994.

——, ed. *The Poems of Andrew Marvell*. New York: Longman, 2013.

Sokol, B. J., and Mary Sokol. *Shakespeare, Law and Marriage*. Cambridge: Cambridge University Press, 2003.

Spitzer, Leo. *Classical and Christian Ideas of World Harmony*. Baltimore: Johns Hopkins University Press, 1963.

Sprott, S. Ernest. *Milton's Art of Prosody*. Oxford: Oxford University Press, 1953.

Stallybrass, Peter. "'We Feaste in Our Defense': Patrician Carnival in Early Modern England and Robert Herrick's 'Hesperides.'" *English Literary Renaissance* 16, no. 1 (Winter 1986): 234–52.

Stapleton, M. L. *Harmful Eloquence: Ovid's Amores from Antiquity to Shakespeare*. Ann Arbor: University of Michigan Press, 1996.

Stein, Arnold. "Donne and the Couplet." *PMLA* 57, no. 3 (September 1942): 676–96.

——. "Donne's Harshness and the Elizabethan Tradition." *Studies in Philology* 41, no. 3 (July 1944): 390–409.

Stewart, Susan. "Rhyme and Freedom." In *The Sound of Poetry / The Poetry of Sound*, edited by Marjorie Perloff and Craig Dworkin, 29–48. Chicago: University of Chicago Press, 2009.

Stiebel, Arlene. "Not since Sappho: The Erotic in Poems of Katherine Philips and Aphra Behn." In *Homosexuality in Renaissance and Enlightenment England: Literary Representations in Historical Context*, edited by Claude J. Summers, 153–71. New York: Harrington Park, 1992.

Stogdill, Nathaniel. "Abraham Cowley's 'Pindaric Way': Adapting Athleticism in Interregnum England." *English Literary Renaissance* 42, no. 3 (Autumn 2012): 482–514.

Strier, Richard. "Bondage and the Lyric: Philosophical and Formal, Renaissance and Modern." In *The Work of Form: Poetics and Materiality in Early Modern Culture*, edited by Ben Burton and Elizabeth Scott-Baumann, 73–87. Oxford: Oxford University Press, 2014.

———. "Radical Donne: 'Satire III.'" *English Literary History* 60, no. 2 (Summer 1993): 283–322.

Summers, Claude J. "*Hero and Leander*: The Arbitrariness of Desire." In *Constructing Christopher Marlowe*, edited by J. A. Downie and J. T. Parnell, 133–47. Cambridge: Cambridge University Press, 2000.

———. "Herrick, Vaughan and the Poetry of Anglican Survivalism." In *New Perspectives on the Seventeenth-Century English Religious Lyric*, edited by John G. Roberts, 46–74. Columbia: University of Missouri Press, 1994.

Summers, Claude J., and Ted-Larry Pebworth, eds. *Classic and Cavalier: Essays on Jonson and the Sons of Ben*. Pittsburgh: University of Pittsburgh Press, 1982.

———, eds. *"The Muses Common-Weale": Poetry and Politics in the Seventeenth Century*. Columbia: University of Missouri Press, 1988.

Summers, Joseph, ed. *The Lyric and Dramatic Milton: Selected Papers from the English Institute*. New York: Columbia University Press, 1965.

Swann, Marjorie. *Curiosities and Texts: The Culture of Collecting in Early Modern England*. Philadelphia: University of Pennsylvania Press, 2001.

Swinburne, A. C. Preface to *The "Hesperides" and "Noble Numbers," by Robert Herrick*. Edited by Alfred Pollard. New York: Charles Scribner's Sons, 1891.

Temperley, Nicholas. *The Music of the English Parish Church*. Cambridge: Cambridge University Press, 1979.

Thain, Marion, ed. *The Lyric Poem: Formations and Transformation*. Cambridge: Cambridge University Press, 2013.

Thompson, John. *The Founding of English Metre*. London: Routledge and Kegan Paul, 1961.

Tillyard, E.M.W. *Elizabethan World Picture: A Study of the Idea of Order in Shakespeare, Donne and Milton*. New York: Random House, 1959.

Tribble, Elizabeth B. "The Partial Sign: Spenser and the Sixteenth-Century Crisis of Semiotics." In *Ceremony and Text in the Renaissance*, edited by Douglas F. Rutledge, 23–34. Newark: University of Delaware Press, 1996.

Trimpi, Wesley. *Ben Jonson's Poems: A Study of the Plain Style*. Stanford, CA: Stanford University Press, 1962.

Trotter, David. *The Poetry of Abraham Cowley*. London: Macmillan, 1979.

Tschann, Judith. "The Layout of 'Sir Thopas' in the Ellesmere, Cambridge Dd.4.24, and Cambridge Gg.4.27 Manuscripts." *Chaucer Review* 20, no. 1 (Summer 1985): 1–13.

Tuck, Jonathan. "'Thou Fall'st, My Tongue': Success and Failure in the Cary-Morison Ode." *George Herbert Journal* 22, no. 1–2 (Fall 1998): 77–93.

Tuck, Richard. *Philosophy and Government 1572–1651*. Cambridge: Cambridge University Press, 1993.

Turner, Henry S. *The English Renaissance Stage: Geometry, Poetics, and the Practical Spatial Arts, 1580–1630*. Oxford: Oxford University Press, 2006.

Tuve, Rosemond. *Elizabethan and Metaphysical Imagery*. Chicago: University of Chicago Press, 1947.

Underdown, David. *Royalist Conspiracy in England, 1649–1660*. New Haven, CT: Yale University Press, 1960.

van den Berg, Sara J. *The Action of Ben Jonson's Poetry*. Newark: University of Delaware Press, 1987.

van den Berg, Sara J., and W. Scott Howard, eds. *The Divorce Tracts of John Milton: Texts and Contexts*. Pittsburgh: Duquesne University Press, 2010.

Vickers, Brian. *Classical Rhetoric in English Poetry*. New York: St. Martin's, 1970.

Villeponteaux, Mary A. "'With Her Own Will Beguyld': The Captive Lady in Spenser's *Amoretti*." *Explorations in Renaissance Culture* 14, no. 1 (1988): 29–39.

Wakelin, Daniel. *Humanism, Reading, and English Literature 1430–1530*. Oxford: Oxford University Press, 2007.

Waller, Gary. *The Sidney Family Romance: Mary Wroth, William Herbert and the Construction of Gender*. Detroit: Wayne State University Press, 1993.

Ward, Thomas. "Abraham Cowley's Odes 'Rightly Repeated.'" *Restoration: Studies in English Literary Culture, 1660–1700* 42, no. 2 (Fall 2018): 39–64.

Watt, Tessa. *Cheap Print and Popular Piety, 1550–1640*. Cambridge: Cambridge University Press, 1991.

Wayne, Don E. "Jonson's Sidney: Legacy and Legitimation in *The Forrest*." In *Sir Philip Sidney's Achievements*, edited by M.J.B. Allen, Dominic Baker-Smith, and Arthur F. Kinney, 227–50. New York: AMS, 1990.

———. *Penshurst: The Semiotics of Place and the Poetics of History*. Madison: University of Wisconsin Press, 1984.

Weisman, Karen, ed. *The Oxford Handbook of the Elegy*. Oxford: Oxford University Press, 2010.

Welch, Anthony. *The Renaissance Epic and the Oral Past*. New Haven, CT: Yale University Press, 2012.

Wesling, Donald. *The Chances of Rhyme: Device and Modernity*. Berkeley: University of California Press, 1980.

Wickert, Max. "Structure and Ceremony in Spenser's *Epithalamion*." *English Literary History* 35, no. 2 (June 1968): 135–57.

Wilcher, Robert. *The Writing of Royalism, 1628–1660*. Cambridge: Cambridge University Press, 2001.

Williams, David. *Milton's Leveller God*. Montreal: McGill-Queen's University Press, 2017.

Wilson, Scott. "The Struggle for Sovereignty in 'Astrophil and Stella.'" *Criticism* 33, no. 3 (Summer 1991): 309–32.

Wilson-Okamura, David Scott. *Spenser's International Style*. Cambridge: Cambridge University Press, 2013.

Wimsatt, W. K. *The Verbal Icon: Studies of the Meaning of Poetry*. Lexington: University of Kentucky Press, 1954.

Winner, Jack D. "Ben Jonson's Epigrammes and the Conventions of Formal Verse Satire." *Studies in English Literature* 23, no. 1 (Winter 1983): 61–76.

Wittreich, Joseph Anthony, Jr. "Circular Rhymes in 'Lycidas'?" *PMLA* 86, no. 5 (October 1971): 1032–35.

———. "Milton's 'Destin'd Urn': The Art of 'Lycidas.'" *PMLA* 84, no. 1 (January 1969): 60–70.

———. "Perplexing the Explanation: Marvell's 'On Mr Milton's Paradise lost.'" In *Approaches to Marvell: The York Tercentenary Lectures*, edited by C. A. Patrides, 280–305. London: Routledge and Kegan Paul, 1978.

Wolfe, Jessica. "Spenser, Homer, and the Mythography of Strife." *Renaissance Quarterly* 58, no. 4 (Winter 2005): 1220–88.

Wolfson, Susan. *Formal Charges: The Shaping of Poetry in British Romanticism*. Stanford, CA: Stanford University Press, 1997.

Woods, Susanne. "Ben Jonson's Cary-Morison Ode: Some Observations on Structure and Form." *Studies in English Literature* 18, no. 1 (Winter 1978): 57–74.

———. "The Context of Jonson's Formalism." In *Classic and Cavalier: Essays on Jonson and the Sons of Ben*, edited by Claude J. Summers and Ted-Larry Pebworth, 77–89. Pittsburgh: University of Pittsburgh Press, 1982.

———. *Milton and the Poetics of Freedom*. Pittsburgh: Duquesne University Press, 2013.

———. *Natural Emphasis: English Versification from Chaucer to Dryden*. San Marino, CA: Huntington Library, 1984.

Worden, Blair. "Milton, *Samson Agonistes*, and the Restoration." In *Culture and Society in the Stuart Restoration: Literature, Drama, History*, edited by Gerald MacLean, 111–36. Cambridge: Cambridge University Press, 1995.

Wright, Gillian. *Producing Women's Poetry, 1600–1730: Text and Paratext, Manuscript and Print*. Cambridge: Cambridge University Press, 2013.

Yeats, W. B. "Edmund Spenser." In *The Collected Works of W. B. Yeats*, edited by Richard J. Finneran and George Bornstein, 4: 257–76. New York: Scribner, 2007.

Young, R. V. "The Elegy." In *The Oxford Handbook of John Donne*, edited by Dennis Flynn, M. Thomas Hester, and Jeanne Shami, 134–48. Oxford: Oxford University Press, 2011.

Zwicker, Stephen N. "John Dryden Meets, Rhymes, and Says Farewell to John Milton: A Restoration Drama in Three Acts." In *Milton in the Long Restoration*, edited by Blair Hoxby and Ann Baynes Coiro, 182–90. Oxford: Oxford University Press, 2016.

———. *Lines of Authority: Politics and English Literary Culture, 1649–1689*. Ithaca, NY: Cornell University Press, 1993.

INDEX

Figures, tables, and notes are indicated, respectively,
with a notation of *fig*, *tab*, or *n* after the page number.

sured couplets of, 136, 138, 149–50, 157–58, 180, 183, 185, 187; vs Milton, 164, 166, 167, 173–74, 175–76, 179; and neoclassical mode, 57, 129, 161, 229n74; and Pindaric ode, 107–20, 122, 156; and poetics of character, 16, 17, 86–91, 105–7, 114–15, 117–18, 124–25; praise poems of, 172, 178–79, 182; Stoicism of, 109, 118, 126–27, 139, 153, 182

WORKS: *Epigrammes,* 91–93, 94, 118, 138; "Epistle to Katherine, Lady Aubigny," 99–100, 102–7, 110, 113, 117; "A Fit of Rhyme against Rhyme," 84–85, 180; *The Forrest,* 91–92, 94–100, 113, 118, 138, 141, 163, 234n118; *Masque of Queens,* 133; "Ode to Sir William Sidney, on his Birth-day," 97; *Poetaster,* 135, 224n112; *Sejanus,* 90–91; "Song. That Women Are But Men's Shadows," 97–98; "Song to Celia," 99; *Timber: Or, Discoveries,* 84, 87, 88, 94, 109, 114, 115, 118; *Time Vindicated,* 86, 87–88; "To Lucy, Countess of Bedford, with Master Donne's Satires," 73; "To My Book," 92; "To Penshurst," 97, 102; "To Sir Robert Wroth," 97, 99–101, 113; "To the Immortal Memory and Friendship of That Noble Pair," 107–18, 119–20, 122, 124, 151, 156, 195; "To the World," 98; *The Underwood,* 91, 107; *Volpone,* 99; "Why I Write Not of Love," 94–96, 97

Jonsonus Virbius, 89
Juvenal, 58, 101, 161

Kahn, Victoria, 165, 196, 205n71, 227n45
Kalas, Rayna, 204n49
Kaplan, Ruth, 212n68
Keach, William, 214n1
Keats, George, 46
Keats, Georgiana, 46
Keats, John, 46–47, 214n1
Kermode, Frank, 227n36
Kerrigan, John, 96

Kerrigan, William, 236n19
Kesler, R. L., 213n101
King, Edward, 167, 168, 170–71
Kinney, Clare, 37
Klein, Lisa M., 212n68, 213n95
Kranidas, Thomas, 205n77
Kuzner, James, 218n69
Kyd, Thomas, 21

laborious art, 88, 158, 163, 180, 188–89
Lamb, Charles, 24, 187
Landino, Cristoforo, 207n96
Langer, Ullrich, 230n114
Language Poets, 25
La Primaudaye, Pierre de, 148, 208n15
Larsen, Kenneth, 49
Latin verse, 7–8, 9, 34, 54, 62, 64, 105–6, 119, 222n55, 223n88. *See also* Greek verse; Horace; Ovid; Virgil
laws, 105–7, 108, 115, 156–57, 175–77, 184, 188
leaping, 108–9, 111, 116–17, 119
Leaver, Robin, 229n72
Leavis, F. R., 184
Leighton, Angela, 19, 206n80, 227n44
Leo, Russ, 195
Leveller movement, 134–35
Levens, Peter, 212n73
Lever, J. W., 41
Levine, Caroline, 11
Lewalski, Barbara Kiefer, 160
lewdness, 61, 92–93
Lewis, C. S., 239n107
libertinism, 57, 72, 92, 106, 124, 149, 175
liberty: ancient state of, 59–60, 63–64, 66–67, 69–70, 72–73, 77–79, 100–101, 175–77; of conscience, 73, 107, 174–75; discursive vs ethical, 73, 99–102, 105–7, 179; measured, 90–91, 112–13, 118, 176–77, 198–200; Milton's views on, 172, 174, 175–79, 192–93, 235n7; poetical, 20, 102–5, 161, 181; private, 142, 145, 148, 151–54, 156–59; and retirement, 91, 99–102, 141–42, 145, 151–52; within bands, 44–46, 49–51. *See also* captivity
licentiousness, 71–72, 83, 106, 175; of couplets, 57–59, 62–63, 64, 77–78, 80, 92–93
ligare, 44, 79–80

triplets, 132, 157, 158, 222n55

Trissino, Gian Giorgio, 207n112

Trotter, David, 125, 156, 224n121

truth: Donne on, 69–70, 79, 80–81, 106–7, 153, 188, 199; Jonson on, 92, 103, 104–5; Milton on, 167, 171

Tschann, Judith, 3

Turner, Henry S., 202n15

tyranny: of custom, 172; of love, 97–99, 124; of passions, 42, 52; refuted, 11, 206n93; of rhyme, 7, 59–60, 84, 95, 157

van den Berg, Sara, 103, 222n76

Van der Noot, Jan, 31

variability, 111–13, 131–32, 141–42, 152, 156–57, 184, 193

Vaughan, Henry, 130, 232n137

Vergil, Polydore, 6

verse, efficacy of, 126–27, 128–30, 132–34, 138–39, 165–66, 173–74, 197

verse letters, 58, 72, 73–74, 81, 103, 149. *See also* epistles

versification, 8–10, 15, 16, 18, 29–32, 172–73

versi sciolti. See blank verse

versus intercalaris, 54–55, 56

Villiers, George, Duke of Buckingham, 137

Virgil: as poetic forefather, 57, 100, 123, 126, 152, 159, 184, 224n112; poetics of, 54–55, 68, 87, 125, 170, 186, 190, 239n107

Waller, Edmund, 130

Walsingham, Francis, 35

Ward, Thomas, 158

Warton, Thomas, 56

Watson, Thomas, 96–97

Watt, Tessa, 216n25

Wayne, Don, 223n102

Webbe, William, 7, 32, 36–37, 54, 204n40

Welch, Anthony, 227n34

Wentworth, Thomas, Earl of Strafford, 121–22, 122, 125, 170

Wesling, Donald, 3, 6–7

Whitfield, Anne, 227n29

Whitgift, John, 83

Wickert, Max, 214n111

Wilson-Okamura, David Scott, 17, 18, 66, 210n36, 215n8

Wimsatt, W. K., 202n12

Winner, Jack D., 92

Wither, George, 85–88, 134, 135, 136

Wittreich, Joseph, 167

wombs, 42, 103, 112–13, 234n190

Woodford, Samuel, 145

Woods, Susanne, 16, 235n7

Woodword, Rowland, 219n100

Wordsworth, William, 165, 172, 178–79

Wright, Gillian, 146

Wroth, Mary, 97

Wroth, Robert, 97, 99–101, 113

Xenophon, 27

Yeats, William Butler, 29

A NOTE ON THE TYPE

THIS BOOK has been composed in Miller, a Scotch Roman typeface designed by Matthew Carter and first released by Font Bureau in 1997. It resembles Monticello, the typeface developed for The Papers of Thomas Jefferson in the 1940s by C. H. Griffith and P. J. Conkwright and reinterpreted in digital form by Carter in 2003.

Pleasant Jefferson ("P. J.") Conkwright (1905–1986) was Typographer at Princeton University Press from 1939 to 1970. He was an acclaimed book designer and AIGA Medalist.

The ornament used throughout this book was designed by Pierre Simon Fournier (1712–1768) and was a favorite of Conkwright's, used in his design of the *Princeton University Library Chronicle*.